AF251965

AN INTRODUCTION TO
COMPUTATIONAL FINANCE

Series in Quantitative Finance – Vol. 1

AN INTRODUCTION TO
COMPUTATIONAL
FINANCE

Ömür Uğur

Middle East Technical University, Turkey

Imperial College Press

Published by

Imperial College Press
57 Shelton Street
Covent Garden
London WC2H 9HE

Distributed by

World Scientific Publishing Co. Pte. Ltd.
5 Toh Tuck Link, Singapore 596224
USA office: 27 Warren Street, Suite 401-402, Hackensack, NJ 07601
UK office: 57 Shelton Street, Covent Garden, London WC2H 9HE

British Library Cataloguing-in-Publication Data
A catalogue record for this book is available from the British Library.

Series in Quantitative Finance — Vol. 1
AN INTRODUCTION TO COMPUTATIONAL FINANCE

ISBN-13 978-1-84816-192-4
ISBN-10 1-84816-192-1
ISBN-13 978-1-84816-193-1 (pbk)
ISBN-10 1-84816-193-X (pbk)

Printed by FuIsland Offset Printing (S) Pte Ltd, Singapore

To My Family,

my little Öykü and my dear Sema

Preface

The theory of stochastic processes is considered to be difficult to understand by those who do not have a sound background in advanced topics of mathematics and mathematical analysis. Indeed, this is true, although exaggerated: option pricing, for instance, is based on sophisticated theory of real and functional analysis, such as measures and integrations. However, to understand the basics of option pricing a relatively modest background in mathematics seems to be sufficient. This book tries to avoid high-level mathematical backgrounds and makes it possible to be accessible to readers from different fields of science, and the practitioners of financial markets.

Although there are several publications on similar subjects, this book mainly focuses on pricing of derivative securities, options in particular, through a variety of approaches in literature: *binomial trees, Monte Carlo simulations,* and *partial differential equations.* By no means is it complete nor does it contain striking new theoretical ideas. This book is based on the lectures I have given on *scientific computing* and *computational finance.* In fact, this book tries to fill the gap between *mathematical finance* and *numerical approaches* by collecting the most appreciated and up-to-date monographs and many other selected literature in these fields, such as [Brandimarte (2002); Higham (2004); Korn and Korn (2001); Seydel (2002); Wilmott *et al.* (1995)].

Not only is this book considered a textbook in related undergraduate or graduate courses, but it also aims to serve those who want to implement and/or learn pricing algorithms by themselves. Indeed, the contents as well as the algorithms with their implementations in MATLAB make this book self-contained on basic methods of option pricing. Hopefully, it will provide an introduction to the essential features of *computational finance* and help those improve their mathematical backgrounds for more advanced topics.

This book contains working MATLAB codes to illustrate the ideas as well as the algorithms presented in the text. These codes and MATLAB functions will hopefully help readers implement their own algorithms and build their own library for pricing options. For ease of access as well as flexibility these codes were written without using sophisticated features of MATLAB so that their implementations in any other programming languages could easily be achieved. Moreover, to ensure the accuracy of the material in this book the codes and functions are also made available on-line. They can be obtained via the world-wide web at

```
http://www.metu.edu.tr/~ougur
```

for those who are already familiar with MATLAB and want to implement the vectorised versions for better performance. The website will also include the *errata* of the book, as well as comments and other material.

The chapters in the book can be followed depending on the readers' interests and their backgrounds. For instance, many students in finance are familiar with *Monte Carlo* methods, while the students of scientific computing are accustomed to *numerical solutions of partial differential equations*, in general. To help readers, this book is organised as follows.

The book starts with *fixed-income* securities and an introduction to *portfolio optimisation* by means of the *mean-variance approach*. Such an introduction is expected to introduce some of the technical terms used in the financial world and to help those who are not familiar with programming in MATLAB. In fact, the introductory chapter is relatively easier and almost independent of the remaining parts of the book.

Binomial methods in Chapter 2 presumes to serve an introduction to options as well as the basics of option pricing. Using the *no-arbitrage* principle and the risk-free interest rate, risk-neutral valuation of *European* options is introduced by the help of binomial models. Other type of options, in particular *American* ones, are also introduced and priced in this chapter.

In Chapter 3, stochastic processes and simulation of stochastic differential equations by means of *numerical methods* are presented. In order to support ideas and methods, the *stochastic Itô integral* and its properties are introduced, but a deep mathematical background is avoided. The *Itô lemma* and its use in evaluating such integrals as well as its applications in finance completes the chapter.

The famous *Black-Scholes* formulae for option pricing are derived in Chapter 4 by solving the transformed *heat equation*. Having such closed-form formulae, the concept of *hedging* is then easily discussed and further illustrated with some implementations in MATLAB.

Chapter 5 starts with *pseudo-random numbers* and discusses the transformation of *random variables* in order to draw *variates* from a given distribution. In particular, the basic algorithms, the *Box-Muller* and the *Marsaglia*, are introduced so as to draw *samples* from a *normal* distribution. The main part of this chapter is devoted to the *Monte Carlo* methods and the use of *variance reduction* techniques for option pricing by simulation. This chapter also contains several examples to illustrate and compare the methods.

Finally, in Chapter 6, after an introduction to *numerical solutions of partial differential equations* (PDEs) by *finite difference* methods, the *Black-Scholes PDEs* in option pricing are solved numerically. First, a relatively easier *heat equation*, which is obtained by transforming the variables in the Black-Scholes setting, is solved numerically. The basic methods, such as *explicit, implicit* and the *Crank-Nicolson*, as well as their stability analysis are investigated. The methods are also illustrated by applications to European options. Then, the finite difference formulae are applied directly to the Black-Scholes PDEs to value several options on *uniform grids*. In this chapter, *American* options are treated by means of the *free-boundary problems*, too. In order to value American options by finite difference methods, the *projected successive over-relaxation* algorithm is introduced. Of course, all examples and topics are enhanced by the presentation of suitable MATLAB codes. Finally, in this last chapter, similarities between *binomial* and *trinomial* methods with finite difference ones are presented.

The book ends with an appendix: *a short introduction to* MATLAB for those who are not familiar to its basic usage, built-in functions and plotting utilities. In the appendix, the use of *m-files* in MATLAB is emphasised.

Acknowledgments

A few years ago, I met Korns, leading seminars at a *workshop* at the *Institute of Applied Mathematics* of the *Middle East Technical University*, Ankara, Turkey. I hardly knew *financial mathematics* and how real and functional analysis were extensively used in finance. Since then I have been gradually learning and figuring out possible applications. All are because of Prof. Ralf Korn. I think I will never be able to repay what he has taught me and I would like to express my great gratitude, to him, as well as to his wife Dipl. Math. Elke Korn.

I would like to thank Prof. Aydın Aytuna, Prof. Bülent Karasözen and Prof. Ersan Akyıldız who had invited Prof. Ralf Korn and Dipl. Math. Elke Korn to the institute.

I would like to extend my thanks to Prof. Hayri Körezlioğlu, our head of the Department of Financial Mathematics at the institute. He had encouraged me to take part in studying financial mathematics, and had taught me the probabilistic nature of it. He had been a great friend who was willing to teach at all times, anywhere, even from his hospital bed. His passing away has deeply affected us all and I devote this piece of work to him, our unforgettable teacher and friend. He is still with us, teaching, studying, and dancing ...

I am grateful to two organisations: DAAD — German Academic Exchange Service, and TÜBİTAK — the Scientific & Technological Research Council of Turkey. Their invaluable support during the preparation of the draft in Kaiserslautern, Germany, was greatly appreciated. Without them it would be almost impossible to start writing this book. At this point, I wish to thank all those in Fraunhofer ITWM and in the Department of Mathematics at the University of Kaiserslautern, for their cordial hospitality during the period of writing the draft of this book.

There are many others, friends, colleagues and students I would like to thank. They are too many to name. I wish to express my gratitude to those who have helped in preparation of this book. However, there is a friend my biggest appreciation goes to: having read the whole manuscript, Prof. Gerhard-Wilhelm Weber has pointed out many typos and errors, and made his valuable comments and corrections. Of course, as many books do, this one will contain such errors and typos for sure. There might be even more. All are my faults and I apologise for them.

Finally, I deeply appreciate the patience and understanding of my dear wife, Sema, and my lovely daughter, Öykü, during this long period of writing the book. With my great pleasure and gratitude I dedicate this book to them.

Ömür Uğur
January 4, 2008

Contents

Chapter 1

Introduction

This chapter introduces some of the financial terminology used in business and literature. It also outlines some basic financial problems that can be tackled numerically, and it provides readers with some background and refreshes their memories. Another aim of this chapter is to help readers be accustomed to the usage of MATLAB and related toolboxes for solution of those problems. Although many of the problems and examples presented in this chapter are rather easy to solve by standard numerical methods, it must be emphasised that there are many other cases in which sophisticated methods are needed. Thus, programming of your own algorithms becomes important, and in that respect, this chapter gradually introduces also some basic programming in MATLAB and tries to complement the appendix of the book.

The present chapter contains both fixed-income securities and risky securities. The former is treated in its simplest form by the notion of *present value of money*. To do so, the *cash flow* associated with fixed income securities, such as default-free bonds, is at the centre. The *term structure* of interest rate is avoided in order to simplify the discussions in this context. Instead, a constant *risk-free* interest rate is assumed over all the investment periods. The cash flow associated with bonds makes it necessary to deal with management of a bond portfolio in order to meet liabilities in future. Durations and convexities are defined and an approach to bond portfolio management is introduced by the help of *linear programming*.

Risky securities, such as stocks that basically form the main part of the book is also introduced in this chapter. The basic *mean-variance* approach to portfolio optimisation in *Markowitz* sense is introduced. A risk measure for the portfolio is defined via the variance and minimised by using *quadratic programming*. As a result of the approach, efficient portfolios and the *efficient frontier* are introduced.

Finally, some prerequisites related to expectations and variances of random variables which will be frequently used in the rest of the book are also introduced in this chapter.

1.1   Fixed-Income Securities

Fixed-income securities are one of the instruments commonly used by firms and public administrations to fund their activities and to meet their liabilities.

The simplest prototype of fixed-income securities is the fixed-coupon bond that is characterised by a *face value*, also called the *par value*, and *maturity* date. The bond is purchased at a price that is not necessarily equal to the face value, but at maturity you are paid this face value.

However, the term *fixed-income* is somewhat misleading, since there are many bonds whose coupon rates depend on some other financial quantities. If the coupon rate is not certain, analysing a bond may be difficult. Even if the coupon rate is fixed and known, bond prices may differ depending on the probability of *default*. Furthermore, some bonds have embedded *options* which complicate the analysis. These complex structures of bonds in financial markets are out of the scope of this section.

Even if the bonds are restricted to be as simple as possible, there are still two fundamental problems to deal with: *valuing* of bonds, and *managing a bond portfolio* constructed according to one's own particular needs or liabilities.

1.1.1   *Valuation*

Consider a zero-coupon bond with a face value F and maturity T (one year from now, for example). The security is purchased at a price P now. At maturity, the *return* will be:

$$R = \frac{F}{P}.$$

Hence, from the *rate of return*,

$$r = R - 1 = \frac{F}{P} - 1,$$

it is easy to calculate the *price* of the bond:

$$P = \frac{F}{1 + r}.$$

If F and r are fixed values, the above relation can be regarded as a *pricing formula*. In fact, this is a *discounting* formula of the face value, given the rate of return r for the zero-coupon bond. What rate r must be used in pricing? If the bond is *default-free*, such as government bonds, this should be the prevailing *risk-free* interest rate.

One can easily show, using the common principle in finance, the *no-arbitrage* principle, that

$$P = \frac{F}{1+r} \qquad (1.1)$$

is the *fair value* of the price of a default free, zero-coupon bond. In this equation, F is the face value and r is the risk-free interest rate which is assumed to be constant for all times until maturity. To show that P in (1.1) is the fair value of the bond, let us explore the no-arbitrage arguments: assume that the bond is under-priced, that is,

$$P_1 < P = \frac{F}{1+r}.$$

Then, you may borrow an amount L and use it to purchase L/P_1 bonds.[1] Note that the net cash flow at the beginning is zero. Until maturity you keep your position and hold the bonds. Then at maturity, you pay back the loan together with the market risk-free rate, $L(1+r)$, and you gain $F\frac{L}{P_1}$ from holding the bonds. In other words, the net profit at maturity is

$$F\frac{L}{P_1} - L(1+r) = L\left(\frac{F}{P_1} - 1 - r\right) > 0.$$

However, this is a (strictly) positive amount without paying anything at the beginning of the investment. Thus, under-priced bonds give you an arbitrage opportunity, hence, the contrary,

$$P_1 \geq P = \frac{F}{1+r},$$

must hold. However, if the bond is over-priced, that is, $P_1 > P$, then you had better borrow the bond rather than the money needed to buy it. Sell the bond and invest the money at risk-free interest rate. However, this would lead to the profit,

$$-F\frac{L}{P_1} + L(1+r) = L\left(-\frac{F}{P_1} + 1 + r\right) > 0,$$

---

[1] In this book it is always assumed that one can borrow any amount of money with the risk-free interest rate r. Furthermore, one can even borrow any fraction of bonds or other securities.

at maturity for $P_1 > P$, which is again positive without spending anything at the beginning: another arbitrage opportunity. Thus, the bond can neither be over-priced nor be under-priced. Hence, only the price P is the fair price of the bond for both parties.

Remark 1.1. The practice of borrowing an asset to sell it immediately is known as *short-selling*. In practice, short-selling has many limitations. However, in pricing it is often reasonable to assume that short-selling is possible.

We all know that one dollar to be acquired in the future, say a year later, is not worth one dollar now, but something less. There are many causes of this, however, interest rates are the formal acknowledgement to that. Moreover, interest rates are not in general constant within a year and they are exposed to changes of the economy of a country. They vary in time. However, in almost all cases in this book the interest rate r will be assumed to be constant unless otherwise is explicitly stated.

Consider a stream of payments c_t at the discrete-time instants $t = 0, 1, \ldots, n$, say in years, as in Fig. 1.1. The *present value*, say PV, of the *cash flow* can be computed as follows:

$$PV = \sum_{t=0}^{n} \frac{c_t}{(1+r)^t} = \sum_{t=0}^{n} d_t c_t,$$

where r is some *interest rate* for a single time period and the $d_t = \frac{1}{(1+r)^t}$ are the *discount factors*.

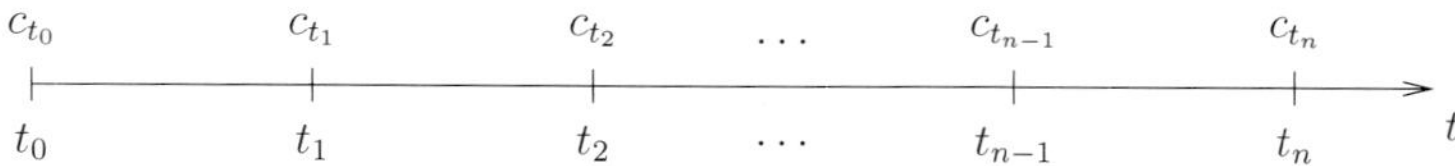

Fig. 1.1   A stream of cash flows

In practice, *different discount rates* should be used for the cash flow occurring in these n different periods. Hence,

$$PV = \sum_{t=0}^{n} \frac{c_t}{(1+r_t)^t},$$

where, in this case, the discount factors d_t and r_t are related to the *term structure of interest rates*. Of course, this formula should be altered if the time periods are not given in years, but months as in the following example.

Example 1.1. Suppose that a one-year, zero-coupon bond is purchased five months after the issue date. The interest rate is assumed to be constant within the year. Then, a plausible pricing formula could be

$$P = \frac{F}{(1+r)^{7/12}},$$

assuming that all months (remaining 7 months to maturity) have the same number of days.

Although the *nominal* interest rate is quoted yearly, the coupon payments of a bond occur more frequently. If there are m payments per year at some regular time intervals, then

$$PV = \sum_{i=0}^{k} \frac{c_{t_i}}{(1+r/m)^i}, \qquad (1.2)$$

where i indexes the periods and k is the number of years times the number of periods within one year. In other words, k is the total number of periods at which the cash flow c_{t_i} occurs.

Consider a default-free bond maturing in n years, paying coupons once a year. The fair price of the bond may be obtained from the cash flow associated to it. The fair price means that one must pay the present value of the future cash flow now. In other words, the amount

$$c_{t_0} = -\sum_{i=1}^{n} \frac{c_{t_i}}{(1+r)^i} - \frac{F}{(1+r)^n}$$

must be paid now so that

$$PV = \sum_{i=0}^{n} \frac{c_{t_i}}{(1+r)^i} + \frac{F}{(1+r)^n} = 0.$$

Note that c_{t_i} is the amount of coupon payments per period for $i = 1, 2, \ldots, n$ and F is the face value that is paid at maturity together with the coupon payment. Therefore, the fair price P of such a default-free bond can be calculated as follows:

$$P = \sum_{i=1}^{n} \frac{c_{t_i}}{(1+r)^i} + \frac{F}{(1+r)^n}. \qquad (1.3)$$

Similarly, if m periods occur within a year the formula above must be adapted to mimic the situation. From a mathematical point of view, the formula implies that all such bonds have the same price. However, this is not the case in real life: the bonds in the market carry different sources of risks, default risks in particular.

Moreover, since interest rates are not constant in general, the bonds are characterised by their *yields*. Indeed, if a bond price P_o is observed at the market, then its yield can be determined from the solution λ of the equation

$$P_o = \sum_{i=1}^{n} \frac{c_{t_i}}{(1+\lambda)^i} + \frac{F}{(1+\lambda)^n},$$

where the c_{t_i} are the coupon payments at times $i = 1, 2, \ldots, n$ and F is the face value. Note that the opposite case is also applicable: depending on the required yield λ, the price P of the bond can be calculated from (1.3) by replacing r with λ. If, however, more than one, say m, coupon payments occur within a year then the formula (1.3) must be adapted to

$$P = \sum_{i=1}^{k} \frac{c_{t_i}}{(1+\lambda/m)^i} + \frac{F}{(1+\lambda/m)^k} \qquad (1.4)$$

in order to reflect the situation, where k is the total number of coupon payments.

From a different perspective, the *yield* is considered the *internal rate of return* of the associated cash flow, which is described in the following definition.

Definition 1.1. For a given stream of cash flows c_t for $t = 0, 1, \ldots, n$, the *internal rate of return* is defined as the value ρ such that the present value of the stream is zero, that is,

$$\sum_{t=0}^{n} \frac{c_t}{(1+\rho)^t} = 0. \qquad (1.5)$$

The problem of finding the internal rate of return associated to a cash flow turns out to be a well-known problem of scientific computing. Let x be defined by $x = \frac{1}{1+\rho}$ so that the equation (1.5) be changed into the following form:

$$0 = c_0 + c_1 x + c_2 x^2 + \cdots + c_n x^n = \sum_{t=0}^{n} c_t x^t. \qquad (1.6)$$

Fortunately, this problem is a special case of *root finding problems* of numerical analysis: finding zeros of polynomials. There are efficient and fast methods for finding zeros of functions, particularly, polynomials.

In this particular case, the zeros of polynomials, n roots of (1.6) including the multiplicities are expected by the *Fundamental Theorem of Algebra*. These roots in general complex numbers, however, the following mathematical remark due to [Luenberger (1998)] is in harmony with the financial world!

Remark 1.2. It can be shown that for a given stream of cash flows c_t with $c_0 < 0$ and $c_t \geq 0$ for $t = 1, 2, \ldots, n$ such that

$$\sum_{t=1}^{n} c_t > 0$$

we have a *unique, real and positive* solution of (1.5):

$$x = \frac{1}{1+\rho} \quad \text{so that} \quad \rho = \frac{1}{x} - 1.$$

Example 1.2. Now, suppose that \$100 is paid for a coupon bond maturing in 5 years with face value \$100 and coupon payments \$6 annually. The internal rate of return of such a stream can easily be computed by the zeros of the related polynomial. An implementation of the calculations is shown in Fig. 1.2, which is considered a MATLAB Command Window. Notice that the cash flow initially is negative: the money that is given to buy the bond. It turns out that the internal rate of return is 6%; or, the other way around, the yield of the bond is 6%. This is also verified by another built-in function in the *Financial toolbox* of MATLAB.

In MATLAB and its toolboxes there are also other built-in functions dealing with financial instruments. In Fig. 1.3, for example, calculations of the present values of a cash flow with two different interest rates are shown by the use of such built-in functions. Interpreting the results in terms of the bond prices with different yields also ensures the calculations in Fig. 1.2 of Example 1.2: The price \$100 paid for the bond was fair!

Moreover, the results shown in Fig. 1.3 also verify the fact that the present value of a cash flow drops if the interest rate is raised. Thus, a special emphasis on the importance of changes in the interest rates, or the yields, in pricing of fixed-income securities must be shown.

```
>> cf = [ -100 6 6 6 6 106 ];
>> x = roots(fliplr(cf)) % type "help roots"
x =
  -0.8090 + 0.5878i
  -0.8090 - 0.5878i
   0.3090 + 0.9511i
   0.3090 - 0.9511i
   0.9434
>> rho = 1 ./ x - 1
rho =
  -1.8090 - 0.5878i
  -1.8090 + 0.5878i
  -0.6910 - 0.9511i
  -0.6910 + 0.9511i
   0.0600
>> irr(cf) % requires Financial Toolbox
ans =
     0.0600
```

Fig. 1.2   Calculation of the internal rate of return

```
>> cf = [0 8 8 8 8 108];
>> pvvar(cf, 0.08) % requires Financial Toolbox
ans =
   100.0000
>> pvvar(cf, 0.09)
ans =
    96.1103
```

Fig. 1.3   Calculation of present values with different yields

1.1.2 *Interest Rate Sensitivity*

Consider a liability of amount L to be paid in five years. If you can find a "safe" zero-coupon bond maturing in five years, with a face value F, then you are in safe: just buy L/F of these bonds. However, unfortunately, one's liabilities cannot be *hedged* in this way, in general, because it will not be easy to find a bond maturing at the time of the liability. Thus, it is almost impossible to buy a single bond to meet your liabilities. Doing so, you face with different risks. For sure, you will have to reinvest money on bonds with different maturities and have to face with *interest rate* risks as a result. Even if a portfolio of bonds is constructed to hedge your liabilities, it is important to know how the changes in the interest rates affect this portfolio.

Therefore, constructing a bond portfolio and protecting it against interest rate uncertainties are two important issues in managing a portfolio. To this end, one must know how a bond price (or a portfolio of bonds) behaves due to changes of the interest rate, or correspondingly, to changes of the underlying yield. When holding a bond one would like to know how sensitive the value of the bond is due to changes in the economic environment: the current interest rate or the yield of the bond. An important quantity, *duration* of a bond, has to be calculated by the practitioners in the bond market.

Mathematically speaking, there is a function, say $P = P(\lambda)$, that maps the yield λ to the price P of a bond. Let

$$P = \sum_{k=1}^{n} \frac{c_k}{(1 + \lambda/m)^k}$$

be the price of a bond with m coupon payments per year. Here, c_k is the value of the cash flow corresponding to the periods $k = 1, \ldots, n$. The *rate of change of P with respect to λ* is simply the derivative:

$$\begin{aligned}
\frac{\mathrm{d}P}{\mathrm{d}\lambda} &= \frac{\mathrm{d}}{\mathrm{d}\lambda}\left(\sum_{k=1}^{n} \frac{c_k}{(1 + \lambda/m)^k}\right) \\
&= \sum_{k=1}^{n} c_k \frac{\mathrm{d}}{\mathrm{d}\lambda}\left(\frac{1}{(1 + \lambda/m)^k}\right) \\
&= -\sum_{k=1}^{n} \frac{k}{m} \frac{c_k}{(1 + \lambda/m)^{k+1}} \\
&= -\frac{1}{(1 + \lambda/m)} \sum_{k=1}^{n} \frac{k}{m} \frac{c_k}{(1 + \lambda/m)^k} \\
&= -D_M\, P,
\end{aligned}$$

where

$$D_M = \frac{1}{(1 + \lambda/m)}\, D, \quad \text{and} \quad D = \frac{1}{P} \sum_{k=1}^{n} \frac{k}{m} \frac{c_k}{(1 + \lambda/m)^k}. \qquad (1.7)$$

Here D is called the *Macaulay duration* and D_M is the *modified duration*. Practically, both durations have a similar property that they are *weighted averages* of the times (k) at which cash flows (c_k) occur.

From the relation,

$$\frac{\mathrm{d}P}{\mathrm{d}\lambda} = -D_M\, P, \qquad (1.8)$$

one can infer that the modified duration is related to the *slope* of the *price-yield* curve at a given point; this is sometimes referred to as the *price elasticity* of the bond with respect to the changes in the yield. Once the slope is known we can easily build a tangent line approximation to the bond price considered to be a function of the yield. This is a *first-order* approximation to the price of a bond, and it is illustrated in Fig. 1.4. If at $\lambda = \lambda_0$ the modified duration D_M is known and the price $P_0 = P(\lambda_0)$ is given, the first-order approximation to the price $P = P(\lambda)$ can then be calculated from

$$P(\lambda) \approx P_0 - D_M P_0(\lambda - \lambda_0) \qquad (1.9)$$

for those λ in the vicinity of λ_0.

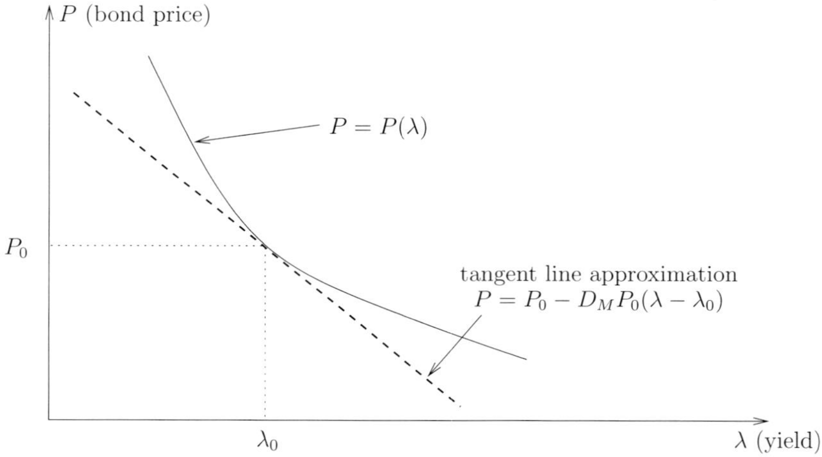

Fig. 1.4   A first-order approximation to the bond price

Moreover, by taking the second derivative of P with respect to λ, one can easily obtain the equation,

$$\frac{\mathrm{d}^2 P}{\mathrm{d}\lambda^2} = C P, \qquad (1.10)$$

which gives a second-order information about the price P. The value of C is called the *convexity* and it is defined by

$$C = \frac{1}{P} \frac{1}{(1 + \lambda/m)^2} \sum_{k=1}^{n} \frac{k(k+1)}{m^2} \frac{c_k}{(1 + \lambda/m)^k}. \qquad (1.11)$$

Note that the unit of convexity is time-squared, while that of duration is time. Further, it is clear from the equations (1.7) and (1.11) that the duration and the convexity of a bond are all positive quantities, at least for reasonable values of yield λ. Therefore, the price of a bond decreases as the yield increases because of positive duration; moreover, it is a convex function of λ due to positive convexity.

Now, having the change $\Delta\lambda := \lambda - \lambda_0$ in the yield, a second-order approximation of the change

$$\Delta P := P - P_0 = P(\lambda) - P(\lambda_0)$$

in the price can be calculated as

$$\Delta P \approx -D_M \, P_0 \, \Delta\lambda + \frac{1}{2} \, C \, P_0 \, (\Delta\lambda)^2. \qquad (1.12)$$

This follows from the classical Taylor's theorem, which is, informally,

$$P(\lambda_0 + \Delta\lambda) = P(\lambda_0) + P'(\lambda_0)\Delta\lambda + \frac{1}{2}P''(\lambda_0)(\Delta\lambda)^2 + \mathcal{O}\left((\Delta\lambda)^3\right),$$

for a sufficiently smooth function P of λ.

Here, it should be noted that the duration D_M and the convexity C as well as P_0 are calculated at $\lambda = \lambda_0$ using their respective formulae. Thus, a *second-order* approximation of the bond price can be written as

$$P(\lambda) \approx P_0 - D_M \, P_0 \, (\lambda - \lambda_0) + \frac{1}{2} \, C \, P_0 \, (\lambda - \lambda_0)^2. \qquad (1.13)$$

The following example illustrates how built-in functions in MATLAB can be used to calculate the sensitivity parameters, duration and convexity, in order to approximate the bond price.

Example 1.3. Assume that the cash flows in the following four years are $10 with the current yield 5%. We may check the quality of the approximate price change, based on duration and convexity, due to an increase in the yield by 0.5%. A detailed MATLAB environment is shown in Fig. 1.5; calculations ensure that the second-order approximation gives satisfactory results while the first-order one is a bit lacking in quality.

On the other hand, Fig. 1.6 depicts these approximations to the bond price as a function of the yield qualitatively. The use of the convexity

```
>> cf = [10 10 10 10]; p1 = pvvar([0, cf], 0.05); p2 = pvvar([0, cf], 0.055);
>> deltaP1 = p2 - p1
deltaP1 =
   -0.4080
>> [d1 dm] = cfdur(cf, 0.05); % returns both Macaulay and modified
>> cv = cfconv(cf, 0.05); % returns convexity
>> first_approx_deltaP1 = -dm*p1*0.005
first_approx_deltaP1 =
   -0.4118
>> second_approx_deltaP1 = -dm*p1*0.005 + 0.5*cv*p1*(0.005)^2
second_approx_deltaP1 =
   -0.4080
```

Fig. 1.5   A Matlab environment testing the price change with the help of duration and convexity

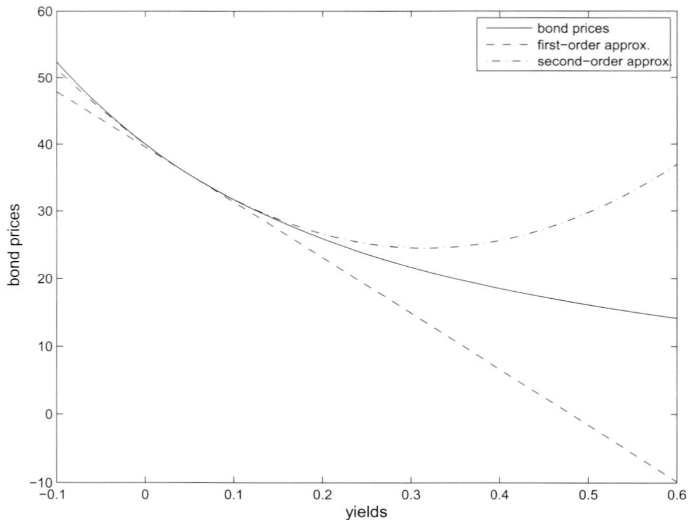

Fig. 1.6   First- and second-order approximations to the bond price

information increases the quality of the approximation when compared with the use of the duration only.

In order to implement the idea and plot these first- and second-order approximations as well as the bond price itself, Fig. 1.7 shows a script file in Matlab.

```
──────────────────────── approxBondPrices.m ────────────────────────
% approximation of bond prices
clear all, close all
coupons = [10 10 10 10]; % given
yields = -0.1:0.01:0.6; howMany = length(yields);
for i = 1:howMany
    prices(i) = pvvar([0 coupons], yields(i));
end

plot(yields, prices) % exact prices
hold on
lambda0 = 0.05; P0 = pvvar([0 coupons], lambda0); % assumed to be given
[duration, modifiedDuration] = cfdur(coupons, lambda0);
convexity = cfconv(coupons, lambda0);

% first-order approximation
P_1 = P0 .* ( 1 - modifiedDuration .* (yields - lambda0) );
plot(yields, P_1, 'r--'), hold on
%second-order approximation
P_2 = P0 .* ( 1 - modifiedDuration .* (yields - lambda0)   ...
    + 0.5 * convexity .* (yields - lambda0).^2 );
plot(yields, P_2, 'g-.'), hold off
ylabel('bond prices','FontSize',12), xlabel('yields','FontSize',12)
legend('bond prices', 'first-order approx.', 'second-order approx.')
print -r900 -deps '../figures/approxBondPrices'
```

Fig. 1.7   A simple MATLAB script to plot first- and second-order approximations

However, readers who cannot access to those built-in functions are encouraged to write their own functions in MATLAB. A glance on the following example might be helpful since it illustrates the calculations of a bond price, its duration and convexity.

Example 1.4. Consider a three year bond with a face value of \$100 and annual coupon payments of 10% of its face value. The yield λ is assumed to be 9%. Then the current price of the bond is

$$P_0 = \sum_{i=1}^{3} \frac{c}{(1+\lambda)^i} + \frac{F}{(1+\lambda)^3} = 102.5313,$$

where $c = 10$, $F = 100$ and $\lambda = 0.09$. The modified duration at the current price can be calculated as,

$$D_M = \frac{1}{1+\lambda} \frac{1}{P_0} \sum_{i=1}^{3} i \frac{c_i}{(1+\lambda)^i} = 2.5128,$$

where in this case, $c_i = c$ for $i = 1, 2$, and $c_3 = c + F$. Note that $c_3 = c + F$

is the cash flow at maturity. Similarly, the convexity of the bond is

$$C = \frac{1}{(1+\lambda)^2} \frac{1}{P_0} \sum_{i=1}^{3} i(i+1) \frac{c_i}{(1+\lambda)^i} = 8.9325.$$

Now, suppose that the yield is subject to change, from $\lambda = 0.09$ to $\lambda = 0.1$. The change in the yield is then $\Delta\lambda = +0.01$. Therefore, an approximate price of the bond can be calculated as

$$P \approx P_0 \left[1 - D_M \Delta\lambda + \frac{1}{2} C (\Delta\lambda)^2 \right] = 100.0007,$$

by using the convexity information beside the duration.

It is advised that you should check the calculations made in (1.4) by a relatively easy function shown in Fig. 1.8 for the bond characteristics. A script file for testing purposes is also presented in Fig. 1.9.

```
———————————————— bondChar_Discrete.m ————————————————
function [BondPrice, BondDuration, BondConvexity, Approx] = ...
    bondChar_Discrete(cashFlows, times, faceValue, yield, changeInYield)

% Insert faceValue into the cash flows.
cashFlows(end) = cashFlows(end) + faceValue;
% Calculate
discountFactor = 1.0/(1+yield);
BondPrice = sum( (discountFactor.^times) .* cashFlows );
BondDuration = discountFactor .* 1/BondPrice ...
        * sum( times .* (discountFactor.^times) .* cashFlows );
BondConvexity = discountFactor^2 .* 1/BondPrice ...
        * sum( times .* (times+1) .* (discountFactor.^times) .* cashFlows );
% Approximate bond price given the change in yield
Approx = BondPrice * (1 - BondDuration * changeInYield ...
            + 0.5 * BondConvexity * changeInYield^2 );
```

Fig. 1.8   A simple MATLAB function for calculating bond characteristics

```
———————————————— testBondChar_Discrete.m ————————————————
% test bondChar_Discrete
clear all;
cashFlows = [10 10 10]'; times = [1 2 3]';
faceValue = 100; yield = 0.09; changeInYield = 0.01;

[BondPrice, BondDuration, BondConvexity, Approx] = ...
    bondChar_Discrete(cashFlows, times, faceValue, yield, changeInYield)
```

Fig. 1.9   A simple MATLAB function for calculating bond characteristics

In order to find a continuously compounding discount factor d_t, suppose that the annual interest rate is r, and interest is paid n times each year.

If one year is divided into n equally spaced subperiods, then the interest rate for each period becomes r/n. Therefore, the discount factor d_m for the mth period is given by

$$d_m = \frac{1}{(1 + r/n)^m} = \left(1 + \frac{r}{n}\right)^{-m}.$$

Note that the time t at the mth period is

$$t = \frac{m}{n}$$

in years, so that the discount factor at time $t = m/n$ becomes

$$d_t = \left(1 + \frac{r}{n}\right)^{-m} = \left(1 + \frac{r}{n}\right)^{-nt}.$$

Thus, taking limit as n tends to infinity and using the well-known *exponential growth* property,

$$\lim_{n \to \infty} \left(1 + \frac{r}{n}\right)^n = e^r,$$

the *continuously compounding discount factor* d_t is found to be

$$d_t = \lim_{n \to \infty} \left[\left(1 + \frac{r}{n}\right)^n\right]^{-t} = e^{-rt}. \tag{1.14}$$

Using the discount factor d_t in (1.14), the present value of a stream of cash flows c_{t_k} turns into the form

$$PV = \sum_{k=0}^{n} e^{-rt_k} c_{t_k}. \tag{1.15}$$

Now, the bond with a face value F, maturing in t_n years, and paying coupons c_{t_k} at times t_k, has the price

$$P = \sum_{k=1}^{n} e^{-\lambda t_k} C_{t_k}, \tag{1.16}$$

with continuously compounding yield λ, where $C_{t_k} = c_{t_k}$ for $t_k = t_1, t_2, \ldots, t_{n-1}$ and $C_{t_n} = c_{t_n} + F$. Similarly, the modified as well as Macaulay duration becomes

$$D_M = D = -\frac{1}{P}\frac{\mathrm{d}P}{\mathrm{d}\lambda} = \frac{1}{P}\sum_{k=0}^{n} t_k e^{-\lambda t_k} C_{t_k}. \qquad (1.17)$$

The convexity of such a bond can be computed by

$$C = \frac{1}{P}\frac{\mathrm{d}^2 P}{\mathrm{d}\lambda^2} = \frac{1}{P}\sum_{k=0}^{n} t_k^2 e^{-\lambda t_k} C_{t_k}. \qquad (1.18)$$

With such formulae at hand it should not be difficult to modify the MATLAB function in Fig. 1.8 to include the case in which the yield is continuously compounding. This is left as an exercise to the readers!

Until now, the duration and the convexity of a single bond have been defined, but practically, a portfolio of bonds is needed and managed to meet the future liabilities. Such a portfolio, in fact, contains many bonds with ranging yields and maturities.

1.1.3 *Portfolio Management*

A common exercise in bond portfolio management, called *immunisation*, is to shape a portfolio with a given (modified) duration D, and possibly a convexity C. Suppose that a set of N bonds in a portfolio with durations D_i and convexities C_i for $i = 1, 2, \ldots, N$ are given. One would like to know the weights $w_1, w_2, \ldots, w_N$ of these bonds in the portfolio.

Although it is not true in general, but for the sake of simplicity, let us assume that both the duration and the convexity of the portfolio can be computed as a weighted linear combination of these bond characteristics, namely, the durations and the convexities. Thus, a set of equations is obtained as

$$\begin{aligned} \sum_{i=1}^{N} D_i w_i &= D, \\ \sum_{i=1}^{N} C_i w_i &= C, \\ \sum_{i=1}^{N} w_i &= 1. \end{aligned} \qquad (1.19)$$

Notice that the weights are summed up to one in the above system. In fact, the system is a $3 \times N$ linear one that has to be solved for the unknown weights $w_1, w_2, \ldots, w_N$. Unfortunately, this system is generally *underdeter-*

mined, and has a unique solution only if the rank of the coefficient matrix

$$A := \begin{bmatrix} D_1 & D_2 & \cdots & D_N \\ C_1 & C_2 & \cdots & C_N \\ 1 & 1 & \cdots & 1 \end{bmatrix}$$

is exactly 3 —the number of independent equations we have for the N unknown weights $w_1, w_2, \ldots, w_N$. Of course, one can use a *least-squares* solution in the case when $N \leq 3$! However, this is rarely the action taken. A simple *immunisation* of a bond portfolio consisting of three bonds only is shown in Fig. 1.10 of the following example.

Example 1.5. Assume that in a portfolio there are only three bonds all of which are settled on the same day. However, their respective maturities, coupon rates and yields are different as it is generally expected. These characteristics of the bonds are given in Fig. 1.10. This example will introduce some more built-in functions in the Financial toolbox of MATLAB that can be used in dealing with bonds, durations and convexities.

```
───────────────────────────── bondPortfolio_DC.m ─────────────────
% the three bonds with
settles      = '02-Sep-2007';
maturities   = ['03-Oct-2008' ; '04-Nov-2010' ; '31-Dec-2015'];
couponRates = [0.06 ;  0.07 ; 0.08]; yields = [0.05 ; 0.075 ; 0.1];
% durations and convexities
durations = bnddury(yields, couponRates, settles, maturities);
convexities = bndconvy(yields, couponRates, settles, maturities);
% the coefficient matrix and the right-hand-side vector
A = [durations' ; convexities' ; 1 1 1];
b = [10; 160; 1];
% solution of the system
weights = A\b
```

Fig. 1.10   A simple MATLAB script for a bond portfolio immunisation

Given the required duration and the convexity of the portfolio, we are mostly interested in the solution of the system (1.19) for immunisation.

Having only three bonds in the portfolio, the system becomes a *square* one: three equations with three unknown weights. The MATLAB script shown in Fig. 1.10 computes the solution to be,

$$w = [w_1, w_2, w_3]^T = [6.0632, \ -10.9833, \ 5.9201]^T,$$

for the 3×3 system. Note that the second bond has to be sold *short*, which may not be feasible in the market, but the other two must be bought as many as required in order to match the given duration and the convexity of the portfolio.

Contrary to the example above, when there are more than 3 bonds in the required portfolio there may be more than one solution, and one has to decide which one is the "best"! A plausible, however simple, idea is to maximise the *average yield* of the portfolio consisting of N bonds with their respective yields λ_i, given that the portfolio must have the duration D and the convexity C. However, yet there is still a *big restriction* on the choices of D and C: they are assumed to be linear combinations of the durations D_i and the convexities C_i of the bonds in the portfolio. In other words, these are given by the first two equalities in (1.19):

$$\sum_{i=1}^{N} D_i w_i = D \quad \text{and} \quad \sum_{i=1}^{N} C_i w_i = C.$$

Assuming such linear combinations are possible the formulation of this maximisation problem can be written as a *linear programming* (LP) problem:

$$\text{maximise } \sum_{i=1}^{N} \lambda_i w_i$$

$$\text{subject to}$$

$$\begin{aligned}
\sum_{i=1}^{N} D_i w_i &= D \\
\sum_{i=1}^{N} C_i w_i &= C \\
\sum_{i=1}^{N} w_i &= 1 \\
w_i &\geq 0, \quad 1 \leq i \leq N.
\end{aligned} \tag{1.20}$$

Note that the weights, over which the maximisation is taken are restricted to be nonnegative in order to avoid short-selling. Indeed, a negative weight, $w_j < 0$ for some $1 \leq j \leq N$, would simply mean that you should *sell* the jth bond *short*, which is not in general possible. So, the nonnegativity requirement $w_i \geq 0$ for all $i = 1, 2, \ldots, N$ forbids short sales of any of the bonds.

The linear programming *maximisation* problem in (1.20) can be written in a "neater" way, in the form as it generally appears in literature, by the use of matrices and vectors:

$$(\mathcal{LP}) \ : \ \begin{cases} \text{maximise } w^T \Lambda \\ \text{subject to} \\ \qquad A w = b \\ \qquad w \geq 0. \end{cases} \tag{1.21}$$

Here the column vectors $w = [w_1, w_2, \ldots, w_N]^T$ and $\Lambda = [\lambda_1, \lambda_2, \ldots, \lambda_N]^T$

consist of the weights and the yields, respectively. The matrix A is

$$A := \begin{bmatrix} D_1 & D_2 & \cdots & D_N \\ C_1 & C_2 & \cdots & C_N \\ 1 & 1 & \cdots & 1 \end{bmatrix},$$

which has already been defined previously, and the right-hand side column vector is $b = [D, C, 1]^T$. The meaning of $w \geq 0$ is given by the component-wise inequalities: $w_i \geq 0$ for all $i = 1, 2, \ldots, N$.

Remark 1.3. In general, instead of maximising an objective function, say $f(x) = w^T \Lambda$, over a domain, we consider the minimising of the negative of it. Hence, we write down the problem in the *standard form* as

$$(\mathcal{LP}) \; : \; \begin{cases} \text{minimise} & -w^T \Lambda \\ \text{subject to} & \\ & A\,w = b \\ & w \geq 0, \end{cases} \tag{1.22}$$

instead of the linear maximisation problem in (1.21). Moreover, the non-negativity condition $w \geq 0$ ensures the boundedness of this minimisation problem.

The following example considers more than three bonds in a portfolio with different maturities, face values, and coupon rates. The MATLAB script in Fig. 1.11 shows the properties of this bond portfolio. The prices of the bonds are given by their *clean prices* presented in the script: the actual price of a bond. The clean price of a bond with a given yield λ is obtained by removing the *accrued interest* from the *dirty* price, DP,

$$DP = \sum_{i=1}^{n} \frac{c_i}{(1 + \lambda/m)^i},$$

where c_i is a coupon payment at each period i, and n is the total number of remaining coupon periods after the settlement date.

Accrued interest may be computed by simply considering the coupon payments over the period between two payments. Roughly speaking, if coupons are paid every six months and you buy a bond four months before the next coupon payment, you owe one-third of the coupon to the previous owner. So, this amount is added to the clean price to find the dirty price of a bond. In other words, clean price and accrued interest sum up to the actual present value of the cash flow associated with the bond.

Example 1.6. Consider more than three bonds in a portfolio immunisation. The properties of these bonds are given in the MATLAB script shown in Fig. 1.11.

```
―――――――――――――――――― bondPortfolio_maximumYield.m ――――――――――――――――――
clear all, close all
% bonds
settle = '01-Jan-2007';
maturity = ['10-Jan-2020'; '20-Oct-2018'; '30-Aug-2025'; ...
            '01-Mar-2020'; '21-Oct-2015'];
face = [300; 1000; 200; 100; 100];
couponRate = [0.08; 0.07; 0.06; 0.05; 0.05];
cleanPrice = [ 256.8205; 688.4300; 121.3829; 69.4931; 66.6912 ];
% for more information on 'cleanPrice' see 'bndprice', or compare
% yieldsExpected = [0.1, 0.12, 0.11, 0.09, 0.11];
% cleanPrice = bndprice(yieldsExpected, couponRate, ...
%    settle, maturity,[],[],[],[],[],[],[],face)

% yields, durations, convexities
yields = bndyield(cleanPrice, couponRate, settle, maturity, ...
            2, 0, [] , [] , [] , [], [] , face);
durations = bnddury(yields, couponRate, settle, maturity, ...
            2, 0, [] , [] , [] , [], [] , face);
convexities = bndconvy(yields, couponRate, settle, maturity, ...
            2, 0, [] , [] , [] , [], [] , face);
% coefficient matrix, and right-hand-side vector
A = [durations'; convexities'; ones(1,5)];
% b vector is near the average values of durations and convexities
b = [ 7.50 ; 80.50 ; 1]; % but the last row is 1!
[weights, maxYield] = maximumYield(yields, A, b)
```

Fig. 1.11   A simple MATLAB script showing the properties of a portfolio of bonds

The resulting linear programming problem (1.21) for maximising the portfolio yield can easily be solved by the help of the built-in functions in the *Optimization Toolbox*. A simple MATLAB function that basically calls such a built-in function from the toolbox is presented in Fig. 1.12.

```
―――――――――――――――――― maximumYield.m ――――――――――――――――――
function [weights, maxYield] = maximumYield(yields, ...
    coeffMatrix, rightSideVector)

n = length(yields);
weights = linprog(-yields,[],[],coeffMatrix,rightSideVector,zeros(1,n));
maxYield = weights' * yields;
```

Fig. 1.12   A simple MATLAB function for solving the linear programming problem

When the script in Fig. 1.11 is run, the optimal portfolio weights in the vector $w = w^*$, are found to be

$$w^* = [0.0000, \ 0.5919, \ 0.0881, \ 0.3200, \ 0.0000]^T.$$

Recall that short-selling of bonds is avoided, hence all the weights are non-negative.

Surprisingly, the number of nonzero weights in the example above is equal to the number of *equality* constraints in the linear programming problem. As long as the optimisation algorithm converges, this situation remains almost the same: the number of nonzero components of the optimal solution vector w^*, if it exists, will be at most equal to the number of equality constraints. Therefore, in this setting the optimal portfolio will always include at most three bonds, even if there are many other bonds in the portfolio. This might be considered a disadvantage of the immunisation approach.

Outlook

As an introductory section to describe basic concepts and terminology used in finance, the contents presented here are very much influenced by [Brandimarte (2002)] which also contains MATLAB codes and many examples of portfolio management.

Fixed-income securities, portfolio management and immunisation are important concepts of practitioners in bond markets. In [Fabozzi (1997); Gup and Brooks (1993); Sundaresan (1997)], detailed discussions on bond markets and derivatives traded as well as associated risks can be found. Interest rate term structure models and pricing interest rate derivatives are extensively considered, for example, in [Brigo and Mercurio (2001); Musiela and Rutkowski (1997)].

1.2 Portfolio Optimisation

This section deals with *asset allocation* decisions with risky securities. Actually we have seen already that *fixed-income* security is somewhat a misleading term. Bonds, which were considered to have a fixed income, have different yields and, in general, these change in time. Moreover, bonds and portfolio of bonds face different sources of risk. In what follows, risky securities, such as stocks, are considered. Such securities are assets to which *random* cash flows are associated.

Consider a set of n assets. You may purchase the asset i ($1 \leq i \leq n$) at a known price P_i; after holding it for a period, you may then sell it for a price Q_i, which is, however, a *random variable*. Loosely speaking, a random variable, although it is a function, may be considered to be a value of a function, but somewhat this value is *unknown*! Less mathematically oriented reader may skip the following formal definition.

Definition 1.2. A real-valued function X on a sample space Ω is called a *random variable* if the set

$$\{X \leq x\} := \{\omega \in \Omega \; : \; X(\omega) \leq x\} = X^{-1}((-\infty, x])$$

is measurable for all $x \in \mathbb{R}$. That is, $\{X \leq x\} \in \mathcal{F}$. Here $\mathcal{F}$ is a σ–algebra or a σ–field and the triplet $(\Omega, \mathcal{F}, \mathbb{P})$ is a probability space.

The following important identities hold for the expectation $\mathbb{E}[X]$, the variance $\mathbb{V}\text{ar}[X]$, and the covariance $\mathbb{C}\text{ov}[X, Y]$ of random variables X and Y. These are

$$\mathbb{V}\text{ar}[X \mp Y] = \mathbb{V}\text{ar}[X] + \mathbb{V}\text{ar}[Y] \mp 2\,\mathbb{C}\text{ov}[X, Y],$$
$$\mathbb{V}\text{ar}[\alpha X] = \alpha^2\,\mathbb{V}\text{ar}[X],$$
$$\mathbb{C}\text{ov}[\alpha X, Y] = \alpha\,\mathbb{C}\text{ov}[X, Y] = \alpha\,\mathbb{C}\text{ov}[Y, X],$$

where

$$\mathbb{V}\text{ar}[X] = \mathbb{C}\text{ov}[X, X],$$
$$\mathbb{C}\text{ov}[X, Y] = \mathbb{E}\left[(X - \mathbb{E}[X])(Y - \mathbb{E}[Y])\right] = \mathbb{E}[XY] - \mathbb{E}[X]\,\mathbb{E}[Y].$$

It is sometimes useful to write the covariance as

$$\mathbb{C}\text{ov}[X, Y] = \rho_{XY}\sqrt{\mathbb{V}\text{ar}[X]}\sqrt{\mathbb{V}\text{ar}[Y]},$$

where ρ_{XY} is the *correlation coefficient* of the random variables X and Y. The identities above are almost considered prerequisites for the rest of the book and will be used frequently.

Turning back to the n assets with prices P_i, both the *return*

$$R_i = \frac{Q_i}{P_i}$$

and the *rate of return*

$$r_i = \frac{Q_i - P_i}{P_i} = R_i - 1$$

become random variables, because Q_i is a random variable. Note that the rate of return may be negative for an asset, but not less than -1. The worst that can happen is that you lose everything invested on that asset.

In this section, our treatment is going to be limited to the single period problem. The possibility of *re-balancing* the portfolio neither after a while nor continuously in time is considered.

Suppose that an initial wealth Π_0 is given, and that it should be allocated on a set of n risky assets at the beginning of the investment period. Then, you would like to maximise the wealth Π at the end of the investment period. However, since returns are random, Π is a random variable as well, and maximising it does not really make sense! Thus, some thought is needed to define a sensible objective function. One possibility is to maximise the expected value, $\mathbb{E}[\Pi]$, of the portfolio wealth. However, in such a case, you would be ignoring risks completely. Indeed, one has to trade off risks and returns by finding a way to quantify risks. Basically, managing a portfolio of risky assets requires a way to trade-off risks and potential returns.

If the rate of return of an asset is assumed to be normally distributed, then the rate of return can be characterised by the two parameters of the normal distribution completely: the expected return $\bar{r}_i = \mathbb{E}[r_i]$ and the standard deviation σ_i or the variance $\sigma_i^2 = \mathbb{V}\text{ar}[r_i]$. The variance may be considered as a measure of risk; the larger the variance, the larger the possibility of having both large positive and large negative returns.

However, constructing a portfolio of risky assets needs special care. Consider a simple example, and suppose that you have two assets with $\bar{r}_1 > \bar{r}_2$ and $\sigma_1 > \sigma_2$. That is, the asset 1 has better potential than the asset 2, but it is riskier. Which one is better? Of course, there is no easy answer, in that it depends on the subjective attitude toward risk.

On the other hand, when choosing a portfolio an investor has the aim of obtaining a return as large as possible. If the only criterion to judge this is the mean of the portfolio return, then this will typically lead to investing the whole wealth in the security with the highest mean return. However, this could be a very risky asset and thus, the return can have big fluctuations. To accommodate this fact, we introduce the idea of minimising the possible risk as a second criterion. As a measure of this risk, the portfolio variance is chosen. The basic idea of *Markowitz* was to look for a balance between risk and return, that is, the variance and the mean of the portfolio.

1.2.1 *Basic Mean-Variance Portfolio Optimisation*

A relatively simple approach to portfolio optimisation is based on the idea of restricting the choice to "reasonable" portfolios. If you fix the expected return you want to get from the investment, you would like to find the portfolio achieving this expected return, but with minimal risk. Similarly, if you fix the level of risk you are willing to take, you would like to select a portfolio maximising the expected return. This approach leads to the theory of *mean-variance* portfolio.

Let us consider the asset allocation problem again, when only two risky assets are available. Apparently, the problem is solved when $\bar{r}_1 > \bar{r}_2$ and $\sigma_1 < \sigma_2$. In this case, the asset 1 has a larger expected return than asset 2, and it is less risky; hence a naïve argument would lead to the conclusion that asset 2 should not be considered at all. However, this may not be the case, since the possible *correlation* between the assets is completely ignored. The inclusion of asset 2 may, in fact, be beneficial in reducing the risk. Choosing the asset with relatively less variance turns out to be the "wrong" action that is to be taken by the ones who do not like risks. Thus, there is a need for a mathematical formulation of the problem in order to decide on "reasonable" portfolio of risky securities.

In general, the interesting quantities are the portfolio weights,

$$w_i = \frac{\varphi_i P_i}{\Pi_0},$$

of n assets with prices P_i ($i = 1, 2, \ldots, n$). Here, φ_i is the number of shares of the asset i and Π_0 is the total initial wealth of the portfolio, say π. Therefore, a natural constraint on the weights is

$$\sum_{i=1}^{n} w_i = w_1 + w_2 + \cdots + w_n = \sum_{i=1}^{n} \frac{\varphi_i P_i}{\Pi_0} = 1.$$

Note that the initial portfolio wealth Π_0 is not considered, but the allocation of fractions of this wealth. In fact, it is obvious that if φ_i is the number of shares of the security i with price P_i, then

$$\Pi_0 = \sum_{i=1}^{n} \varphi_i P_i$$

holds for the n-asset portfolio π with weights

$$w_i = \frac{\varphi_i P_i}{\Pi_0}, \qquad i = 1, 2, \ldots, n.$$

Hence, knowing the weight w_i will help us decide on what positions to take for the asset i. If, further, *short-selling* is ruled out, then the requirement on the weights is that

$$w_i \geq 0, \qquad i = 1, 2, \ldots, n.$$

Now, the *rate of return* of the portfolio π is

$$r_\pi = r_\pi(w) = \sum_{i=1}^{n} w_i\, r_i = w^T r,$$

where

$$w = [w_1, w_2, \ldots, w_n]^T \quad \text{and} \quad r = [r_1, r_2, \ldots, r_n]^T$$

are column vectors in $\mathbb{R}^n$, of weights and rate of returns, respectively. The *expected return* of the portfolio can easily be calculated to give

$$\bar{r}_\pi = \bar{r}_\pi(w) = \sum_{i=1}^{n} w_i\, \bar{r}_i = w^T \bar{r}. \tag{1.23}$$

The vector $\bar{r} \in \mathbb{R}^n$ for the expected rate of return is similarly defined.

The variance σ_π^2 of r_π of the portfolio can be computed by using the basic properties of variance. For the two-asset case, this is relatively easy:

$$\begin{aligned}
\sigma_\pi^2 = \sigma_\pi^2(w) &= \mathrm{Var}\,[w_1 r_1 + w_2 r_2] \\
&= w_1^2 \sigma_1^2 + 2 w_1 w_2 \sigma_{12} + w_2^2 \sigma_2^2 \\
&= w^T \Sigma w.
\end{aligned}$$

Here the matrix Σ is the covariance matrix of the returns r_1 and r_2, and it is defined by

$$\Sigma = \begin{bmatrix} \sigma_{11} & \sigma_{12} \\ \sigma_{21} & \sigma_{22} \end{bmatrix} \quad \text{such that} \quad \begin{aligned} \sigma_{ii} &= \sigma_i^2, \\ \sigma_{ij} &= \sigma_{ji}, \end{aligned}$$

where σ_{12} is the covariance of r_1 and r_2. Carrying out the same calculations in the case of n assets, you obtain

$$\sigma_\pi^2 = \sigma_\pi^2(w) = \sum_{i=1}^{n} \sum_{j=1}^{n} w_i \sigma_{ij} w_j = w^T \Sigma w, \tag{1.24}$$

where $\Sigma \in \mathbb{R}^{n \times n}$ is the covariance matrix of the returns of the n assets. Note that the covariance matrix Σ is symmetric, namely, $\sigma_{ij} = \sigma_{ji}$ for all i and j.

For different choices of the vector w of weights, different portfolios are characterised by the expected value of their returns in (1.23), and the variances in (1.24). The latter is assumed to be a measure for the portfolio that carries risk. Therefore, an investor would like both to minimise the variance, and to maximise the expected return. However, these two objectives are, in general, conflicting, and a trade-off must be found. Essentially, the *mean-variance* approach of Markowitz to portfolio optimisation can be summarised as follows:

- For a given *lower* bound $\bar{r}_T$ for the mean of the portfolio return we must choose an admissible portfolio π so that the variance σ_π^2 is *minimal* with $\bar{r}_\pi \geq \bar{r}_T$.
- For a given *upper* bound σ_T^2 for the variance of the portfolio return we must choose an admissible portfolio π so that the return $\bar{r}_\pi$ is *maximal* with $\sigma_\pi^2 \leq \sigma_T^2$.

In Fig. 1.13 a typical set for the attainable pairs $(\sigma_\pi^2, \bar{r}_\pi)$ for all admissible portfolios is plotted. Only the portfolios π whose pairs $(\sigma_\pi^2, \bar{r}_\pi)$ are on the bold (upper-left) part of the curve has the specific property that it is not possible to obtain a higher expected return without increasing the variance. In general, there are infinitely many such portfolios and it is reasonable to assume that an investor would like to choose one of them.

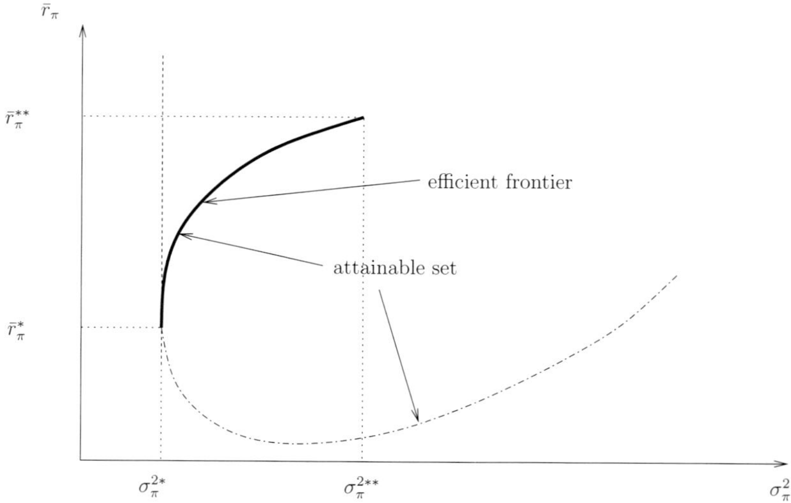

Fig. 1.13   Efficient frontier

Definition 1.3. A portfolio is called *efficient* if it is not possible to obtain a higher expected return without increasing risk. The set of efficient portfolios is called *efficient set* or *efficient frontier*.

It is reasonable, at first, if minimising the variance of the portfolio is chosen for a given fixed lower bound $\bar{r}_T$ for the expected return. This is achieved by solving the following optimisation problem:

$$
(\mathcal{QP}) \ : \ \begin{cases} \text{minimise} \quad \sigma_\pi^2 = w^T \Sigma w \\ \text{subject to} \\ \qquad\qquad w^T \bar{r} \geq \bar{r}_T \\ \qquad\qquad \sum_{i=1}^n w_i = 1 \\ \qquad\qquad w_i \geq 0, \quad 1 \leq i \leq N. \end{cases} \tag{1.25}
$$

This is a *quadratic programming* problem (QP), moreover, with a positive semi-definite[2] matrix Σ. This problem can be solved very efficiently by using standard quadratic programming algorithms.

On the other hand, one may choose the other side of the coin and consider the task of maximising the expected portfolio return $\bar{r}_\pi$, under a given upper bound σ_T^2 for the variance σ_π^2. In this case, the problem is formulated as

$$
(\mathcal{LP})_q \ : \ \begin{cases} \text{minimise} \quad \bar{r}_\pi = w^T \bar{r} \\ \text{subject to} \\ \qquad\qquad w^T \Sigma w \leq \sigma_T^2 \\ \qquad\qquad \sum_{i=1}^n w_i = 1 \\ \qquad\qquad w_i \geq 0, \quad 1 \leq i \leq N. \end{cases} \tag{1.26}
$$

The problem is now a *linear programming* one, however, with a *quadratic* constraint. For such problems there are no special standard algorithms. Of course, one could treat this problem with general methods of nonlinear optimisation, but this would lead to inefficient algorithms.

Therefore, in the following, the first principle of the Markowitz mean-variance approach is considered. That is, we consider the quadratic minimisation problem $(\mathcal{QP})$ in (1.25) that reduces the risk associated with the portfolio. The example below shows that under the mean-variance approach it can be optimal to invest on a relatively risky security. Moreover, it presents a way to find the optimal solution, for simplicity, in the case of two dimensions. Of course, applying numerical methods in case of large dimensions is unavoidable.

---

[2]A real matrix $\Sigma \in \mathbb{R}^{n \times n}$ is called *positive semi-definite* if $x^T \Sigma x \geq 0$ for all $x \in \mathbb{R}^n$.

Example 1.7. Suppose that we have two risky securities, such as stocks, whose respective expected rate of returns and their variances are as follows:

$$\bar{r}_1 = \mathbb{E}\left[r_1\right] = 1, \quad \bar{r}_2 = \mathbb{E}\left[r_2\right] = 0.9,$$
$$\sigma_1^2 = \sigma_{11} = \mathrm{Var}\left[r_1\right] = 0.1, \quad \sigma_2^2 = \sigma_{22} = \mathrm{Var}\left[r_2\right] = 0.2.$$

Moreover, these two securities are assumed to be negatively correlated with the covariance

$$\mathbb{C}\mathrm{ov}\left[r_1, r_2\right] = \sigma_{12} = \sigma_{21} = -0.1.$$

Constructing a very simple portfolio π_s of a very simple form,

$$r_{\pi_s} = \frac{1}{2}r_1 + \frac{1}{2}r_2,$$

shows that the risk of having invested only on one of the securities is considerably reduced. However, the decrease in the expected return is relatively small despite a relatively small decrease in the expected return. The expected rate of return of such a portfolio is

$$\bar{r}_{\pi_s} = \mathbb{E}\left[r_{\pi_s}\right] = \frac{1}{2} + \frac{0.9}{2} = 0.95 < 1 = \max\{\bar{r}_1, \bar{r}_2\}.$$

However, its variance becomes

$$\sigma_{\pi_s}^2 = \frac{0.1}{4} + \frac{0.2}{4} - \frac{0.2}{4} = 0.025 < 0.1 = \min\{\sigma_1^2, \sigma_2^2\}.$$

In other words, the risk is reduced by 75% although the drop in the return is just 5% of investing in the first security.

In fact, an investor would be more interested in the solution of the quadratic problem $(\mathcal{QP})$ in (1.25) by specifying a lower bound $\bar{r}_T$ for the expected return of the portfolio. Now, suppose that such a target return is prescribed as

$$\bar{r}_T = 0.98,$$

and we are interested in finding the *optimal* portfolio π^* having the minimal variance with the weights $w^* = [w_1^*, w_2^*]^T$. So, in this case, the quadratic programming problem turns out to be minimising the objective function

$$\sigma_\pi^2 = (0.1)w_1^2 + (0.2)w_2^2 - (0.2)w_1 w_2,$$

on the feasible region

$$D = \{(w_1, w_2) \; : \; w_1 + w_2 = 1, \; w_1 + (0.9)w_2 \geq 0.98, \; w_1, w_2 \geq 0\}.$$

This region is shown in Fig. 1.14 by the bold line segment on $w_1 + w_2 = 1$.

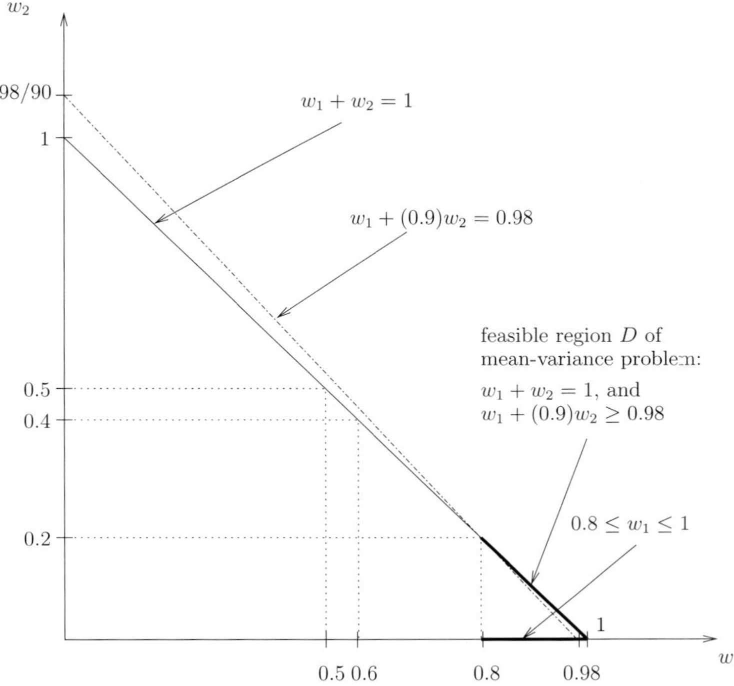

Fig. 1.14 Domain and optimal solution for the quadratic programming problem in Example 1.7

The equality constraint $w_1 + w_2 = 1$ helps us reduce the problem into a one-dimensional one by rewriting the objective function as follows:

$$\sigma_\pi^2 = (0.1)w_1^2 + (0.2)(1 - w_1)^2 - (0.2)w_1(1 - w_1)$$
$$= (0.5)w_1^2 - (0.6)w_1 + (0.2).$$

This is again a quadratic function, but only in the variable w_1. Moreover, w_1 is restricted to the closed region,

$$0.8 \leq w_1 \leq 1,$$

because of the inequality constraint, $w_1 + (0.9)(1 - w_1) \geq 0.98$, which is also shown in Fig. 1.14 by another bold line on the w_1-axis. First, observe that the critical point $w_1 = 0.6$ is not in the considered region and hence is not feasible. In fact, at such a critical point, $\bar{r}_\pi(0.6, 0.4) = 0.96 < 0.98$, although the variance is reduced to $\sigma_\pi^2(0.6, 0.4) = 0.02$. Therefore, in the feasible region, $w_1 \geq 0.8$, the optimal solution occurs at the left-end point $w_1 = 0.8$ of the interval $[0.8, 1]$. So,

$$w_1 = w_1^* = 0.8 \quad \text{and} \quad w_2 = w_2^* = 0.2$$

are the values of the weights for the optimal portfolio π^*. At these optimal weights, the variance of the portfolio return is computed to give

$$\sigma_\pi^{2*} = (0.5)(0.8)^2 - (0.6)(0.8) + (0.2) = 0.4,$$

and the expected rate of return becomes

$$\bar{r}_\pi^* = (0.8) + (0.9)(0.2) = 0.98.$$

Table 1.1 summarises some of the portfolios of this example.

Table 1.1 Portfolios observed in Example 1.7

$[w_1, w_2]$	$\bar{r}_\pi$	σ_π^2
$[0.5, 0.5]$	0.95	0.025
$[0.6, 0.4]$	0.96	0.02
$[0.8, 0.2]$	0.98	0.04*

*optimal solution.

The example above and Table 1.1 suggest a way in order to find possible admissible portfolios by changing the inequality constraint to an equality constraint systematically. Instead of the quadratic minimisation problem $(\mathcal{QP})$ in (1.25) for a given target $\bar{r}_T$, the following *modified* one is considered:

$$(\mathcal{QP})_{eq} \ : \ \begin{cases} \text{minimise} \quad \sigma_\pi^2 = w^T \Sigma w \\ \text{subject to} \\ \qquad\qquad w^T \bar{r} = \bar{r}_T \\ \qquad \sum_{i=1}^n w_i = 1 \\ \qquad\qquad w_i \geq 0, \quad 1 \leq i \leq N. \end{cases} \tag{1.27}$$

Note that in this problem there are *equality constraints* $w^T \bar{r} = \bar{r}_T$ instead of the inequality ones. Therefore, given the lower and the upper bound for the expected return, we discretize the possible returns, say by $\bar{r}_T(\ell)$, where ℓ is in some index set. Then, at each of these discrete levels, the optimal weights that are associated with the portfolio are solved by considering the following problem,

$$\underset{w}{\text{minimise}} \quad \sigma_\pi^2(\ell) = w^T \Sigma w$$

subject to

$$w^T \bar{r} = \bar{r}_T(\ell) \tag{1.28}$$
$$\sum_{i=1}^n w_i = 1$$
$$w_i \geq 0, \quad 1 \leq i \leq N$$

for every ℓ in the index set. For each target $\bar{r}_T(\ell)$, the points in the mean-variance attainable set are then computed. The portfolios $\pi = \pi(w, \ell)$, depending also on ℓ, with the vector $w = w(\ell)$ of weights, will indeed have minimum variance $\sigma_\pi^2(\ell)$ at the ℓth level.

It is possible to use a MATLAB built-in function for the purpose of selecting efficient portfolios, especially in cases where there are a large number of assets. For instance, in Fig. 1.15 a MATLAB script that plots the mean-variance *efficient frontier* is shown, which also calculates the parameters of five possible efficient portfolios. Although the script is written for two-asset case, it is easy to modify it to include more assets. The output of the script is summarised in Table 1.2 and the readers are advised to check the corresponding data with the ones given in Table 1.1 of Example 1.7.

```
 ──────────────────── efficient_frontier.m ────────────────────
% Efficient Portfolios
clear all, close all
expectedReturns = [1, 0.9]; covarianceMatrix = [0.1, -0.1; -0.1, 0.2];
% frontcon(expectedReturns, covarianceMatrix) % plots efficient frontier
[standardDev, returns, weights] = ...
    frontcon(expectedReturns, covarianceMatrix, 5);
variances = standardDev .^ 2; [weights, returns, variances]
```

Fig. 1.15   A simple MATLAB script that sets up the *efficient frontier*

Table 1.2   Output from the script in Fig. 1.15

$[w_1, w_2]$	$\bar{r}_\pi$	σ_π^2
$[0.6000, 0.4000]$	0.9600	0.0200
$[0.7000, 0.3000]$	0.9700	0.0250
$[0.8000, 0.2000]$	0.9800	0.0400
$[0.9000, 0.1000]$	0.9900	0.0650
$[1.0000, 0.0000]$	1.0000	0.1000

Inspired by the built-in function, we wish to find the set of attainable portfolios within a given range of expected rate of returns as targets. The following example illustrates the idea of minimum variance approach by solving the modified problem $(\mathcal{QP})_{eq}$ in (1.27).

Example 1.8. This example focuses on recursively solving the quadratic programming problem $(\mathcal{QP})_{eq}$ in (1.25) with the equality constraints. Here the target $\bar{r}_T$ ranges from a lower bound of possible expected rate of returns, say $\bar{r}_l$, to an upper one, $\bar{r}_h$. Hence, all attainable portfolios will be characterised by their weights. Among those portfolios one can then extract the ones which are also efficient, that is, on the *efficient frontier*. The values of $\bar{r}_l$ and $\bar{r}_h$ are chosen as the minimum and the maximum values of the expected rate of returns of the assets, respectively. In Fig. 1.16, the idea of discretizing the expected rate of returns by the required number of attainable portfolios is presented. After preparing the necessary input data, we recursively solve for the weights in the quadratic programming problem $(\mathcal{QP})_{eq}$ for each discretized level of expected rate of returns.

```
――――――――――――――――――― attainablePortfolios.m ―――――――――――
function [standardDev, returnLevels, weights] = ...
    attainablePortfolios(expectedReturns, covarianceMatrix,nPoints)

n = length(expectedReturns);
% discretize the portfolio expected target returns
lowest = min(expectedReturns); highest = max(expectedReturns);
step = (highest-lowest) / (nPoints-1); returnLevels = (lowest:step:highest)';
m=length(returnLevels); variances = zeros(1,m); weights = zeros(n,m);

% set up the quadratic programming
c = zeros(n,1); Aeq = [expectedReturns; ones(1,n)];
vlb = zeros(n,1); vub = ones(n,1); x0 = zeros(1,n);

for i = 1:m
    beq = [returnLevels(i,1);1];
        x = quadprog(covarianceMatrix, c, [], [], Aeq, beq, vlb, vub, x0);
        variances(i) = x' * covarianceMatrix * x; weights(:,i) = x;
end
standardDev = sqrt(variances);
```

Fig. 1.16   A simple MATLAB function for the attainable portfolios

In order to test the approach and point a portfolio with arbitrary weights, the script in Fig. 1.17 is executed. The output of the script, the graphs of the mean-variance attainable set and the efficient frontier, are plotted in Fig. 1.18.

The portfolio with weights $w = [0.5, 0.5]^T$ of the example is not an

```
_________________________ testAttainablePortfolios.m _________________________
% testAttainablePortfolios
clear all, close all
expectedReturns = [1, 0.9]; covarianceMatrix = [0.1, -0.1; -0.1, 0.2];

[standardDevM, returnsM, weightsM] = ...
    frontcon(expectedReturns, covarianceMatrix,20);
[standardDev, returns, weights] = ...
    attainablePortfolios(expectedReturns, covarianceMatrix,50);

myWeights = [0.5, 0.5]; myReturn = myWeights * expectedReturns';
myStandardDev = sqrt(myWeights * covarianceMatrix * myWeights');
plot(standardDevM, returnsM, 'r', 'LineWidth',2), hold on
plot(standardDev, returns, 'gx-.'), plot(myStandardDev, myReturn, 'bo')
text(myStandardDev, myReturn, '  my Portfolio','Fontsize',12),
legend('using "frontcon"', 'attainablePortfolios'),
ylabel('Portfolio expected return','Fontsize',12)
xlabel('Portfolio standard deviation','Fontsize',12)
print -r900 -deps '../figures/testAttainablePortfolios'
```

Fig. 1.17   A simple MATLAB script for the attainable portfolios

efficient portfolio, for sure, and it has to be adjusted. To do so, one needs the solution of the quadratic programming ($\mathcal{QP}$) in (1.25) together with a desired target value $\bar{r}_T$ for the lower bound of the expected rate of return. Even if the rate of return of the portfolio is satisfactory, it must still be adjusted to the desired position on the efficient frontier: the quadratic programming problem ($\mathcal{QP}$) must be solved for the optimal weights. Note also that in the above example, the expected rate of returns, variances and the covariances are as the same as the ones given in Example 1.7. Recall that the vector of optimal weights was found to be $w^* = [0.8, 0.2]^T$. Therefore, the portfolio should be adjusted with those optimal weights.

Exercise 1.1. Suppose that we have a set of *time series* $S_i^{(j)}$ for the values of n assets $S^{(j)}$, where $j = 1, 2, \ldots, n$ and $i = 1, 2, \ldots, N$. Considering the time series for $r^{(j)}$ and using the *sample mean* and the basic properties of $\mathrm{Cov}\left[r^{(j)}, r^{(s)}\right]$, calculate the average expected rate of return of each asset and the covariance matrix. Having computed these parameters you can then use the algorithm presented in Fig. 1.16 to find the attainable portfolios, and hence, the efficient frontier.

Outlook

An alternative approach to mean-variance portfolio optimisation is the so-called *utility maximisation*. This approach considers obtaining an optimal portfolio by using a suitably chosen *utility function* instead of minimising

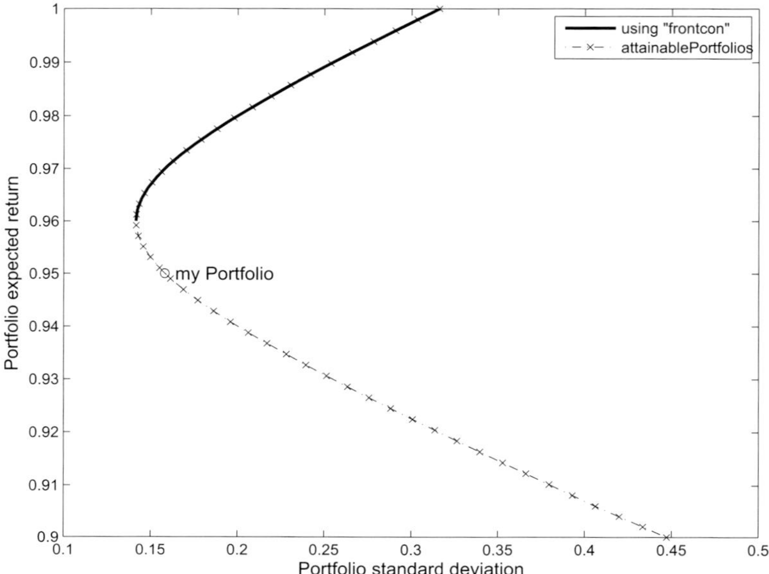

Fig. 1.18　The *efficient frontier* and a current portfolio of the MATLAB script in Fig. 1.17

the variance. In other words, the problem

$$
\begin{cases}
\underset{w\in\mathbb{R}}{\text{maximise}} \; \mathbb{E}\left[U(\bar{r}_\pi)\right] \\
\text{subject to} \\
\qquad \sum_{i=1}^{n} w_i = 1 \\
\qquad\quad w_i \geq 0, \quad 1 \leq i \leq N
\end{cases}
$$

is considered, where U is an utility function. More information and discussions on the choices of the utility functions as well as the utility approach to optimal portfolios can be found in [Elton and Gruber (1995); Korn (1997); Merton (1990)]. These also include *dynamic programming* approaches for optimal portfolios due to the lack of mean-variance portfolio optimisation.

References on theoretical and practical aspects of optimisation in general consist of [Fletcher (1987); Nash and Sofer (1996); Sundaram (1996)]. For applications of optimisation, especially, for the use of integer and multistage stochastic programming in finance and economics, we refer to [Brandimarte (2002)].

Chapter 2

Option Pricing and Binomial Methods

Financial markets have created many instruments that assist and regulate agreements on delivery of certain goods in the future. These instruments are generally contracts, written on an underlying asset, between two parties. They are simply called *derivatives* since their values and characteristic features depend on the underlying asset, which can be stocks, indexes, currencies and so on.

This chapter introduces such derivatives, but mainly it focuses on *options* and their basic properties. Pricing derivatives, especially options, is the central theme in financial engineering and computational finance. The no-arbitrage principle is again very helpful in the calculation of the *fair value* of the premium that is to be paid when signing a derivative contract.

In order to price an option, the dynamics of the underlying asset is of great importance. Although this dynamics is generally described by (continuous) stochastic models, this chapter contains discrete binomial models. The methods derived from such models are called the *tree* or the *lattice* methods. The parameters of these methods are obtained from the corresponding continuous stochastic models or their approximations, hence, there are a variety of different binomial methods in literature. Since their implementations are relatively easier than other methods in option pricing, tree methods are very popular among academics as well as practitioners of the market.

2.1 Options

An *option* is the right, but not the obligation, to buy or sell an asset (mostly, a risky one) at a prescribed fixed price within a specified period. An option is also a financial instrument that allows to make a bet on rising or falling

35

values of an underlying asset. The underlying asset typically is a stock. However, the underlying can be any other: shares of a company, stock indexes, currencies, or commodities. Since the value of an option depends on the value of the underlying asset, options and many other related financial instruments, such as *futures, forwards, swaps*, are simply called *derivatives*.

Being a financial derivative, an option is an agreement between two parties on trading the asset at a "certain" future time. One party is the *writer*, often a bank, who fixes the terms of the option contract and sells the option. The other party is the *holder*, who purchases the option, paying the *market price*, which is called the *premium*. Calculation of a *fair value* of this premium that has to be paid when entering the contract is a central theme in finance.

When you buy a *call* option, you get the right to buy the underlying asset for a price K, called the *exercise price* (or *strike*) at a certain date T, known as the *expiration date* (or *maturity*). Suppose that the underlying asset is a stock whose price is a *random variable* $S_t := S(t)$, depending on the time t. If at maturity the actual price S_T is larger than the exercise price K, you would exercise the option and buy the stock, since you may sell the stock immediately and gain $S_T - K$. Of course, if the contrary happens, you would not exercise the option and let it expire worthless. Thus, the *payoff* of such a call option is

$$P = \max\{S_T - K, 0\} =: (S_T - K)^+ . \tag{2.1}$$

An illustration of the payoff function in (2.1) is shown in Fig. 2.1(a).

With a *put* option, on the other hand, you have the right to sell the stock. In this case, you would exercise the option only if the strike price is larger than the market value S_T at maturity T. So the payoff of such a put option becomes

$$P = \max\{K - S_T, 0\} =: (K - S_T)^+ . \tag{2.2}$$

The payoff of a put option is depicted in Fig. 2.1(b).

Depending on the time of exercise, there are two basic types of options: with a *European* option you may exercise your right only at maturity T; an *American* option, however, may be exercised whenever you wish within the life time of the option. These are called *vanilla* options, owing their name to their simplicity. Unlike European and American options, a *Bermudan* option gives its holder the right to exercise at a set of prescribed dates within

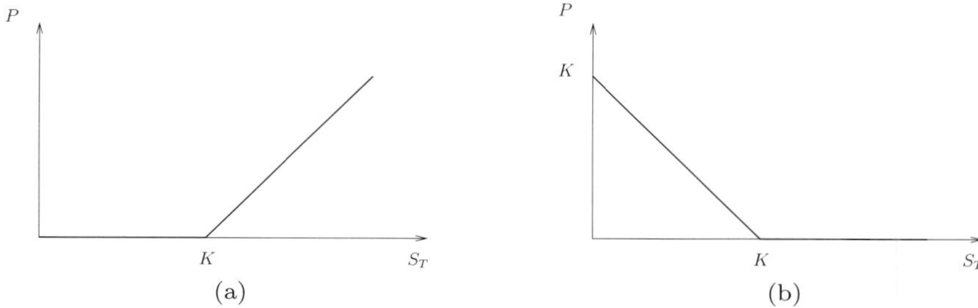

Fig. 2.1   Payoff functions. (a) for a call option, (b) for a put option

the time *horizon*. There are many other types of options, some of which depend on the asset's path, some do not. *Asian* options, for example, have a payoff depending on the average price of the underlying stock; thus they depend on the *path* of the stock movement before the maturity. Generally, they are called *exotic* options. European vanilla options, on the other hand, do not depend on the path of the underlying, while American options implicitly do.

Indeed, quite complex exotic options are actually designed and traded (we refer to [Zhang (1998)]) due to the fact that options are used to control risks of having a portfolio of risky assets, such as stocks. For instance, holding such a portfolio may carry the risk that stock price may decline. In such cases, one can protect himself, or reduce the risk of a large loss, by buying a put option on the same underlying. On the other hand, a similar protection against rising of the underlying stock prices can be achieved by buying call options on the same underlying, generally a stock.

Moreover, since gains from options may be more than those of holding the underlying asset, options attract speculators. Here is an example of such a situation, the so-called *leverage* effect of trading options.

Example 2.1. Suppose that a stock price is \$50 per share, and you believe that it will "rise" in the future. Then you buy a share of the stock and put it in a safe. You were right; a month later the stock price becomes \$55, you sell your shares and gain the rate of return

$$\frac{55 - 50}{50} = 0.1, \qquad (\text{i.e., } 10\%).$$

On the other hand, in view of your judgement of the stock price, you may choose to buy a call option instead, with strike $K = \$50$, on that underlying stock maturing one month later. The option price is most probably cheaper than a share of the stock itself, say it costs \$2.5. Hence, one month later you would exercise the option and your rate of return would be

$$\frac{55 - 50 - 2.5}{2.5} = 1, \qquad \text{(i.e., 100\%)}.$$

This effect is called *leverage* or *gearing*. Of course, there is the other side of the coin: consider what happens if the stock price drops to \$45.

There are two basic issues in dealing with derivatives. The first issue is *pricing*: a key role in pricing is played by the *no-arbitrage* argument. One assumes that arbitrage is not possible. In fact, in an idealised market, information spreads rapidly and arbitrage opportunities become apparent so that arbitrage cannot last for long. The second issue is *hedging*: an important application of derivatives. Hedging is fundamental, for the writer of a call (option), for example, to avoid being hit by rising asset prices. Although pricing of options is the central theme of this book, players of the market are, in general, interested in trading strategies to reduce and, if possible, to avoid risks by hedging.

2.1.1   *The No-Arbitrage Principle*

The use of the no-arbitrage argument has already been applied in pricing bonds, which were regarded as riskless securities. This argument, or rather the principle, is of great importance in pricing options as well. Roughly speaking, *arbitrage* means a risk-free profit; in a more involved setting, *arbitrage* means the existence of a portfolio or a self-financing strategy constructed initially with no capital, but, with a probability of gain at maturity. An arbitrage opportunity can loosely be stated as a *free lunch*.

In an idealised market, existence of arbitrage opportunities would be realised by all *arbitrageurs* and other players so that it will not last long. The market would lead to adjustments of prices and wipe out the possible arbitrage opportunities. For modelling of financial markets this leads to the postulate, the *no-arbitrage principle*: the *absence of arbitrage* is assumed in a "good" market. In order to distinguish possible arbitrage it is also assumed that there is a *risk-free* or *risk-neutral*, continuously compounding interest rate, which is considered to be positive throughout the time horizon. For pricing purposes it is accepted that one can borrow and lend money in any amount at the risk-free interest rate. Among possible candidates for such an interest rate are LIBOR or EURIBOR rates, which can also be found in financial papers.

To illustrate the idea and make use of the *no-arbitrage* principle in pricing derivatives, consider the fair price of a *forward* contract written at time $t_0 = 0$. Unlike options, a forward contract binds the two parties, the holder and the writer, to buy and sell one share of a certain asset at a certain date T in future and for a price F. Although the price S_0 of the asset is known when the contract is signed, the price S_T at time T is a random variable. Therefore, it seems that the forward price F is a random variable, too. Apparently, a simple arbitrage argument shows that this is not the case, and a fair price,

$$F = S_0 e^{rT}, \tag{2.3}$$

can be assigned and written to the contract today. Here, r is the risk-free interest rate.

In order to show that the price in (2.3) is an arbitrage-free, fair price for both parties involved, we consider the writer (seller) of the contract, who is obliged to deliver the asset at time T in exchange for F. He can simply borrow S_0 amount of money, buy the asset and put it in a safe. When the contract expires at maturity T he delivers the asset to the buyer and gets his F. With F he must be able to pay his debt, which has grown to $S_0 e^{rT}$ due to the continuously compounding, risk-free interest rate. Hence, the price F written to the contract should not be less than $S_0 e^{rT}$, otherwise he would lose money with certainty. The buyer would then be taking the advantage of a low price. Therefore, to avoid arbitrage, it must be true that

$$F \geq S_0 e^{rT}.$$

However, the buyer of the contract can simply reverse the strategy of the seller: if what is written into the contract is more than $S_0 e^{rT}$, then he would certainly have a loss at maturity. Thus, F must not be more than $S_0 e^{rT}$, that is,

$$F \leq S_0 e^{rT}.$$

Therefore, $F = S_0 e^{rT}$ is the fair value for the price of a forward, which should be written into the contract at time $t_0 = 0$ to avoid arbitrage. Otherwise, an arbitrage opportunity exists for one of the parties for sure.

Here is an important application of the *no-arbitrage* argument, applied to European options. The conclusion of the example below is the so-called *put-call parity* for European options, and it will be used frequently in subsequent parts of the book.

Example 2.2. Consider a stock with spot price S_0 at time $t_0 = 0$. Suppose that there are European type call and put options on that stock, both maturing at T, with the same strike K. Denote the values of these call and put options, respectively, by V_C and V_P, and construct the following two portfolios.

$\Pi^{(1)}$: Consists of one European call and Ke^{-rT} amount of cash, where r is the risk-free interest rate.

$\Pi^{(2)}$: Consists of one European put and one share of the underlying stock.

At time $t = 0$ these portfolios have the respective values,

$$\Pi_0^{(1)} = V_C + Ke^{-rT}, \quad \Pi_0^{(2)} = V_P + S_0.$$

At the maturity $t = T$, however, due to the unknown stock price S_T, there are two cases to consider:

(i) $S_T > K$. In such a case, the call option is exercised and the cash earns the risk-free interest rate. Hence, the value of the first portfolio at maturity T is

$$\Pi_T^{(1)} = S_T - K + Ke^{-rT}e^{rT} = S_T.$$

On the other hand, the second portfolio has the value

$$\Pi_T^{(2)} = 0 + S_T = S_T.$$

Here, in the portfolio $\Pi^{(2)}$, the put option expires worthless. These two portfolios have the same value S_T at maturity T.

(ii) $S_T \leq K$. A similar argument made in (i) shows that the values of those two portfolios are again the same:

$$\Pi_T^{(1)} = 0 + K = K,$$

and

$$\Pi_T^{(2)} = K - S_T + S_T = K.$$

In each of the cases, (i) and (ii), the portfolios have the same value at time T. Hence, their values at time $t_0 = 0$ must be equal; otherwise there will be an arbitrage opportunity: one would simply buy the portfolio that is cheaper and sell the other, putting the difference into his pocket. Since both portfolios are worth the same at maturity no matter what the stock price S_T becomes, the investor would gain the risk-free interest rate. Therefore, in order to avoid arbitrage, the following equality must hold,

$$\Pi_0^{(1)} = \Pi_0^{(2)},$$

at time $t = t_0$. This implies the *put-call parity* for European options:

$$V_C + Ke^{-rT} = V_P + S_0. \tag{2.4}$$

Equivalently, the *put-call parity* for European options is written, sometimes, in the form:

$$S_0 + V_P - V_C = Ke^{-rT}.$$

This equation can also be interpreted as follows: construct a portfolio, say Π, consisting of one share stock, a put option, and a short position in a call option on the same stock. Hence, such a portfolio will earn the strike price K at maturity T for sure, that is, the constructed portfolio is a riskless one.

Conventionally, at a given time t such that $t_0 \le t \le T$ the stock price is denoted by S_t, and it is assumed to be known. One can easily modify the *put-call parity* to reflect this conventional situation: Denoting the values of call and put options by $V_C(S_t, t)$ and $V_P(S_t, t)$, respectively, and noting that $T - t$ is the remaining time to maturity, the put-call parity in (2.4) for European options changes to

$$S_t + V_P(S_t, t) - V_C(S_t, t) = Ke^{-r(T-t)}. \tag{2.5}$$

Further generalisation of the put-call parity considers the stocks that pay *dividends* to the share holders. When dividends are paid the price S_t of the asset instantaneously drops by the amount of payment, because of the no-arbitrage principle. Although dividends can be paid at certain discrete times we assume a continuous dividend yield, $D \ge 0$. The continuous flow of dividends is modelled by a decrease of S_t in each infinitesimal time interval dt by the amount $DS_t dt$. In such a case, a dynamic strategy for continuously updating (balancing) the constructed portfolio Π_t as time passes is needed: you buy $e^{-D(T-t)}$ number of shares of the stock with the price S_t and then keep buying the stock by the dividends paid until maturity so that at maturity T you have exactly one share of the underlying. That is, the portfolio,

$$\Pi_t = S_t e^{-D(T-t)} + V_P(S_t, t) - V_C(S_t, t),$$

constructed at time t, is a riskless one and earns the strike K at maturity for sure. If the no-arbitrage principle is applied to this portfolio, then the modified *put-call parity* for European options becomes

$$S_t e^{-D(T-t)} + V_P(S_t, t) - V_C(S_t, t) = Ke^{-r(T-t)} \tag{2.6}$$

in the case when the underlying stock pays dividends with continuous dividend rate D.

Outlook

The use of the no-arbitrage principle is very common in pricing financial derivatives. Some of the classical books on options, futures, and other financial products as well as financial institutions are [Cox and Rubinstein (1985); Hull (2000); Kwok (1998); Pliska (1997)], the latter of which may be regarded as a comprehensive guide to the theory of arbitrage in discrete-time models. The theory of arbitrage in continuous-time models, however, is considered, for instance, in [Björk (1998)].

2.2 The Binomial Model

The use of arbitrage arguments leads to pricing equations in the form of *partial differential equations* (PDEs). These equations rarely have closed-form solutions, and hence, numerical methods are of great help in solving PDEs. Some of the numerical methods used extensively in literature will be studied later in the book. However, the no-arbitrage principle can also be used in deriving *tree methods*. In this respect, binomial methods are easy to implement and understand pricing of derivative securities.

The major part of this book is devoted to continuous-time models of the underlying assets' dynamics and their discretization. However, a discrete approach to asset prices may provide us with a short way to establish a first algorithm for calculating fair values of options as an introduction.

To begin with, let us discretize the time horizon $[0, T]$ with steps of width δt. If $\delta t = T$, then the model is called *one-period* model (see Fig. 2.2). Likewise, if $\delta t < T$ the global model is called *multi-period* model (see Fig. 2.4).

Now consider a single time step. Although the asset price at the beginning of the time step is known; the price at the end of the period, after δt time step, is a random variable. For a simple discrete model we may think only two possible values; accounting for the probabilities, p_u, of an increase and, $p_d := 1 - p_u$, of a decrease in the asset price as shown in Fig. 2.2.

Consider an asset with price S_0 at time $t_0 = 0$. At the end of the time step the new asset price, say $S_{\delta t}$, is either risen to $S_{\delta t} = uS_0$ $(u > 1)$ with respect to some underlying probability p_u, or dropped to $S_{\delta t} = dS_0$ $(d < 1)$ with probability p_d. Such a model is called a (one-period) *binomial*

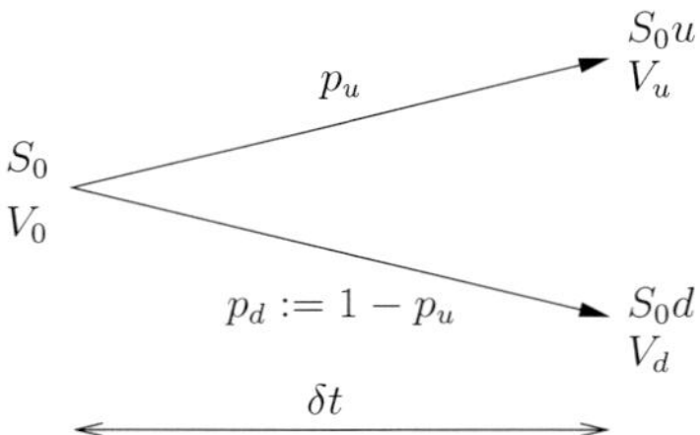

Fig. 2.2   One-period binomial model

model. In the case of a multi-period model, continuation of this procedure forms a *binomial lattice*: at each step two outcomes are possible with their respective probabilities p_u and p_d. Lattice methods are also known as *tree* methods.

Imagine, now, an option (depending on the asset) with an unknown price denoted by V_0. If the option can only be exercised after δt in a one-period model, it is easy to find its values V_u and V_d from the payoff corresponding to the two outcomes of the asset price. In order to find a fair value V_0 of the option, the no-arbitrage principle is exploited again. Let us set up a portfolio Π with the initial wealth (value)

$$\Pi_0 = V_0 - \Delta\, S_0. \tag{2.7}$$

This portfolio in (2.7) consists of an option and a *short position* in Δ number of shares of the asset. The two possible outcomes of the portfolio are either

$$\Pi_u = V_u - u\,\Delta\, S_0 \quad \text{or} \quad \Pi_d = V_d - d\,\Delta\, S_0, \tag{2.8}$$

depending on the possible price $S_{\delta t}$ of the asset at the end of the time period δt. The strategy to construct such a portfolio helps us choose Δ in such a way that the portfolio is riskless, that is,

$$\Pi_u = \Pi_d.$$

Hence, the number of shares of the asset is

$$\Delta = \frac{V_u - V_d}{S_0(u - d)}. \tag{2.9}$$

Moreover, due to no-arbitrage, if this portfolio is riskless it must earn the risk-free interest rate r. Assuming continuously compounding risk-free interest rate r, it must be true that

$$\Pi_{\delta t} = e^{r\delta t}\Pi_0 = e^{r\delta t}\left(V_0 - \Delta\, S_0\right) = \Pi_u = \Pi_d,$$

at the end of the time period δt. Using either Π_u or Π_d in (2.8), we obtain

$$V_0 e^{r\delta t} = e^{r\delta t} \Delta S_0 + V_u - u \Delta S_0.$$

Substituting the expression for Δ and simplifying the terms, it is easy to obtain the value of the option as follows:

$$V_0 = e^{-r\delta t} \{qV_u + (1-q)V_d\}, \tag{2.10}$$

where

$$q = \frac{e^{r\delta t} - d}{u - d}. \tag{2.11}$$

It is interesting to note that the probabilities p_u and p_d do not play any role, but q does. In fact, the existence of such a q introduces a *fundamental* concept: q may be considered the *risk-neutral probability*, say $\mathbb{Q}$, in the sense that under this probability measure, the expected asset return is the risk-free interest rate. This follows from the fact that

$$\begin{aligned}
\mathbb{E}_{\mathbb{Q}}[S_{\delta t}] &= qS_0 u + (1-q)S_0 d \\
&= \left(e^{r\delta t} - d\right) S_0 + S_0 d \\
&= S_0 e^{r\delta t}.
\end{aligned} \tag{2.12}$$

Indeed, the equality in (2.12) is of great importance. The *continuous (stochastic) model*[1] for the asset prices gives the same expectation under the *risk-neutral measure* $\mathbb{Q}$. Moreover, under this measure, the option value V_0 is computed as the expected value of the payoff discounted at the risk-free rate. In other words,

$$V_0 = \mathbb{E}_{\mathbb{Q}}\left[e^{-r\delta t}V_{\delta t}\right] = e^{-r\delta t}\mathbb{E}_{\mathbb{Q}}[V_{\delta t}], \tag{2.13}$$

where

$$\mathbb{E}_{\mathbb{Q}}[V_{\delta t}] = qV_u + (1-q)V_d. \tag{2.14}$$

Here, it should be emphasised that $V_{\delta t}$, that is, the values V_u and V_d are the payoffs at the maturity $\delta t = T$ for the one-period binomial model. As long as the values of the parameters u and d are known, the corresponding

---

[1] The model is assumed to be the *geometric Brownian motion* for the asset prices.

payoff values V_u and V_d can easily be calculated. Consequently, the value of the option is determined from (2.13) by using (2.14) and (2.11).

Exercise 2.1. Consider a European vanilla call option with a strike K. Using the payoff function, write down an explicit formula for V_0 in (2.13) in terms of the parameters u and d. Use the one-period binomial model and $q = \frac{e^{r\delta t} - d}{u - d}$.

In order to find the parameters u and d, we equate the variances of the continuous model and the binomial model, but under the risk-neutral measure. This is plausible since by the choice of q in (2.11) the expectations of both model match. Hence, from (2.12) it follows that

$$qu + (1 - q)d = e^{r\delta t}. \tag{2.15}$$

Once more, referring to *continuous model* for the asset prices, from the *lognormal distribution* it is not difficult to show the identity:

$$\mathbb{E}_{\mathbb{Q}}\left[S_{\delta t}^2\right] = S_0^2 e^{(2r+\sigma^2)\delta t}.$$

Hence, for the continuous model the variance is

$$\mathrm{Var}\left[S_{\delta t}\right] = S_0^2 e^{2r\delta t}\left(e^{\sigma^2 \delta t} - 1\right),$$

where σ is the *volatility* of the asset prices. On the other hand, the required variance for the one-period binomial model satisfies

$$\begin{aligned}
\mathrm{Var}\left[S_{\delta t}\right] &= \mathbb{E}_{\mathbb{Q}}\left[S_{\delta t}^2\right] - \left(\mathbb{E}_{\mathbb{Q}}\left[S_{\delta t}\right]\right)^2 \\
&= qS_0^2 u^2 + (1 - q)S_0^2 d^2 - S_0^2\left[qu + (1 - q)d\right]^2.
\end{aligned}$$

Therefore, equating the variances of the continuous and the binomial models, the relation

$$e^{2r\delta t}\left(e^{\sigma^2 \delta t} - 1\right) = qu^2 + (1 - q)d^2 - \left(e^{r\delta t}\right)^2$$

is obtained by using the equation for the expectation in (2.12), or (2.15) in particular. Simplifying this relation yields the following equation for the variances,

$$qu^2 + (1 - q)d^2 = e^{(2r+\sigma^2)\delta t}. \tag{2.16}$$

This is the first equation that is to be used for determining the parameters u and d. Thus, another equation is needed in order to determine the parameters, u and d. Fortunately, such an equation can be chosen arbitrarily provided that it is independent of the one in (2.16).

Here, we choose a convenient assumption on the parameters u and d:

$$u\,d = 1 \tag{2.17}$$

so that an up-step followed by a down-step yields the same price as a down-step followed by an up-step, moreover,

$$S_0\,u\,d = S_0\,d\,u = S_0.$$

Indeed, such an assumption will prove useful later in simplifying the structure of the multi-period binomial model and the notion of recombining lattice (see Fig. 2.4).

Consequently, we have to solve a system of nonlinear equations

$$\begin{cases} qu^2 + (1-q)d^2 = e^{(2r+\sigma^2)\delta t} \\ \qquad\quad ud = 1 \end{cases} \tag{2.18}$$

in order to fix the free parameter u and d of the one-period binomial model, where $q = \frac{e^{r\delta t}-d}{u-d}$. Fortunately, it is not difficult to get the quadratic equation

$$u^2 - 2\beta u + 1 = 0$$

from the system (2.18). Here, the simplifying parameter β is

$$\beta = \frac{1}{2}\left(\frac{1}{\alpha} + \alpha e^{\sigma^2 \delta t}\right),$$

where $\alpha = e^{r\delta t}$. The quadratic equation above can easily be solved for u to give

$$u = \beta \pm \sqrt{\beta^2 - 1}.$$

Using the fact that $u > 1$ and $d < 1$ for an up- and down-movements, respectively, we deduce that

$$u = \beta + \sqrt{\beta^2 - 1}, \quad d = \beta - \sqrt{\beta^2 - 1}. \tag{2.19}$$

In view of the calculation above, the parameters of the one-period binomial model are fully determined and they can be summarised as follows:

$$\begin{aligned} \beta &= \tfrac{1}{2}\left(e^{-r\delta t} + e^{(r+\sigma^2)\delta t}\right), \\ u &= \beta + \sqrt{\beta^2 - 1}, \\ d &= \beta - \sqrt{\beta^2 - 1} = 1/u, \\ q &= \frac{e^{r\delta t}-d}{u-d}. \end{aligned} \tag{2.20}$$

Remark 2.1. In fact, these parameters will also be valid for the multi-period binomial method (lattice).

Here is an example that illustrates pricing an option by the one-period binomial method identified by the parameters in (2.20).

Example 2.3. Suppose that we have a European option with strike $K = 50$, maturing in $T = 5$ months. The underlying asset price is initially $S_0 = 50$, and has the volatility $\sigma = 40\%$. The risk-free interest rate is constant and $r = 10\%$. First, the parameters of the one-period binomial model are computed as

$$
\begin{aligned}
\delta t &= \tfrac{5}{12} \approx 0.4167, \\
\beta &= \tfrac{1}{2}\left(e^{-r\delta t} + e^{(r+\sigma^2)\delta t}\right) \approx 1.0368, \\
u &= \beta + \sqrt{\beta^2 - 1} \approx 1.3106, \\
d &= \beta - \sqrt{\beta^2 - 1} = 1/u \approx 0.7630, \\
q &= \tfrac{e^{r\delta t} - d}{u - d} = 0.5105.
\end{aligned}
$$

The corresponding tree for the movement of the asset prices is shown in Fig. 2.3. At maturity T the payoff values, V_u and V_d, are easily calculated as

$$
\begin{aligned}
V_u &= \max\{0, S_0 u - K\} \approx 15.5299, \\
V_d &= \max\{0, S_0 d - K\} = 0,
\end{aligned}
$$

from the corresponding asset prices.

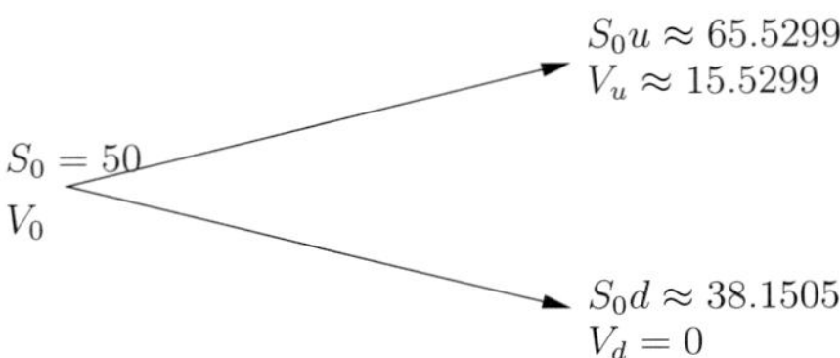

Fig. 2.3   One-period binomial model: asset prices and payoff values

What remains is to find the discounted value of the expected payoff by the use of formula (2.10). Hence, the option price is

$$
\begin{aligned}
V_0 &= e^{-r\delta t}\, \mathbb{E}_\mathbb{Q}\left[V_{\delta t}\right] = e^{-r\delta t}\{qV_u + (1-q)V_d\} \\
&\approx e^{-(0.1)(0.4167)}\{(0.5105)(15.5299) + (0.4895)(0)\} \\
&= 7.6044.
\end{aligned}
$$

In order to make the discrete binomial method useful, we should try to allow a wider range of prices, henceforth, pass to the *multi-period* binomial lattice: the easiest way to do it is to increase the number of time steps as shown in Fig. 2.4.

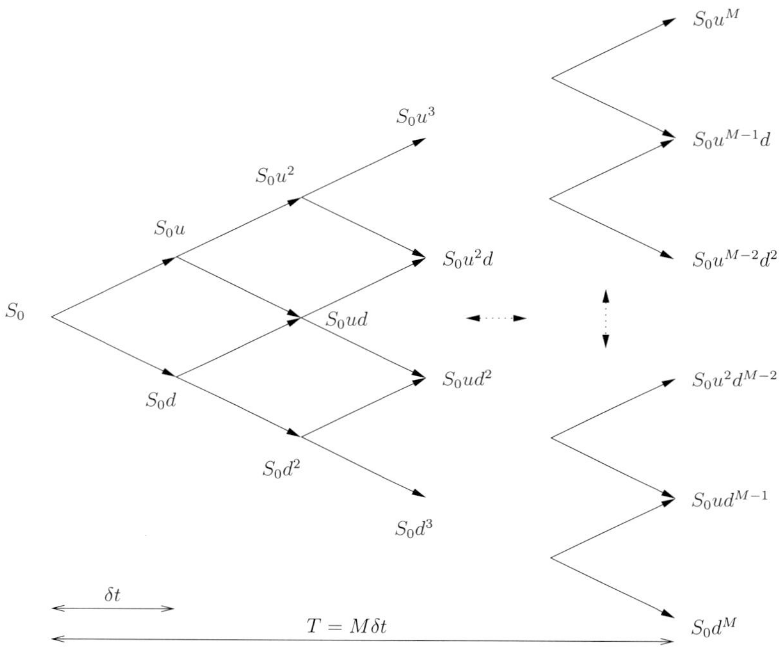

Fig. 2.4   Recombining binomial lattice

To understand the notations used in Fig. 2.4, let us denote:

$$\delta t := \frac{T - t_0}{M},$$
$$t_i := t_0 + i\,\delta t, \quad i = 0, 1, \ldots, M,$$
$$S_i := S_{t_i}.$$

Here, M is the number of time steps, T is the maturity of the option, and S_i is the asset price at time t_i. At each time $t = t_i$ the nodes of the lattice are ordered and the values

$$S_{ji} := S_0\, u^j\, d^{i-j}, \tag{2.21}$$

are assigned for each $i = 0, 1, \ldots, M$ and $j = 0, 1, \ldots, i$. Because at each time step t_i there corresponds $i + 1$ values of the asset price S_i due to up- and down-movements. For example, in Fig. 2.4,

$$S_{13} := S_0 u d^2, \quad S_{03} := S_0 d^3, \quad S_{12} := S_0 u d, \quad S_{33} := S_0 u^3.$$

For simplicity, we also denote the asset price S_0 at t_0 by $S_{00} := S_0$.

Now that the grid points (t_i, S_{ji}) are fixed, the option values

$$V_{ji} := V(S_{ji}, t_i)$$

are to be determined at each point of the grid. Fortunately, at maturity $T = M\delta t$ the payoff $P_{jM} := P(S_{jM}, t_M)$ of the option is known and, hence,

$$V_{jM} = V(S_{jM}, t_M) = P_{jM}$$

for every $j = 0, 1, \ldots, M$. Now, we have to trace the lattice backward in time starting from $i = M - 1$ until $i = 0$ to find the value of $V_{00} = V(S_{00}, t_0)$, which corresponds to an approximation of the option price V_0 at time $t_0 = 0$. Note that for every $i = M - 1, M - 2, \ldots, 0$ and $j = 0, 1, \ldots, i$ the relations,

$$S_{ji}\, u = S_{j+1,i+1} \quad \text{and} \quad S_{ji}\, d = S_{j,i+1},$$

are valid between the nodes in the binomial lattice shown in Fig. 2.4.

Therefore, the backward phase consists of dealing with one-period bi-nomial models as in Fig. 2.5. Similar to the one in (2.10), starting from the payoffs V_{jM}, the values V_{ji} associated to the nodes (S_{ji}, t_i) can easily be calculated recursively for $i = M - 1, M - 2, \ldots, 0$ and $j = 0, 1, \ldots, i$.

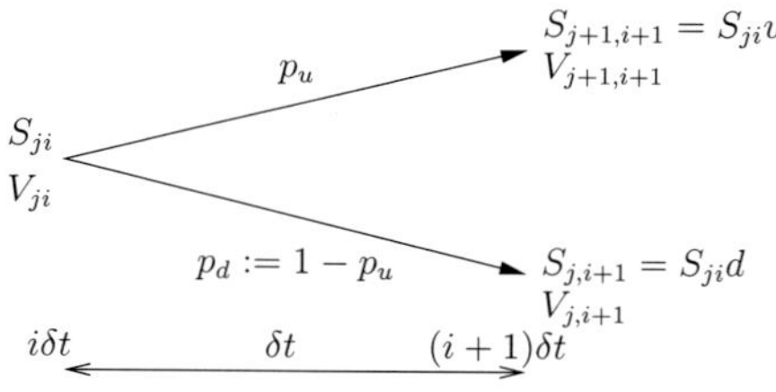

Fig. 2.5   One-period binomial model that begins at the node (t_i, S_{ji})

In order to simplify the discussion, assume that exercising the option before maturity, that is, at times t_i, $i < M$, is not allowed. In other words, consider a European option, no matter whether it is a call or a put. Moreover, suppose that the underlying asset never pays a dividend. At each time step, therefore, preserving the risk-neutrality condition, $q = \frac{e^{r\delta t} - d}{u - d}$, as before, the pricing formula in (2.10) is generalised to

$$V_{ji} = e^{-r\delta t}\left\{qV_{j+1,i+1} + (1 - q)V_{j,i+1}\right\} \tag{2.22}$$

for $j = 0, 1, \ldots, i$, while $i = M - 1, M - 2, \ldots, 0$.

Note also that under the risk-neutrality, the asset prices follow the rule,

$$\begin{aligned}
qS_{j+1,i+1} + (1 - q)S_{j,i+1} &= qS_{ji}u + (1 - q)S_{ji}d \\
&= e^{r\delta t}S_{ji}.
\end{aligned} \tag{2.23}$$

Hence, the relation (2.15) in the one-period binomial model remains valid for the multi-period case. This is true because of the relations $S_{ij}\,u = S_{j+1,i+1}$ and $S_{ij}\,d = S_{j,i+1}$, of the nodes in the recombining binomial lattice in Fig. 2.4. Moreover, equating the variances of the continuous and the binomial models ensures the validity of (2.16). Therefore, when the convenient assumption, $ud = 1$, is made all the parameters, q, u and d of multi-period binomial model can be determined. The parameters of the multi-period binomial model are exactly the ones defined in (2.20).

The recursion (2.22) for European option values V_{ji} starts from the values of the payoff V_{jM} and terminates at V_{00}. The value of V_{00} is an approximation for the value $V(S_0, t_0)$ of the continuous-time model. The accuracy of this approximation clearly depends on the time steps δt chosen, and the method is expected to converge to the value of the option at time t_0 as M tends to infinity.

Algorithm 2.1 summarises the multi-period binomial method for European options, where the underlying asset pays no dividends. An implementation of the algorithm is given in Fig. 2.6. It also calculates the prices at each node of the grid although this is not necessary for pricing path independent options.

The following example illustrates how to apply the multi-period binomial lattice method step by step. To compare the values computed by the implementation in Fig. 2.6 and investigate the convergence of the method, a built-in function in MATLAB for the closed-form solution is used.

Example 2.4. This example extends the previous example to the multi-period case. Consider a European vanilla call option with the strike price $K = 50$, and time to maturity $T = 5$ months. The asset price initially

---

Algorithm 2.1 Binomial Method for European Options

Given: $S_0, t_0, K, r, T, \sigma, M, put.$

Optional: $put = 0$

Calculate:

$$\delta t = \tfrac{T-t_0}{M},$$
$$\beta = \tfrac{1}{2}\left(e^{-r\delta t} + e^{(r+\sigma^2)\delta t}\right),$$
$$u = \beta + \sqrt{\beta^2 - 1},$$
$$d = 1/u = \beta - \sqrt{\beta^2 - 1},$$
$$q = \tfrac{e^{r\delta t}-d}{u-d}.$$

if $put = 1$ **then**
    for $j = 0, 1, \ldots, M$ **do**
        $V_{jM} = \max\{0,\ K - S_0 u^j d^{M-j}\}$ % payoff values for put
    end for
else
    for $j = 0, 1, \ldots, M$ **do**
        $V_{jM} = \max\{0,\ S_0 u^j d^{M-j} - K\}$ % payoff values for call
    end for
end if
for $i = M - 1, M - 2, \ldots, 0$ **do**
    for $j = 0, 1, \ldots, i$ **do**
        $V_{ji} = e^{-r\delta t}\{qV_{j+1,i+1} + (1-q)V_{j,i+1}\}$ % values at the nodes
    end for
end for
Return: $V_{00}.$

---

is $S_0 = 50$, and has the volatility $\sigma = 0.4$. The risk-free interest rate is constant $r = 0.1$.

First, the parameters of the binomial lattice are calculated to form the values of the asset. Suppose that each time step is a month so that a 5-period binomial model is considered. Hence, the values of the parameters of interest are

$$\delta t = \tfrac{1}{12} \approx 0.0833,$$
$$\beta = \tfrac{1}{2}\left(e^{-r\delta t} + e^{(r+\sigma^2)\delta t}\right) \approx 1.0068,$$
$$u = \beta + \sqrt{\beta^2 - 1} \approx 1.1236,$$
$$d = \beta - \sqrt{\beta^2 - 1} = 1/u \approx 0.8900,$$
$$q = \tfrac{e^{r\delta t}-d}{u-d} = 0.5067.$$

Therefore, the asset prices at the end of each month can easily be calculated

```
                                  BinomialExactQ.m
function [price, lattice, latticeS] = BinomialExactQ(S0, K, r, T, sigma, M, put)

if nargin < 7
    put = 0;
end
dt = T/M; beta = 0.5 * ( exp(-r*dt) + exp((r+sigma^2)*dt) );
u = beta + sqrt( beta^2 -1 ); d=1/u; q = (exp(r*dt) - d) / (u-d);
lattice = zeros(M+1,M+1); latticeS = zeros(M+1,M+1);

for j = 0:M
    latticeS(j+1,M+1) = S0*u^j*d^(M-j);
    if (put)
        lattice(j+1,M+1) = max(0, K - latticeS(j+1,M+1)); % Put Payoff
    else
        lattice(j+1,M+1) = max(0, latticeS(j+1,M+1) - K); % Call Payoff
    end
end

for i=M-1:-1:0
    for j=0:i
        latticeS(j+1,i+1) = S0*u^j*d^(i-j);
        lattice(j+1,i+1) = exp(-r*dt) * ...
            (q * lattice(j+2,i+2) + (1-q) * lattice(j+1,i+2));
    end
end
price = lattice(1,1);
```

Fig. 2.6   Binomial lattice method for European call and put options

to form the binomial lattice in Fig. 2.7. This is achieved by the use of (2.21) defined for the values of asset prices at the nodes of the grid.

The payoff values of the European call option with strike $K = 50$ can be calculated from those values of the asset prices at maturity. At time $t = t_5$ the values of the payoff are obtained as

$$V_{j,5} := P_{j,5} = P(t_5, S_{j,5}) := \max\left\{S_{j,5} - K,\ 0\right\},$$

for each $j = 0, 1, \ldots, 5$. Having computed these values, the formula (2.22) is used backward in time for $t = t_4, t_3, \ldots, t_0$. This recursive iteration terminates with the value V_{00}, an approximation to the option price today. The values V_{ji} obtained are shown in Fig. 2.8. However, we emphasise that the values are calculated by using the MATLAB function in Fig. 2.6 rather than a calculator. Then, the results are rounded off to four decimal digits.

In order to clarify the Fig. 2.8, let us consider the calculation of the value $V_{4,4} = 30.1182$: inserting the lattice parameters into (2.22) we obtain approximately that

$$\begin{aligned}
V_{4,4} &= e^{-r\delta t}\left\{qV_{5,5} + (1-q)V_{4,5}\right\} \\
&= e^{-(0.1)(0.0833)}\left\{(0.5067)(39.5576) + (0.4933)(20.9332)\right\} \\
&\approx 30.1182.
\end{aligned}$$

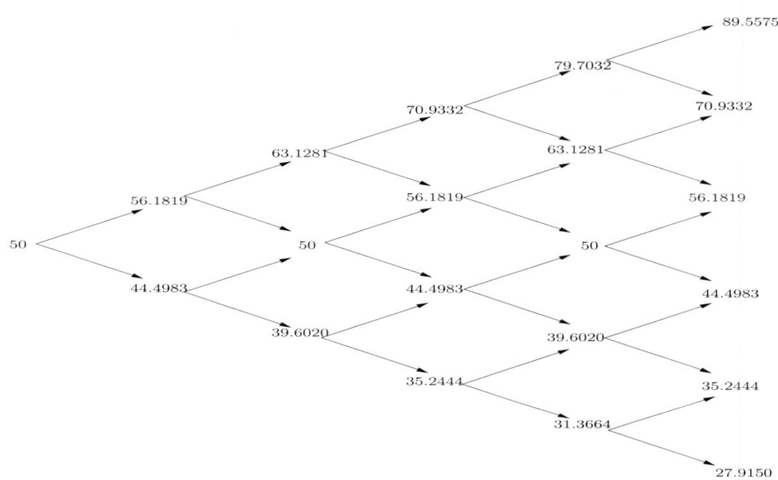

Fig. 2.7   Multi-period binomial model: asset prices at the nodes

Careful readers will certainly notice that the calculations above, using four decimal digits, will not produce the result 30.1182, but something close. This happens due to round-off errors! As indicated, the calculations are done using the procedure in Fig. 2.6 first, and then, rounded. A MATLAB script is presented in Fig. 2.9 to illustrate the use of this procedure. This script also produces a graph in order to test how good the approximations are when compared to built-function that computes the exact values from the Black-Scholes closed-form formula.

The graph in Fig. 2.10 as well as the values in Table 2.1 points out the convergence of the binomial method and compares the values V_{00} calculated for a number of periods with the Black-Scholes exact value.

You might have observed that the script in Fig. 2.9 calls another binomial method, whose output is also summarised in Table 2.1. In fact, this method differs from the one that has already been derived in that the former uses approximations to the parameters u and d. These approximations are extensively used in literature and proved useful for their simple forms avoiding the computation of the square-root function.

To derive these approximations we recall the Taylor's expansion for e^x, namely, the power series:

$$e^x = 1 + x + \frac{1}{2!}x^2 + \mathcal{O}\left(x^3\right).$$

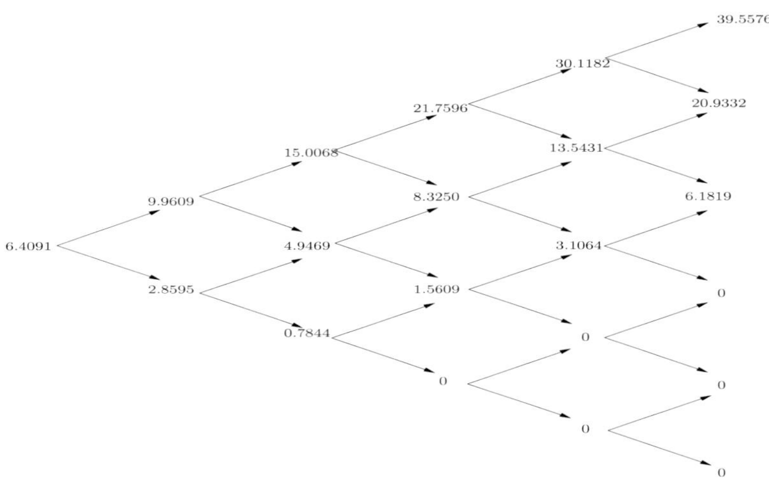

Fig. 2.8   Multi-period binomial model: option values at the nodes

```
                           ____________ testBinomialExactQ.m ____________
% testBinomialExactQ
clear all, close all
S0 = 50; K = 50; r = 0.1; sigma = 0.4; T = 5/12; flag = 0;
[BS_call, BS_put] = blsprice(S0,K,r,T,sigma); % calculates exact price

maxM = 100;
for M = 1:maxM
    priceApprox(M) = BinomialApproxUD(S0,K,r,T,sigma, M, flag);
    price(M) = BinomialExactQ(S0,K,r,T,sigma, M, flag);
end
plot(1:maxM, ones(1,maxM)*BS_call, 'g-'), hold on;
plot(1:maxM, price, 'r-o'); xlabel('M','FontSize',12), ylabel('V','FontSize',12)
print -r900 -deps '../figures/testBinomialExactQ'
```

Fig. 2.9   A MATLAB script for testing multi-period binomial method

In order to find some approximate solutions for u and d of some order, the right-hand-side of the system in (2.18) is replaced by the following alternative approximation:

$$\begin{aligned} e^{(2r+\sigma^2)\delta t} &= 1 + (2r + \sigma^2)\delta t + \mathcal{O}\left((\delta t)^2\right) \\ &= e^{2r\delta t} + \sigma^2\delta t + \mathcal{O}\left((\delta t)^2\right). \end{aligned}$$

Indeed, by using the Taylor's expansion, one can easily show that the variance, $\mathbb{V}\mathrm{ar}\,[S_{\delta t}]$, can be approximated as

$$\mathbb{V}\mathrm{ar}\,[S_{\delta t}] = S_0^2 e^{2r\delta t}\left(e^{\sigma^2\delta t} - 1\right) = \left[\sigma^2\delta t + \mathcal{O}\left((\delta t)^2\right)\right]S_0^2.$$

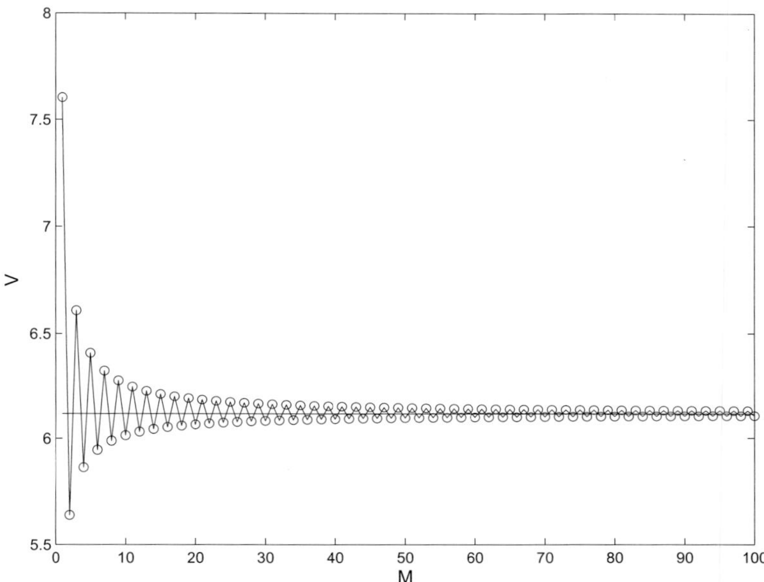

Fig. 2.10 European call by binomial lattice: M is the number of periods considered until maturity $T = 5/12$

Table 2.1 Values obtained from Binomial Method

M	V_{00}	V_{00}^*
1	7.6043	7.3086
2	5.6413	5.5370
128	6.1084	6.1066
2048	6.1160	6.1159
4096	6.1163	6.1162
Black-Scholes	6.1165	6.1165

*obtained by using (2.25)

Thus, the system of nonlinear equations becomes

$$\begin{cases} qu^2 + (1-q)d^2 = e^{2r\delta t} + \sigma^2 \delta t \\ ud = 1 \end{cases} \tag{2.24}$$

so that the free parameters u and d of the binomial lattice can be solved.

Note that the system (2.24) is an approximation of order $\mathcal{O}\left((\delta t)^2\right)$. So, the solutions will be at most of that order. Using $ud = 1$ and $q = \frac{e^{r\delta t}-d}{u-d}$ the left-hand-side of the first equation in (2.24) can be rewritten as follows:

$$\begin{aligned}
qu^2 + (1-q)d^2 &= q(u+d)(u-d) + d^2 \\
&= \left(e^{r\delta t} - d\right)(u+d) + d^2 \\
&= e^{r\delta t}(u+d) - 1 \\
&= e^{r\delta t}\left(u + \tfrac{1}{u}\right) - 1
\end{aligned}$$

Then, equating the both sides yields a quadratic equation in u, which is of order $\mathcal{O}\left((\delta t)^2\right)$. This quadratic equation is then simplified to

$$u^2 - \left(2 + \sigma^2 \delta t\right)u + 1 = 0.$$

Although such an equation can be solved exactly, one can easily verify, by direct substitution, that

$$u = e^{\sigma\sqrt{\delta t}}$$

satisfies the equation, but only up to of order $\mathcal{O}\left(\sqrt{(\delta t)^3}\right)$. Such a solution is consistent with the equation, since the latter is of order $\mathcal{O}\left((\delta t)^2\right)$. Consequently,

$$\boxed{\begin{aligned}
u &= e^{\sigma\sqrt{\delta t}} + \mathcal{O}\left(\sqrt{(\delta t)^3}\right) \approx e^{\sigma\sqrt{\delta t}} \\
d &= e^{-\sigma\sqrt{\delta t}} + \mathcal{O}\left(\sqrt{(\delta t)^3}\right) \approx e^{-\sigma\sqrt{\delta t}}
\end{aligned}} \qquad (2.25)$$

are approximations of order $\mathcal{O}\left(\sqrt{(\delta t)^3}\right)$ to the parameters of the binomial lattice.

Indeed, it is a matter of choice to use either the ones in (2.20) or the approximate ones in (2.25) for the parameters u and d. You may prefer the approximate ones, for their simplicity and less complexity, since they use fewer floating-point operations.

Remark 2.2. If the underlying asset pays continuous dividend yield with rate D, then it is possible, by a simple arbitrage argument, to introduce the dividend rate into the binomial method. Because the continuous dividend provides a return of D, the asset price must provide a instantaneous return of $\mu = r - D$ under the risk-neutral measure, where r is the risk-free interest rate. Otherwise, an arbitrage opportunity exists.

In this case the system we solved for u and d changes, because the expectations and the variances of asset prices change. However, it turns out that it is enough to replace r in the above formulae by

$$\mu := r - D, \qquad (2.26)$$

but only in those parameters u, d, and q. That is, the formula (2.22),

$$V_{ji} = e^{-r\delta t}\left\{qV_{j+1,i+1} + (1-q)V_{j,i+1}\right\},$$

which computes the option price at each node of the grid, is still valid; but q is changed to

$$q = \frac{e^{(r-D)\delta t} - d}{u - d}.$$

The following example illustrates the use of approximate formulae for the parameters of the binomial method. Further, it will verify the idea raised in Remark 2.2 and help us draw some obvious conclusions.

Example 2.5. In this example, a European call option with strike $K = 50$ and maturity $T = 1$ is considered. The interest rate is assumed to be $r = 0.2$. The underlying asset has the volatility $\sigma = 0.5$ and it pays a continuous dividend with yield $D = 0.2$. The script file in Fig. 2.11 shows the characteristic features of the option, and it selects a varying range for the asset prices at time $t = t_0 = 0$. On the other hand, the modified binomial method that uses the approximate formulae for the parameters is implemented in Fig. 2.12.

Once the script in Fig. 2.11 is run, some facts can be realised from the output:

- When the underlying asset pays dividends, the option value is less the corresponding option where the underlying asset pays no dividend. This fact is verified by comparing Fig. 2.13(a) and (b).
- The value of a European vanilla call option can never be below its payoff, no matter what the asset price is today, as long as the underlying asset does not pay dividends. See Fig. 2.13(a), for example.
- However, this is not the case for options with the underlying paying dividends, and Fig. 2.13(b) is an illustration of this fact.

Exercise 2.2. Try to modify the MATLAB function shown in Fig. 2.6 in order to include the dividends paid with rate D. Try to draw similar conclusions as in Example 2.5 by plotting some graphs for European vanilla put options.

```
                              testBinomialApproxUD_Dividend.m
% testBinomialApproxUD_Dividend
clear all, close all
S = [0:150]'; K = 50; r = 0.2; sigma = 0.5; T = 1; flag = 0; D=0.2;
[BS_call, BS_put] = blsprice(S,K,r,T,sigma, D); % calculates BS price
[BS_call0, BS_put0] = blsprice(S,K,r,T,sigma, 0); % with no dividend

M = 100; i=1; dS = 5;
for S0 = S(1):dS:S(end)
    price0(i) = BinomialApproxUD_Dividend(S0,K,r,T,sigma, M, flag, 0);
    price(i) = BinomialApproxUD_Dividend(S0,K,r,T,sigma, M, flag, D);
    i = i+1;
end
payoffCall = max(S-K, 0); payoffPut = max(K-S, 0);
figure(1), plot(S, payoffCall, '-.'), hold on
plot(S, BS_call0, 'c-'), plot(S(1):dS:S(end),price0, 'rx'),
xlabel('S','FontSize',12), ylabel('V','FontSize',12), hold off
print -r900 -deps '../figures/testBinomialApproxUD_Dividend0'
figure(2), plot(S, payoffCall, '-.'), hold on
plot(S, BS_call, 'c-'), plot(S(1):dS:S(end),price, 'rx'),
xlabel('S','FontSize',12), ylabel('V','FontSize',12), hold off
print -r900 -deps '../figures/testBinomialApproxUD_Dividend'
```

Fig. 2.11   A MATLAB script to test binomial lattice method for European options when
the underlying asset pays dividends

2.2.1 *Pricing American Options by Binomial Methods*

For American options, the recursion formula (2.22) must be modified by
adding a *test* whether early exercise is to be preferred. To do so, the value
of the option V_{ji} at the node (t_i, S_{ji}) must be compared with the option's
intrinsic value P_{ji}. The intrinsic value of the option is the immediate payoff
obtained from exercising the option, thus, calculated from the formulae:

$$P_{ji} := P(S_{ji}, t_i) := \max\{0,\ S_0 u^j d^{M-j} - K\}, \qquad (2.27)$$

for a call option, and

$$P_{ji} := P(S_{ji}, t_i) := \max\{0,\ K - S_0 u^j d^{M-j}\}, \qquad (2.28)$$

for a put option.

Due to the possibility of an early exercise, the value of an American
option can never be smaller than that of its counterpart European option.
In addition, an American option has at least the value of its payoff due to
the no-arbitrage principle. Because we trace the binomial lattice backward
in time, from $t = T$ to $t = t_0$, the absence of arbitrage implies that the
value V_{ji} of an American option must be chosen so that

```
──────────────────────── BinomialApproxUD_Dividend.m ────────────
function [price, lattice, latticeS] = ...
    BinomialApproxUD_Dividend(S0, K, r, T, sigma, M, put, D)

if nargin < 7
    put = 0;
end
dt = T/M; u=exp(sigma.*sqrt(dt)); d = 1./u; q=(exp((r-D).*dt) - d) ./ (u-d);
lattice = zeros(M+1,M+1); latticeS = zeros(M+1,M+1);
if (put)
    for j=0:M
        latticeS(j+1,M+1) = S0*u^j*d^(M-j);
        lattice(j+1,M+1) = max(0, K - latticeS(j+1,M+1)); % Put Payoff
    end
else
    for j=0:M
        latticeS(j+1,M+1) = S0*u^j*d^(M-j);
        lattice(j+1,M+1) = max(0, latticeS(j+1,M+1) - K); % Call Payoff
    end
end
for i=M-1:-1:0
    for j=0:i
        latticeS(j+1,i+1) = S0*u^j*d^(i-j);
        lattice(j+1,i+1) = exp(-r*dt) * ...
            (q * lattice(j+2,i+2) + (1-q) * lattice(j+1,i+2));
    end
end
price = lattice(1,1);
```

Fig. 2.12 Binomial lattice method for European call and put options when the underlying asset pays dividends

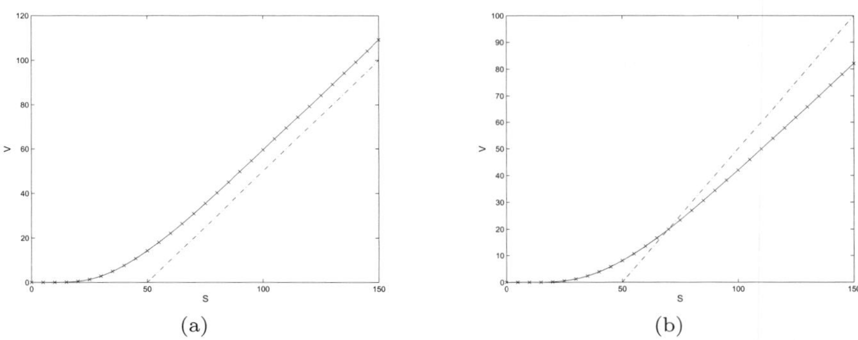

Fig. 2.13 European vanilla call option values (a) underlying pays *no* dividends, (b)
underlying pays dividends

$$V_{ji} = \max\left\{ e^{-r\delta t}\left[qV_{j+1,i+1} + (1-q)V_{j,i+1} \right], P_{ji} \right\} \qquad (2.29)$$

for every $i = M-1, M-2, \ldots, 0$, and $j = 0, 1, \ldots, i$. Hence, equation (2.29) is crucial and it must be inserted into Algorithm 2.1 in order to price an American option. An implementation of the binomial lattice for American options is presented in Fig. 2.14, in which the approximate values of u and d in (2.25) are used.

```
                                  BinomialApproxUD_Am.m
function [price, lattice, latticeS] = ...
    BinomialApproxUD_Am(S0, K, r, T, sigma, M, put, D)

if nargin < 7
    put = 0;
end
dt = T/M; u = exp(sigma.*sqrt(dt)); d = 1./u; q = (exp((r-D)*dt) - d) ./ (u-d);
lattice = zeros(M+1,M+1); latticeS = zeros(M+1,M+1);
for j = 0:M
    latticeS(j+1,M+1) = S0*u^j*d^(M-j);
    if (put)
        lattice(j+1,M+1) = max(0, K - latticeS(j+1,M+1)); % Put Payoff
    else
        lattice(j+1,M+1) = max(0, latticeS(j+1,M+1) - K); % Call Payoff
    end
end
for i=M-1:-1:0
    for j=0:i
        latticeS(j+1,i+1) = S0*u^j*d^(i-j);
        if (put)
            Pji = K - latticeS(j+1,i+1);
        else
            Pji = latticeS(j+1,i+1) - K;
        end
        lattice(j+1,i+1) = max( Pji, ...
        exp(-r*dt) * (q*lattice(j+2,i+2) + (1-q)*lattice(j+1,i+2)) );
    end
end
price = lattice(1,1);
```

Fig. 2.14   Binomial lattice method for American call and put option

Example 2.6. In this example, pricing an American option is illustrated and compared with its European counterpart. The parameters of the option are as the same as the ones in Example 2.4, also shown in the script file in Fig. 2.15. Differently from Example 2.4, we will now consider an American put option. An implementation of the binomial method is shown in Fig. 2.14, which includes the condition in (2.29) to price American options.

It should be emphasised that there is no closed form solution for the price of an American vanilla option. However, as it can be seen in Fig. 2.16(b), the price of an American put option is always greater than the corresponding European one and it seems the binomial method converges to that price. In fact, the value of an American option can never be

```
_______________________ testBinomialApproxUD_Am.m _______________________
% testBinomialApproxUD_Am
clear all, close all
SO = 50; K = 50; r = 0.1; sigma = 0.4; T = 5/12; flag = 1; D = 0;
[BS_call, BS_put] = blsprice(SO,K,r,T,sigma, D); % calculates exact price

maxM = 100;
for M = 1:maxM
    price_AmPut(M) = BinomialApproxUD_Am(SO,K,r,T,sigma, M, flag, D);
    price_EuCall(M) = BinomialApproxUD_Dividend(SO,K,r,T,sigma, M, 0, D);
    price_AmCall(M) = BinomialApproxUD_Am(SO,K,r,T,sigma, M, 0, D);
end
figure(1), plot(1:maxM, ones(1,maxM)*BS_call, 'r-'), hold on
plot(1:maxM, price_EuCall, 'b-.'); plot(1:maxM, price_AmCall, 'ko');
xlabel('M','FontSize',12), ylabel('V','FontSize',12);
legend('European call (Black-Scholes)','European call (Binomial)',...
    'American call (Binomial)'), hold off
print -r900 -deps '../figures/testBinomialApproxUD_Am_a'
figure(2), plot(1:maxM, ones(1,maxM)*BS_put, 'r-'), hold on;
plot(1:maxM, price_AmPut, 'b-.o');
xlabel('M','FontSize',12), ylabel('V','FontSize',12);
legend('European put (Black-Scholes)', 'American put (Binomial)');
print -r900 -deps '../figures/testBinomialApproxUD_Am_b'
```

Fig. 2.15 Testing the binomial lattice method for both European and American call and put options

below the value of the corresponding European one due to the condition in (2.29).

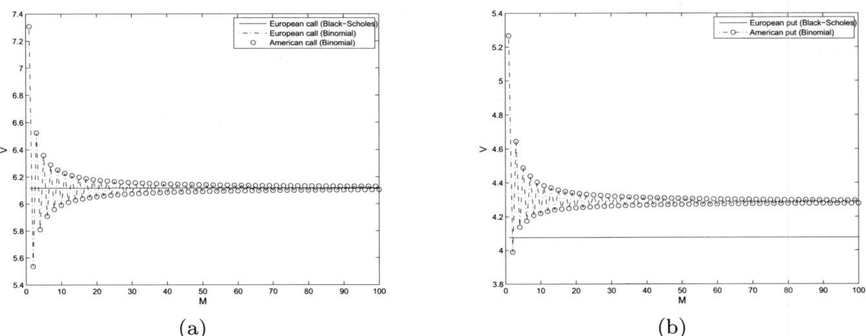

(a)   (b)

Fig. 2.16 Binomial method applied to American and European call options (a) call options (b) put options

On the other hand, surprisingly the values of the European and the American call options coincide! See Fig. 2.16(a). As a matter of fact, as long as the underlying asset pays no dividends an American and the corresponding European call options have the same unique price. Thus, *it is never favourable to exercise an American call option* on an underlying that does not pay dividends. This can easily be shown by the use of the no-arbitrage principle and the condition in (2.29).

The following example considers again American options, but assumes that the underlying asset pays dividends. It is advised that the reader should have a glance on Fig. 2.13(b) of Example 2.5, which depicts the graph of the price of a European call option when the underlying pays dividends.

Example 2.7. This example is very similar to Example 2.5, however, we investigate American call and put options on an underlying that now pays dividends with rate D. The data used for these options are the ones given in Example 2.5, and now the script in Fig. 2.17 is run.

```
                          testBinomialApproxUD_Am_Dividend.m
% testBinomialApproxUD_Am_Dividend
clear all, close all
S = [0:150]'; K = 50; r = 0.2; sigma = 0.5; T = 1; flag = 0; D = 0.2;
[BS_call, BS_put] = blsprice(S,K,r,T,sigma, D); % calculates BS price
[BS_call0, BS_put0] = blsprice(S,K,r,T,sigma, 0); % with no dividend

M = 100; i=1; dS = 2.5;
for S0 = S(1):dS:S(end)
    price0(i) = BinomialApproxUD_Am(S0,K,r,T,sigma, M, flag, D);
    price(i) = BinomialApproxUD_Am(S0,K,r,T,sigma, M, 1, D);
    i = i+1;
end
payoffCall = max(S-K, 0); payoffPut = max(K-S, 0);
figure(1), plot(S, BS_call, 'c-'), hold on, plot(S(1):dS:S(end),price0, 'rx'),
xlabel('S','FontSize',12), ylabel('V','FontSize',12),
legend('Eu (Black-Scholes)', 'Am (Binomial)', 'Location', 'NorthWest'),
plot(S, payoffCall, '-.'), hold off
print -r900 -deps '../figures/testBinomialApproxUD_Am_Dividend0'
figure(2), plot(S, BS_put, 'c-'), hold on, plot(S(1):dS:S(end),price, 'rx'),
xlabel('S','FontSize',12), ylabel('V','FontSize',12),
legend('Eu (Black-Scholes)', 'Am (Binomial)'),
plot(S, payoffPut, '-.'), hold off
print -r900 -deps '../figures/testBinomialApproxUD_Am_Dividend'
```

Fig. 2.17 A MATLAB script to test binomial lattice method for American options when the underlying asset pays dividends

The values of American call and put options versus the asset prices are shown in Fig. 2.18(a) and (b), respectively. Both graphs indicate that the price of the American options are above the payoff no matter if the option is a call or a put.

On the other hand, the graph in Fig. 2.18(b) is typical for an American put option, in general. Qualitative behaviour does not change if the underlying asset pays no dividends. In other words, the values of an American put option would be again more than the payoff if there were no dividends. This is in contrast with the American call option. Note that if the underlying asset does not pay dividends, then the value of an American call is the same as that of the corresponding European call. To this end, compare Fig. 2.18(a) with Fig. 2.13(b), in particular.

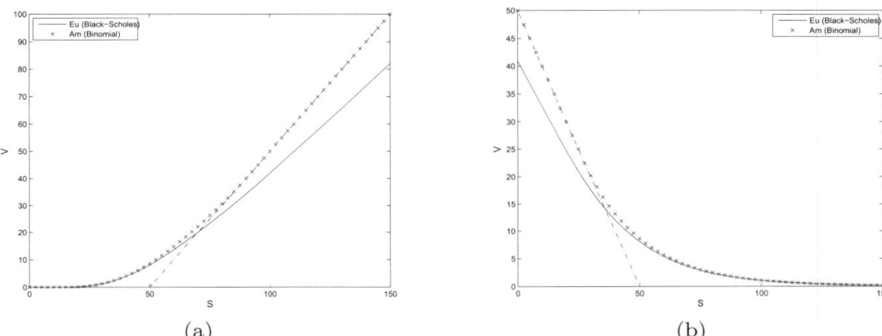

(a)   (b)

Fig. 2.18 American call and put option values where the underlying asset pays dividends: (a) call option, (b) put option

In both graphs depicted in Fig. 2.18, although it is not so obvious, there are values of the option prices that are also equal to the values of the payoffs. Thus, the options must be exercised. For American call option, the values for which exercise must be chosen occur when $S \geq S_f$ for some critical value S_f at time t_0. Similarly, for American put options, the *region of exercise* is $S \leq S_f$. Note that S_f is the value of S at which the two curves, the payoff and the option values, meet. The readers are advised to find those values and observe the trajectory of S_f as time to maturity T approaches zero.

Outlook

The binomial method presented here in option pricing is extensively used by practitioners. This simple, but powerful, method was originally developed in [Cox *et al.* (1979)] and shown to converge the Black-Scholes closed-form formulae for vanilla options.

In [Pliska (1997)], a complete discussion on risk-neutral probability versus the no-arbitrage argument in discrete-time models can be found. There are many other textbooks on mathematical finance which include binomial methods and risk-neutral valuation principle, such as [Hull (2000); Kwok (1998); Seydel (2002); Shreve (2004a); Wilmott *et al.* (1995)].

For the rate of convergence of the binomial method we refer to [Jiang and Dai (2004); Leisen and Reimer (1996); Walsh (2003)]. A case study on implementations of binomial method in MATLAB is given in [Higham (2002)] together with the codes.

2.3   An Alternative Binomial Method

This section introduces an alternative binomial method that has been frequently used in literature. The approach to derive this alternative method is in fact quite similar to the one that has been investigated in Section 2.2. However, in this case, the probabilities p_u and $p_d = 1 - p_u$ of up- and down-movements, respectively, are also unknown parameters to be determined in the binomial lattice.

This alternative method depends basically on matching the expectations and variances of the asset prices in the continuous and the binomial models. The latter model is considered to be a discrete one. In fact, having constructed a riskless portfolio and giving a meaning to q, these expectations and the variances of the asset prices involved in the discrete and continuous models have been equated. Fortunately, the expectations have already been matched by the definition of q, namely,

$$q = \frac{e^{r\delta t} - d}{u - d}.$$

Then, to fix the parameters u and d of the binomial lattice, variances have been used together with a plausible assumption

$$u\,d = 1.$$

In the subsequent alternative approach this plausible assumption is avoided. Also, the risk-neutral interpretation of q is lost in the following alternative binomial model, since we do not construct a riskless portfolio. However, the use of expectation, under the risk-neutral measure, of the continuous model for the asset prices may be used to obtain another equation in order to determine the parameters of this new binomial method.

Consider Fig. 2.5, where p_u is the probability of an up-movement of the underlying asset price, and denote $p := p_u$. Assume that the market has its own "risk-neutral" probability measure $\mathbb{P}$, which does not reflect the expectations of an individual in the market: The expected return is that of the risk-free interest rate r to avoid arbitrage opportunities. Under this probability, therefore, the expectation and the variance of the binomial model are

$$\begin{aligned}
\mathbb{E}_{\mathbb{P}}\left[S_{t_{i+1}}\right] &= = pS_{t_i}u + (1-p)S_{t_i}d, \\
\mathbb{V}\mathrm{ar}_{\mathbb{P}}\left[S_{t_{i+1}}\right] &= pS_{t_i}^2 u^2 + (1-p)S_{t_i}^2 d^2 - S_{t_i}^2\left[pu + (1-p)d\right]^2,
\end{aligned} \tag{2.30}$$

respectively. Thus, in this setting, another parameter p of the binomial lattice has to be determined apart from the ones, u and d.

On the other hand, the expectation and the variance of asset prices in the continuous model under the risk-neutral measure $\mathbb{Q}$ are defined as

$$\begin{aligned}
\mathbb{E}_{\mathbb{Q}}\left[S_{t_{i+1}}\right] &= S_{t_i}e^{r\delta t}, \\
\mathbb{V}\mathrm{ar}_{\mathbb{Q}}\left[S_{t_{i+1}}\right] &= S_{t_i}^2 e^{2r\delta t}\left(e^{\sigma^2\delta t} - 1\right).
\end{aligned} \tag{2.31}$$

Fortunately, solving p in (2.30) by equating the corresponding expectations yields that

$$p = \frac{e^{r\delta t} - d}{u - d}, \tag{2.32}$$

which is, surprisingly, the definition for q in the previous section. However, p stands for the probability of an up-movement of asset price, rather than for a risk-neutral probability measure $\mathbb{Q}$. Moreover, it is a parameter, like u and d, that is to be determined. Of course, to be a valid model for probability, the relation

$$0 \le p \le 1$$

must hold. This is equivalent to

$$d \le e^{r\delta t} \le u, \tag{2.33}$$

which directly follows from (2.32), and relates the up- and down-movements of asset price to the riskless interest rate. The relation (2.33) seems artificial at a first glance, however, the inequalities easily follow from the no-arbitrage principle.

What remains next is to equate the variances of both the binomial and the continuous models for the asset prices. Using the relations (2.30) and (2.31), it follows that

$$pu^2 + (1-p)d^2 = e^{(2r+\sigma^2)\delta t}, \tag{2.34}$$

which is the same as the one in (2.16), but includes p instead of q.

Therefore, for the three free parameters, p, u and d, of the binomial lattice we have only two equations to be solved. Thus, there is still a free parameter that can be chosen arbitrarily in the system,

$$\begin{cases} pu + (1-p)d = e^{r\delta t} \\ pu^2 + (1-p)d^2 = e^{(2r+\sigma^2)\delta t}. \end{cases} \qquad (2.35)$$

Note that the system in (2.35) consists of the equations (2.15) and (2.16), in the previous section, but with a simple difference: q is replaced by p. As a consequence, introducing the plausible assumption on u and d such as $ud = 1$ will ensure $p := p_u = q$. Hence, the same values of u and d of the previous section will be obtained.

The alternative approach in literature is to introduce

$$p := p_u = \frac{1}{2}, \qquad (2.36)$$

rather that $ud = 1$. This new assumption indicates that the probabilities of up- and down-movements of the asset price are the same: 50% for each. This seems another plausible assumption: using (2.36), the system in (2.35) reduces to a simpler form,

$$\begin{cases} u + d = 2e^{r\delta t} \\ u^2 + d^2 = 2e^{(2r+\sigma^2)\delta t}. \end{cases} \qquad (2.37)$$

Moreover, it is easy to eliminate d in the second equation by using the first and get the quadratic equation,

$$u^2 - 2e^{r\delta t}u + e^{2r\delta t}\left(2 - e^{\sigma^2\delta t}\right) = 0,$$

in u. Therefore, under the assumption that $0 < d < u$, the solution of the system in (2.37) becomes

$$u = e^{r\delta t}\left(1 + \sqrt{e^{\sigma^2\delta t} - 1}\right), \qquad d = e^{r\delta t}\left(1 - \sqrt{e^{\sigma^2\delta t} - 1}\right). \qquad (2.38)$$

One can easily verify this by direct substitution.

To sum up, all the parameters of the alternative binomial method are determined as follows:

$$p = \tfrac{1}{2},$$
$$u = e^{r\delta t}\left(1 + \sqrt{e^{\sigma^2\delta t} - 1}\right),$$
$$d = e^{r\delta t}\left(1 - \sqrt{e^{\sigma^2\delta t} - 1}\right). \tag{2.39}$$

Of course, it is possible to use approximations to these values of u and d: the following exercise presents two such approximations that are widely used.

Exercise 2.3. Calculate an approximate solution, of order $\mathcal{O}\left(\sqrt{(\delta t)^3}\right)$, for the system in (2.37). In other words, use Taylor's theorem to show that

$$u = e^{(r-\sigma^2/2)\delta t + \sigma\sqrt{\delta t}} + \mathcal{O}\left(\sqrt{(\delta t)^3}\right) = e^{r\delta t + \sigma\sqrt{\delta t}} + \mathcal{O}\left(\sqrt{(\delta t)^3}\right),$$

and

$$d = e^{(r-\sigma^2/2)\delta t - \sigma\sqrt{\delta t}} + \mathcal{O}\left(\sqrt{(\delta t)^3}\right) = e^{r\delta t - \sigma\sqrt{\delta t}} + \mathcal{O}\left(\sqrt{(\delta t)^3}\right),$$

are such solutions.

Example 2.8. Consider a *pay-later* contract. For simplicity, assume that it is a European call: the feature of this contract is that no *premium* is paid when the contract is entered. If the contract is *in the money* at maturity, the contract must be exercised and a premium is paid to the writer. Otherwise, if the contract is *out of the money*, then the option expires worthless without any charge. Notice that, unlike the classical options, you are obliged to pay the premium in case the contract is in the money. In other words, at maturity you may have a negative profit due to the obligation to exercise.

In order to find the premium that is to be paid at maturity makes the binomial method difficult to use. Because, it is initialised by the payoff. However, the premium is unknown, and so is the payoff. The binomial method should trace the lattice backward in time starting from the known values of the payoff at maturity. On the other hand, it is possible to write this premium to the payoff in the related part of the binomial method: a premium, the value of the contract, is paid only if the asset price is greater than the strike price K. Therefore, the following code segment

```
if ( S0*(u^j)*(d^(M-j)) > K )
   lattice(M+1,j+1) = S0*(u^j)*(d^(M-j)) - K - premium;
end
```

may be inserted in order to initialise the payoff, although the premium is not known yet. The resulting code, shown in Fig. 2.19, will then price the contract only if the *premium* is given.

```
———————————————— LatticeEurCall_PayLater.m ————————————————
function [price, lattice] = ...
    LatticeEurCall_PayLater(premium,S0,K,r,T,sigma,M)

dt = T/M; erdt = exp(r*dt); sqt = sqrt( exp(sigma^2*dt) - 1 );
u = erdt * (1 + sqt);
d = erdt * (1 - sqt); % or u=exp(sigma * sqrt(dt)); d=1/u;
q = 0.5;  % or q=(exp(r*dt) - d)/(u-d);
lattice = zeros(M+1,M+1);
for j=0:M
   if (S0*(u^j)*(d^(M-j)) > K)
       lattice(M+1,j+1)=S0*(u^j)*(d^(M-j)) - K - premium;
   end
end
for i=M-1:-1:0
   for j=0:i
       lattice(i+1,j+1) = exp(-r*dt) * ...
           (q * lattice(i+2,j+2) + (1-q) * lattice(i+2,j+1));
   end
end
price = lattice(1,1);
```

Fig. 2.19 Binomial lattice method for a pay-later option

Since no premium is paid when entering the contract today, due to the *no-arbitrage* principle we ask the question: *what must be the* premium *that has to be paid at maturity, $t = T$, so that the* value of the contract *is zero today, $t = t_0$?* An answer to this question, and to similar ones, lies in the *root-finding* problems. Thus, if $f(x)$ represents the value of the option, given the premium x, then we look for the roots of the equation

$$f(x) = 0.$$

To put it in another way, the zeros x of the function f are the values of the premium that has to be paid if the contract is in the money at maturity.

These zeros can be found in MATLAB by the following code

```
fzero(inline('LatticeEurCall_PayLater(x,50,50,0.1,5/12,0.4,100)'),10)
```

for a given asset with price \$50 and volatility 40%, the risk-free interest rate is 10%, the strike \$50, and the option is maturing in 5 months. In Fig. 2.20 the built-in function `fsolve` instead of `fzero` is used, both of which basically do the same: they find the zeros of the given function near a given initial guess.

```
———————————————— LatticeEurCall_PayLater_Ex.m ————————————
% Pay-Later Option Valuation by Binomial Lattice
clear all, close all

M = 25;
for i = 1:M
    [premium(i), value(i)] = fsolve(@(x) ...
        LatticeEurCall_PayLater(x,50,50,0.1,5/12,0.4,100*i), 10);
    payLater(i) = LatticeEurCall_PayLater...
                    (premium(i),50,50,0.1,5/12,0.4,100*M);
end
[ premium(end), value(end) ]

figure(1), plot(1:M, premium, '-o');
xlabel('M (x100)','FontSize',12), ylabel('Premium','FontSize',12)
print -r900 -deps '../figures/LatticeEurCall_PayLater_Ex_a'
figure(2), plot(1:M, payLater, '-o'), hold on, plot(1:M, zeros(M),'r-.'),
xlabel('M (x100)','FontSize',12), ylabel('PayLater','FontSize',12)
print -r900 -deps '../figures/LatticeEurCall_PayLater_Ex_b'
```

Fig. 2.20   Pay-later option by finding zeros

Fig. 2.21(a) shows the values from the *root-finding* problem versus the number of steps used in the binomial lattice. These are the premiums that have to be paid at maturity. On the other hand, at those premiums, the values calculated by the function in Fig. 2.19 by using 2500 number of periods are shown in Fig. 2.21(b). These values seem to converge to zero, which should be expected.

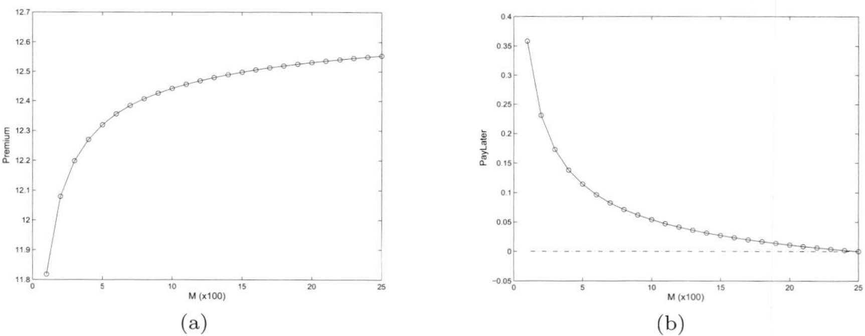

(a)   (b)

Fig. 2.21   Pay-later option values from binomial lattice. (a) premium versus the number periods, (b) values obtained from `LatticeEurCall_PayLater.m` using 2500 periods

Table 2.2 shows the results of the root finding procedure depending on the number of periods used in the binomial model.

Table 2.2   Premiums of the pay-later contract using binomial lattice with different periods M

M	Premium	$\epsilon^{\dagger}$	$\mathcal{E}^{\dagger}$
100	11.8182	-0.1356×10^{-8}	0.3583
200	12.0797	-0.7904×10^{-8}	0.2309
300	12.1984	-0.9232×10^{-8}	0.1731
1000	12.4426	1.4085×10^{-8}	0.0541
2300	12.5454	2.3151×10^{-8}	0.0040
2400	12.5496	0.2288×10^{-8}	0.0019
2500	12.5536	-0.0857×10^{-8}	0.0000

†Using `LatticeEurCall_PayLater.m`; ϵ is calculated at Premium by using M periods, and $\mathcal{E}$ is calculated by using 2500 periods.

Outlook

The choice $p_u = 1/2$ for up- and down-movements is widely used and investigated in literature. Detailed analysis of the binomial methods as well as the approximations of u and d can be found in [Cox and Rubinstein (1985); Hull (2000)]. For more advanced binomial methods we refer to [Breen (1991); Klassen (2001)].

An extension of the binomial method is the multinomial, in particular, the *trinomial trees* [Cox *et al.* (1979); Hull and White (1994a)], in which the stock price may not change within the time interval δt. Trinomial methods can give higher accuracy when compared to the binomial ones. It is possible to derive a trinomial lattice method by the use of hedging strategy, or risk-neutral valuation. However, such a trinomial model will be derived later in Section 6.6 as a consequence of *finite difference* approximation to the Black-Scholes partial differential equation.

Chapter 3

Stochastic Differential Equations

Stochastic differential equations (SDEs) play an important role in a wide variety of branches in applied mathematics, including biology, chemistry, mechanics, and of course, finance. Theoretical aspects of SDEs require familiarity with advanced mathematical topics, such as probability, real and functional analysis. However, with the help of numerical methods for simulations, this chapter can be regarded as a first step towards the underlying theory of SDEs.

Having experience with the *Wiener* process, the Stochastic Itô processes, which are described by SDEs, follow in this chapter. Approximations and simulations of solution paths of SDEs are carried out by the well-known *Euler-Maruyama* method, which is consistent with the Stochastic Itô integral.

Further in the chapter, the *Itô integral* is defined and some features of the integral are presented by keeping the theoretical aspects to a minimum. This is achieved by considering the *Riemann-Stieltjes* sums for integrals, but investigating the *convergence in the mean*. Although the theory behind is extensive, the stochastic integrals are restricted mainly to the integrals of *simple processes*. The extension should then be made possible by considering certain limits of these simple processes.

Naturally, a stochastic process may depend on other processes. This means, a particular chain rule is needed for stochastic processes: introducing the well-known *Itô lemma* for this purpose leads to many applications of stochastic processes. Moreover, this lemma can also be used to compute the integrals of some particular stochastic processes and represent closed-forms solutions of some of the SDEs used in finance: being a plausible, governing model for the stock prices, the SDEs that describe the *geometric Brownian motions* are solved and illustrated by some applications.

3.1 Stochastic Itô Processes

A *stochastic process* is a family of random variables X_t, which are defined on a set of parameters t. Here, we consider the variable $t \in \mathbb{R}$ as the time that varies continuously in an interval $I \subseteq \mathbb{R}$, which typically represents the finite time horizon $I = [0, T]$. Other notations for a stochastic process include $\{X_t,\ t \in I\}$, $(X_t)_{0 \leq t \leq T}$, and if it is clear from the context, just by X. If t varies in a given time interval, then the resulting function X_t is called a *realisation* or a *path* of the stochastic process.

With their own specific properties, there are many stochastic processes that are widely used in the literature of finance. Among them are Gaussian and Markov processes, and more importantly, Wiener processes, which are also called *Brownian motions*. The term *Brownian motion* originally meant irregular motion of a (pollen) particle on a surface of a fluid, caused by tiny impulses of molecules. Later, Wiener suggested a model and formulated the mathematical definition of a *Wiener process*. A Brownian motion, for instance, is both Gaussian and Markov. The following definition is not standard, and equivalent definitions of a Wiener process can be found in standard textbooks of financial mathematics.

Definition 3.1. A one-dimensional (standard) Wiener process (or a Brownian motion) W_t is a process that is continuous in time and has the following properties.

(1) $W_0 = 0$, with probability one.
(2) $W_t \sim \mathcal{N}(0, t)$ for all $t \geq 0$. That is, for each t the random variable W_t is normally distributed with mean $\mathbb{E}\left[W_t\right] = 0$ and variance $\mathbb{V}\mathrm{ar}\left[W_t\right] = \mathbb{E}\left[W_t^2\right] = t$.
(3) All increments $\Delta W_t := W_{t+\Delta t} - W_t$ on nonoverlapping time intervals are independent. That is, the displacements $W_{t_2} - W_{t_1}$ and $W_{t_4} - W_{t_3}$ are independent for all $0 \leq t_1 < t_2 \leq t_3 < t_4$. In other words, W_t has *independent increments*.

Multi-dimensional Wiener processes are similarly defined. The notation $\mathcal{N}(\mu, \Sigma)$ in the definition is commonly used for the *normal distribution*, where $\mu \in \mathbb{R}^n$ is a mean vector and $\Sigma \in \mathbb{R}^n$ is a covariance matrix. In the particular case when $\mu = 0$ and $\Sigma = I$, then the normal distribution, $\mathcal{N}(0, I)$, is called the *standard normal distribution*. The corresponding density function, denoted by $\phi_{\mu, \sqrt{\Sigma}}(x)$, of the normal distribution $\mathcal{N}(\mu, \Sigma)$

is given by,

$$\phi_{\mu,\sqrt{\Sigma}}(x) = \frac{1}{(2\pi)^{n/2}} \frac{1}{(\det \Sigma)^{1/2}} \exp\left\{ -\frac{1}{2}(x-\mu)^T \Sigma^{-1}(x-\mu) \right\} \quad (3.1)$$

for $x \in \mathbb{R}^n$. In particular, when $n = 1$ and $\Sigma = \sigma^2 \in \mathbb{R}$ the density of the normal distribution is, for $x \in \mathbb{R}$,

$$\phi_{\mu,\sigma}(x) = \frac{1}{\sigma\sqrt{2\pi}} e^{-\frac{1}{2}\left(\frac{x-\mu}{\sigma}\right)^2}. \quad (3.2)$$

In this case, the corresponding distribution function $\Phi_{\mu,\sigma}(x)$ of the normal distribution with parameters, mean μ and standard deviation σ, becomes

$$\Phi_{\mu,\sigma}(x) = \frac{1}{\sigma\sqrt{2\pi}} \int_{-\infty}^{x} e^{-\frac{1}{2}\left(\frac{\xi-\mu}{\sigma}\right)^2} d\xi. \quad (3.3)$$

Of course, there is a close relation between the distribution functions $\mathcal{N}(\mu,\sigma^2)$ and $\mathcal{N}(0,1)$. For instance, if Z is a random variable from the standard normal distribution, then $X = \mu + \sigma Z$ is a random variable from the normal distribution with mean μ and standard deviation σ. This is because, the distribution function of the latter, denote it to be $F_X(x)$ for now, can be computed as

$$F_X(x) := \mathbb{P}\left\{ X \le x \right\} = \mathbb{P}\left\{ \mu + \sigma Z \le x \right\}$$

$$= \mathbb{P}\left\{ Z \le \frac{x-\mu}{\sigma} \right\} =: \Phi_{0,1}\left(\frac{x-\mu}{\sigma} \right).$$

The function $\Phi_{0,1}\left(\frac{x-\mu}{\sigma}\right)$ above can further be integrated to give

$$\Phi_{0,1}\left(\frac{x-\mu}{\sigma} \right) := \frac{1}{\sqrt{2\pi}} \int_{-\infty}^{\frac{x-\mu}{\sigma}} e^{\xi^2/2} d\xi$$

$$= \frac{1}{\sigma\sqrt{2\pi}} \int_{-\infty}^{x} e^{-\frac{1}{2}\left(\frac{\eta-\mu}{\sigma}\right)^2} d\eta =: \Phi_{\mu,\sigma}(x).$$

Thus, these two calculations can be summarised as follows:

$$\text{if } Z \sim \mathcal{N}(0,1), \text{ then } X = \mu + \sigma Z \sim \mathcal{N}(\mu,\sigma^2), \quad (3.4)$$

and conversely,

$$\text{if } X \sim \mathcal{N}(\mu,\sigma^2), \text{ then } Z = \frac{X-\mu}{\sigma} \sim \mathcal{N}(0,1). \quad (3.5)$$

Furthermore, the relation between the two distribution functions can be written as

$$\Phi_{\mu,\sigma}(x) = \Phi_{0,1}\left(\frac{x-\mu}{\sigma}\right), \qquad (3.6)$$

which is, in fact, clear from either of the calculations.

Now, returning back to the Wiener processes, for $0 \leq s < t$ the following property is generally regarded as the most important consequence of the definition of a Wiener process W_t and the normal distribution. This is,

$$W_t - W_s \sim \mathcal{N}(0, t - s). \qquad (3.7)$$

Due to this property of the increments of Wiener processes W_t, we say, W_t has *stationary increments*. Immediately this property yields,

$$\mathbb{E}\left[W_t - W_s\right] = 0$$

and

$$\mathbb{V}\mathrm{ar}\left[W_t - W_s\right] = \mathbb{E}\left[(W_t - W_s)^2\right] = t - s.$$

In particular, for $s = 0$, the preceding two properties can be written as

$$\mathbb{E}\left[W_t\right] = 0 \qquad \text{and} \qquad \mathbb{E}\left[(\Delta W_t)^2\right] = \Delta t. \qquad (3.8)$$

In order to run a computer simulation of a Wiener (or any other stochastic or deterministic, but continuous) process, a time discretization or a discrete version of the model itself is needed. So, let $\Delta t > 0$ be a constant time increment, and let the points

$$t_j = j\,\Delta t, \quad \text{for} \quad j = 0, 1, \ldots$$

be the nodes at which the values of $W_{t_i} := W_{i\Delta t}$ are to be obtained. Luckily, the rearrangement of the terms in the form of a telescoping sum,

$$W_{j\Delta t} = \sum_{k=1}^{j}\left[W_{k\Delta t} - W_{(k-1)\Delta t}\right] = \sum_{k=1}^{j}\Delta W_{(k-1)\Delta t},$$

shows that $W_{j\Delta t}$ can be written as a sum of the increments

$$\Delta W_{t_{k-1}} := W_{t_k} - W_{t_{k-1}} \qquad (3.9)$$

of the Wiener process W_t. These increments are independent by definition, and are normally distributed with mean zero and variance Δt by the property (3.7). Thus, this gives the opportunity to simulate at least these increments ΔW_{t_k} by drawing "standard normally distributed random numbers", say Z_k for each k. Those numbers Z_k are assumed to be *independent* "random" realisations of a random variable $Z \sim \mathcal{N}(0, \Delta t)$. Whenever this is the case for the numbers Z_k, the notation $Z_k \sim \mathcal{N}(0, \Delta t)$ will be used, but we will assume implicitly that they are independent realisations of a random variable $Z \sim \mathcal{N}(0, \Delta t)$, without loss of generality. Moreover, such a sequence of random numbers Z_k is said to be a *sample*[1] from the underlying distribution. Here, the distribution is the normal distribution with mean zero and variance Δt, namely, $\mathcal{N}(0, \Delta t)$.

Using the density function of the normal distribution, if Z is a random variable that is normally distributed with $Z \sim \mathcal{N}(0, 1)$, then $Z\sqrt{\Delta t}$ is again normally distributed. Furthermore, it satisfies the property,

$$Z\sqrt{\Delta t} \sim \mathcal{N}(0, \Delta t).$$

Thus, this leads to the *discretized* version of a Wiener process:

$$W_{t_k} = W_{t_{k-1}} + \Delta W_{t_{k-1}}, \quad \Delta W_{t_{k-1}} = Z_k\sqrt{\Delta t}, \quad Z_k \sim \mathcal{N}(0, 1), \quad (3.10)$$

for each $k \in \mathbb{N}$. Using (3.9) and the fact that $W_0 = 0$ this is equivalent to Algorithm 3.1 for simulating the paths of a Wiener process.

Algorithm 3.1 Paths of a Wiener Process

   Given: M, $t_0 = 0$, $W_0 = 0$, $\Delta t \geq 0$.
   for $k = 1, 2, \ldots, M$ **do**
      $Z_k \sim \mathcal{N}(0, 1)$ % sequence Z_k is a sample from $\mathcal{N}(0, 1)$
      $W_k = W_{k-1} + Z_k\sqrt{\Delta t}$
   end for

Two quick implementations of Algorithm 3.1 are shown in Fig. 3.1 and Fig. 3.2. Notice that the latter is a vectorised version and runs faster than the former, a nonvectorised one. The corresponding discretized paths of a Wiener process are shown in Fig. 3.3.

The histograms corresponding to a given number of paths of a Wiener process are depicted in Fig. 3.4. The density functions of the corresponding

---

[1]See Definition 5.1 on page 140 for more details.

```
———————————————— WienerProcess_slow.m ————————————————
% WienerProcess
clear all, close all, randn('state',13)
T = 1; N = 300; dt = T/N; dW = zeros(1,N); W = zeros(1,N);
dW(1) = sqrt(dt)*randn; W(1) = dW(1);
for j = 2:N
    dW(j) = sqrt(dt)*randn; % increment
    W(j) = W(j-1) + dW(j); % next
end
plot([0:dt:T],[0,W]) % W(0) = 0
xlabel('t', 'FontSize', 12), ylabel('W(t)', 'FontSize', 12)
print -r900 -deps '../figures/WienerProcess_slow'
```

Fig. 3.1   Wiener process

```
———————————————— WienerProcess_HistFit.m ————————————————
% WienerProcess Histogram (vectorised)
clear all, close all, randn('state',13)
T = 1; N = 300; dt = T/N; M = 10000; % number of paths
for i = 1:M
    dW = sqrt(dt)*randn(1,N); W = cumsum(dW);
    phi(i) = W(end);
end
histfit(phi, 50);
xlabel('W(T)','FontSize',12), ylabel('M number of W(T) Values','FontSize',12)
print -r900 -depsc -cmyk '../figures/hist10000'
```

Fig. 3.2   Wiener process (vectorised)

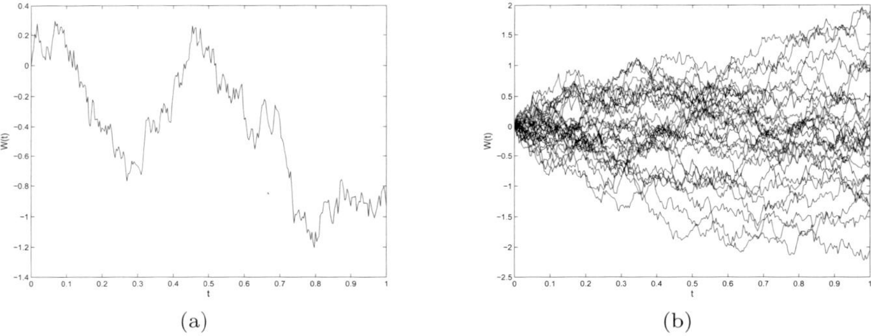

(a)   (b)

Fig. 3.3   Paths of a Wiener process: (a) a single path, (b) numerous paths

normal distributions are also shown for comparison. As the number of paths increases, the histograms fit better to the superimposed density function.

There are many libraries that allow you to draw a random number from a specified distribution. In finance, the calculation of $Z_k \sim \mathcal{N}(0, 1)$ is particularly important in simulations of stochastic processes that are described by

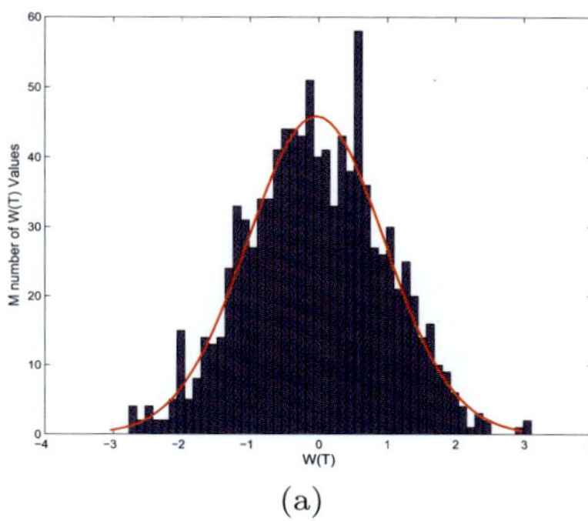 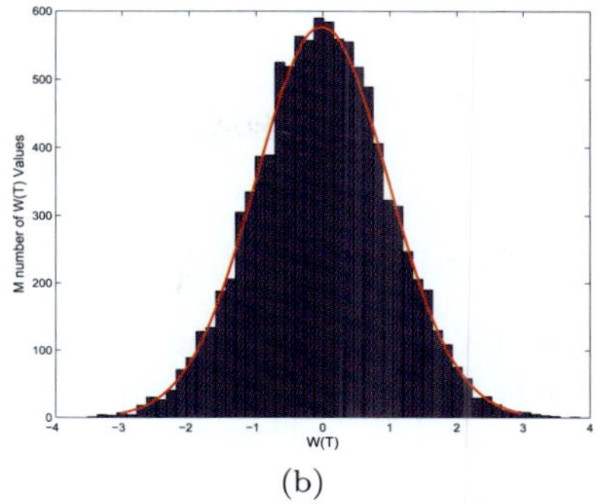

(a)   (b)

Fig. 3.4   Histogram corresponding to (a) 1000 paths (b) 10000 paths of a Wiener process

the Wiener processes. Thus, knowing at least the basics of random number generation will prove useful whenever the available libraries lack in choosing random numbers from a distribution. Generating random numbers and transformation of random variables are investigated later in Chapter 5, which presents the Monte Carlo simulations.

Almost all realisations of a Wiener process are *nowhere* differentiable. This becomes "intuitively" clear when the difference quotient

$$\frac{\Delta W_t}{\Delta t} = \frac{W_{t+\Delta t} - W_t}{\Delta t}$$

is considered. Due to $\mathbb{E}\left[(\Delta W_t)^2\right] = \Delta t$, the standard deviation of the numerator is $\sqrt{\Delta t}$. Hence, as Δt approaches zero the normal distribution of the difference quotient disperses and no convergence can be expected.

Observations in financial markets show some kind of uncertainty, *stochastic fluctuations*, such as the quoted data for asset prices, for instance. The models to describe these fluctuations generally include Wiener processes. However, due to almost nowhere differentiability of Wiener processes, it becomes impossible to define the dynamics by using ordinary or partial differential equations. Hence, defining a new type of differential equation is inevitable.

Definition 3.2. An equation of the form

$$dX_t = a(X_t, t)\, dt + b(X_t, t)\, dW_t \tag{3.11}$$

is called an Itô stochastic differential equation (SDE). The SDE together with the *initial condition*

$$X_{t_0} = X_0,$$

is a "symbolic" representation of the integral equation,

$$X_t = X_0 + \int_{t_0}^{t} a(X_s, s)\, ds + \int_{t_0}^{t} b(X_s, s)\, dW_s. \qquad (3.12)$$

The solution of (3.12) is called an *Itô process*. Furthermore,

- $a(X_t, t)$ is called the *drift* term or the drift coefficient,
- $b(X_t, t)$ is the *diffusion* term,
- the integral $\int_{t_0}^{t} b(X_s, s)\, dW_s$ refers to the stochastic Itô integral.

Stochastic integrals will be investigated in Section 3.2. Here, the focus will be on numerically solving the SDE for an Itô process, since an intuitive understanding of the underlying dynamics and the paths of an Itô process seems to be an advantage.

Note that a Wiener process itself is a special case of an Itô process; in fact, from $X_t = W_t$, the *trivial* SDE,

$$dX_t = dW_t, \quad X_0 = W_0 = 0$$

follows. Hence, $a \equiv 0$ and $b \equiv 1$ are assumed in the definition. Note that if $b \equiv 0$ and X_0 is constant (deterministic), then the SDE becomes an *ordinary differential equation* (ODE):

$$\frac{dX_t}{dt} = a(X_t, t),$$

which is also equivalent to the *ordinary* integral equation,

$$X_t = X_0 + \int_{t_0}^{t} a(X_s, s)\, ds,$$

provided that $X_{t_0} = X_0$.

Now, think of a discretized path of an Itô process governed by the SDE (3.11), and consider

$$t_{j+1} = t_j + \Delta t_j, \quad \text{for} \quad j = 0, 1, \ldots, k,$$

where $t_0 = 0$ is assumed. In other words, all the values of X_{t_j} are known for $t_0, t_1, \ldots, t_k$. Then, an approximation to $X_{t_{k+1}}$ can be written as

$$X_{t_{k+1}} = X_{t_k} + a(X_{t_k}, t_k)\, \Delta t_k + b(X_{t_k}, t_k)\, \Delta W_{t_k}. \qquad (3.13)$$

It must be emphasised that the time increments are defined by

$$\Delta t_k = t_{k+1} - t_k,$$

while the increments of the Wiener process W_t are

$$\Delta W_{t_k} = W_{t_{k+1}} - W_{t_k}.$$

Therefore, as long as a discretized path of the underlying Wiener process is known up to some time $t = t_M$, one can calculate, or rather approximate, the value of $X_{t_{k+1}}$ from the equation (3.13). In fact, this calculation describes a well-known method, the *Euler-Maruyama* method, for approximating solutions to Itô SDEs. The Algorithm 3.2 shows the pseudo-code of this method.

Algorithm 3.2 Euler-Maruyama Method

  Given: $M, t_0,\ X_0,\ \Delta t_k,\ W_0 = 0$
  for $k = 0, 1, \ldots, M$ **do**
    $t_{k+1} = t_k + \Delta t_k$
    $\Delta W_k = Z_k \sqrt{\Delta t_k},$ with $Z_k \sim \mathcal{N}(0, 1)$
    $X_{k+1} = X_k + a(X_k, t_k)\Delta t_k + b(X_k, t_j)\Delta W_k$
  end for

If a path of a Wiener process W_t is given, then the solution X_t of the SDE is called a *strong* solution. On the other hand, if we are free to select any of the paths of a Wiener process, then the solution is called a *weak* solution. In this sense, the Euler-Maruyama method described in Algorithm 3.2 can be used to approximate both, strong and weak, solutions, depending on whether the sequence of random numbers Z_k are prescribed or not.

Example 3.1. As an illustration of the Euler-Maruyama method, consider the following SDE:

$$dX_t = \mu X_t\, dt + \sigma \sqrt{X_t}\, dW_t, \qquad X_0 = 1, \tag{3.14}$$

which is called a *square-root asset price model.* Here, the drift and the diffusion terms are given by

$$a(X_t, t) = \mu X_t, \qquad b(X_t, t) = \sigma \sqrt{X_t},$$

respectively, and μ and σ are assumed to be constant, which represent, respectively, the drift and the volatility. The parameters of the model are taken to be

$$S_0 = 1, \ \mu = 0.1, \ \sigma = 0.5, \ \text{and } T = 1.$$

By using $M = 2^8$ discrete points, an implementation of the Euler-Maruyama method in Algorithm 3.2 is shown in Fig. 3.5 for the square-root asset process.

```
────────────────────── Euler_sqrtAsset.m ──────────────────────
% Euler-Maruyama
% dX = mu*X dt + sigma*sqrt(X) dW,    X_0 = 1
clear all, close all, randn('state',13)
T = 1; M = 2^8; dt = T/M; mu = 0.1; sigma = 0.5; XO = 1;
X = zeros(1,M+1); X(1) = XO;
for j = 1:M
    dW = sqrt(dt)*randn;
    a = mu*X(j); b = sigma*sqrt(X(j)); % calculate coefficients
    X(j+1) = X(j) + a*dt + b*dW;
end
plot([0:dt:T],X,'r-'), xlabel('t','FontSize',12), ylabel('X','FontSize',12)
print -r900 -deps '../figures/EM_sqrtAsset'
```

Fig. 3.5 Euler-Maruyama method

Fig. 3.6 shows the paths of the square-root asset price model (3.14), which are obtained by the Euler-Maruyama algorithm.

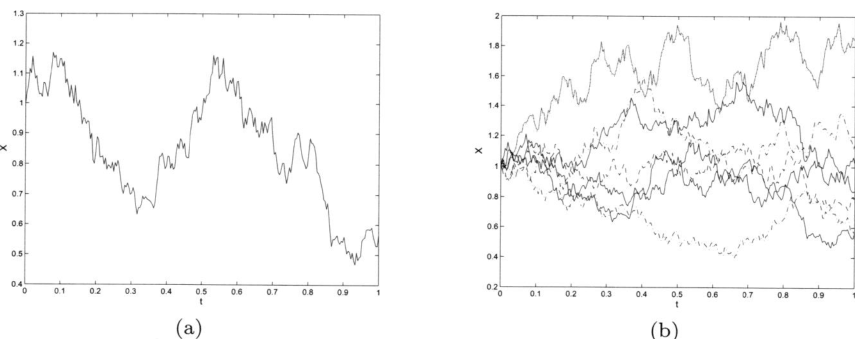

     (a)   (b)

Fig. 3.6 Paths of the solution of SDE (3.14) by Euler-Maruyama method: (a) a single path, (b) some more paths

Depending on the drift and the diffusion terms, there are specific names for the SDEs. The most important one, at least in this book, is the *geometric Brownian motion*,

$$dS_t = \mu S_t \, dt + \sigma S_t \, dW_t, \tag{3.15}$$

that describes the dynamics of the asset prices S_t. The geometric Brownian motion, where μ and σ are considered as constants, is the reference model on which the Black-Scholes-Merton approach to the stock prices is based. The following example will illustrate the Euler-Maruyama method on this reference model.

Example 3.2. Consider the SDE for the geometric Brownian motion,

$$dS_t = \mu S_t \, dt + \sigma S_t \, dW_t,$$

whose *closed-form* solution will be proved to be

$$S_t = S_0 e^{\left(\mu - \frac{1}{2}\sigma^2\right)t + \sigma W_t}, \tag{3.16}$$

where $S_{t_0} = S_0$ is the initial value of the asset price. This solution might be regarded as a strong solution, for a given realisation of the Wiener process W_t.

By choosing a fixed path of the Wiener process W_t for t in the interval $[0, T]$, let us apply the Euler-Maruyama method to approximate the closed-form solution. To do so, consider the implementation in Fig. 3.7, which could be optimised, of course. It computes several paths of a geometric Brownian motion by Euler-Maruyama method with small step sizes. The parameters of the model are taken to be

$$S_0 = 1, \ \mu = 0.1, \ \sigma = 0.5, \ \text{and } T = 1.$$

In Fig. 3.8(a) some of the paths of the geometric Brownian motion are shown, while in Fig. 3.8(b) a histogram corresponding to the final values S_T for the 10000 paths is depicted. The superimposed curve in Fig. 3.8(b) is the corresponding density function of the *lognormal* distribution.

It must be emphasised that the histogram shown in Fig. 3.8(b) is normalised so that the total area is unity, and the superimposed function is the density function of the lognormal distribution. An example of a MAT-LAB function that transforms the given data to a normalised histogram is implemented in Fig. 3.9.

Exercise 3.1. Compare the solution obtained in Example 3.2 with the closed-form solution in (3.16). Also, compare the histograms for the final values of the asset prices defined by the geometric Brownian motion (3.15) and the square-root process (3.14).

The *lognormal* distribution mentioned in Example 3.2 is the distribution of a random variable X of the form $X = e^Z$, where Z is normally distributed

```
—————————————— GeometricBrownianMotion.m ——————————————
% Euler-Maruyama for Geometric Brownian Motion
% dS = mu*S*dt + sigma*S*dW, S_0 = 1
clear all, close all, randn('state',13)
T = 1; M = 2^8; dt = T/M; mu = 0.1; sigma = 0.5; SO = 1; N = 10000;
HS = zeros(N,1); S = zeros(N,M+1); S(:,1) = SO*ones(1,N);
for k = 1:N % for a path
    for j = 1:M
        dW = sqrt(dt)*randn;
        a = mu*S(k,j); b = sigma*S(k,j); % calculate coefficients
        S(k,j+1) = S(k,j) + a*dt + b*dW;
    end
end
figure(1), plot( [0:dt:T], S(1:1000:N, :) ),
xlabel('t','FontSize',12), ylabel('S','FontSize',12)
print -r900 -depsc -cmyk '../figures/GeometricBM_Paths'
figure(2), HS = S(:,end);
histNormalized(HS, 0.05, min(min(HS)), max(max(HS))); hold on
x = (0:0.02:6); y = lognpdf(x, (mu - 0.5*sigma^2), sigma); % lognormal pdf
plot(x, y, 'r-', 'LineWidth', 2); xlabel('x','FontSize',12), ylabel('y','FontSize',12)
print -r900 -depsc -cmyk '../figures/GeometricBM'
```

Fig. 3.7   Paths of a Geometric Brownian Motion and a histogram corresponding to final values

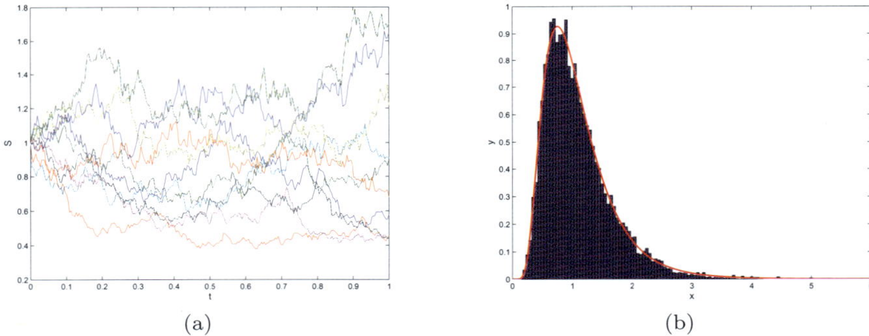

(a)   (b)

Fig. 3.8   Geometric Brownian Motion: (a) some paths, (b) histogram corresponding to final values of 10000 paths

with mean μ and standard deviation σ. Indeed, this definition follows from the fact that $\log(X)$ is normally distributed, $\log(X) \sim \mathcal{N}(\mu, \sigma^2)$. In order to derive the corresponding distribution and the probability density functions, let Z be a normally distributed random variable such that $Z \sim \mathcal{N}(\mu, \sigma)$. Then, the distribution function of $X = e^Z$, say $\Psi_{\mu,\sigma}(x)$ for > 0, can be

```
————————————————— histNormalized.m —————————————————
function [h,hn,xspan] = histNormalized(data, binSize, xi, xf)
% Normalized Histogram Plot

xspan = [xi:binSize:xf]; h = hist(data, xspan);
hn = h / (length(data)*binSize);
bar(xspan, hn, 1); % no space between bars
```

Fig. 3.9   Normalisation of a histogram

computed as

$$\Psi_{\mu,\sigma}(x) = \mathbb{P}\left\{X \le x\right\} = \mathbb{P}\left\{Z \le \log x\right\}$$

$$= \frac{1}{\sigma\sqrt{2\pi}} \int_{-\infty}^{\log x} e^{-\frac{(\xi-\mu)^2}{2\sigma^2}}\, d\xi$$

$$= \frac{1}{\sigma\sqrt{2\pi}} \int_0^x \frac{1}{s} e^{-\frac{(\log s - \mu)^2}{2\sigma^2}}\, ds.$$

Therefore, the probability density function of the lognormal distribution is defined by

$$\psi_{\mu,\sigma}(x) = \frac{1}{x\sigma\sqrt{2\pi}} e^{-\frac{(\log x - \mu)^2}{2\sigma^2}}, \qquad x > 0. \tag{3.17}$$

The following exercise will prove useful later in finding the expectation and the variance of geometric asset prices. Recall that the expectation and the variance of continuous model for asset prices were used in deriving the binomial models in Chapter 2. So, readers are advised to calculate the moments $\mathbb{E}\left[X^n\right]$ for any $n \in \mathbb{N}$ of a lognormally distributed random variable X.

Exercise 3.2. Let X be a lognormally distributed random variable with parameters μ and σ. To be more specific, let $X = e^Z$ be a random variable such that $Z \sim \mathcal{N}(\mu, \sigma^2)$. Show that the moments are defined by

$$\mathbb{E}\left[X^n\right] = \exp\left\{n\mu + \frac{n^2\sigma^2}{2}\right\}, \qquad n = 1, 2, \ldots. \tag{3.18}$$

In particular, show that

$$\mathbb{E}\left[X\right] = e^{\mu + \sigma^2/2} \quad \text{and} \quad \mathbb{E}\left[X^2\right] = e^{2\mu + 2\sigma^2}$$

so that the variance of X is

$$\mathbb{V}\mathrm{ar}\left[X\right] = e^{2\mu + \sigma^2}\left(e^{\sigma^2} - 1\right). \tag{3.19}$$

Outlook

Existence and uniqueness theorems for solutions to stochastic differential equations are not covered in this book, however, many standard textbooks on numerical solutions of SDEs, such as [Kloeden and Platen (1992); Kloeden *et al.* (1997)] include theoretical aspects of SDEs, too. The former has many applications ranging from genetics to physics. An introduction to numerical methods and codes for programmers can also be found in [Cyganowski *et al.* (2002); Higham (2001); Platen (1999)].

Apart from Euler-Maruyama method described in this section there are many other numerical methods for solutions of SDEs. They are mainly derived from *stochastic Taylor expansion* which generalises the classical Taylor series for deterministic functions to stochastic processes. A well-known numerical scheme is the so-called *Milstein* method. While the Euler-Maruyama method has the order of (strong) convergence 1/2, the Milstein method has 1: we can regard the Milstein method as the proper generalisation of the deterministic Euler method which has also the same order of convergence. Higher order Runge-Kutta schemes are also available for solution of SDEs in [Kloeden and Platen (1992)].

3.2 Stochastic Itô Integral

Let $P^{(n)}$ be a sequence of partitions of the interval $[t_0, T]$, defined by

$$P^{(n)} := \left\{ t_0 = t_0^{(n)} < t_1^{(n)} < \cdots < t_{m_n}^{(n)} = T \right\},$$

with the convention that $t_0 = 0$. Assume that the mesh sizes

$$\delta^{(n)} := \max_{1 \leq j \leq m_n} \left| t_j^{(n)} - t_{j-1}^{(n)} \right| \longrightarrow 0$$

as $m_n \to \infty$ for every $n \in \mathbb{N}$. Suppose that we are interested in defining the integral

$$\mathcal{I}_T := \int_{t_0}^{T} W_s \, dW_s,$$

by the Riemann-Stieltjes sum

$$R_n := \sum_{j=1}^{m_n} W_{\tau_{j-1}^{(n)}} \Delta W_{t_{j-1}^{(n)}} = \sum_{j=1}^{m_n} W_{\tau_{j-1}^{(n)}} \left(W_{t_j^{(n)}} - W_{t_{j-1}^{(n)}} \right), \qquad (3.20)$$

where $\tau_{j-1}^{(n)} \in [t_{j-1}^{(n)}, t_j^{(n)}]$. First, let us consider the case when $\tau_{j-1}^{(n)} = t_{j-1}^{(n)}$, that is, the evaluation of the integrand W_t is at the beginning of the subintervals. It is easy to calculate the expectation of R_n by using the basic properties of the Wiener processes as follows:

$$\mathbb{E}\left[\sum_{j=1}^{m_n} W_{t_{j-1}^{(n)}}\left(W_{t_j^{(n)}} - W_{t_{j-1}^{(n)}}\right)\right] = \sum_{j=1}^{m_n} \mathbb{E}\left[W_{t_{j-1}^{(n)}}\left(W_{t_j^{(n)}} - W_{t_{j-1}^{(n)}}\right)\right]$$

$$= \sum_{j=1}^{m_n} \mathbb{E}\left[W_{t_{j-1}^{(n)}}\right]\mathbb{E}\left[W_{t_j^{(n)}} - W_{t_{j-1}^{(n)}}\right]$$

$$= 0.$$

On the other hand, if the integrand is evaluated at the end of the subintervals, that is, at $\tau_{j-1}^{(n)} = t_j^{(n)}$, then, unlike our first calculations, the sum in (3.20) would give the expectation as $T - t_0$. In fact,

$$\mathbb{E}\left[\sum_{j=1}^{m_n} W_{t_j^{(n)}}\left(W_{t_j^{(n)}} - W_{t_{j-1}^{(n)}}\right)\right] = \sum_{j=1}^{m_n} \mathbb{E}\left[\left(W_{t_{j-1}^{(n)}} + \Delta W_{t_{j-1}^{(n)}}\right)\Delta W_{t_{j-1}^{(n)}}\right]$$

$$= \sum_{j=1}^{m_n} \mathbb{E}\left[\left(\Delta W_{t_{j-1}^{(n)}}\right)^2\right]$$

$$= \sum_{j=1}^{m_n}\left(t_j^{(n)} - t_{j-1}^{(n)}\right) = t_{m_n} - t_0$$

$$= T - t_0.$$

Note that the increments of the Wiener process are defined by

$$\Delta W_{t_{j-1}^{(n)}} = W_{t_j^{(n)}} - W_{t_{j-1}^{(n)}},$$

as usual. These two calculations simply show that the evaluation of the integrand at different points of the subintervals in the partition produces different expectations of the corresponding Riemann-Stieltjes sums.

Indeed, Wiener processes are not of *bounded variation*; in other words, the limit of

$$V_n := \sum_{j=1}^{m_n}\left|W_{t_j^{(n)}} - W_{t_{j-1}^{(n)}}\right| \tag{3.21}$$

is unbounded even if $\delta^{(n)} \to 0$. Hence, defining a stochastic integral in the sense of Riemann-Stieltjes integral by using the sums R_n is impossible.

Although the variation V_n of W_t is unbounded, the *quadratic variation*

$$Q_n := \sum_{j=1}^{m_n}\left|W_{t_j^{(n)}} - W_{t_{j-1}^{(n)}}\right|^2 \tag{3.22}$$

converges to $T - t_0$ *in the (quadratic) mean;*[2] that is,

$$\underset{\delta^{(n)} \to 0}{\text{l.i.m}} \sum_{j=1}^{m_n} \left| W_{t_j^{(n)}} - W_{t_{j-1}^{(n)}} \right|^2 = T - t_0. \qquad (3.23)$$

In order to show this limit, the *limit in the mean*, the following equivalent lemma has to be proved.

Lemma 3.1. *The quadratic variation Q_n defined by (3.22) converges to $T - t_0$ in the mean. That is,*

$$\mathbb{E}\left[(Q_n - (T - t_0))^2 \right] \longrightarrow 0 \quad \text{as} \quad \delta^{(n)} \to 0. \qquad (3.24)$$

Proof. Using the basic properties of expectations and variances, the following identity can easily be obtained:

$$\mathbb{E}\left[(Q_n - (T - t_0))^2 \right] = (\mathbb{E}\left[Q_n - (T - t_0) \right])^2 + \mathbb{V}\text{ar}\left[Q_n - (T - t_0) \right]. \qquad (3.25)$$

On one hand, the expectation $\mathbb{E}\left[Q_n - (T - t_0) \right]$ involved in (3.25) can be shown to be zero. This simply follows from

$$\begin{aligned}
\mathbb{E}\left[Q_n \right] &= \sum_{j=1}^{m_n} \mathbb{E}\left[\left| W_{t_j^{(n)}} - W_{t_{j-1}^{(n)}} \right|^2 \right] \\
&= \sum_{j=1}^{m_n} \left(t_j^{(n)} - t_{j-1}^{(n)} \right) \\
&= T - t_0.
\end{aligned}$$

On the other hand, the variance $\mathbb{V}\text{ar}\left[Q_n - (T - t_0) \right]$, which is equivalent to

---

[2]A sequence X_n is said to converge in the (quadratic) mean to X, if $\mathbb{E}\left[X_n^2 \right] < \infty$, $\mathbb{E}\left[X^2 \right] < \infty$, and if

$$\lim_{n \to \infty} \mathbb{E}\left[(X_n - X)^2 \right] = 0.$$

We will write this limit generally in the form

$$\underset{n \to \infty}{\text{l.i.m}}\, X_n = X$$

$\mathrm{Var}\left[Q_n\right]$, can be computed as

$$
\begin{aligned}
\mathrm{Var}\left[Q_n\right] &= \sum_{j=1}^{m_n} \mathrm{Var}\left[\left|W_{t_j^{(n)}} - W_{t_{j-1}^{(n)}}\right|^2\right] \\
&= \sum_{j=1}^{m_n}\left\{\mathbb{E}\left[\left(\Delta W_{t_{j-1}^{(n)}}\right)^4\right] - \left(\mathbb{E}\left[\left(\Delta W_{t_{j-1}^{(n)}}\right)^2\right]\right)^2\right\} \\
&= \sum_{j=1}^{m_n}\left\{3\left(t_j^{(n)} - t_{j-1}^{(n)}\right)^2 - \left(t_j^{(n)} - t_{j-1}^{(n)}\right)^2\right\} \\
&= 2\sum_{j=1}^{m_n}\left(t_j^{(n)} - t_{j-1}^{(n)}\right)^2.
\end{aligned}
$$

In the calculations above, the identity

$$
\mathbb{E}\left[\left(\Delta W_{t_{j-1}^{(n)}}\right)^4\right] = 3\left(t_j^{(n)} - t_{j-1}^{(n)}\right)^2
$$

is used, which can also be proved easily. Finally, substituting $\mathbb{E}\left[Q_n\right]$ and $\mathrm{Var}\left[Q_n\right]$ in (3.25) gives

$$
\begin{aligned}
\mathbb{E}\left[\left(Q_n - (T - t_0)\right)^2\right] &= 2\sum_{j=1}^{m_n}\left(t_j^{(n)} - t_{j-1}^{(n)}\right)^2 \\
&\leq 2\delta^{(n)}\sum_{j=1}^{m_n}\left(t_j^{(n)} - t_{j-1}^{(n)}\right) \\
&= 2\delta^{(n)}(T - t_0) \longrightarrow 0 \quad \text{as} \quad \delta^{(n)} \to 0.
\end{aligned}
$$

Hence, this completes the proof. $\qquad\square$

Lemma 3.1 admits an immediate corollary that is widely used in literature. This is also known as the *quadratic variation* of Wiener processes. An indirect proof of the following corollary considers the special case when $Q_n = W_t - W_{t_0}$ and $\Delta t = t - t_0$.

Corollary 3.1. *Let W_t be a Wiener process. Then,*

$$
\mathbb{E}\left[(\Delta W_t)^2 - \Delta t\right] = 0, \quad \text{and} \quad \mathrm{Var}\left[(\Delta W_t)^2 - \Delta t\right] = 2\left(\Delta t\right)^2,
$$

which is symbolically written as

$$
(dW_t)^2 = dt.
$$

Referring back to the quadratic variation Q_n defined by (3.22), it is easy to give an upper bound to it as

$$Q_n \leq \max_{1 \leq j \leq m_n} \left| \Delta W_{t_{j-1}^{(n)}} \right| \times \sum_{j=1}^{m_n} \left| \Delta W_{t_{j-1}^{(n)}} \right|.$$

Thus, the first term of the bound above vanishes as $\delta^{(n)} \to 0$. That is,

$$\max_{1 \leq j \leq m_n} \left| \Delta W_{t_{j-1}^{(n)}} \right| \longrightarrow 0 \quad \text{as} \quad \delta^{(n)} \to 0,$$

which simply follows from the continuity of W_t.

Therefore, in view of Lemma 3.1, the other factor of the bound for Q_n, the *first variation*,

$$V_n = \sum_{j=1}^{m_n} \left| W_{t_j^{(n)}} - W_{t_{j-1}^{(n)}} \right| = \sum_{j=1}^{m_n} \left| \Delta W_{t_{j-1}^{(n)}} \right|,$$

must be unbounded in order to compensate the boundedness of the quadratic variation Q_n as $\delta^{(n)} \to 0$.

Now, let us return back to the integral

$$\mathcal{I}_T := \int_{t_0}^{T} W_s \, dW_s$$

and consider taking the *limit in the mean* of the Riemann-Stieltjes sum R_n in (3.20). That is, we are now interested in the limit

$$\lim_{\delta^{(n)} \to \infty} R_n = \lim_{\delta^{(n)} \to \infty} \sum_{j=1}^{m_n} W_{\tau_{j-1}^{(n)}} \left(W_{t_j^{(n)}} - W_{t_{j-1}^{(n)}} \right). \tag{3.26}$$

Furthermore, let us pick the points

$$\tau_{j-1}^{(n)} = (1 - \lambda) t_{j-1}^{(n)} + \lambda \tau_j^{(n)},$$

arbitrarily in the intervals $[t_{j-1}^{(n)}, t_j^{(n)}]$ for $0 \leq \lambda \leq 1$ in order to seek a generalised formula for the integration. First, we note that the Riemann-Stieltjes sum R_n may be decomposed also in the form

$$R_n = \tfrac{1}{2} \left(W_T^2 - W_{t_0}^2 \right) - \tfrac{1}{2} \sum_{j=1}^{m_n} \left(W_{t_j^{(n)}} - W_{t_{j-1}^{(n)}} \right)^2$$

$$+ \sum_{j=1}^{m_n} \left(W_{\tau_{j-1}^{(n)}} - W_{t_{j-1}^{(n)}} \right)^2 \tag{3.27}$$

$$+ \sum_{j=1}^{m_n} \left(W_{t_j^{(n)}} - W_{\tau_{j-1}^{(n)}} \right) \left(W_{\tau_{j-1}^{(n)}} - W_{t_{j-1}^{(n)}} \right).$$

Second, by the help of Lemma 3.1, the first sum in (3.27) converges to $T - t_0$ in the mean. Third, similar to the proof of Lemma 3.1, one can easily show that the second sum converges to $\lambda(T - t_0)$. Finally, the last one converges to zero in the mean. Hence, the limit in the mean of R_n can be calculated as

$$\underset{\delta^{(n)} \to 0}{\text{l.i.m}} \sum_{j=1}^{m_n} W_{\tau_{j-1}^{(n)}} \Delta W_{t_{j-1}^{(n)}} = \frac{1}{2} \left(W_T^2 - W_{t_0}^2 \right) + \left(\lambda - \frac{1}{2} \right) (T - t_0). \quad (3.28)$$

Unfortunately, in this generalised case, the limit in the mean of R_n also depends on λ. In other words, it depends on the choice of the points $\tau_{j-1}^{(n)}$ of the intervals $[t_{j-1}^{(n)}, t_j^{(n)}]$ in evaluating the integrand.

In particular, if $\lambda = 0$, that is, if the left-end points $\tau_{j-1}^{(n)} = t_{j-1}^{(n)}$ of the subintervals are used, the limit in the mean becomes

$$\underset{\delta^{(n)} \to 0}{\text{l.i.m}} \sum_{j=1}^{m_n} W_{\tau_{j-1}^{(n)}} \Delta W_{t_{j-1}^{(n)}} = \frac{1}{2} \left(W_T^2 - W_{t_0}^2 \right) - \frac{1}{2}(T - t_0). \quad (3.29)$$

However, if $\lambda = \frac{1}{2}$, that is, if the midpoints $\tau_{j-1}^{(n)} = \frac{1}{2} \left(t_{j-1}^{(n)} + t_j^{(n)} \right)$ of the subintervals are chosen, then a relatively "simpler" form,

$$\underset{\delta^{(n)} \to 0}{\text{l.i.m}} \sum_{j=1}^{m_n} W_{\tau_{j-1}^{(n)}} \Delta W_{t_j^{(n)}} = \frac{1}{2} \left(W_T^2 - W_{t_0}^2 \right), \quad (3.30)$$

is obtained. The choices of τ_{j-1} as above are particularly important:

- The choice of the left-end points, $\tau_{j-1}^{(n)} = t_{j-1}^{(n)}$ is due to *Itô*, while
- the choice of the midpoints, $\tau_{j-1}^{(n)} = \frac{1}{2} \left(t_{j-1}^{(n)} + t_j^{(n)} \right)$ is due to *Stratonovich*.

The integrals that use these points define the *stochastic Itô* and the *Stratonovich integrals*, respectively.

To sum up, for a given $t \in [t_0, T]$, the integral

$$\mathcal{I}_t := \int_{t_0}^{t} W_s \, dW_s = \frac{1}{2} \left(W_t^2 - W_{t_0}^2 \right) - \frac{1}{2}(t - t_0) \quad (3.31)$$

is the *Itô integral* of W_t. On the other hand,

$$\mathcal{I}_t^{\circ} = \int_{t_0}^{t} W_s \circ dW_s = \frac{1}{2}\left(W_t^2 - W_{t_0}^2\right) \qquad (3.32)$$

is called the *Stratonovich integral* of W_t. Notice that to distinguish between the integrals, the symbol "$\circ$" is used when the stochastic integral in the sense of Stratonovich is assumed.

These two definitions of the stochastic integrals have their own advantages and disadvantages in applications of finance and of other branches of science. Although it seems plausible to decide on the choice of Stratonovich and take the midpoints, however, the key point on the choice lies in the so-called *martingale* property. This is defined via the conditional expectation of a stochastic process X_t as

$$\mathbb{E}\left[X_t \mid \mathcal{F}_s\right] = X_s \quad \text{for all} \quad s < t.$$

Here, the σ–algebra $\mathcal{F}_s$ is called the *filtration*, to which the process X_t is *adapted*. That is, the process X_t is $\mathcal{F}_t$–measurable for all $t \geq 0$. In the naïve sense, the martingale property means that all future variations of X_t for $t > s$ are unpredictable, or not available in the information set, $\mathcal{F}_s$. Therefore, the martingale property is in line with financial terms: decisions are taken *today* rather than *tomorrow*. As long as the processes are driven by the Wiener process W_t, the filtration $\mathcal{F}_t$ is generally considered to be the smallest σ–algebra generated by the underlying Wiener process. The information set, in this case, is referred to as the *natural filtration* defined by

$$\mathcal{F}_t = \sigma\left\{W_s : s \leq t\right\}, \quad t \geq 0.$$

Therefore, a Wiener process itself satisfies the *martingale* property with respect to the natural filtration. For, W_t and the increments $\Delta W_t := W_{t+\Delta t} - W_t$ for $\Delta t > 0$ are independent random variables. Consequently, defining a stochastic integral which also satisfies this property, and choosing the Itô integral is appreciated.

Note that if the stochastic Itô integral $\mathcal{I}_t$ above is considered, then it can be represented via the stochastic differential equation,

$$d\mathcal{I}_t = W_t\, dW_t, \qquad \mathcal{I}_{t_0} = 0. \qquad (3.33)$$

Hence, in order to simulate the stochastic Itô process defined by $\mathcal{I}_t$ the Euler-Maruyama method can be used. For instance, if the discretization

$t_i = t_0 + i\Delta t_i$ is used for $i \in \mathbb{N}$ and $\Delta t_i > 0$, then the Euler-Maruyama method gives

$$\mathcal{I}_{t_i} = \mathcal{I}_{t_{i-1}} + W_{t_{i-1}} \Delta W_{t_{i-1}}, \tag{3.34}$$

where $\Delta W_{t_{i-1}} = W_{t_i} - W_{t_{i-1}}$.

Furthermore, note also that in Euler-Maruyama method, the integrand W_t is evaluated at the beginning of the intervals $[t_{i-1}, t_i]$. Consequently, the Euler-Maruyama method is *consistent* with the stochastic Itô integral.

Exercise 3.3. Provided that W_{t_0} is given, or simply assuming $t_0 = 0$, simulate the paths of the Itô integral

$$\mathcal{I}_t = \int_{t_0}^{t} W_s \, dW_s$$

and compare them with the explicit form

$$\mathcal{I}_t = \frac{1}{2} \left(W_t^2 - W_{t_0}^2 \right) - \frac{1}{2}(t - t_0).$$

3.2.1 *Definition and Properties of the Itô Integral*

The preceding discussion on defining the stochastic Itô integral by the convergence in the mean is practically useful in evaluating the integrals. However, for theoretical purposes a more sound definition of stochastic integrals is needed. This section briefly explains how this may be done. The idea is rather similar to defining a Lebesgue integral of functions. First, define the integral for *simple* functions with respect to a Lebesgue measure. Then, extend it to the integration of certain class of functions.

In stochastic integration, however, we have processes instead of functions, and the integration is taken with respect to a (Wiener) process, rather than a Lebesgue measure. In what follows, we will consider the stochastic Itô integral with respect to a Wiener process W_t with the *natural filtration*

$$\mathcal{F}_t = \sigma \left\{ W_s \; : \; s \leq t \right\}, \quad t \leq 0,$$

which is the smallest σ–algebra generated by W_t. Moreover, all the processes will be adapted to this filtration, that is, if X_t is adapted to $\mathcal{F}_t$, then X_t is $\mathcal{F}_t$–measurable, and $\mathbb{E}\left[X_t^2 \right] < \infty$.

Let $P = \{t_0, t_1, \ldots, t_n\}$ be a partition of $[0, t]$ such that

$$0 = t_0 \leq t_1 \leq t_2 \leq \cdots \leq t_n = T.$$

Assume that a process C_t, for $t \in [0, T]$, is defined by

$$C_t := \begin{cases} C(t_i), & \text{if } t \in [t_{i-1}, t_i), \ i = 1, 2, \ldots, n, \\ C(t_n), & \text{if } t = T, \end{cases} \qquad (3.35)$$

where $C(t_i)$, for each $i = 1, 2, \ldots, n$ is a random variable and adapted to the filtration $\mathcal{F}_{t_{i-1}}$. Such a process C_t is called a *simple process*. See Fig. 3.10 for a single path, which is continuous from the right, of a simple process. It is also possible to define simple processes having left-continuous paths. However, in the following discussion we will assume that C_t is as described by (3.35).

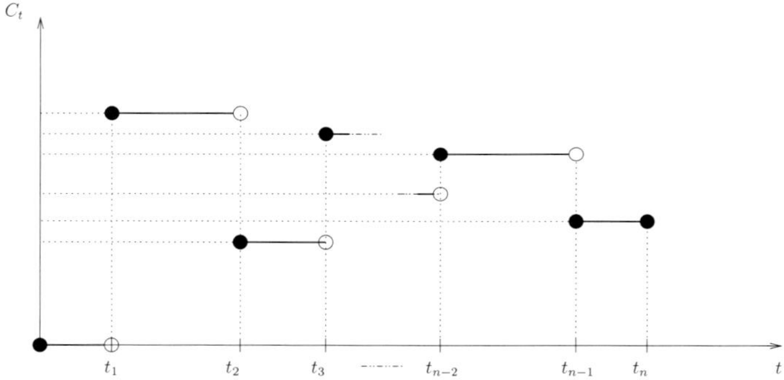

Fig. 3.10   A path of a simple process

The stochastic Itô integral of a simple process with respect to a Wiener process W_t is then defined as

$$\begin{aligned} I_t(C_t) &:= \int_{t_0}^{t} C_s \, dW_s \\ &= \sum_{j=0}^{k-1} C(t_j) \left(W_{t_{j+1}} - W_{t_j} \right) + C(t_k) \left(W_t - W_{t_k} \right) \end{aligned} \qquad (3.36)$$

for $t \in [t_k, t_{k+1}]$. If $k = 0$, then the sum in (3.36) is assumed to be zero.

It is possible to extend this definition of the stochastic integral described for simple processes to the integral of general processes. Let f_t be a general process such that it is adapted to the natural filtration $\mathcal{F}_t$ and it satisfies the *square-integrability* condition,

$$\mathbb{E}\left[\int_0^T f_t^2 \, dt\right] < \infty. \tag{3.37}$$

The idea of the extension is based on approximating the process f_t by simple processes C_t. The approximating simple processes $C_t^{(\kappa)}$ may be constructed by choosing a set of partitions

$$0 = t_0^{(\kappa)} \le t_1^{(\kappa)} \le t_2^{(\kappa)} \le \cdots \le t_n^{(\kappa)} = T$$

and then setting

$$C_t^{(\kappa)} := \begin{cases} f_{t_i^{(\kappa)}}, & \text{if } t \in [t_{i-1}^{(\kappa)}, t_i^{(\kappa)}), \ i = 1, 2, \ldots, n, \\ f_{t_n^{(\kappa)}}, & \text{if } t = T. \end{cases} \tag{3.38}$$

In the partition above we implicitly assume a dependency between the indexes κ and n, for the sake of simplicity. As the step size of the partition approaches zero, the simple processes will approximate the process f_t "better", in the sense that

$$\lim_{\kappa \to \infty} \mathbb{E}\left[\int_0^T \left|C_t^{(\kappa)} - f_t\right|^2 dt\right] = 0. \tag{3.39}$$

Then, the stochastic Itô integral of f_t with respect to a Wiener process W_t for $0 \le t \le T$ is defined by the following limit in the mean:

$$I_t(f_t) := \int_{t_0}^t f_s \, dW_s = \underset{\kappa \to \infty}{\text{l.i.m}} \int_{t_0}^t C_s^{(\kappa)} \, dW_s. \tag{3.40}$$

This integral exists, since the integrals

$$I_t(C_t^{(\kappa)}) = \int_{t_0}^t C_s^{(\kappa)} \, dW_s$$

are integrals of simple processes and the sequence $\left\{I_t(C_t^{(\kappa)})\right\}_{\kappa=0}^{\infty}$ becomes a *Cauchy* sequence (in a complete Hilbert space of square-integrable processes) due to a property, so-called *isometry*, which will be described in the sequel. Interested readers are advised to refer to advanced textbooks on stochastic integrals for more on the existence of such approximating sequences and the properties of integrals.

Indeed, the following properties of a stochastic Itô integral follow from the corresponding properties of integrals of simple processes. The proofs are omitted.

Theorem 3.1 (Properties of Stochastic Itô Integral). *Let f_t and g_t be adapted processes that satisfy the square-integrability condition (3.37). Then, the stochastic Itô integral*

$$I_t(f_t) := \int_{t_0}^{t} f_s \, dW_s$$

has the following properties.

(1) **Continuity.** *As a function of t, the paths of $I_t(f_t)$ are continuous.*
(2) **Adaptivity.** *For each t, $I_t(f_t)$ is $\mathcal{F}_t$-measurable.*
(3) **Linearity.** *For every constant c,*

$$cI_t(f_t) + I_t(g_t) = \int_{0}^{t} (cf_s + g_s) \, dW_s.$$

(4) **Martingale.** *$I_t(f_t)$ satisfies the martingale property.*
(5) **Itô Isometry.**

$$\mathbb{E}\left[I_t^2(f_t)\right] = \mathbb{E}\left[\int_{0}^{t} f_t^2 \, ds\right].$$

(6) **Quadratic Variation.** *The quadratic variation of $I_t(f_t)$, which is denoted by $[I_t(f_t), I_t(f_t)]$ satisfies*

$$[I_t(f_t), I_t(f_t)] = \int_{0}^{t} f_s^2 \, ds.$$

In the following example the definition of the stochastic Itô integral is directly applied to the integral of a Wiener process. This is indeed what has been proved before, however, it shows how to construct the approximating simple processes.

Example 3.3. In order to compute the Itô integral

$$I_t(W_t) = \int_{0}^{T} W_s \, dW_s$$

we define the simple processes for each κ as

$$C_t^{(\kappa)} := \begin{cases} W_0, & \text{if } 0 \leq t < \frac{T}{\kappa}, \\ W_{t_1}, & \text{if } \frac{T}{\kappa} \leq t < \frac{2T}{\kappa}, \\ \vdots & \\ W_{t_{\kappa-1}}, & \frac{(\kappa-1)T}{\kappa} \leq t < T, \\ W_{t_\kappa}, & \text{if } t = T, \end{cases} \tag{3.41}$$

for the sequence of partitions

$$t_i = t_0 + i\Delta t, \quad \Delta t = \frac{T}{\kappa}, \quad i = 1, 2, \ldots, \kappa = n.$$

See Fig. 3.11 for an illustration of the constructed simple processes on the partitions.

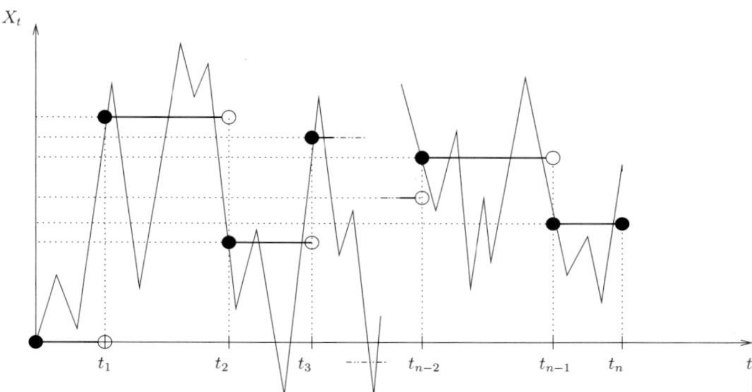

Fig. 3.11   Approximating a path of a Wiener process by using a simple process

Therefore, one can easily show that

$$\lim_{\kappa \to \infty} \mathbb{E}\left[\int_0^T \left|C_t^{(\kappa)} - W_t\right|^2 dt\right] = 0,$$

and hence, by definition the integral of W_t with respect to W_t is

$$I_t(W_t) := \int_0^T W_s \, dW_s = \underset{\kappa \to \infty}{\mathrm{l.i.m}} \int_0^T C_s^{(\kappa)} \, dW_s$$

$$= \underset{\kappa \to \infty}{\mathrm{l.i.m}} \sum_{j=1}^{\kappa} W_{t_{j-1}} \left(W_{t_j} - W_{t_{j-1}}\right).$$

However, this is what we computed and summarised in (3.28) (for $\lambda = 0$) and (3.31). Thus,

$$I_t(W_t) := \int_{t_0}^T W_s \, dW_s = \frac{1}{2}W_T^2 - \frac{1}{2}T.$$

We conclude this section by the following example, whose result will also be shown by another method in the sequel. The method is an application of the well-known Itô lemma.

Exercise 3.4. By using the definition of the Itô integral, show that

$$\int_0^t s \, dW_s = tW_t - \int_0^t W_s \, ds$$

for $t \in [0, T]$.

Outlook

Although, a thorough mathematical approach to stochastic integrals consists of measure theoretic concepts and certain function and probability spaces, we restricted the theory to the *convergence in the mean* and the integration of simple processes. This is is due to the similarities of the classical theory of Riemann-Stieltjes integration and its practical usage. Depending on readers background we refer to [Evans (2008); Kloeden and Platen (1992); Korn and Korn (2001); Mikosch (1998); Shreve (2004b)] for a complete discussion.

There is a close relation between the Itô and the Stratonovich integrals, however, each integral has its own particular applications in mathematical sciences. See, for instance, [Kloeden and Platen (1992); Mikosch (1998); Øksendal (2002)]. In finance, Itô integrals are preferred due to the *martingale* property of stochastic processes and the calculus derived is named after Itô: *Itô calculus* has some simple rules for products of dW_t and dt.

3.3 Itô Lemma

This section presents the well-known lemma of Itô and its several applications, such as computing stochastic Itô integrals and solutions of SDEs. The lemma, given below without proof, is fundamental in stochastic processes and compositions of such processes: it is regarded as the *chain rule* for stochastic Itô processes.

Lemma 3.2 (Itô Lemma). *Let X_t for $t \geq 0$ be a stochastic Itô processes defined by*

$$dX_t = a(X_t, t) \, dt + b(X_t, t) \, dW_t, \tag{3.42}$$

and let $f : (x, t) \mapsto f(x, t)$ be a function for which the partial derivatives,

$$f_x := \frac{\partial f}{\partial x}, \quad f_{xx} := \frac{\partial^2 f}{\partial x^2}, \quad \text{and} \quad f_t := \frac{\partial f}{\partial t},$$

are defined and continuous. Then, for every $t \geq 0$, $Y_t := f(X_t, t)$ is an Itô process, and

$$dY_t = A(X_t, t)\, dt + B(X_t, t)\, dW_t, \qquad (3.43)$$

where

$$A(X_t, t) = f_t(X_t, t) + f_x(X_t, t)\, a(X_t, t) + \tfrac{1}{2} f_{xx}(X_t, t)\, b^2(X_t, t),$$
$$B(X_t, t) = f_x(X_t, t)\, b(X_t, t). \qquad (3.44)$$

Here are some classical examples that illustrate the Itô lemma for stochastic processes and its applications in evaluating stochastic integrals as well as solutions of SDEs.

Example 3.4. Let $f(x, t) = x^2 - t$. Then, $f_x = 2x$, $f_{xx} = 2$, and $f_t = -1$. Let Y be the new random variable defined by $Y := f(X, t) = X^2 - t$, where X is the Wiener process, that is, $X = W$. In other words, X satisfies the trivial SDE,

$$dX = dW, \quad X_0 = 0.$$

Therefore, by the Itô lemma, the stochastic process Y satisfies the following SDE:

$$dY = \left(2 \cdot X \cdot 0 + (-1) + \tfrac{1}{2} \cdot 2 \cdot 1^2\right) dt + 2 \cdot X \cdot 1\, dW$$
$$= 2X\, dW.$$

In terms of the Wiener process, this means

$$d(W_t^2 - t) = 2W_t\, dW_t.$$

Thus, using the stochastic integral form, it is equivalent to

$$W_t^2 - t = W_0^2 - 0 + 2 \int_0^t W_u\, dW_u,$$

from which one can deduce the well-known integral of W_t, that is,

$$\int_0^t W_u\, dW_u = \frac{1}{2}\left(W_t^2 - t\right).$$

Example 3.5. In this example, we want to show that $Y_t = tW_t$ is a solution of the SDE,

$$dY_t = W_t\, dt + t\, dW_t.$$

We start with assuming $X_t = W_t$, and guess the function f in Lemma 3.2 as $f(X_t, t) = tX_t$, presuming that it will work. Applying the Itô lemma to $Y_t := f(X_t, t)$ leads us to the SDE for Y_t as

$$dY_t = X_t\, dt + t\, dW_t,$$

which is equivalent to

$$d(tW_t) = W_t \, dt + t \, dW_t.$$

Luckily, this guess has worked, and shown that $Y_t = tW_t$ is in fact a solution of the SDE. Note that Y_t for $t = 0$ is zero, that is, $Y_0 = 0$.

In particular, considering the integral equation corresponding to the SDE for Y_t, it follows that the Itô integral of t satisfies

$$\int_0^t s \, dW_s = t \, W_t - \int_0^t W_s \, ds,$$

where the integral on the right-hand-side of the equality is the usual Lebesgue integral of W_t. It is *not* a stochastic integral.

Example 3.6. An *Ornstein-Uhlenbeck* X_t is defined for $t \geq 0$ via the SDE,

$$dX_t = -\gamma X_t \, dt + \sigma \, dW_t,$$

where γ and σ are assumed to be constant. For a wish to find an *explicit* form to represent the process X_t we apply the Itô lemma to the proposed function,

$$f(x,t) = x \, e^{\gamma t},$$

which is continuous in $\mathbb{R}^2$, for sure. The partial derivatives,

$$f_t = \gamma x e^{\gamma t}, \qquad f_x = e^{\gamma t}, \qquad f_{xx} = 0,$$

are also continuous. Hence, applying the Itô lemma gives,

$$\begin{aligned}
A(X_t, t) &= \gamma X_t + e^{\gamma t}(-\gamma X_t) = 0, \\
B(X_t.t) &= e^{\gamma t}\sigma,
\end{aligned}$$

so that the SDE for $f(X_t, t)$ becomes

$$d\left(X_t e^{\gamma t}\right) = \sigma e^{\gamma t} \, dW_t.$$

However, this is equivalent to

$$X_t e^{\gamma t} - X_0 = \sigma \int_0^t e^{\gamma s} \, dW_s,$$

from which an explicit form of the Ornstein-Uhlenbeck process X_t is given by

$$X_t = X_0 e^{-\gamma t} + \sigma \int_0^t e^{\gamma(s-t)} \, dW_s.$$

Note that this explicit form involves a stochastic Itô integral of a deterministic function $e^{\gamma(s-t)}$ with respect to dW_s, which is a stochastic process.

An important consequence of the Itô lemma is the application to the asset prices S_t defined by a geometric Brownian motion. The following exercise will show implicitly that the asset price S_t is *lognormally* distributed under the basic assumption of a geometric Brownian motion:

$$dS_t = \mu S_t\, dt + \sigma S_t\, dW_t, \tag{3.45}$$

where μS_t is the *drift rate* with the *expected rate of return* μ, σS_t is the *diffusion* and σ is the *volatility* of the asset prices.

Although geometric Brownian motions are going to be investigated in the next section, readers are encouraged to work on the following exercise, and apply the Itô lemma.

Exercise 3.5. Let $f(x,t) = \exp\{\alpha t + \beta x\}$ and $Y_t = f(W_t,t)$ where W_t is a Wiener process, and α and β are constant. Find the SDE for the process Y_t. Then, show that

- $Y_t = \exp\left\{\left(\mu - \frac{1}{2}\sigma^2\right)t + \sigma W_t\right\}$ solves the SDE for the geometric Brownian motion, $dS_t = \mu S_t\, dt + \sigma S_t\, dW_t$, with constants μ and σ; and

- $e^{-\frac{1}{2}\theta^2 t + \theta W_t} = 1 + \theta \int_0^t e^{-\frac{1}{2}\theta^2 s + \theta W_s}\, dW_s$, where θ is constant.

Note that the random variable Y_t is then lognormally distributed.

Outlook

Generalisation of the Itô lemma may be the *Itô-Doeblin formula*, see [Shreve (2004b)], for example. This leads, in two dimensions, to the *Itô product rule* for stochastic processes X_t and Y_t:

$$d(X_t\, Y_t) = X_t\, dY_t + Y_t\, dX_t + dX_t \cdot dY_t.$$

The Itô calculus can then be simplified by using the following table, which appears in some textbooks and regarded as the product rules for the infinitesimal changes dt and dW_t:

$\cdot$	dt	dW_t
dt	0	0
dW_t	0	dt

3.4   Applications in Stock Market

In this section, the most important continuous models for the dynamics of asset prices S_t, which is an Itô process, is discussed. This standard model assumes that the relative return dS_t/S_t of an asset in the time interval dt is composed of a *drift* term μ plus *stochastic* fluctuations in the form of σdW. To be specific, the geometric Brownian motion described by

$$dS_t = \mu S_t\, dt + \sigma S_t\, dW_t, \tag{3.46}$$

is considered, where μ and σ are assumed to be constant. The process S_t stands for the asset or stock prices though, the geometric Brownian motion is widely used in financial applications. For instance, the model is even used to describe the dynamics of the *firm value* of a company in risk management applications.

The importance of this model is indeed due to the lemma below, which is in fact a corollary of the Itô lemma. Apparently, the solution of the geometric Brownian motion is given explicitly in the lemma.

Lemma 3.3. *The solution of the geometric Brownian motion,*
$$dS_t = \mu S_t\, dt + \sigma S_t\, dW_t,$$
where μ and σ are constant, is given by

$$S_t = S_0 \exp\left\{ \left(\mu - \frac{1}{2}\sigma^2\right) t + \sigma W_t \right\}. \tag{3.47}$$

Proof.   Let W_t be an arbitrary Wiener process and f be the function defined by $f(x,t) = \log(x)$, which is continuous for all $x > 0$. Applying the Itô lemma to $f(S_t, t) = \log(S_t)$ leads to the SDE

$$d(\log S_t) = \left(\mu - \frac{1}{2}\sigma^2\right) dt + \sigma\, dW_t,$$

for the so-called *log-prices*. However, this SDE is equivalent to an integral equation, which is easily solved:

$$\begin{aligned}
\log S_t &= \log S_0 + \int_0^t \left(\mu - \frac{1}{2}\sigma^2\right) ds + \int_0^t \sigma\, dW_s \\
&= \log S_0 + \left(\mu - \frac{1}{2}\sigma^2\right) t + \sigma\, W_t.
\end{aligned} \tag{3.48}$$

Hence, taking the exponential of both sides completes the proof. $\square$

Following the lemma it is easy to find the distribution of the asset prices S_t by simply defining the random variable, which is indeed a stochastic process, X_t by

$$X_t := \left(\mu - \frac{1}{2}\sigma^2 \right) t + \sigma W_t. \tag{3.49}$$

Thus, the properties of a Wiener process imply that the random variable X_t is normally distributed and, specifically,

$$X_t = \log S_t - \log S_0 \sim \mathcal{N}\left(\left(\mu - \frac{1}{2}\sigma^2 \right) t, \ \sigma^2 t \right). \tag{3.50}$$

Denoting the mean and the variance, respectively, by $\hat{\mu}$ and $\hat{\sigma}$,

$$\hat{\mu}(t) = \log S_0 + \left(\mu - \frac{1}{2}\sigma^2 \right) t, \tag{3.51}$$

$$\hat{\sigma}^2(t) = \sigma^2 t, \tag{3.52}$$

it follows that the log-prices are normally distributed with mean $\hat{\mu}$ and variance $\hat{\sigma}^2$. That is,

$$\log S_t \sim \mathcal{N}\left(\hat{\mu}(t), \hat{\sigma}^2(t) \right) \tag{3.53}$$

and hence,

$$S_t \sim \Psi_{\hat{\mu},\hat{\sigma}}, \tag{3.54}$$

where $\Psi_{\hat{\mu},\hat{\sigma}}$ is the lognormal distribution function with the specified parameters $\hat{\mu}$ and $\hat{\sigma}$. Thus, from equation (3.17) of Section 3.1 the distribution function of the lognormal distribution can be written as

$$\Psi_{\hat{\mu},\hat{\sigma}}(x) = \int_0^t \psi_{\hat{\mu},\hat{\sigma}}(\xi) \, d\xi,$$

where the density function $\psi_{\hat{\mu},\hat{\sigma}}$ of the distribution is defined by

$$\psi_{\hat{\mu},\hat{\sigma}}(x) = \frac{1}{x\hat{\sigma}\sqrt{2\pi}} e^{-\frac{(\log x - \hat{\mu})^2}{2\hat{\sigma}^2}}, \qquad x > 0. \tag{3.55}$$

Therefore, returning back to the original parameters μ for the drift and σ for the volatility of the asset prices, it turns out that the density function of the random variable S_t can be represented by

$$\psi_{\mu,\sigma}(s) = \frac{1}{s\sigma\sqrt{2\pi t}} \exp\left\{ -\frac{\left[\log(s/S_0) - \left(\mu - \frac{1}{2}\sigma^2\right) t\right]^2}{2\sigma^2 t} \right\}, \tag{3.56}$$

for $s > 0$.

On the other hand, referring back to Example 3.2 in Section 3.1, it is easy to calculate the expectation and the variance of the asset prices. Using the parameters μ and σ that stand for the drift coefficient and the volatility term, respectively, of the asset prices S_t, the expectation $\mathbb{E}\,[S_t]$ of the prices becomes

$$\mathbb{E}\,[S_t] = e^{\hat{\mu} + \frac{\hat{\sigma}^2}{2}} = e^{\log S_0 + \mu t} = S_0 e^{\mu t}. \tag{3.57}$$

The variance of the asset prices S_t, however, can be computed to give

$$\mathbb{V}\mathrm{ar}\,[S_t] = e^{2\hat{\mu} + \hat{\sigma}^2}\left(e^{\hat{\sigma}^2} - 1\right) = S_0^2 e^{2\mu t}\left(e^{\sigma^2 t} - 1\right). \tag{3.58}$$

We emphasise that these are the relations we had borrowed when the parameters of the binomial methods of Sections 2.2 and 2.3 were computed. Under the condition that the drift μ is the risk-free interest rate, the parameters were found by matching the expectations and the variances of both the continuous and the discrete models. The former stands for the use of the geometric Brownian motion to describe the asset prices, while the latter stands for the binomial models of Chapter 2.

The following exercise may be useful to extend the definition of a geometric Brownian motion to include stochastic processes as the coefficients. In such a case, a geometric Brownian motion may not be a family of random variables distributed lognormally.

Exercise 3.6. A more general form of a geometric Brownian motion can be described by the SDE

$$dS_t = \mu(t)S_t\,dt + \sigma(t)S_t\,dW_t,$$

where $\mu = \mu(t)$ and $\sigma = \sigma(t)$ are adapted stochastic processes that are integrable, respectively, in the sense of Lebesgue and Itô. Show that

$$S_t = S_0 \exp\left\{\int_0^t \left(\mu(s) - \frac{1}{2}\sigma^2(s)\right)ds + \int_0^t \sigma(s)\,dW_s\right\}$$

is an explicit representation of the geometric Brownian motion. Determine also the conditions under which S_t is lognormally distributed.

Now, having been equipped with a good tool for the asset prices S_t that follow the geometric Brownian motion, simulation of the paths of the process may easily be done. Since S_0 is the current asset price and W_t is a random variable that is normally distributed with mean zero and variance t, the terminal asset prices at time t can be represented by

$$S_t = S_0 \exp\left\{ \left(\mu - \frac{1}{2}\sigma^2\right) t + \sigma Z \sqrt{t}\right\}, \qquad (3.59)$$

where $Z \sim \mathcal{N}(0, 1)$. Of course, here Z means a sample from the standard normal distribution. Thus, this is an easier way to simulate asset prices rather than solving the associated SDE numerically. For instance, it is sufficient just to draw samples from the standard normal distribution in order to simulate the asset prices S_T at maturity $t = T$, rather than solving the SDE numerically by the Euler-Maruyama method.

Moreover, due to the independent and identically distributed increments of the Wiener process, simulation of the whole path can easily be done. In cases when the options are path dependent, for instance, the whole path can be obtained from (3.59) recursively. A simple recursive procedure for simulating the values S_{t_i} at times $t = t_i$ is given in Algorithm 3.3.

Algorithm 3.3 Paths of the Asset Price

   Given: M, S_{t_0}
   for $i = 0, 1, \ldots, M$ **do**
      draw $Z_k \sim \mathcal{N}(0, 1)$
      $S_{t_{i+1}} = S_{t_i} \exp\left\{ \left(\mu - \frac{1}{2}\sigma^2\right)(t_{i+1} - t_i) + \sigma Z_k \sqrt{t_{i+1} - t_i}\right\}$
   end for

A relatively easy MATLAB implementation of Algorithm 3.3 is shown in Fig. 3.12, it verifies that the asset prices are *lognormally* distributed. See Fig. 3.13, where several paths of the process S_t as well as a histogram corresponding to the final values S_T together with the superimposed density function of the lognormal distribution are shown.

One can also compare the Fig. 3.13 with Fig. 3.8 on page 82. The latter was obtained by the Euler-Maruyama method for solving numerically the associated SDE for the geometric Brownian motion.

Although, applying the Euler-Maruyama method to a geometric Brownian motion gives a satisfactory result for the final values of the asset prices, we must avoid the calculation of the whole path if only the final values are required. In such cases, neither the script in Fig. 3.7 nor the one in Fig. 3.12 must be used, but the equation (3.59) must be evaluated at time $t = T$:

```
───────────────── AssetPaths_gBM.m ─────────────────
function SPaths = AssetPaths_gBM(S0,mu,sigma,T,NSteps,NRepl)
% Calculates the asset paths using the exact formula
% NSteps = number of time steps to be taken
% NRepl  = number of paths to be simulated

dt = T/NSteps; mudt = (mu-0.5*sigma^2)*dt; sidt = sigma*sqrt(dt);
Increments = mudt + sidt*randn(NRepl, NSteps);
LogPaths = cumsum([log(S0)*ones(NRepl,1) , Increments] , 2);
SPaths = exp(LogPaths);
```

Fig. 3.12   An implementation of Algorithm 3.3 for asset prices

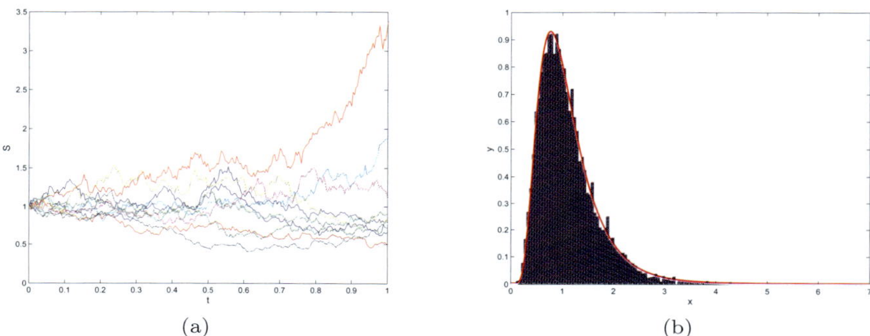

(a)   (b)

Fig. 3.13   Asset Prices: (a) some paths, (b) histogram corresponding to final values of 10000 paths

$$S_T = S_0 \exp\left\{ \left(\mu - \frac{1}{2}\sigma^2 \right) T + \sigma Z \sqrt{T} \right\}, \qquad (3.60)$$

for a given sample Z from the standard normal distribution. This means, in other words, a sample from the lognormal distribution with the required parameters is just what is needed. Samples from a distribution will be investigated, and the use of the script in Fig. 3.12 will become clear in Chapter 5 for pricing path dependent options.

The discrete version of the geometric Brownian motion can be written in the form

$$\frac{\Delta S}{S} = \mu \, \Delta t + \sigma Z \sqrt{\Delta t},$$

where $Z \sim \mathcal{N}(0,1)$ and, consequently, the returns of the asset prices satisfy

$$\frac{\Delta S}{S} \sim \mathcal{N}(\mu\Delta t, \sigma^2 \Delta t).$$

Although this distribution matches the actual market data in a rough approximation, there are many other models that weaken the requirements of this model.

In fact, the assumptions of a constant interest rate r and a constant volatility σ are quite restrictive, for example. To overcome this simplification, stochastic interest rates r_t and volatility σ_t are considered. To describe either of these, a class of models is given by considering the following SDEs for each $\beta \in \mathbb{R}$:

$$dr_t = \alpha(R - r_t)\,dt + \sigma_r r_t^\beta\,dW_t, \quad \alpha > 0, \tag{3.61}$$

where W_t is again a Brownian motion and α is a positive constant. Note that the drift term $\alpha(R - r_t)$ is positive for $r_t < R$ and negative for $r_t > R$. This causes a pull toward to R, which may be thought to be the *market mean* of the interest rate. This effect is called *mean reversion*. There are two important models derived from the class given by (3.61):

- *Vasicek model* is obtained by letting $\beta = 0$, and assuming a constant volatility σ_r.
- *Cox-Ingersoll-Ross model*, on the other hand, assumes $\beta = 1/2$.

Note that in the Cox-Ingersoll-Ross model, the volatility $\sigma_r \sqrt{r_t}$ vanishes when r_t tends to zero, provided that $r_0 > 0$ and $R > 0$. This ensures the nonnegativity of the interest rates, that is, $r_t \geq 0$ for all t. Moreover, the condition

$$2\alpha R \geq \sigma_r^2$$

ensures that $r_t > 0$. See, for instance, [Kwok (1998); Mao (2007)] for more details.

In order to study the models in which interest rate or volatility are not constant, but stochastic, the Itô stochastic processes must be generalised to multi-dimensions. Similar to the *one-factor* scalar SDE, the general *multi-factor* vector version of the equation can be written by using the same notation,

$$dX_t = a(X_t, t)\,dt + b(X_t, t)\,dW_t. \tag{3.62}$$

This is, however, equivalent to the integral equation,

$$X_t = X_0 + \int_{t_0}^t a(X_s, s)\,ds + \int_{t_0}^t b(X_s, s)\,dW_s, \tag{3.63}$$

where $X_{t_0} = X_0$. Here, the stochastic vector process X_t may consist of n stochastic processes $X_t^{(1)}, X_t^{(2)}, \ldots, X_t^{(n)}$ so that

$$\left[X_t^{(1)}, X_t^{(2)}, \ldots, X_t^{(n)} \right]^T \in \mathbb{R}^n.$$

The vector $a = a(X_t, t)$ is then an n-dimensional vector

$$a(X_t, t) = \left[a_1(X_t, t), a_2(X_t, t), \ldots, a_n(X_t, t) \right]^T \in \mathbb{R}^n,$$

which stands for the *drift vector*. The matrix $b = b(X_t, t)$ is of size $n \times m$, and

$$b(X_t, t) = \begin{bmatrix} b_{11}(X_t, t) & b_{12}(X_t, t) & \cdots & b_{1m}(X_t, t) \\ b_{21}(X_t, t) & b_{22}(X_t, t) & \cdots & b_{2m}(X_t, t) \\ \vdots & \vdots & \ddots & \vdots \\ b_{n1}(X_t, t) & b_{n1}(X_t, t) & \cdots & b_{nm}(X_t, t) \end{bmatrix} \in \mathbb{R}^{n \times m}$$

is called the *volatility matrix*. The process W_t, however, is an m-*dimensional Wiener process*:

$$W_t = \left[W_t^{(1)}, W_t^{(2)}, \ldots, W_t^{(m)} \right]^T \in \mathbb{R}^m,$$

where each $W_t^{(i)}$ is a one-dimensional Wiener process.

There is, of course, a corresponding Itô lemma for vector processes. The Itô lemma for multi-factor models is out of the scope of this book, however, interested readers can refer to advanced textbooks on stochastic processes.

On the other hand, the components of the vector process X_t in (3.62) are Itô processes that satisfy

$$dX_t^{(i)} = a_i(X_t, t)\, dt + \sum_{k=1}^{m} b_{ik}(X_t, t)\, dW_t^{(k)} \tag{3.64}$$

for every $i = 1, 2, \ldots, n$. Equivalently, in terms of integrals this correspondence can be written as

$$X_t^{(i)} = X_0^{(i)} + \int_{t_0}^{t} a_i(X_s, s)\, ds + \sum_{k=1}^{m} \int_{t_0}^{t} b_{ik}(X_s, s)\, dW_s^{(k)}, \tag{3.65}$$

where $X_{t_0}^{(i)} = X_0^{(i)}$ for each $1 \leq i \leq n$.

Note that neither the SDEs nor the integral equations above are decoupled, since the functions $a_i = a_i(X_t, t)$ and $b_{ik}(X_t, t)$ *do* depend on the components of the vector process X_t. Also note that each SDE, for a fixed i, consists of a linear combination of one-dimensional Wiener processes $W_t^{(1)}, W_t^{(2)}, \ldots, W_t^{(m)}$. These Wiener processes may or may not be dependent. In case they are dependent, so are their increments. Thus, this raises the problem of drawing random numbers from the standard normal distribution that are also dependent. Such cases will be considered in Section 5.3.3 of Chapter 5.

The Euler-Maruyama method for numerical solutions of multi-dimensional SDEs can still be applied. To do so, each of the n SDEs involved in (3.64) is considered separately: for a given $\Delta t > 0$, these SDEs are then discretized by the Euler-Maruyama method. At each time step, all the components of the stochastic vector process X_t are computed before advancing to the next time step. The following example will show how this is done, and will illustrate the concept of *mean reversion* and the *square-root asset process*.

Example 3.7. Consider a 2-dimensional stochastic process, given by the following system of SDEs:

$$
\begin{aligned}
dS_t &= \mu S_t \, dt + \sigma_t \sqrt{S_t} \, dW_t^S, \\
d\sigma_t &= (\sigma_0 - \sigma_t) \, dt + \sqrt{\sigma_t} \, dW_t^\sigma,
\end{aligned}
\tag{3.66}
$$

where μ is a constant. The processes W_t^S and W_t^σ are assumed to be *independent* Wiener processes. The initial condition is given by

$$
S_t\big|_{t=0} = S_0, \qquad \sigma_t\big|_{t=0} = \sigma_0.
$$

Here S_t stands for the asset prices and follows the so-called square-root process. The volatility σ_t, on the other hand, is given by a mean-reverting stochastic process, which is also a square-root processes. Recall the Cox-Ingersoll-Ross model based on the class of models represented by (3.61) when $\beta = 1/2$.

We would like to show how the Euler-Maruyama method can be applied to multi-dimensional SDEs, in particular, to 2-dimensional stochastic process given by (3.66). Let t_i, for $i = 0, 1, \ldots, N$, be the discrete times for which the values of the paths are desired, then the time discretized versions of the SDEs for S_t and σ_t can be written as

$$
\boxed{
\begin{aligned}
\Delta S_{t_i} &= \mu S_{t_i} \Delta t_i + \sigma_{t_i} \sqrt{S_{t_i}} \, \Delta W_{t_i}^S, \\
\Delta \sigma_{t_i} &= (\sigma_0 - \sigma_{t_i}) \Delta t_i + \sqrt{\sigma_{t_i}} \, \Delta W_{t_i}^\sigma.
\end{aligned}
}
\tag{3.67}
$$

It must be emphasised that the increments of the stochastic processes involved in the above discretization are

$$\Delta S_{t_i} := S_{t_{i+1}} - S_{t_i},$$

$$\Delta \sigma_{t_i} := \sigma_{t_{i+1}} - \sigma_{t_i},$$

$$\Delta W_{t_i} := W_{t_{i+1}} - W_{t_i},$$

for $i = 0, 1, \ldots, N - 1$. As usual, the time steps are defined by

$$\Delta t_i := t_{i+1} - t_i$$

for every $i = 1, 2, \ldots, N$, and $t_0 = 0$ is assumed. Therefore, only samples from a normal distribution are needed to interpret the increments of the independent Wiener processes in order to advance to the time level $i + 1$ from the level i. An implementation of the Euler-Maruyama method is shown in Fig. 3.14.

```
_________________ Euler_Maruyama_Sqrt_MeanReverting.m _________________
% Euler-Maruyama_Sqrt_MeanReverting (Vectorized across samples)
clear all, close all, randn('state',13)

K = 1; mu = 0.05; T = 1; N = 2^16; dt = T/N; M = 10;
S_0 = 1; Sig_0 = 0.8; Sigma0 = 0.8; S = S_0*ones(M,N); Sig = Sig_0*ones(M,N);
for j = 1:N
    dW_1 = sqrt(dt)*randn(M,1); dW_2 = sqrt(dt)*randn(M,1); % independent of dW_1
    % To be safe!
    S(:,j+1) = abs(S(:,j) + dt*mu*S(:,j) + sqrt(S(:,j)).*Sig(:,j).*dW_1);
    Sig(:,j+1) = abs(Sig(:,j) + dt*(Sigma0 - Sig(:,j)) + sqrt(Sig(:,j)).*dW_2);
end
figure(1), plot([0:dt:1], Sig(1,:), 'g', [0:dt:1], Sigma0*ones(1,size(Sig,2)), 'r' )
xlabel('time','FontSize',12), ylabel('volatility','FontSize',12),
print -r900 -depsc -cmyk '../figures/EM_tv'

figure(2), plot( [0:dt:1], S(1,:), 'b',[0:dt:1], 1+mu*[0:dt:1], 'r' )
xlabel('time','FontSize',12), ylabel('stock prices','FontSize',12)
print -r900 -depsc -cmyk '../figures/EM_ts'

figure(3), plot( S(1,:), Sig(1,:), 'r' ), grid on
xlabel('stock prices','FontSize',12), ylabel('volatility','FontSize',12)
print -r900 -depsc -cmyk '../figures/EM_sv'

figure(4), plot3( [0:dt:1], S(1,:), Sig(1,:), 'k' ), hold on
plot3( [0:dt:1], S(1,:), zeros(size(Sig(1,:))), 'b' )
plot3( ones(size([0:dt:1])), S(1,:), Sig(1,:), 'r' )
plot3( [0:dt:1], 3*ones(size(S(1,:))), Sig(1,:), 'g' ), grid on
xlabel('time','FontSize',12), ylabel('stock prices','FontSize',12)
zlabel('volatility','FontSize',12)
print -r900 -depsc -cmyk '../figures/EM_tsv'
```

Fig. 3.14   An implementation of the Euler-Maruyama method for a 2-dimensional SDE in (3.66)

It should be emphasised that when a numerical method, such as the Euler-Maruyama, is applied to the square-root processes there may be negative values supplied to the square-root function. To be on the safe side we simply update the terms by their absolute values in Fig. 3.14 due to [Higham and Mao (2005)].

The graphs in Fig. 3.15 show the paths of the asset prices and the volatility defined by the system of SDEs in (3.66). Although it is not necessary, the path of the volatility is reverting to the mean σ_0 shown in Fig. 3.15(b).

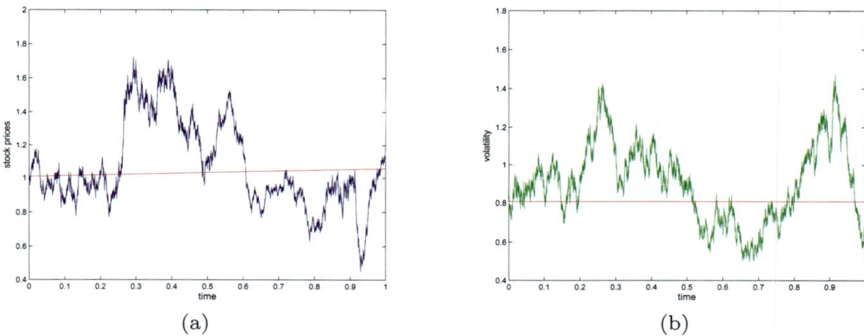

(a)   (b)

Fig. 3.15   A single realisation of a path: (a) asset prices S_t, (b) volatility σ_t defined by the SDEs in (3.66)

A realisation of the paths of the stochastic vector process $X_t = [S_t, \sigma_t]^T$ in $\mathbb{R}^3$ is shown in Fig. 3.16(a). The projection of the path on the (S, σ)-plane is depicted in Fig. 3.16(b).

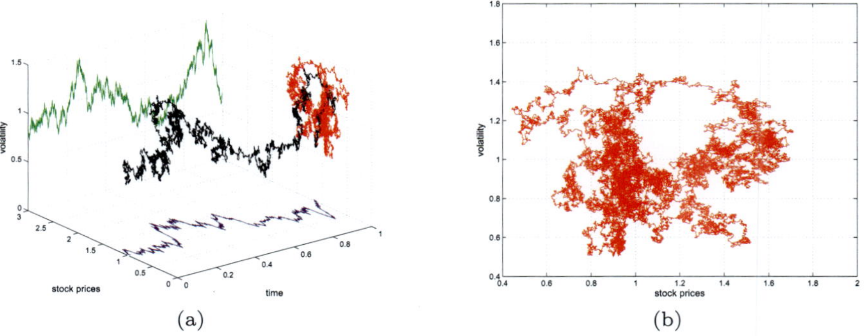

(a)   (b)

Fig. 3.16   A single realisation of a path of the vector process $[S_t, \sigma_t]^T$: (a) in space, (b) projected on the plane

Outlook

Among the applications of stochastic SDEs, we have discussed only the ones related to option pricing. Possible applications of stochastic processes and their simulations, or numerical solutions, cover a diversity of disciplines. The book [Kloeden and Platen (1992)] is a good reference to some of these disciplines other than mathematical finance.

Financial applications, on the other hand, include not only options on stocks but also term structure models and interest rate linked derivatives, optimal portfolios, risk and risk management, etc.. Although we cannot embrace the entire literature, readers may refer to any or some of [Arnold (1974); Björk (1998); Brigo and Mercurio (2001); Elton and Gruber (1995); Glasserman (2004); Hull and White (1994a,b); Kijima (2003); Korn (1997); Kwok (1998); Luenberger (1998); Merton (1990); Mikosch (1998); Øksendal (2002); Rogers and Talay (1997); Wilmott *et al.* (1995)] for a further outlook.

Chapter 4

The Black-Scholes Equation

The most important application of the Itô calculus, derived from the *Itô lemma*, in financial mathematics is the *pricing of options*. The most famous result in this area is the *Black-Scholes formulae* for pricing European vanilla call and put options. As a consequence of the formulae, both in theoretical and practical applications, *Robert Merton* and *Myron Scholes* were awarded the *Nobel Prize* for Economics in 1997 to honour their contributions to option pricing. Unfortunately, Fischer Black, who has also given his name and contributions, had passed away two years before.

In their famous work, in 1973, Black and Scholes transformed the option pricing problem into the task of solving a (parabolic) partial differential equation (PDE) with a final condition. The main conceptual idea of Black and Scholes lies in the construction of a riskless portfolio taking positions in bonds (cash), option, and the underlying stock. Such an approach strengthens the use of the *no-arbitrage* principle as well.

Derivation of a closed-form solution to the Black-Scholes equation depends on the fundamental solution of the *heat equation*. Hence, it is important, at this point, to transform the Black-Scholes equation to the heat equation by *change of variables*. Having found the closed-form solution to the heat equation, it is possible to transform it back to find the corresponding solution of the Black-Scholes PDE.

The connection between an *initial and/or boundary value problem* for differential equations, the so-called a *Cauchy problem*, and the computation of the *expected value* of a functional of a solution of an SDE is covered by the *Feynman-Kac* representation theorem. However, we leave it to interested readers, but apply the celebrated closed-form solutions to various examples.

Indeed, an important consequence of these closed-form solutions is the use of the *Greeks*: the partial derivatives of the value of an option with respect to the variables. The Greeks are used for *hedging* purposes, which is related to the sensitivity of the option prices to the parameters, such as the underlying asset prices, interest rates, time, and the volatility of the asset prices. Having solved the Black-Scholes equation, we have the opportunity to maintain the closed-form representations of these *Greeks*.

4.1 Derivation of the Black-Scholes Equation

This section applies the *Itô lemma* to derive the Black-Scholes equation, whose basic and the first assumption is a geometric Brownian motion for the asset price.

A direct consequence of the Itô lemma, Lemma 3.2 on page 96, follows for the geometric Brownian motion of the asset prices, where we have $X_t = S_t$, $a = \mu S_t$, and $b = \sigma S_t$. Hereafter, we will drop the subscript t for both a better understanding and simplicity. Assume that the asset price S follows the geometric Brownian motion,

$$dS = \mu S \, dt + \sigma S \, dW,$$

where μ and σ are constant, and W is a Wiener process. Let $V = V(S,t)$ denote the value of an option (or a contingent claim) that is sufficiently smooth, namely, its second-order derivatives with respect to S and first-order derivative with respect to t are continuous in the domain

$$\mathcal{D}_V = \{(S,t) : S \geq 0, \quad 0 \leq t \leq T\}. \tag{4.1}$$

Then, it immediately follows from the Itô lemma that

$$dV = \left(\frac{\partial V}{\partial S} \mu S + \frac{\partial V}{\partial t} + \frac{1}{2} \frac{\partial^2 V}{\partial S^2} \sigma^2 S^2 \right) dt + \frac{\partial V}{\partial S} \sigma S \, dW. \tag{4.2}$$

This is in fact nothing more than a rephrasing of the Itô lemma, however, it will be used to derive the celebrated Black-Scholes equation in the sequel by applying the no-arbitrage principle.

Since both stochastic processes S and V are driven by the same Wiener process W, the stochastic term, $\sigma S \frac{\partial V}{\partial S} \, dW$, can be eliminated by constructing a portfolio that consists of the option and the underlying asset: a common exercise in finance. Let Π be the wealth of the portfolio that consists of one short position with value V and Δ units of the underlying asset with the price S. Assume that initially the portfolio wealth is Π_0, and hence, the value of the portfolio at time t can be determined from

$$\Pi = -V + \Delta\, S.$$

Therefore, the infinitesimal change in the portfolio becomes

$$d\Pi = -dV + \Delta\, dS$$

$$= -\left(\mu S\left[\Delta - \frac{\partial V}{\partial S}\right] + \frac{\partial V}{\partial t} + \frac{1}{2}\sigma^2 S^2 \frac{\partial^2 V}{\partial S^2}\right) dt + \left(-\frac{\partial V}{\partial S} + \Delta\right)\sigma S\, dW.$$

Note that the fluctuations caused by the increments of the underlying Wiener process have a coefficient, $\left(-\frac{\partial V}{\partial S} + \Delta\right)$, that depends on Δ, the number of shares of the underlying asset. Hence, by

$$\Delta = \frac{\partial V}{\partial S}$$

shares of asset, the infinitesimal change $d\Pi$ of the portfolio within the time interval dt is

$$d\Pi = -\left(\frac{\partial V}{\partial t} + \frac{1}{2}\sigma^2 S^2 \frac{\partial^2 V}{\partial S^2}\right) dt, \tag{4.3}$$

and it is purely *deterministic*. Indeed, more than that: *the drift rate μ has been cancelled out!* This represents the gain when Π_0, the initial wealth, is invested in the *risky*, but *frictionless* market[1] that consists of the option with value V and the underlying asset with S.

Furthermore, choosing $\Delta = \frac{\partial V}{\partial S}$ provides a strategy (*hedging*) to eliminate the risk in the portfolio due to the stochastic fluctuations and the drift coefficient μ of the underlying asset that has disappeared. In this sense, the modelling of V is risk-neutral. The remaining parameter σ reflects the stochastic behaviour in the Black-Scholes equation. Although it is assumed to be constant, its estimation is an important concept, known as the *implied volatility* in finance.

The same amount of wealth Π of the portfolio should gain the riskless interest rate in infinitesimal time. Under the assumption of a frictionless market without arbitrage and a constant risk-free interest rate r, the amount Π would grow to $\Pi = \Pi_0\, e^{r(t-t_0)}$. Hence, the change in infinitesimal time would be

$$d\Pi = r\Pi\, dt,$$

which is equivalent to

---

[1] This means that there are no transaction costs, the interest rates for borrowing and lending money are equal, all parties have immediate access to any information, and all securities and credits are available at any time and in any size. Further, individual trading will not influence the price.

$$d\Pi = r\left(-V + \Delta\,S\right)dt$$
$$= \left(-rV + rS\frac{\partial V}{\partial S}\right)dt. \tag{4.4}$$

This infinitesimal change $d\Pi$ in the portfolio is due to the investment in the risk-free interest rate r, unlike the one in (4.3).

By the no-arbitrage principle and the possibility of an early exercise of an option, it is required that the riskless gain in (4.4) cannot be more than the gain in the risky market given by (4.3). Hence,

$$-rV + rS\frac{\partial V}{\partial S} \leq -\left(\frac{\partial V}{\partial t} + \frac{1}{2}\sigma^2 S^2 \frac{\partial^2 V}{\partial S^2}\right).$$

Consequently, the inequality, due to Black and Scholes,

$$\frac{\partial V}{\partial t} + \frac{1}{2}\sigma^2 S^2 \frac{\partial^2 V}{\partial S^2} + rS\frac{\partial V}{\partial S} - rV \leq 0 \tag{4.5}$$

must hold in the domain $\mathcal{D}_V$. This inequality is valid no matter if the considered option is European or American. Hence, an option price generally satisfies this *partial differential inequality.*

If the option is assumed to be a European one, then there is no possibility of early exercise, and the no-arbitrage principle implies that these gains must be equal at the end of the infinitesimal investment time interval. Hence, for European options the partial differential inequality in (4.5) is reduced to the celebrated *Black-Scholes* equation,

$$\frac{\partial V}{\partial t} + \frac{1}{2}\sigma^2 S^2 \frac{\partial^2 V}{\partial S^2} + rS\frac{\partial V}{\partial S} - rV = 0 \tag{4.6}$$

in the domain $\mathcal{D}_V$.

Therefore, an option price $V = V(S,t)$ must solve either of the inequality or the equality depending on whether the option is, respectively, American or European. However, in (4.5) and (4.6) there is no μ, the drift rate of the asset. The drift rate μ has been replaced by the risk-free interest rate r under the assumption of no-arbitrage. This is known as the *risk-neutral valuation principle,* which is summarised in the following remark.

Remark 4.1. For pricing options the return rate μ of the underlying asset that pays no dividend is replaced by the risk-free interest rate r. In other words, $\mu = r$ is assumed.

The remark above still remains valid if, further, *dividends* are assumed to be paid with continuously compounding yield, say δ. The continuous flow of dividends, however, can be modelled easily by a decrease of the asset price, S, in each infinitesimal time interval dt. This decrease in S is equal to the amount paid out by the dividend: $\delta S \, dt$ with a constant $\delta \geq 0$. This is due to the no-arbitrage principle: otherwise, by purchasing the asset at time t and selling it immediately after receiving the dividend one would make a risk-free profit of amount $\delta S \, dt$. The continuously compounding dividend yield can easily be inserted into the Black-Scholes framework: the drift coefficient of the asset price model changes to $\mu - \delta$ rather than μ only. That is, the geometric Brownian motion of the asset price is generalised to

$$dS = (\mu - \delta)S \, dt + \sigma S \, dW. \qquad (4.7)$$

Hence, carrying out a similar argument,[2] the corresponding Black-Scholes equation for a European option price $V(S,t)$ with the domain $\mathcal{D}_V$ becomes

$$\frac{\partial V}{\partial t} + \frac{1}{2}\sigma^2 S^2 \frac{\partial^2 V}{\partial S^2} + (r - \delta)S\frac{\partial V}{\partial S} - rV = 0 \qquad (4.8)$$

instead of the Black-Scholes PDE in (4.6). For American options, the equality sign "=" in (4.8) must be changed to an inequality sign "$\leq$" to allow possible early exercise opportunities.

Outlook

Derivation of the Black-Scholes equation is originally proposed in [Black and Scholes (1973)] and [Merton (1973)] based on the no-arbitrage principle or the *delta-hedging* argument. The riskless portfolio

$$\Pi = -V + \Delta S \quad \text{with} \quad \Delta = \frac{\partial V}{\partial S},$$

is sometimes called the *delta-hedge* portfolio. See Section 4.3 for more on hedging.

It is important to emphasise again that in the Black-Scholes equation μ does not appear due to the riskless portfolio. The risk-neutral valuation principle in Remark 4.1 is indeed based on a more mathematical

---

[2]Readers are encouraged to derive the Black-Scholes equation with continuous dividend yield by considering a portfolio strategy.

setting: existence of a *risk-neutral* measure. Girsanov theorem (see for instance (Shreve, 2004b, p. 212)) states that there exists a unique measure $\mathbb{Q}$ under which

$$\tilde{W}_t = W_t + \frac{\mu - r}{\sigma}\, t$$

becomes a Brownian motion. Here, the term $(\mu - r)/\sigma$ is called the *market price of risk*. Rearranging the terms and using the geometric Brownian motion for the asset prices S_t driven by the standard Brownian motion W_t, we obtain

$$dS_t = rS_t\, dt + \sigma S_t\, d\tilde{W}_t.$$

In this setting the pricing is maintained by the risk-neutral probability $\mathbb{Q}$ rather than the market probability $\mathbb{P}$.

4.2   Solution of the Black-Scholes Equation

The Black-Scholes equation admits a closed-form solution and, hence, this solution made the founders well-known and respected. In fact, the Black-Scholes equation

$$\frac{\partial V}{\partial t} + \frac{1}{2}\sigma^2 S^2 \frac{\partial^2 V}{\partial S^2} + (r - \delta)S\frac{\partial V}{\partial S} - rV = 0 \tag{4.9}$$

for a European option $V(S, t)$ is of the type of a *parabolic* partial differential equation in the domain $\mathcal{D}_V$, where

$$\mathcal{D}_V = \{(S, t) : S > 0, \quad 0 \le t \le T\}. \tag{4.10}$$

Hence, by a suitable transformation of the variables the Black-Scholes equation is equivalent to the *heat* equation,

$$\frac{\partial u}{\partial \tau} = \frac{\partial^2 u}{\partial x^2} \tag{4.11}$$

for $u = u(x, \tau)$ for x and t in the domain

$$\mathcal{D}_u = \left\{(x, \tau) : -\infty < x < \infty, \quad 0 \le \tau \le \frac{\sigma^2}{2}T\right\}. \tag{4.12}$$

In general, the classical heat equation may be considered in a larger domain, $x \in \mathbb{R}$ and $\tau \ge 0$. However, since the option expires at maturity T, and the time when the option contract is signed is assumed to be $t_0 = 0$, then the transformed heat equation will naturally have a bounded τ. On the other hand, although in the domain of the Black-Scholes equation the variable S lies on the positive real axis, the variable x in the domain of the heat equation lies on the whole real axis. These are all due to the transformations used in the sequel.

4.2.1 *Transforming to the Heat Equation*

Consider the transformations of the *independent* variables

$$S = K\,e^x, \quad \text{and} \quad t = T - \frac{\tau}{\sigma^2/2},$$

and the *dependent* variable

$$v(x,\tau) = \frac{1}{K}V(S,t) = \frac{1}{K}V\left(Ke^x, T - \frac{\tau}{\sigma^2/2}\right).$$

In fact, the change of the independent variables ensures that the domain of the new dependent variable $v = v(x,\tau)$ is $\mathcal{D}_u$.

By the chain rule for functions of several variables, these changes of variables give

$$\frac{\partial V}{\partial t} = K\frac{\partial v}{\partial \tau}\frac{\partial \tau}{\partial t} = -\frac{\sigma^2}{2}K\frac{\partial v}{\partial \tau},$$

$$\frac{\partial V}{\partial S} = K\frac{\partial v}{\partial x}\frac{\partial x}{\partial S} = \frac{K}{S}\frac{\partial v}{\partial x},$$

$$\frac{\partial^2 V}{\partial S^2} = \frac{\partial}{\partial S}\left(\frac{\partial V}{\partial S}\right) = \frac{K}{S^2}\left(\frac{\partial^2 v}{\partial x^2} - \frac{\partial v}{\partial x}\right).$$

Inserting the derivatives in the Black-Scholes equation (4.9) transforms it to a *constant coefficient* one:

$$v_\tau = v_{xx} + \left(\frac{r-\delta}{\sigma^2/2} - 1\right)v_x - \frac{r}{\sigma^2/2}v,$$

where the subscripts represents the partial derivatives with respect to the corresponding variables. Define the following new constants,

$$\kappa = \frac{r-\delta}{\sigma^2/2}, \quad \text{and} \quad \ell = \frac{\delta}{\sigma^2/2},$$

so that the transformed PDE turns into a simpler form

$$v_\tau = v_{xx} + (\kappa - 1)v_x - (\kappa + \ell)v, \tag{4.13}$$

the coefficients of which involve the new two constants κ and ℓ. This constant coefficient PDE must be transformed further to the heat equation by some other change of the independent variables.

In order to simplify the final transformation of the dependent variable v, let us first define the following constants:

$$\gamma = \frac{1}{2}(\kappa - 1), \quad \text{and} \quad \beta = \frac{1}{2}(\kappa + 1) = \gamma + 1,$$

so that

$$\beta^2 = \gamma^2 + \kappa.$$

In terms of these new constants, now the transformation can be defined by

$$v(x, \tau) = e^{-\gamma x - (\beta^2 + \ell)\tau} u(x, \tau),$$

for all (x, τ) in $\mathcal{D}_u$. Hence, the partial derivatives with respect to τ and x can be calculated as

$$v_\tau = e^{-\gamma x - (\beta^2 + \ell)\tau} \left\{ -(\beta^2 + \ell)u + u_\tau \right\},$$
$$v_x = e^{-\gamma x - (\beta^2 + \ell)\tau} \left\{ -\gamma u + u_x \right\},$$
$$v_{xx} = e^{-\gamma x - (\beta^2 + \ell)\tau} \left\{ \gamma^2 u - 2\gamma u_x + u_{xx} \right\}.$$

Thus, substituting these derivatives into (4.13) yields

$$u_\tau = u_{xx} + (-2\gamma + \kappa - 1) u_x + \gamma (2\gamma - \kappa + 1) u,$$

after having used the fact that $\beta^2 = \gamma^2 + \kappa$. Notice that the coefficients of the terms u_x and u in the equation above vanishes by the choice of γ as $\frac{1}{2}(\kappa - 1)$. Consequently, the equation that is to be satisfied by the transformed dependent variable $u = u(x, \tau)$ is the dimensionless form of the heat equation,

$$\frac{\partial u}{\partial \tau} = \frac{\partial^2 u}{\partial x^2}, \qquad (4.14)$$

that is to be solved on the domain $\mathcal{D}_u$. This shows the equivalence between the Black-Scholes equation (4.9) and the heat equation (4.11).

To sum up, in order to transform the Black-Scholes equation to the classical dimensionless heat equation, the constants used above are defined to be

$$\kappa = \frac{r - \delta}{\sigma^2/2}, \qquad \ell = \frac{\delta}{\sigma^2/2},$$
$$\gamma = \frac{1}{2}(\kappa - 1), \qquad \beta = \frac{1}{2}(\kappa + 1) = \gamma + 1. \qquad (4.15)$$

On the other hand, the transformations of the dependent and the independent variables that use those constants are given by

$$
\begin{aligned}
S &= K\,e^x, & t &= T - \frac{\tau}{\sigma^2/2}, \\
V(S,t) &= K\,v(x,\tau), & v(x,\tau) &= e^{-\gamma x - (\beta^2 + \ell)\tau}\,u(x,\tau).
\end{aligned}
\tag{4.16}
$$

Under these changes of variables, the domain $\mathcal{D}_V$ is mapped to $\mathcal{D}_u$.

The *fundamental solution* of the dimensionless heat equation $u_\tau = u_{xx}$ is given by

$$
G(x,\tau) = \frac{1}{\sqrt{4\pi\tau}}\,\exp\left\{-\frac{x^2}{4\tau}\right\}
\tag{4.17}
$$

which satisfies the equation for all $\tau > 0$ and $x \in \mathbb{R}$. This can be easily shown by direct substitution into the equation. Note also that $G(x,\tau) = \phi_{0,\sqrt{2\tau}}(x)$, that is, it is the probability density function of the normal distribution with mean zero and variance 2τ.

Moreover, for a given *initial* condition,

$$
u(x,0) = u_0(x), \qquad -\infty < x < \infty,
\tag{4.18}
$$

at $\tau = 0$, the solution of the heat equation can be written as a convolution integral of G and u_0 as

$$
u(x,\tau) = \int_{-\infty}^{\infty} G(x - \xi, \tau)\,u_0(\xi)\,d\xi
\tag{4.19}
$$

for $\tau > 0$. With this representation, the function $G(x - \xi, \tau)$ is also called the *Green's function* for the diffusion equation. It is not too difficult to show that $u = u(x,\tau)$ represented by the convolution integral above is indeed a solution of the heat equation and satisfies

$$
\lim_{\tau \to 0^+} u(x,\tau) = u_0(x).
$$

We leave these details to the readers.

Consequently, the solution of the heat equation which satisfies the initial condition (4.18) can be represented by (4.19) or, using (4.17), by

$$
u(x,\tau) = \frac{1}{\sqrt{4\pi\tau}} \int_{-\infty}^{\infty} e^{-\frac{(x-\xi)^2}{4\tau}}\,u_0(\xi)\,d\xi.
\tag{4.20}
$$

Therefore, in order to solve the Black-Scholes equation we need to determine what the initial function $u_0(x) = u(x,0)$ corresponds to in the original setting. This initial function is given for $\tau = 0$, and hence, there is the corresponding given function at maturity $t = T$, the payoff function. Due to the transformations in (4.16), the payoff function of the contingent claim stands for the *terminal condition* of the Black-Scholes equation.

If the terminal condition of the Black-Scholes equation is given by $V(S,T) = P(S)$ at maturity $t = T$, then it must be transformed to find the corresponding initial condition, $u(x,0) = u_0(x)$, of the heat equation. By plugging it in (4.20) and, if possible, performing the integration, the solution to the heat equation can be found. Consequently, using the transformations (4.16), the computed solution must be interpreted using the original variables S, t and V involved in the Black-Scholes PDE.

4.2.2 *Closed-Form Solutions of European Call and Put Options*

The well-known Black-Scholes formulae for European call and put options can be derived from the solution represented in (4.20) for the heat equation. In fact, there are many cases where closed-form solutions can be derived by using these integral representations. However, in most cases, the closed-form solutions of the European call and put options are at the centre, and they can be used to derive others. Moreover, due to the *put-call parity* of European options, it is preferable to look for a closed-form solution of either a call or a put option. Using the solution of the heat equation, however, the corresponding closed-form solutions of both, call and put options, can easily be derived.

In order to derive these formulae the payoff functions must be transformed by the change of variables in (4.16) into the corresponding initial conditions for the heat equation. Let us denote by $V_C(S,t)$ and $V_P(S,t)$ the values of the European call and put options, respectively. Then, the payoff functions are

$$V_C(S,T) = \max\left\{S - K,\, 0\right\}, \qquad (4.21)$$
$$V_P(S,T) = \max\left\{K - S,\, 0\right\}, \qquad (4.22)$$

where K is the strike price. Using the transformations in (4.16), the payoff of a call option, for instance, is easily converted to

$$u_C(x,0) = \frac{1}{K}e^{\gamma x}V_C(Ke^x, T)$$

$$= \frac{1}{K}e^{\gamma x}\max\{Ke^x - K,\, 0\}$$

$$= \max\left\{e^{(\gamma+1)x} - e^{\gamma x},\, 0\right\}.$$

Similar calculations can be carried out for the payoff function of a put option. Using the constant $\beta = \gamma + 1$ in (4.15), the corresponding initial conditions at $\tau = 0$ for the heat equation become

$$u_C(x,0) = \max\left\{e^{\beta x} - e^{\gamma x},\, 0\right\}, \tag{4.23}$$

$$u_P(x,0) = \max\left\{e^{\gamma x} - e^{\beta x},\, 0\right\}. \tag{4.24}$$

Substitution of these functions into the integral solution in (4.20) will then yield the solution $u = u(x, \tau)$ for the transformed dependent variable. For example, substituting the initial condition (4.23) for a European call option into the solution formula gives

$$u_C(x,\tau) = \frac{1}{\sqrt{4\pi\tau}}\int_{-\infty}^{\infty} e^{-\frac{(x-\xi)^2}{4\tau}}\max\left\{e^{\beta x} - e^{\gamma x},\, 0\right\}d\xi$$

$$= \frac{1}{\sqrt{4\pi\tau}}\int_{0}^{\infty} e^{-\frac{(x-\xi)^2}{4\tau}}\left(e^{\beta x} - e^{\gamma x}\right)d\xi$$

$$= I_\beta - I_\gamma, \tag{4.25}$$

where the last integrals are defined by

$$I_\alpha = \frac{1}{\sqrt{4\pi\tau}}\int_{0}^{\infty} e^{-\frac{(x-\xi)^2}{4\tau}+\alpha\xi}\,d\xi \tag{4.26}$$

for each $\alpha = \beta, \gamma$. Calculation, or simplification of the integral I_α can further be carried out by a change of variables as follows:

$$I_\alpha = \frac{1}{\sqrt{4\pi\tau}}\int_{0}^{\infty} e^{-\frac{[(x+2\tau\alpha)-\xi]^2}{4\tau}+\alpha\xi}\,e^{\alpha x + \alpha^2\tau}\,d\xi$$

$$= e^{\alpha x + \alpha^2\tau}\int_{-\infty}^{\frac{x+2\tau\alpha}{\sqrt{2\pi}}}\frac{1}{\sqrt{2\pi}}e^{-\eta^2/2}\,d\eta,$$

where the change of variable $\eta = \frac{x+2\tau\alpha-\xi}{\sqrt{2\pi}}$ is used. Note that the last integral contains the probability density function of the standard normal distribution. Hence, using the distribution function Φ,

$$\Phi(\zeta) = \int_{-\infty}^{\zeta} \phi(\eta)\,d\eta = \frac{1}{\sqrt{2\pi}}\int_{-\infty}^{\zeta} e^{-\eta^2/2}\,d\eta, \tag{4.27}$$

of the normal distribution with mean zero and variance one, the integral I_α can be written in closed-form as

$$I_\alpha = e^{\alpha x + \alpha^2 \tau} \, \Phi\left(\frac{x + 2\tau\alpha}{\sqrt{2\pi}}\right). \tag{4.28}$$

Therefore, the solution $u_C(x, \tau)$ represented by the difference of two integrals, as in (4.25), is simplified to

$$u_C(x, \tau) = e^{\beta x + \beta^2 \tau} \, \Phi\left(\frac{x + 2\tau\beta}{\sqrt{2\pi}}\right) - e^{\gamma x + \gamma^2 \tau} \, \Phi\left(\frac{x + 2\tau\gamma}{\sqrt{2\pi}}\right). \tag{4.29}$$

Similar calculations carried out for the transformed initial condition $u_P(x, 0)$ in (4.24) for the put option shows that

$$u_P(x, \tau) = e^{\gamma x + \gamma^2 \tau} \, \Phi\left(-\frac{x + 2\tau\gamma}{\sqrt{2\pi}}\right) - e^{\beta x + \beta^2 \tau} \, \Phi\left(-\frac{x + 2\tau\beta}{\sqrt{2\pi}}\right). \tag{4.30}$$

What remains only is that the solutions represented by equations (4.29) and (4.30) must be transformed back in order to write the solutions of the Black-Scholes equation for the European call and put options, respectively. This can be done by using the transformations defined by (4.16) that are accompanied with the notations in (4.15). Let us define

$$d_1 = \frac{x + 2\tau\beta}{\sqrt{2\pi}}, \quad \text{and} \quad d_2 = \frac{x + 2\tau\gamma}{\sqrt{2\pi}}. \tag{4.31}$$

Then, in terms of the original variables $S = Ke^x$ and $t = T - \frac{\tau}{\sigma^2/2}$ of the Black-Scholes equation, d_1 and d_2 can easily be obtained as

$$d_1 = \frac{\log(S/K) + \left(r - \delta + \frac{1}{2}\sigma^2\right)(T - t)}{\sigma\sqrt{T - t}}, \tag{4.32}$$

$$d_2 = \frac{\log(S/K) + \left(r - \delta - \frac{1}{2}\sigma^2\right)(T - t)}{\sigma\sqrt{T - t}}. \tag{4.33}$$

Recall that the constants β and γ were defined by (4.15). For ease of reference, they were

$$\gamma = \frac{1}{2}(\kappa - 1), \quad \text{and} \quad \beta = \frac{1}{2}(\kappa + 1) = \gamma + 1,$$

where $\kappa = \frac{r - \delta}{\sigma^2/2}$. Note also that d_2 can be defined via d_1 as

$$d_2 = d_1 - \sigma\sqrt{T-t}. \tag{4.34}$$

On the other hand, the transformation used for the dependent variable $V(S,t)$, the value of an option, was

$$V(S,t) = K\,v(x,t), \qquad v(x,\tau) = e^{-\gamma x - (\beta^2 + \ell)\tau}\,u(x,\tau),$$

where $\ell = \frac{\delta}{\sigma^2/2}$. Hence, the value of a European call option can be converted back from (4.29) as

$$V_C(x,t) = Ke^{-\gamma x - (\beta^2 + \ell)\tau}\left\{ e^{\beta x + \beta^2 \tau}\,\Phi(d_1) - e^{\gamma x + \gamma^2 \tau}\,\Phi(d_2) \right\}$$

$$= Ke^{(\beta - \gamma)x - \ell\tau}\Phi(d_1) - Ke^{(\gamma^2 - \beta^2 - \ell)\tau}\Phi(d_2).$$

Here, notice that

$$\beta - \gamma = 1 \quad \text{and} \quad \ell\tau = \delta(T-t)$$

so that $Ke^{(\beta - \gamma)x - \ell\tau} = Se^{-\delta(T-t)}$. Moreover,

$$(\gamma^2 - \beta^2 - \ell)\tau = -(\ell + \kappa)\tau = -r(T-t),$$

hence, $Ke^{(\gamma^2 - \beta^2 - \ell)\tau} = Ke^{-r(T-t)}$. Therefore, replacing the values of the parameters and the independent variables x and τ with the original ones, S and t, gives

$$V_C(S,t) = Se^{-\delta(T-t)}\Phi(d_1) - Ke^{-r(T-t)}\Phi(d_2), \tag{4.35}$$

which is the celebrated *Black-Scholes formula* for a European call option.

Similar calculations show that the value of a European put option $V_P(S,t)$ can be written as

$$V_P(S,t) = Ke^{-r(T-t)}\Phi(-d_2) - Se^{-\delta(T-t)}\Phi(-d_1). \tag{4.36}$$

On the other hand, this closed-form formula for the value of a European put option can also be obtained from the *put-call* parity

$$V_P(S,t) = V_C(S,t) - Se^{-\delta(T-t)} + Ke^{-r(T-t)} \tag{4.37}$$

by using the relation $\Phi(-\zeta) = 1 - \Phi(\zeta)$, which can be proved easily, and is left as an exercise.

Exercise 4.1. Using the definition of Φ show that

$$\Phi(-\zeta) = 1 - \Phi(\zeta) \tag{4.38}$$

holds for all $\zeta \in \mathbb{R}$.

Exercise 4.2. Show that the closed-form solution $V_{con}(S,t)$ of a *cash-or-nothing* option is given by

$$V_{con}(S,t) = B\,e^{-r(T-t)}\,\Phi(d_2).$$

A cash-or-nothing option has the payoff function

$$V_{con}(S,T) = \begin{cases} B & \text{if } S > K, \\ 0 & \text{if } S \le K. \end{cases}$$

That is, the reward B is paid if the asset price is more than the bet K at maturity T.

Exercise 4.3. Show that the value $V(S,t)$ of a European option can be expressed as the discounted, expectation of the payoff $V(S,T)$ under the risk-neutrality condition: $\mu = r$. In other words, show that

$$\begin{aligned} V(S,t) &= e^{-r(T-t)}\mathbb{E}_{\mathbb{Q}}\left[V(S,T)\right] \\ &= e^{-r(T-t)}\int_0^\infty V(s,T)\,p(s;T,S,t)\,ds, \end{aligned}$$

where $p = p(s;T,S,t)$ is the density function of a lognormal distribution, and it is defined by

$$p(s;T,S,t) = \frac{1}{s\sigma\sqrt{2\pi(T-t)}}\,e^{-\frac{\left[\log(s/S)-\left(r-\delta-\frac{1}{2}\sigma^2\right)(T-t)\right]^2}{2\sigma^2(T-t)}}.$$

This is sometimes called the *transition probability* density.

Although the formulae (4.35) and (4.36) are the closed-form solutions of the Black-Scholes equation for European call and put options, respectively, they still require evaluation of improper integrals. This can be done, however, numerically, in most cases. Hence, truncation of the domains of the integrals is unavoidable for numerical calculations.

Fortunately, a numerous numerical software includes libraries to calculate the *error function*, which is denoted by erf, and is defined by

$$\operatorname{erf}(x) = \frac{2}{\sqrt{\pi}}\int_0^x e^{-t^2}\,dt. \tag{4.39}$$

In fact, this error function is rather similar to the distribution function of the standard normal distribution. It is easy to write the latter in terms of the former. For,

$$\Phi(x) = \frac{1}{\sqrt{2\pi}} \int_{-\infty}^{x} e^{-\frac{1}{2}\xi^2}\, d\xi = \frac{1}{\sqrt{\pi}} \int_{-\infty}^{x/\sqrt{2}} e^{-t^2}\, dt$$

$$= \frac{1}{\sqrt{\pi}} \left(\int_{-\infty}^{0} e^{-t^2}\, dt + \int_{0}^{x/\sqrt{2}} e^{-t^2}\, dt \right).$$

By using the well-known integral

$$\int_{-\infty}^{\infty} e^{-t^2}\, dt = \sqrt{\pi},$$

as well as the definition (4.39) of the error function, it follows that

$$\Phi(x) = \frac{1}{2} \left\{ 1 + \mathrm{erf}\left(x/\sqrt{2} \right) \right\}. \tag{4.40}$$

In most cases, since the error function is available in MATLAB, calculation of the value $\Phi(x)$ at x will be done by using (4.40). However, there is no explicit form for the calculation of neither $\Phi(x)$ nor $\mathrm{erf}(x)$, but there are some well-known approximations collected in [Abramowitz and Stegun (1972)]. The algorithm given in the exercise below is frequently used and relatively fast besides its accuracy. The implementation of the algorithm is left to the readers.

Exercise 4.4. Write a program that computes the value of the standard normal distribution function $\Phi(x)$ at a given point x. First, by using (4.40) if possible. Second, by using the following procedure.

(1) Let $\gamma = 0.2316419$.

(2) Calculate $z = \dfrac{1}{1 + \gamma x}$, for $x \geq 0$.

(3) Let the coefficients be

$$a_1 = 0.319381530, \quad a_2 = -0.356563782,\ a_3 = 1.781477937,$$
$$a_4 = -1.821255978,\ a_5 = 1.330274429.$$

(4) Then, the approximate value of $\Phi(x)$ for $x \geq 0$ is

$$\Phi(x) \approx 1 - \phi(x)\, z\left((((a_5 z + a_4)z + a_3)z + a_2)z + a_1 \right),$$

where $\phi(x)$ is the value of the density function at x. If $x < 0$, then apply $\Phi(x) = 1 - \Phi(-x)$.

Outlook

Within a more general mathematical setting, the risk-neutral expected discounted payoff is linked to the solution of the Black-Scholes equation by the Feynman-Kac theorem. To see this close relation we refer to (Shreve, 2004b, pp. 268–272). For an intuitive and well-illustrated introduction to the relation between partial differential equations and stochastic processes, [Neftci (2000)] seems to be a good reference.

A clear and concise reference for the heat equation and its qualitative properties we refer to [John (1991)], which also includes the Green's functions, *fundamental* solutions, and Fourier transforms.

For similar transformations applied to the Black-Scholes equation in order to get the classical heat equation, readers can refer to [Barraquand and Pudet (1996); Seydel (2002); Wilmott *et al.* (1995)]. In this section, we skipped the transformations of the boundary conditions for options in order to avoid some technical definitions for function spaces in which the solutions are sought. However, readers may have a glance on the literature referenced above, or Chapter 6 in advance, for detailed discussions on some specific options; preferably, European call and put options.

4.3 Hedging Portfolios: The Greeks

This section briefly considers the sensitivity of option price to the underlying parameters, such as asset prices, volatility, interest rates, and so on. Changes in the values of these parameters will certainly change values of the options considerably. A portfolio consisting of options is liable to changes of these parameters and, thus, should be hedged, and the risk it is exposed to should be reduced.

Recall that the portfolio

$$\Pi = -V + \Delta\, S \tag{4.41}$$

was considered in Section 4.1 when deriving the Black-Scholes PDE. This portfolio was made riskless, in other words, it did not change its value by the stochastic fluctuations caused by the asset prices. This was achieved by choosing a Δ number of shares from the underlying asset as

$$\Delta = \frac{\partial V}{\partial S}. \tag{4.42}$$

However, mathematically, this corresponds to the *rate of change* of the option value due to the changes of the underlying asset prices. It is a measure of the *sensitivity* of an option price to the asset prices, which is called by the Greek name: the *delta* of the option.

The *delta* of an option is particularly important in *hedging* portfolios. For instance, an investor likes to have a portfolio that is not affected by the changes in the asset prices. That is, he wishes to manage a portfolio Π whose rate of change

$$\Delta_\Pi = \frac{\partial \Pi}{\partial S} \tag{4.43}$$

with respect to asset prices S is *zero*: $\Delta_\Pi = 0$. This is called the *delta-hedging* of the portfolio.

Suppose that you are in a *short* position in an option with the value V, and you want to protect yourself by taking positions in the asset because of the changes of the underlying asset prices S. Then, you would construct the portfolio in (4.41), where the Δ represents the number of shares of the asset that you need to purchase. Thus, in order to hedge the portfolio with respect to the changes of the prices, you would require the delta of the portfolio to vanish. That is,

$$0 = \frac{\partial \Pi}{\partial S} = -\frac{\partial V}{\partial S} + \Delta.$$

However, this leads to the same Δ defined in (4.42), the delta of the *option* in the portfolio.

A portfolio that has to be hedged may contain several parameters, even if it has only a single option. Of course, a portfolio may have many other financial derivatives and, hence, completely different parameters than that of an option. However, the sensitivities of a portfolio to the parameters of an option are particularly important in hedging. These sensitivities are named after Greek names, and simply called the *Greeks* of a portfolio. The Greeks for a portfolio Π are defined as

$$\textbf{Delta: } \Delta_\Pi = \frac{\partial \Pi}{\partial S}, \quad \textbf{Gamma: } \Gamma_\Pi = \frac{\partial^2 \Pi}{\partial S^2}, \quad \textbf{Theta: } \Theta_\Pi = \frac{\partial \Pi}{\partial t},$$

$$\textbf{Vega: } \mathcal{V}_\Pi = \frac{\partial \Pi}{\partial \sigma}, \quad \textbf{Rho: } \rho_\Pi = \frac{\partial \Pi}{\partial r}.$$

Remark 4.2. Sometimes, the Greek *theta*, Θ_Π, of a portfolio Π is defined to be

$$\Theta_\Pi = \frac{\partial \Pi}{\partial \tau_m},$$

where $\tau_m = T - t$ is the time to maturity. It is easy to use the chain rule and obtain the relation,

$$\frac{\partial \Pi}{\partial t} = \frac{\partial \Pi}{\partial \tau_m} \frac{\partial \tau_m}{\partial t} = -\frac{\partial \Pi}{\partial \tau_m}.$$

Depending on his preferences, an investor may wish to hedge a portfolio that is liable to the changes in any, or several of the parameters. Thus, knowing the Greeks for the options is particularly important. Thanks to the closed-form solutions of the Black-Scholes equation. By using the closed-form solutions, it is possible to derive the corresponding closed-form representations for the Greeks of the European call and put options.

In fact, due to the *put-call* parity (4.37) for European options it is sufficient to know the Greeks only for call options in closed-form. The corresponding Greeks for put options can then be derived by using the put-call parity. The Black-Scholes closed-form solution for a European call option has been given in (4.35). For ease of reference, it is

$$V_C(S, t) = Se^{-\delta(T-t)}\Phi(d_1) - Ke^{-r(T-t)}\Phi(d_2), \qquad (4.44)$$

where Φ is the distribution function of the standard normal distribution whose density is $\Phi' = \phi$. Differentiating V_C with respect to S gives the delta Greek for the call option, which we will denote it by Δ_C, and

$$\Delta_C = \frac{\partial V_C}{\partial S} = e^{-\delta(T-t)}\Phi(d_1) + Se^{-\delta(T-t)}\phi(d_1)\frac{\partial d_1}{\partial S}$$
$$- Ke^{-r(T-t)}\phi(d_2)\frac{\partial d_2}{\partial S}.$$

The partial derivatives of d_1 and d_2 can be easily calculated by using their definitions in (4.32) and (4.33), respectively, and noticing the relation

$$d_2 = d_1 - \sigma\sqrt{T - t}$$

in (4.34). Thus,

$$\frac{\partial d_1}{\partial S} = \frac{\partial d_2}{\partial S} = \frac{1}{S\sigma\sqrt{T - t}}.$$

The delta Δ_C of a call option can further be simplified by the use of the following fact:

$$Se^{-\delta(T-t)}\phi(d_1) - Ke^{-r(T-t)}\phi(d_2) = 0. \qquad (4.45)$$

This can be proved by considering the relation,

$$\log\left(\frac{Se^{-\delta(T-t)}\phi(d_1)}{Ke^{-r(T-t)}\phi(d_2)}\right) = \log\left(S/K\right) + (r-\delta)(T-t) + \log\left(\frac{\phi(d_1)}{\phi(d_2)}\right) \quad (4.46)$$

and the definition of the probability density function which is

$$\phi(\xi) = \frac{1}{\sqrt{2\pi}}\,e^{-\xi^2/2}.$$

First, note that the last logarithm in (4.46) is simplified to

$$\log\left(\frac{\phi(d_1)}{\phi(d_2)}\right) = -\frac{1}{2}\left(d_1^2 - d_2^2\right)$$

by use of the definition of ϕ. Second, the difference $d_1^2 - d_2^2$ may be written as

$$d_1^2 - d_2^2 = 2d_1\sigma\sqrt{T-t} - \sigma^2(T-t)$$
$$= 2\log\left(S/K\right) + 2(r-\delta)(T-t)$$

by using (4.32) and (4.34). Therefore, (4.46) is simplified as

$$\log\left(\frac{\phi(d_1)}{\phi(d_2)}\right) = -\log\left(S/K\right) - (r-\delta)(T-t).$$

Plugging the last expression into (4.46) proves the relation,

$$\log\left(\frac{Se^{-\delta(T-t)}\phi(d_1)}{Ke^{-r(T-t)}\phi(d_2)}\right) = 0,$$

which is equivalent to (4.45).

Hence, summarising the calculations above shows that the delta Δ_C of a European call option is simply

$$\Delta_C = \frac{\partial V_C}{\partial S} = e^{-\delta(T-t)}\Phi(d_1). \quad (4.47)$$

Note also that as $\tau_m = T - t$ approaches zero, d_1 and d_2 defined, respectively, by (4.32) and (4.33) are unbounded from above (tend to ∞) for $S > K$. Similarly, when $S < K$, they are unbounded from below (tend to $-\infty$) as $\tau_m = T - t$ approaches zero. Therefore, from (4.47) it follows that the delta of a call option has the limits:

$$\Delta_C \longrightarrow \begin{cases} 1, & \text{if } S > K \\ 0, & \text{if } S < K \end{cases} \quad \text{as} \quad \tau_m = T - t \to 0. \quad (4.48)$$

On the other hand, from the put-call parity (4.37) of European options, it is easy to calculate the corresponding delta Greek Δ_P for the put option. Differentiating both sides of the parity,

$$V_P(S,t) = V_C(S,t) - Se^{-\delta(T-t)} + Ke^{-r(T-t)},$$

with respect to S yields

$$\Delta_P = \frac{\partial V_P}{\partial S} = \Delta_C - e^{-\delta(T-t)}$$

$$= -e^{-\delta(T-t)}\left\{1 - \Phi(d_1)\right\}.$$

Hence, using the relation $\Phi(-\zeta) = 1 - \Phi(\zeta)$ the delta Δ_P of a European put option is

$$\Delta_P = \frac{\partial V_P}{\partial S} = -e^{-\delta(T-t)}\Phi(-d_1). \tag{4.49}$$

Furthermore, a similar argument as above shows that

$$\Delta_P \longrightarrow \begin{cases} 0, & \text{if } S > K \\ -1, & \text{if } S < K \end{cases} \quad \text{as} \quad \tau_m = T - t \to 0. \tag{4.50}$$

The closed-form representations for the other Greeks for European options can be calculated similarly. The following formulae are left as exercise to the readers. Let us define

$$\tau_m = T - t, \quad \text{and} \quad \eta = \begin{cases} 1, & \text{if } V \text{ is a European call} \\ -1, & \text{if } V \text{ is a European put} \end{cases} \tag{4.51}$$

for simplicity. Then, all the Greeks for a European option, no matter if it is a call or a put, are given by the following closed-form formulae.

Delta: $\Delta := \dfrac{\partial V}{\partial S}$,

$$\Delta = \eta e^{-\delta\tau_m}\, \Phi(\eta d_1), \tag{4.52}$$

Gamma: $\Gamma := \dfrac{\partial^2 V}{\partial S^2}$,

$$\Gamma = e^{-\delta\tau_m}\frac{1}{S\sigma\sqrt{\tau_m}}\phi(d_1), \tag{4.53}$$

Theta: $\Theta := \dfrac{\partial V}{\partial \tau_m}$,

$$\Theta = -\eta \left\{ \delta S e^{-\delta \tau_m} \Phi(\eta d_1) - r K e^{-r \tau_m} \Phi(\eta d_2) \right\} \\ - e^{-\delta \tau_m} \frac{\sigma S}{2\sqrt{\tau_m}} \phi(d_1), \tag{4.54}$$

Vega: $\mathcal{V} := \dfrac{\partial V}{\partial \sigma}$,

$$\mathcal{V} = \sqrt{\tau_m} S e^{-\delta \tau_m} \phi(d_1), \tag{4.55}$$

Rho: $\rho := \dfrac{\partial V}{\partial r}$,

$$\rho = \eta \tau_m K e^{-\delta \tau_m} \Phi(\eta d_2). \tag{4.56}$$

There are, of course, other parameters in the Black-Scholes formulae, such as the strike price K and the dividend yield δ. However, they do not have Greek names, although they can effectively be used in hedging portfolios. For instance, the sensitivity of a portfolio may depend on the changes of the underlying strike prices. If this is to be hedged, then the sensitivity of the option value V to strike price K may be represented by the partial derivative $\frac{\partial V}{\partial K}$. The following exercise that considers this derivative, and the derivative with respect to the dividend yield, is helpful in this respect.

Exercise 4.5. For European call and put options, show that

$$\frac{\partial V}{\partial K} = -\eta e^{-r \tau_m} \Phi(\eta d_2)$$

and

$$\frac{\partial V}{\partial \delta} = -\eta \tau_m S e^{-\delta \tau_m} \Phi(\eta d_1)$$

hold, where η is 1 for call, and -1 for put options. Explain also how to use these sensitivity parameters in hedging.

Fig. 4.1 shows the calculation of the exact formulae of the prices of a European call as well as a put option. It also provides the values of the deltas corresponding to those options. In Fig. 4.2 we show the corresponding values versus the asset price S.

```
———————————— CallPut_Delta.m ————————————
function [C, Cdelta, P, Pdelta] = CallPut_Delta(S,K,r,sigma,tau,div)
% tau = time to expiry (T-t)

if nargin < 6
    div = 0.0;
end
if tau > 0
    d1 = (log(S/K) + (r + 0.5*sigma^2)*(tau)*ones(size(S))) / (sigma*sqrt(tau));
    d2 = d1 - sigma*sqrt(tau);
    N1 = 0.5*(1+erf(d1/sqrt(2))); N2 = 0.5*(1+erf(d2/sqrt(2)));
    C = exp(-div*tau) * S.*N1-K*exp(-r*(tau))*N2; Cdelta = exp(-div*tau) * N1;
    P = C + K*exp(-r*tau) - exp(-div*tau)*S; Pdelta = Cdelta - exp(-div*tau);
else
    C = max(S-K,0); Cdelta =  0.5*(sign(S-K) + 1);
    P = max(K-S,0); Pdelta = Cdelta - 1;
end
```

Fig. 4.1   The use of closed-form solution of the Black-Scholes equation, and the *delta* hedging parameter

As time to maturity approaches zero, the values of the options become closer to the corresponding payoff functions. On the other hand, the deltas of the options have a jump at the strike price $(K = 2)$ when the maturity $(T = 5)$ is reached.

The following example illustrates the delta Greeks for a portfolio of options. However, for simplicity, the options considered have the same underlying asset and the strike prices.

Example 4.1. Consider a portfolio Π consisting of a European call and a put option. Suppose the strike prices are the same: $K = 2$ for each. Let the interest rate r be $r = 0.03$ and the volatility σ of the underlying asset be $\sigma = 0.25$. Furthermore, assume that time to maturity is also the same: $T = 5$ for both options. A MATLAB script is shown in Fig. 4.3, which uses the function in Fig. 4.1.

The graphs of the values of the options and the portfolio are depicted in Fig. 4.4. First row in the figure shows the values, respectively, of the options and of the portfolio. The second row contains the graphs of the corresponding deltas of the options and the portfolio.

Notice that the delta of the portfolio, $\Delta_\Pi = \Delta_C + \Delta_P$, shown in Fig. 4.4 is *zero* for a nonzero value of the asset price. Indeed, adding some number of shares of the asset to the portfolio makes the portfolio riskless. Not a surprise! This number is $\Delta = -(\Delta_C + \Delta_P)$, which is obtained immediately

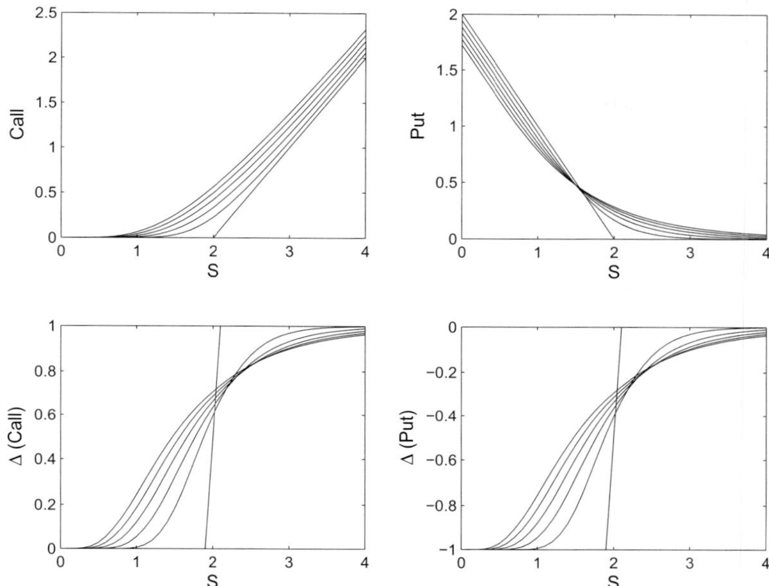

Fig. 4.2   Solutions obtained from the closed-form formulae of the Black-Scholes equation for the European option with varying time to maturity

by constructing the portfolio Π that includes a call and a put option, and Δ number of shares of the asset.

Outlook

In finance, a *hedge* is an investment that is taken out specifically to reduce or cancel out the risk in another investment. We refer to [Higham (2004); Joshi (2004)] for practical applications and brief discussions of the Greeks for hedging the risks associated with having a portfolio of derivatives. For more information on the Greeks, see also [Hull (2000); Kwok (1998)].

4.4   Implied Volatility

The Black-Scholes model has some restrictions. A constant risk-free interest rate r and a constant volatility σ do not seem to be realistic. After all, the derivation of the Black-Scholes equation, and hence, the closed-form solutions for some options, assume a continuously trading strategy which

```
———————————————————— sumOfCallPut_Eg.m ——————————————————
% sumOfCallPut_Eg
clear all, close all
S = 0:0.1:4; K = 2; r = 0.03; sigma = 0.25; T = 5;

[c, cd, p, pd] = CallPut_Delta(S, K, r, sigma, T);
subplot(2,2,1), plot(S, c), hold on, plot(S, p, 'r--')
xlabel('S','Fontsize',12), ylabel('V','Fontsize',12); legend('V_C', 'V_P');
subplot(2,2,2), plot(S, c+p), xlabel('S','Fontsize',12)
ylabel('V_\Pi = V_C + V_P','Fontsize',12)
subplot(2,2,3), plot(S, cd), hold on, plot(S, pd, 'r--')
xlabel('S','Fontsize',12), ylabel('\Delta','Fontsize',12)
legend('\Delta_C', '\Delta_P');
subplot(2,2,4), plot(S, cd+pd), hold on, plot([0 4], [0 0], 'g-.')
xlabel('S','Fontsize',12), ylabel('\Delta_\Pi = \Delta_C + \Delta_P','Fontsize',12);
print -r900 -deps '../figures/sumOfCallPut_Eg'
```

Fig. 4.3   Value of a portfolio consisting of a call and a put option

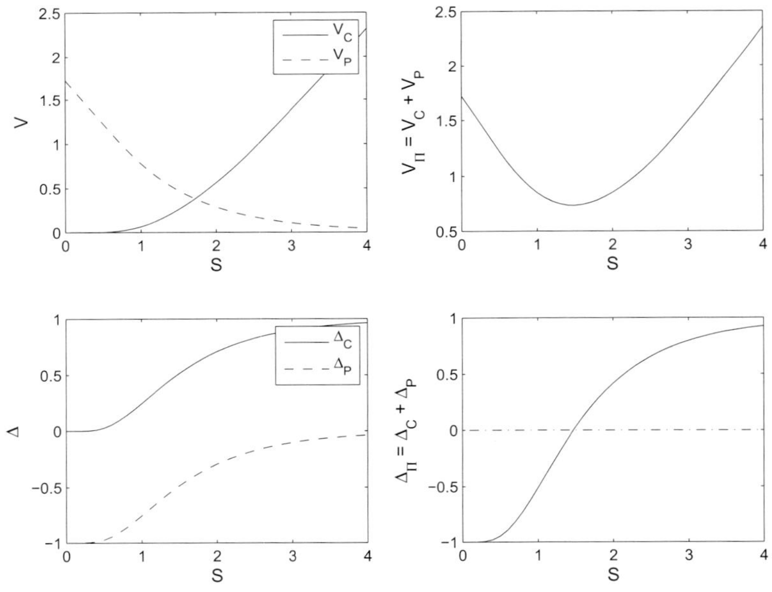

Fig. 4.4   Values and deltas of a portfolio consisting of a call and a put option

is not feasible in the market in order to hedge the portfolio that has been constructed. This is simply due to the changing number of shares $\Delta = \frac{\partial V}{\partial S}$ continuously in time. Furthermore, the model does not assume the presence of transaction costs.

In fact, you may possibly add more drawbacks to these deficiencies of the Black-Scholes setting. Despite these restrictions and deficiencies, however, the Black-Scholes model has become so popular and was awarded with a Nobel Prize! This is mainly due to the existence of a concrete, closed-form solutions to some options whose variants are traded at the market. Beyond professionals and experts in mathematical finance, a closed-form solution means a lot for academics and, especially, for practitioners, the actual players of the market. The Black-Scholes formulae have also the benefit of being very easy to use and understand: given the parameters that are involved in the Black-Scholes formulae, you may directly compute the price of the options.

The only trouble seems to be the estimation of the parameters, especially the estimation of the volatility σ from historical data. The estimation of μ may be easier than that of σ, even more, for pricing purposes μ disappears, and it is replaced by the risk-free interest rate r. It may be easier to estimate r for short term periods, and it may be a part of the option contract.

As it turns out, the empirical performance of the Black-Scholes formulae is reasonably good. For options with a strike price that is not too far from the current price of the underlying asset price, the Black-Scholes formulae anticipates the *observed prices* at the market rather well. However, for options that are deep *out of the money*, the observed prices are, in most cases, higher than the ones suggested by the formulae. This might be partly because of the difficulty of estimation of the parameters r and especially σ, which are assumed to be constant in the Black-Scholes setting. It does not appear to be the case that the volatility is constant over the life time of an option.

However, the option prices are quoted in the market so that the market implicitly knows or presumes the volatility. The volatility $\hat{\sigma}$ derived from these quoted prices for an option is called the *implied volatility*. Due to the closed-form solutions, the Black-Scholes setting is a good candidate model to estimate the volatility implied by the market.

If $\hat{V}$ denotes the quoted prices of an option, then the implied volatility $\hat{\sigma}$ is the value of the σ for which

$$\hat{V} = V(S, t, T, K, r, \sigma), \tag{4.57}$$

where $V = V(S, t, T, K, r, \sigma)$ denotes the model value of the option, which is mostly referred to as the *theoretical price*. Although the underlying model can be any challenging one, the use of the Black-Scholes formulae is easy and illustrative. Thus, it follows from (4.57) that the implied volatility $\hat{\sigma}$ is any of the zeros of the function

$$f(\sigma) = \hat{V} - V(S, t, T, K, r, \sigma), \qquad (4.58)$$

which represents the difference between the observed and the theoretical prices. In other words, the roots of the equation $f(\sigma) = 0$ are sought. Indeed, a similar root finding problem was discussed in Example 2.8 on page 67. The premium of a pay-later contract was found to be the root of a certain function.

Example 4.2. This example presents the root finding problem for the implied volatility. The data shown in Table 4.1 are totally artificial and assumed to be observed for 9 call options in the market. Each row in the table shows the corresponding values of an option with the strike price K.

Table 4.1   Observed data

Option #	Strike price K	Call Option V_C
1	1.00	1.2098
2	1.25	1.0280
3	1.50	0.8677
4	1.75	0.7298
5	2.00	0.6132
6	2.25	0.5157
7	2.50	0.4349
8	2.75	0.3682
9	3.00	0.3134

Assume that the current price of the underlying asset of the options is $S = 2.00$ and the interest rate is $r = 3\%$. Also, suppose that the time to maturity of all options considered is the same: $T = 5$. These values and the observed data are also shown in Fig. 4.5.

The values of the implied volatility for the call options in Table 4.1 are calculated as

$$\hat{\sigma}_1 = 0.3507, \ \hat{\sigma}_2 = 0.3153, \ \hat{\sigma}_3 = 0.2973, \ \hat{\sigma}_4 = 0.2878, \ \hat{\sigma}_5 = 0.2826,$$
$$\hat{\sigma}_6 = 0.2798, \ \hat{\sigma}_7 = 0.2784, \ \hat{\sigma}_8 = 0.2780, \ \hat{\sigma}_9 = 0.2783,$$

respectively. The curve corresponding to the values of the implied volatility is depicted in Fig. 4.6.

```
                         ─────────── impliedVola.m ───────────
% impliedVola
clear all, close all
K = [1.00 1.25 1.50 1.75 2.00 2.25 2.50 2.75 3.00];
Obs = [1.2098 1.0280 0.8677 0.7298 0.6132 0.5157 0.4349 0.3682 0.3134];
S = 2; r = 0.03; T = 5;
for i = 1:length(K)
    [implVola(i), value(i)] = fsolve(@(x) ...
        Obs(i) - CallPut_Delta(S, K(i), r, x, T), 0.3);
end
[implVola', value']
plot(K,implVola,'-o', S*ones(1,length(K)), implVola, 'r--'), hold on
text(S, 0.32, 'Current Asset Price');
xlabel('Strike Price','FontSize',12), ylabel('Implied Volatility','FontSize',12)
print -r900 -deps '../figures/impliedVola'
```

Fig. 4.5   Implied volatility calculation

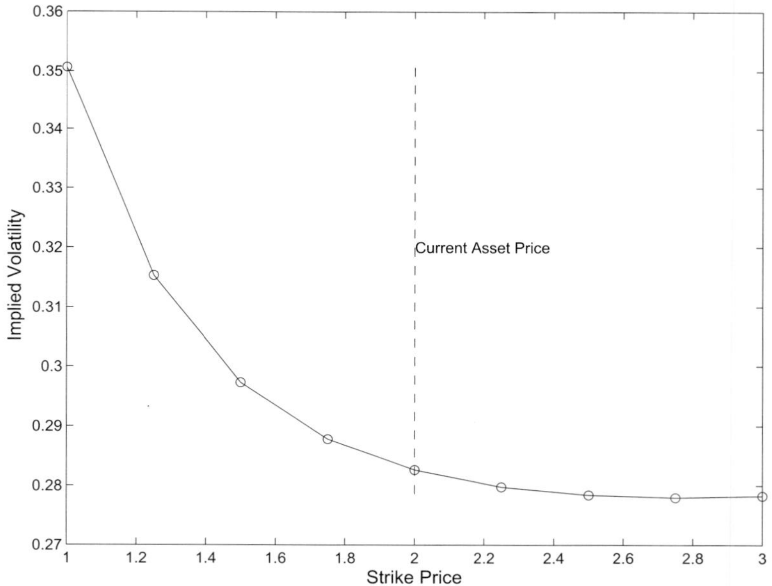

Fig. 4.6   Implied volatility due to data in Table 4.1

In fact, actual data from a market is expected to yield a similar graph
for the implied volatility as in Fig. 4.6, which is called a *volatility smile*
due to its shape. Of course, other shapes, such as *frowns* are possible for
different options. However, it shows that the volatility is not constant at
all, unlike the assumption in the Black-Scholes closed-form solutions.

Outlook

The changes of the volatility during the life time of the options cause hedging costs, hence, the volatility implied by the market has to be estimated by the traders. There are alternative models to the Black-Scholes model under which options are priced and used to estimate the implied volatility. See [Joshi (2004); Hull (2000); Kwok (1998)] for those alternative models, some of which assume a *stochastic* volatility.

Chapter 5

Random Numbers and Monte Carlo Simulation

The basic idea of *Monte Carlo* methods is to simulate a large number of *trajectories* of a process and then average over the desired quantities in order to have information on the behaviour of the process as well as its underlying distribution. Typically, we want to *estimate* an expected value of a random variable with respect to the underlying probability distribution; for instance, an option price may be evaluated by computing the expected value of the payoff with respect to a *risk-neutral* probability measure.

Monte Carlo simulation is of great importance for general models, for instance, models which do not satisfy some (or all) assumptions of the Black-Scholes framework. If, for instance, the interest rate r is modelled by another SDE (that is, not constant at all, but even stochastic), then one should solve a system of SDEs, whose solution may not be written in closed-form. Similarly, a stochastic volatility violates the assumptions of the Black-Scholes equation. In such cases, a Monte Carlo simulation may be the (only) method of choice.

Random numbers play an important role in Monte Carlo methods. In simulations via computers, there is a need to draw a sequence of pseudo-random numbers that accounts for independent realisations of random variable from a specified distribution. There are several methods to generate random numbers digitally, however, to find a good generator is not easy. This chapter introduces some of the basic features of generating pseudo-random numbers. Although the sequence of numbers generated must be statistically tested, the random numbers generated by a *linear congruential generator* will be assumed to be random and independent realisations of a random variable from a uniform distribution.

However, in many financial applications of Monte Carlo method, simulation of a random variable from a normal distribution is necessary. Transforming of random variables and, hence, the sequences of random numbers become important. Besides the *inverse transform* method, there are two other important ones: the *Box-Muller* method and the *polar method of Marsaglia*. While the former is based on transformation of random variables only, the latter involves also the *acceptance-rejection* method. However, both methods are used for generating uncorrelated pseudo-random numbers. For a specified covariance matrix, the *Cholesky factorisation* exists and is used to transform the independent random variables to the correlated ones.

Convergence of the plain Monte Carlo method is based on the *law of large numbers* and the *central limit theorem*. Hence, the rate of convergence is slow and the method requires large samples from the underlying distributions. Among many methods that try to increase the rate of convergence, without the need of large samples, two methods on *variance reduction techniques* are presented in this chapter: the *antithetic* and the *control variates*. The plain Monte Carlo method and the use of variance reduction in option pricing are discussed and illustrated by several examples.

Finally, the use of *low-discrepancy* sequences of random numbers in Monte Carlo methods is described by the end of this chapter. An example of such sequences is the so-called *Halton* sequences. The *quasi-Monte Carlo* method that uses Halton sequences is also illustrated by an example in option pricing.

5.1 Pseudo-Random Numbers

For simulation and valuation of financial instruments, numbers with specified distributions are required. For example, when simulating a path of an SDE (or the Wiener process itself) the numbers $Z_k \sim \mathcal{N}(0,1)$ were introduced, which were drawn from a standard normal distribution. If possible, these numbers must *really* be random, however, the generation of "random numbers" by digital computers is done in a deterministic and entirely predictable way. If this point is to be stressed, one uses the term *pseudo-random* for computed random numbers; otherwise, we will not distinguish between the two and simple say *random numbers*, omitting the prefix *pseudo*.

Definition 5.1. A sequence of random numbers is said to be a *sample* from F if the numbers are independent realisations of a random variable with distribution function F. Sometimes, samples from a distribution are also called *deviates* or *variates*.

Notice that the name of a distribution is implicitly given by its distribution function in the above definition. Generally, if F is the uniform distribution over $(0, 1)$, then we call the sample, say U_k, from F *uniform deviates* and denote this by $U_k \sim \mathcal{U}(0, 1)$. If F is the (standard) normal distribution, on the other hand, then we call the sample, say Z_k, from F *(standard) normal deviates*; as a notation we have already used $Z_k \sim \mathcal{N}(0, 1)$. In case when the mean μ and the variance σ^2 of a normal distribution have to be specified the notation $Z_k \sim \mathcal{N}(\mu, \sigma^2)$ is preferred.

Remark 5.1. We will not distinguish the notation for a sample X_k from F, which is in fact a sequence $\{X_k\}$, from the corresponding random variable X that has the same distribution F. In both cases, we will use the same notation, that is, $X_k \sim F$ and $X \sim F$.

The basis of random number generation is to draw uniform deviates, for example, by the so-called *linear congruential generator*,

$$N_i = a\, N_{i-1} + b \quad \mathrm{mod}\ M, \tag{5.1}$$

an algorithm for which is shown in Algorithm 5.1.

Algorithm 5.1 Linear Congruential Generator

Require: $N_0 \neq 0$
    for $i = 1, 2, \ldots$ **do**
        $N_i = a\, N_{i-1} + b \quad \mathrm{mod}\ M$
    end for

Because of the *modulo* congruence between the numbers, the N_i are in the set $\{0, 1, \ldots, M - 1\}$. Here, $a \neq 0$ is implicitly assumed, otherwise the sequence is too simple! The number N_0 is called the *seed* and, in fact, it is very important to generate the same sequence of numbers whenever it is necessary. Since $N_i \in \{0, 1, \ldots, M - 1\}$, the numbers $U_i \in [0, 1)$ may be defined by

$$U_i = \frac{N_i}{M}, \qquad i = 0, 1, 2, \ldots.$$

These numbers will be regarded as candidates for uniform deviates, $U_i \sim \mathcal{U}[0, 1)$; whether they are suitable will depend on the choice of M, a and b.

In any case, a *statistical* testing may be required for these *pseudo-random* numbers. In this book, we do not deal with neither statistical testing nor hypothesis testing. However, the choice of M, for instance, must be as large as possible due to periodic behaviour of the numbers, sequence $\{N_i\}_{i=1}^{\infty}$. An implementation of a linear congruential generator is shown in Fig. 5.1, which uses $M = 714025$, $a = 1366$, $b = 150889$. Another generator was used by IBM's mainframe computers in the 60s by letting $M = 2^{31}$, $a = 65539$, $b = 0$.

```
                               LCG.m
function ud = LCG(seed, howMany)
% generates uniform random variates ud(1:howMany) given the seed

a = 1366; b = 150889; M = 714025; ud = seed*ones(1,howMany);
for i=2:howMany
    ud(i) = mod(a*ud(i-1) + b, M);
end
ud = ud ./ M;
```

Fig. 5.1　An implementation of the *Linear Congruential Generator*

In most cases MATLAB built-in function **rand** will generally be used to generate samples from the uniform distribution over the unit interval. This built-in function, **rand**, that is used to generate numbers by assuming

$$M = 2^{31} - 1 = 2147483647, \quad a = 7^5 = 16807, \quad b = 0$$

was proposed in [Park and Miller (1988)]. With the new versions of MATLAB, another method is used to recover some of the deficiencies of the former. We will assume, in this chapter, that these generated pseudo-random numbers are independent realisations of a random variable from the uniform distribution over $[0, 1)$. In most cases, no emphasis will be placed on the intervals, and the random variable U or the sample U_i will be denoted simply by $U \sim \mathcal{U}(0, 1)$ or $U_i \sim \mathcal{U}(0, 1)$, respectively. In fact, for numerical implementations we will mostly discard the value zero from the generated pseudo-random numbers.

Random numbers N_i can also be arranged in m-tuples to form a vector sample, as $(N_i, N_{i+1}, \ldots, N_{i+m-1})$ for $i \geq 1$ in order to draw samples from a distribution. Then the tuples or the corresponding points $(U_i, U_{i+1}, \ldots, U_{i+m-1}) \in (0, 1)^m$ need to be analysed with respect to the correlation and their joint and marginal distributions.

Another easy to implement random number generator is the so-called *lagged Fibonacci generator* based on choosing the N_i form the recursion

$$N_{i+1} = N_{i-\ell} - N_{i-\kappa} \qquad \mod M, \tag{5.2}$$

for suitable lags ℓ and κ in $\mathbb{N}$. Note that some initial *seeds* must be given to start the lagged Fibonacci generator. If $\ell \geq \kappa$ is assumed, then the algorithm must be initialised by another random number generator to set the seeds $U_{-\ell}, U_{-\ell+1}, \ldots, U_1, U_0$. As an example of such a Fibonacci generator with $\ell = 17$ and $\kappa = 5$ is

$$U_i = U_{i-17} - U_{i-5}, \qquad \text{if } U_i < 0, \text{ then set } U_i \leftarrow U_i + 1, \tag{5.3}$$

for $i \geq 18$. This algorithm produces pseudo-random numbers directly from $U_i \sim \mathcal{U}(0,1)$. Here the generator requires 17 initial $U_1, U_2, \ldots, U_{17}$ random numbers by means of another method, such as linear congruential generator.

The Fibonacci generators can also be run with varying lags ℓ and κ. One such generator is recommended in [Kahaner *et al.* (1989)], for which a pseudo-code is shown in Algorithm 5.2. An implementation of this algorithm in MATLAB can also be seen in Fig. 5.2.

Algorithm 5.2 Fibonacci Generator (varying lags)

Require: $U_1, U_2, \ldots, U_{17}$, $i = 17, j = 5$
  loop
    $\zeta = U_i - U_j$
    if $\zeta < 0$ **then**
      $\zeta = \zeta + 1$
    end if
    $U_i = \zeta$, $i = i - 1$, $j = j - 1$
    if $i = 0$ **then**
      $i = 17$
    end if
    if $j = 0$ **then**
      $j = 17$
    end if
  end loop

In Fig. 5.3, two-dimensional plots of the pseudo-random numbers as well as the corresponding histograms are shown. The linear congruential, lagged Fibonacci generators, and the MATLAB **rand** are used to generate these samples from the uniform distribution over the unit interval.

```
_________________________ FibonacciLagged.m _________________________
function ud = FibonacciLagged(seed, howMany)
% See  LCG

i = 17; j = 5; ud = LCG(seed,17);
for k = 1:howMany
    zeta = ud(i) - ud(j);
    if (zeta < 0)
        zeta = zeta + 1;
    end
    ud(k) = zeta; ud(i) = zeta; i = i-1; j = j-1;
    if (i==0)
        i = 17;
    end
    if (j==0)
        j = 17;
    end
end
ud = ud(1:howMany); % in case howMany < 17
```

Fig. 5.2   An implementation of Fibonacci (Lagged) random number generator with varying lags. Initial 17 uniform random variates are drawn by the *Linear Congruential Generator*: (LCG)

Outlook

For more on linear congruential random number generators as well as recommendations, see [Niederreiter (1992); Ripley (2006); Seydel (2002); Tezuka (1995)].

It is possible to use a MATLAB built-in function, `kstest`, from the *Statistics toolbox*, which applies the Kolmogorov-Smirnov *goodness-of-fit* test to the given sample. Also, `chi2gof` can be applied to perform a chi-square goodness-of-fit test. See, for instance, [Chakravarti *et al.* (1967); D'Agostino and Stephens (1986)] for details on statistical tests. Other good references include [Cyganowski *et al.* (2002); Knuth (1997)] for those who are interested in statistical testing of the pseudo-random numbers.

On Fibonacci generators and their periods we refer to [Brent (1994)] and the references therein. However, for numerical implementations of congruential and Fibonacci generators, see (Kahaner *et al.*, 1989, Chapter 10).

5.2   Transformation of Random Variables

In the previous section, the samples were drawn from a uniform distribution over $[0, 1)$ by a linear congruential or Fibonacci generators. These random samples that are realisations of a random variable $U \sim \mathcal{U}(0, 1)$ must be transformed to other samples for realisations of random variables

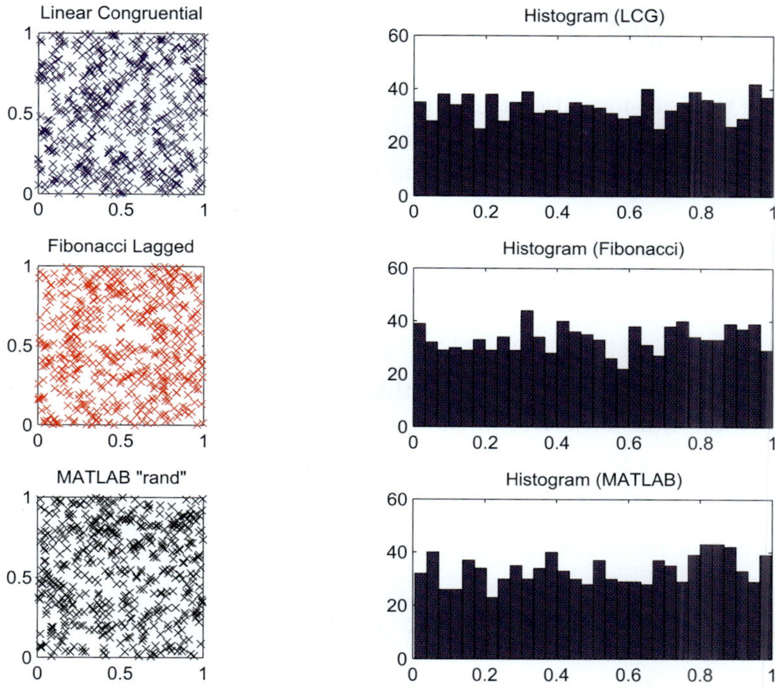

Fig. 5.3   Simulating the pseudo-random numbers drawn from the uniform distribution with different generators

from different distributions. A trivial linear transformation defined by

$$X = a + (b - a)U$$

maps the random variable $U \sim \mathcal{U}(0,1)$ to the random variable $X \sim \mathcal{U}(a,b)$. Such a transformation remains valid for the samples as well:

$$X_i = a + (b - a)U_i,$$

where U_i represents the samples (pseudo-random numbers) from $\mathcal{U}(0,1)$. The transformed random numbers X_i can therefore be regarded as samples from $\mathcal{U}(a,b)$.

Especially for numerical simulations in finance, pseudo-random numbers that are considered as samples from a normal distribution are of main importance. This is because of the underlying Wiener process in modelling the stock price for the valuation of options. For the realisation of random variables from a distribution it is necessary to draw samples from that distribution. In ranging applications of finance, it is, however, necessary to simulate random variables from various distributions. This section presents some of the transformation techniques used in literature, but focuses on the generation of samples from a normal distribution. For pricing of options these samples are the most important ones in Monte Carlo simulations.

5.2.1 *Inverse Transform Method*

Let F be a given distribution function such that

$$F(x) = \mathbb{P}\left\{X \le x\right\}.$$

The aim is to generate samples from this distribution.[1] This can be achieved by a simple transformation of the random variable from a uniform distribution. If U is a random variable from a uniform distribution $\mathcal{U}(0,1)$, then

$$\mathbb{P}\left\{F^{-1}(U) \le x\right\} = \mathbb{P}\left\{U \le F(x)\right\} = F(x),$$

which proves the following theorem.

Theorem 5.1. *Suppose* $U \sim \mathcal{U}(0,1)$ *and* F *be a continuous strictly increasing distribution function. Then,* $F^{-1}(U)$ *is a sample from* F.

Therefore, the theorem above can be summarised by Algorithm 5.3, which is called the *inverse transform method*, in order to draw samples from a given distribution F. As long as a closed-form for the inverse of the distribution function F is available, it is easy to implement this algorithm.

Algorithm 5.3 Inverse Transform Method

    Draw $U \sim \mathcal{U}(0,1)$,

    Return $X = F^{-1}(U)$.   % or solve for X in $F(X) = U$

Example 5.1. Let $F(x) = 1 - e^{-\mu x}$. That is, we want to draw variates from the *exponential distribution*, $X \sim \text{Exp}(\mu)$, where $1/\mu$ is the expected value of X. Direct application of the inverse transform, Algorithm 5.3, yields

$$X = -\frac{1}{\mu}\ln(1 - U),$$

---

[1]We will not distinguish the name of distribution from its distribution function, and denote both by the same notation. Namely, F will denote either the distribution function or the distribution itself, unless we have a common notation for the distribution.

where $U \sim \mathcal{U}(0,1)$. On the other hand, practically it is enough to return

$$X = -\frac{1}{\mu} \ln(U), \qquad U \sim \mathcal{U}(0,1),$$

due to the fact that $(1 - U) \sim \mathcal{U}(0,1)$ for $U \sim \mathcal{U}(0,1)$. The exponential distribution, $\text{Exp}(\mu)$, is important in simulation of *jump-diffusion processes*, and *credit risk* calculations.

It is not easy to use the inverse transform method in case of drawing variates from a normal distribution. Recall that in Section 4.2 on page 124 the error function was defined as,

$$\text{erf}(x) = \frac{2}{\sqrt{\pi}} \int_0^x e^{-t^2}\, dt, \tag{5.4}$$

so that the distribution function of the standard normal distribution function could be written in terms of $\text{erf}(x)$. If $\Phi(x)$ denotes the distribution function of the standard normal distribution, then

$$\Phi(x) = \frac{1}{2}\left\{ 1 + \text{erf}\left(x/\sqrt{2} \right) \right\} \tag{5.5}$$

for $-\infty < x < \infty$. Now, if we denote the inverse of the error function by erf^{-1}, then it is possible to write the inverse $\Phi^{-1}(x)$ of the standard distribution as

$$\Phi^{-1}(x) = \sqrt{2}\, \text{erf}^{-1}\left(2x - 1 \right) \tag{5.6}$$

for $0 \leq x \leq 1$. So, this may be used to transform a uniformly distributed random variable to a standard normally distributed one. However, this still includes approximation to the inverse of the error function. Generally, the inverse error function and, hence, the inverse of the normal distribution function, is given by a rational approximation. In MATLAB, the built-in function **norminv**, which is based on Example 5.1, takes care of this approximation, considering also the tails of the distribution.

The exercise below illustrates how such an approximation to the inverse of the normal distribution function may be used, in case MATLAB is not the choice for a programming language. See [Acklam (2004)] for more details of the algorithm and its implementations in other programming languages. For some other approximations to the inverse of the normal distribution we refer to [Abramowitz and Stegun (1972); Moro (1995)].

Exercise 5.1. Write a program that calculates $x = \Phi^{-1}(p)$ approximately at a point $p \in (0, 1)$ by using the following steps.

(1) Let the coefficients in rational approximations be

$$a_1 = -3.969683028665376 \times 10, \quad a_2 = 2.209460984245205 \times 10^2,$$
$$a_3 = -2.759285104469687 \times 10^2, \, a_4 = 1.383577518672690 \times 10^2,$$
$$a_5 = -3.066479806614716 \times 10, \quad a_6 = 2.506628277459239,$$

$$b_1 = -5.447609879822406 \times 10, \quad b_2 = 1.615858368580409 \times 10^2,$$
$$b_3 = -1.556989798598866 \times 10^2, \, b_4 = 6.680131188771972 \times 10,$$
$$b_5 = -1.328068155288572 \times 10,$$

$$c_1 = -7.784894002430293 \times 10^{-3}, \, c_2 = -3.223964580411365 \times 10^{-1},$$
$$c_3 = -2.400758277161838, \qquad\qquad c_4 = -2.549732539343734,$$
$$c_5 = 4.374664141464968, \qquad\qquad c_6 = 2.938163982698783,$$

$$d_1 = 7.784695709041462 \times 10^{-3}, \, d_2 = 3.224671290700398 \times 10^{-1},$$
$$d_3 = 2.445134137142996, \qquad\qquad d_4 = 3.754408661907416.$$

(2) Define break-points for tails as

$$p_{low} = 0.02425, \quad p_{high} = 1 - p_{low}.$$

(3) Rational approximation for lower region: if $0 < p < p_{low}$,

$$q = \sqrt{-2\log(p)},$$
$$x = \frac{((((c_1 q + c_2)q + c_3)q + c_4)q + c_5)q + c_6}{(((d_1 q + d_2)q + d_3)q + d_4)q + 1}.$$

(4) Rational approximation for central region: if $p_{low} \le p \le p_{high}$,

$$q = p - 0.5, \quad r = q^2,$$
$$x = \frac{(((((a_1 r + a_2)r + a_3)r + a_4)r + a_5)r + a_6)q}{(((((b_1 r + b_2)r + b_3)r + b_4)r + b_5)r + 1}.$$

(5) Rational approximation for upper region: if $p_{high} < p < 1$,

$$q = \sqrt{-2\log(1 - p)},$$
$$x = -\frac{((((c_1 q + c_2)q + c_3)q + c_4)q + c_5)q + c_6}{(((d_1 q + d_2)q + d_3)q + d_4)q + 1}.$$

Consequently, $x \approx \Phi^{-1}(p)$.

Unfortunately, however, it may not be possible to apply the inverse transform method when F does not have an inverse in the classical sense, which is the case with *discrete distributions*. Nevertheless, it is still possible, in an approximate sense, to modify the method to include discrete distributions. Consider a discrete empirical distribution with a finite support, for instance,

$$\mathbb{P}\left\{X = x_j\right\} = p_j, \qquad j = 1, 2, \ldots, n.$$

Then, generate a uniform random variate, $U \sim \mathcal{U}(0, 1)$ and return X that is calculated by

$$X = \begin{cases} x_1, & \text{if } U < p_1, \\ x_2, & \text{if } p_1 \leq U < p_1 + p_2, \\ \vdots \\ x_j, & \text{if } \sum_{k=1}^{j-1} p_k \leq U < \sum_{k=1}^{j} p_k, \\ \vdots \\ x_n, & \text{if } \sum_{k=1}^{n-1} p_k \leq U < \sum_{k=1}^{n} p_k. \end{cases}$$

Since $U \sim \mathcal{U}(0, 1)$ we have

$$\mathbb{P}\left\{X = x_j\right\} = \mathbb{P}\left\{\sum_{k=1}^{j-1} p_k \leq U < \sum_{k=1}^{j} p_k\right\}$$
$$= \sum_{k=1}^{j} p_k - \sum_{k=1}^{j-1} p_k = p_j.$$

In many relevant distributions, the distribution function is invertible; but it may not be as easy as in Example 5.1 to compute the inverse in closed-form. One may then choose to apply some numerical algorithms from *root-finding* problems of scientific computing. However, this may be too costly for some distributions, moreover, it may not be the desired approach. In such cases, a possibility is to resort to the *acceptance-rejection* method.

5.2.2 *Acceptance-Rejection Method*

Let f be a probability density function of the distribution F, whose inverse neither cannot be computed in closed-form nor is desired at all. Assume, further, that we know a function g such that

$$g(x) \geq f(x), \qquad \text{for all } x \in I,$$

where I being the *support*[2] of f. It is therefore possible to obtain a probability density function from the function g by defining

$$r(x) = \frac{1}{c}\, g(x), \qquad c = \int_I g(x)\, dx.$$

Now, if we can simulate the distribution R (with density r), it can be shown that the *acceptance-rejection method*, Algorithm 5.4 generates a random variate X, distributed according to the density f.

Algorithm 5.4 Acceptance-Rejection Method

---

  repeat

    Draw $X \sim R$, where R is the distribution with the density r,

    Draw $U \sim \mathcal{U}(0,1)$, but independent of X,

  until $U \le f(X)/g(X)$

  Return: X

If the support I of the density f is bounded, a natural choice for $r(x)$ is simply the uniform distribution on I, $\mathcal{U}(I)$. If this is the case then simply

$$g(x) = \max_{x \in I} f(x)$$

is chosen.

The underlying idea of acceptance-rejection is that a point x is accepted if the ratio $f(x)/g(x)$ is close to 1, while it is rejected if the ratio is small (near 0, say).

Example 5.2. Consider the density

$$f(x) = 20x(1-x)^3, \qquad x \in [0,1].$$

The inverse transform method would be difficult to apply due to the problem of inverting a polynomial of degree four at each step. The use of acceptance-rejection forces us to find a function $g(x)$ such that $g(x) \ge f(x)$ for $x \in [0,1]$. However, since the function $f(x)$ is bounded on a closed interval and attains its maximum at a critical point $x^* = 1/4$, we choose

$$g(x) = \max_{x \in [0,1]} f(x) = f(x^*) = 135/64$$

so that $f(x) \le g(x)$ for all $x \in [0,1]$. Using the uniform density as the density r, that is, $r(x) = \frac{g(x)}{135/64} = 1$ on $[0,1]$, the following steps will then produce the required variates from the specified distribution:

---

[2]The support of a function is, in general, the set of points for which the function is not zero. More specifically, support of a function f from a set A to the real numbers $\mathbb{R}$ is a subset S of A such that $f(x)$ is zero for all x in A that are not in S.

(1) Draw two independent and uniformly distributed random variates U_1 and U_2, corresponding to X and U in Algorithm 5.4, respectively.
(2) If $U_2 \leq \frac{20U_1(1-U_1)^3}{135/64}$, *accept* $X = U_1$; otherwise, *reject* and go back to step (1).

Outlook

Inverse transform method of this section [Seydel (2002)] is widely applied in financial engineering to generate nonuniform random samples due to its simplicity. In general, the method does not require a distribution function with a classical inverse, but a *generalised* inverse,

$$F^{-1}(u) = \inf \{x \ : \ F(x) = u, \ 0 < u < 1\}.$$

See [Devroye (1986)][3], for instance, for many applications (including algorithms) of the inverse transformation and the acceptance and rejection methods on a variety of distributions.

5.3 Generating Normal Variates

Since the normal distribution plays an important role in financial derivatives, this section specifically deals with transformations that are commonly used in literature in order to generate *normal variates*.

The inverse transform method of the previous section may be generalised by the use of the following theorem that concerns the transformation of random variables in $\mathbb{R}$. The theorem is actually a consequence of the *inverse mapping theorem* of functional/real analysis.

Theorem 5.2 (Transformation in $\mathbb{R}$). *Suppose X is a random variable with density f and distribution F. Let $h : S \longrightarrow B$ be a given function with $S, B \subseteq \mathbb{R}$, where S is the support of f. Assume that h is strictly monotonous. If $Y := h(X)$, then*

(1) Y is a random variable with the distribution $F(h^{-1}(y))$, and
(2) if, further, h^{-1} is continuously differentiable, then the density of Y is given by

$$f(h^{-1}(y)) \left| \frac{dh^{-1}(y)}{dy} \right|.$$

---

[3]See the author's page `http://cg.scs.carleton.ca/~luc/rnbookindex.html` for an online copy.

Proof. Without details, a sketch of the proof may be given as follows: First, observe that

$$\mathbb{P}\{h(X) \leq y\} = \mathbb{P}\{X \leq h^{-1}(y)\} = F(h^{-1}(y)).$$

Then, since h^{-1} is assumed to be continuously differentiable, the density of $Y = h(X)$ is equal to the derivative of the distribution function. Thus, applying the *chain rule* concludes the proof. $\qquad\square$

Unfortunately, however, this theorem cannot directly be applied to find a transformation h, in closed-form, so that $F(h^{-1}(y))$ is the normal distribution function in $\mathbb{R}$. However, the generalisation of Theorem 5.2 to the transformation of random variables in $\mathbb{R}^n$ can be used for this purpose. This generalisation reads as follows.

Theorem 5.3 (Transformation in $\mathbb{R}^n$). *Suppose X is a random variable in $\mathbb{R}^n$ with density $f(x) > 0$ on the support $\mathcal{S}$. Let the transformation $h : \mathcal{S} \longrightarrow \mathcal{B}$ be given, where $\mathcal{S}$, $\mathcal{B} \subseteq \mathbb{R}^n$. Suppose that h is invertible and the inverse is continuously differentiable on $\mathcal{B}$. Then, the transformed random variable $Y := h(X)$ has the density*

$$f\left(h^{-1}(y)\right) \left| \frac{\partial(x_1, x_2, \ldots, x_n)}{\partial(y_1, y_2, \ldots, y_n)} \right|,$$

where $y = (y_1, y_2, \ldots, y_n) \in \mathcal{B}$, $x = h^{-1}(y)$, *and*

$$\frac{\partial(x_1, x_2, \ldots, x_n)}{\partial(y_1, y_2, \ldots, y_n)} = \det \begin{bmatrix} \frac{\partial x_1}{\partial y_1} & \frac{\partial x_1}{\partial y_2} & \cdots & \frac{\partial x_1}{\partial y_n} \\ \vdots & \vdots & \ddots & \vdots \\ \frac{\partial x_n}{\partial y_1} & \frac{\partial x_n}{\partial y_2} & \cdots & \frac{\partial x_n}{\partial y_n} \end{bmatrix}$$

is the so-called Jacobian *of* h^{-1}.

This theorem is the basis of the transform methods described in what follows. By finding a suitable mapping h that satisfies the requirements of Theorem 5.3, it is possible to generate random variates from a normal distribution.

5.3.1   *Box-Muller Method*

The method of Box and Muller is a clever application of Theorem 5.3 in $\mathbb{R}^2$. To begin with, let $\mathcal{S} = (0, 1)^2$ and the density of the uniform distribution $f(x) = 1 > 0$ on $\mathcal{S}$. Let the transformation h be defined by

$$\begin{cases} y_1 = \sqrt{-2\log x_1}\,\cos(2\pi x_2) =: h_1(x_1, x_2), \\ y_2 = \sqrt{-2\log x_1}\,\sin(2\pi x_2) =: h_2(x_1, x_2), \end{cases} \tag{5.7}$$

so that $h : \mathcal{S} \longrightarrow \mathbb{R}^2$. The inverse h^{-1} can easily be calculated by solving the system in (5.7) for x_1 and x_2. This yields

$$\begin{cases} x_1 = \exp\left\{-\tfrac{1}{2}\left(y_1^2 + y_2^2\right)\right\}, \\ x_2 = \tfrac{1}{2\pi}\arctan\left(\tfrac{y_2}{y_1}\right), \end{cases} \tag{5.8}$$

where the main branch of the inverse of the *tangent* function, $\arctan(\xi)$, is used. Therefore, the Jacobian of the inverse transformation can be computed as

$$\frac{\partial(x_1, x_2)}{\partial(y_1, y_2)} = \det \begin{bmatrix} \dfrac{\partial x_1}{\partial y_1} & \dfrac{\partial x_1}{\partial y_2} \\[2mm] \dfrac{\partial x_2}{\partial y_1} & \dfrac{\partial x_2}{\partial y_2} \end{bmatrix}$$

$$= \frac{1}{2\pi}\exp\left\{-\frac{1}{2}\left(y_1^2 + y_2^2\right)\right\} \times \left\{-\frac{1}{1 + y_2^2/y_1^2} - \frac{1}{1 + y_2^2/y_1^2}\frac{y_2^2}{y_1^2}\right\}$$

$$= -\frac{1}{2\pi}\exp\left\{-\frac{1}{2}\left(y_1^2 + y_2^2\right)\right\}.$$

Note that $\left|\frac{\partial(x_1, x_2)}{\partial(y_1, y_2)}\right|$ is the density of the standard distribution in $\mathbb{R}^2$, but also it is the product of *two* one-dimensional densities. That is,

$$\left|\frac{\partial(x_1, x_2)}{\partial(y_1, y_2)}\right| = \frac{1}{\sqrt{2\pi}}e^{-\frac{1}{2}y_1^2} \times \frac{1}{\sqrt{2\pi}}e^{-\frac{1}{2}y_2^2} = \phi(y_1)\,\phi(y_2)$$

and, hence, the two components of $y = (y_1, y_2)$ are independent and normally distributed random variables. In other words, if the components of the vector $X = (X_1, X_2)$ are independent and such that $X_i \sim \mathcal{U}(0, 1)$ for $i = 1, 2$, then

$$Y = (Y_1, Y_2) = (h_1(X_1, X_2),\ h_2(X_1, X_2)) = h(X)$$

consists of two independent standard normal variates. The use of the transformation defined in (5.7) is known as the *Box-Muller* method. Algorithm 5.5 summarises the Box-Muller method, and an implementation of the method is shown in Fig. 5.4.

Another way of obtaining the Box-Muller method for generating normally distributed random variates depends on the following exercise.

Algorithm 5.5 Box-Muller Method

Draw independent $U_1 \sim \mathcal{U}(0,1)$ and $U_2 \sim \mathcal{U}(0,1)$

Set $\theta := 2\pi U_2, \quad \rho = \sqrt{-2\log U_1},$

Return: Z_1 and Z_2, where

$\quad Z_1 = \rho \cos\theta$ $\qquad\qquad\qquad\qquad\qquad$ % a normal variate,

$\quad Z_2 = \rho \sin\theta$ $\quad$ % another normal variate, which is independent of Z_1.

```
———————————————— BoxMuller.m ————————————————
function z = BoxMuller(u1, u2, join)
% join: joins the two normals into one.
% u1, u2 : are two (sequence of) uniform random numbers

if (nargin == 2)
        join = 1;
end
rho = sqrt ( -2 * log(u1) );
z1 = rho .* cos (2*pi*u2); z2 = rho .* sin (2*pi*u2);
if (join)
        z = [z1; z2];
else
        z = [z1 z2];
end
```

Fig. 5.4 An implementation of the *Box-Muller* algorithm to draw normally distributed random variates

Exercise 5.2. Let X and Y be independent standard normal random variables and let R and θ be the polar coordinates of X and Y,

$$X = R\cos\theta, \qquad Y = R\sin\theta.$$

In other words,

$$R^2 = X^2 + Y^2, \qquad \theta = \arctan\frac{Y}{X}.$$

Show that the joint density of R^2 and θ is

$$f(d,\theta) = \frac{1}{2}e^{-d/2} \times \frac{1}{2\pi},$$

where $d = R^2$. Deduce that R^2 and θ are independent and $R^2 \sim \text{Exp}(1/2)$ and $\theta \sim \mathcal{U}(0, 2\pi)$, and hence, re-derive the Box-Muller algorithm using Example 5.1.

5.3.2 *The Polar Method of Marsaglia*

In practice, the algorithm of Box-Muller may be improved by avoiding the costly evaluation of trigonometric functions and integrating the approach of

Box and Muller with the acceptance-rejection approach. The idea results in the so-called *polar rejection method,* shown in Algorithm 5.6. The algorithm is also known as the *method of Marsaglia.*

Algorithm 5.6 Polar Method of Marsaglia

---

  repeat

    Generate independent $U_1, U_2 \sim \mathcal{U}(0,1)$

    $V_i := 2U_i - 1$, for $i = 1, 2$

  until $0 < W := V_1^2 + V_2^2 < 1$ % in implementation, $W \neq 0$

  Return: Z_1 and Z_2, where

$$Z_1 = V_1 \sqrt{-2 \, \tfrac{\log W}{W}}$$

$$Z_2 = V_2 \sqrt{-2 \, \tfrac{\log W}{W}} \qquad\qquad \text{\% } Z_2 \text{ is independent of } Z_1.$$

Although the probability of $W := V_1^2 + V_2^2 < 1$, provided that $W \neq 0$, is $\pi/4 \approx 0.785 \cdots$, the method of Marsaglia (polar rejection method) is generally more efficient than the Box-Muller method.

Indeed, the random variables $V_i = 2U_i - 1$ are uniformly distributed on $(-1, 1)$, namely, $V_i \sim \mathcal{U}(-1, 1)$. If we define the disk $\mathcal{D}$ by

$$\mathcal{D} = \left\{ (V_1, V_2) \; : \; 0 < W := V_1^2 + V_2^2 < 1 \right\},$$

then the surviving (V_1, V_2) of the Marsaglia's algorithm are uniformly distributed on $\mathcal{D}$ with density $f(V_1, V_2) = \frac{1}{\pi}$ for $(V_1, V_2) \in \mathcal{D}$. Thus, defining a transformation from the disk $\mathcal{D}$ into the unit square $\mathcal{S} := (0, 1)^2$ by

$$\begin{bmatrix} X_1 \\ X_2 \end{bmatrix} = \begin{bmatrix} V_1^2 + V_2^2 \\ \frac{1}{2\pi} \arctan \frac{V_2}{V_1} \end{bmatrix},$$

makes it possible to apply Theorem 5.3. It is easy to show that (X_1, X_2) is uniformly distributed on the unit square $\mathcal{S}$. Therefore, the transformation that describes the Box-Muller method defined in (5.7) can be applied. However, from the transformation above it is easy to conclude that the relations

$$\cos(2\pi X_2) = \frac{V_1}{\sqrt{V_1^2 + V_2^2}}, \qquad \sin(2\pi X_2) = \frac{V_2}{\sqrt{V_1^2 + V_2^2}} \qquad (5.9)$$

hold, which means that it is no longer necessary to evaluate trigonometric functions appearing in (5.7). Inserting (5.9) into (5.7) and simplifying the equations give

$$Y_1 = V_1 \sqrt{-2 \frac{\log W}{W}}, \qquad Y_2 = V_2 \sqrt{-2 \frac{\log W}{W}}. \tag{5.10}$$

With these relations, the method of Marsaglia, shown in Algorithm 5.6, modifies the Box-Muller method by preparing the inputs X_1 and X_2 in a clever way, by using the acceptance-rejection method. An implementation of the method of Marsaglia is shown in Fig. 5.5.

```
——————————————————— Marsaglia.m ———————————————————
function nor = Marsaglia(seed, howMany)

rand('state', seed); nor = zeros(howMany+1, 1); k = 0;
while (k < howMany)
    u1 = rand; u2 = rand; v1 = 2*u1 - 1; v2 = 2*u2 - 1; rad = v1^2 + v2^2;
    if ((0 < rad) && (rad < 1))
        z1 = v1 * sqrt ( -2*log(rad)/rad ); z2 = v2 * sqrt ( -2*log(rad)/rad );
        nor(k+1) = z1; nor(k+2) = z2; k = k+2;
    end
end
nor = nor(1:howMany);
```

Fig. 5.5   An implementation of the *Marsaglia* method to draw normally distributed random variates

5.3.3   *Multivariate Normal Variables*

The previous sections and the algorithms therein provide us with drawing independent normal deviates. In many applications, however, one has to generate random samples that are somehow *dependent* of each other: there is a need to draw correlated random variates.

Now, let us first recall the general n-dimensional density function

$$\phi_{\mu, \sqrt{\Sigma}}(x) = \frac{1}{(2\pi)^{n/2}} \frac{1}{(\det \Sigma)^{1/2}} \exp\left\{ -\frac{1}{2}(x - \mu)^T \Sigma^{-1} (x - \mu) \right\}$$

of the *multivariate normal distribution* with expected mean vector

$$\mu = \mathbb{E}\left[X\right], \qquad [X_1, X_2, \ldots, X_n]^T,$$

and the covariance matrix $\Sigma = (\sigma_{ij})$,

$$\sigma_{ij} = (\mathbb{Cov}\left[X\right])_{ij} := \mathbb{E}\left[(X_i - \mu_i)(X_j - \mu_j)\right].$$

The correlation coefficients and the variances are

$$\rho_{ij} = \frac{\sigma_{ij}}{\sigma_i \sigma_j}, \qquad \sigma_i^2 = \sigma_{ii},$$

respectively. The matrix Σ is *symmetric* and *positive definite* in case $\det \Sigma \neq 0$. That is, the matrix Σ satisfies

$$\Sigma^T = \Sigma, \quad \text{and} \quad x^T \Sigma x > 0$$

for all nonzero vector $x \in \mathbb{R}^n$. So, it is possible to use a fast algorithm, the *Cholesky factorisation*, to split Σ into its *LU-decomposition* as

$$\Sigma = LL^T,$$

where L is a *lower triangular matrix*. This factorisation of Σ exists and is unique if $\det \Sigma \neq 0$. See Example 5.3 below for an illustration of the Cholesky factorisation.

Now, let $Z \sim \mathcal{N}(0, I)$ and use the transformation

$$y = L z,$$

where z is a realisation of Z. Here, I denotes the identity matrix of size n. Then, it is easy to show that

$$dy = |\det L| \, dz = (\det \Sigma)^{1/2} \, dz. \tag{5.11}$$

Moreover,

$$z^T z = (L^{-1} y)^T (L^{-1} y) = y^T \left(L^{-1} \right)^T L^{-1} y = y^T (LL^T)^{-1} y$$
$$= y^T \Sigma^{-1} y. \tag{5.12}$$

The use of these last two equalities shows that

$$\phi_{0,I}(z) \, dz = \frac{1}{(2\pi)^{n/2}} \exp\left\{ -\frac{1}{2} z^T z \right\} dz$$
$$= \frac{1}{(2\pi)^{n/2}} \frac{1}{(\det \Sigma)^{1/2}} \exp\left\{ -\frac{1}{2} y^T \Sigma^{-1} y \right\} dy$$
$$= \phi_{0,\sqrt{\Sigma}}(y) \, dy.$$

In other words,

$$\text{if } Z \sim \mathcal{N}(0, I), \quad \text{then} \quad LZ \sim \mathcal{N}(0, \Sigma)$$

and, hence, the translation by the mean vector μ satisfies

$$X := \mu + LZ \sim \mathcal{N}(\mu, \Sigma). \tag{5.13}$$

Out of this observation, we build an algorithm to generate normal samples for a given mean vector $\mu \in \mathbb{R}^n$ and a covariance matrix $\Sigma \in \mathbb{R}^{n \times n}$: generate standard normal variates and apply Cholesky decomposition to the covariance matrix. Then apply the transformation in (5.13). An algorithm for generating correlated normal variates and an implementation of it are shown, respectively, in Algorithm 5.7 and Fig. 5.6.

Algorithm 5.7 Correlated Normal Random Variates

Calculate the Cholesky factorisation, $\Sigma = L L^T$,

Generate $Z \sim \mathcal{N}(0, I)$ componentwise by drawing independent variates

$$Z_i \sim \mathcal{N}(0, 1), \quad \text{for } i = 1, 2, \ldots, n,$$

Return $X := \mu + L Z$

```
                         ──── MultivariateNormalRandom.m ────
function z = MultivariateNormalRandom(mu, Sigma, howMany)
% generates multivariate normal variates with given mu (vector), Sigma (matrix)

n = length(mu); z = zeros(howMany, n); mu = mu(:); % column vector
L = chol(Sigma); % Cholesky factorization of Sigma
% Remark: in Matlab chol produces an upper triangular matrix
for i = 1:howMany
    z(i,:) = mu' + randn(1,n) * L;
end
```

Fig. 5.6   An implementation of Algorithm 5.7 for generating correlated normal vector random variates

Notice that in the case of a one-dimensional distribution, we have

$$\Sigma = \sigma^2 \in \mathbb{R} \quad \text{and} \quad \mu \in \mathbb{R}$$

so that

$$Z \sim \mathcal{N}(0, 1) \implies X := \mu + \sigma Z \sim \mathcal{N}(\mu, \sigma^2).$$

This was shown and has been used in previous sections of the text. In case of two dimensions, for instance, the following example illustrates the factorisation of the covariance matrix.

Example 5.3. Let $\Sigma = (\sigma_{ij}) \in \mathbb{R}^{2 \times 2}$ be the covariance matrix, writing the Cholesky decomposition of $\Sigma = L L^T$ in the form,

$$\Sigma = \begin{bmatrix} \sigma_{11} & \sigma_{21} \\ \sigma_{21} & \sigma_{22} \end{bmatrix} = \begin{bmatrix} \ell_{11} & 0 \\ \ell_{21} & \ell_{22} \end{bmatrix} \begin{bmatrix} \ell_{11} & \ell_{21} \\ 0 & \ell_{22} \end{bmatrix} = LL^T$$

implies a set of equations that have to be solved. These are

$$\ell_{11}^2 = \sigma_{11},$$
$$\ell_{11}\ell_{21} = \sigma_{12},$$
$$\ell_{21}^2 + \ell_{22}^2 = \sigma_{22}.$$

Solving these equations for ℓ_{ij} implies that

$$\ell_{11}^2 = \sigma_{11},$$
$$\ell_{21} = \frac{\sigma_{12}}{\ell_{11}},$$
$$\ell_{22}^2 = \sigma_{22} - \ell_{21}^2.$$

Thus, using the relations $\sigma_{ii} = \sigma_i^2$ and $\sigma_{ij} = \rho_{ij}\sigma_i\sigma_j$, it is deduced that

$$L = \begin{bmatrix} \sigma_1 & 0 \\ \rho\sigma_2 & \sigma_2\sqrt{1-\rho^2} \end{bmatrix}.$$

Thus, if Z_1 and Z_2 are two independent standard normally distributed random variables, then

$$X_1 = \sigma_1 Z_1,$$
$$X_2 = \sigma_2\left(\rho Z_1 + \sqrt{1-\rho^2}Z_2\right)$$

are two independent normally distributed random variables with zero mean vector and Σ variance-covariance matrix. This simple observation will be used later in the sequel when simulating two asset prices that are correlated.

Exercise 5.3. Let the covariance matrix Σ be defined as

$$\Sigma = \begin{bmatrix} \sigma_{11} & \sigma_{21} & \sigma_{31} \\ \sigma_{21} & \sigma_{22} & \sigma_{32} \\ \sigma_{31} & \sigma_{32} & \sigma_{33} \end{bmatrix} = \begin{bmatrix} \ell_{11} & 0 & 0 \\ \ell_{21} & \ell_{22} & 0 \\ \ell_{31} & \ell_{32} & \ell_{33} \end{bmatrix} \begin{bmatrix} \ell_{11} & \ell_{21} & \ell_{31} \\ 0 & \ell_{22} & \ell_{32} \\ 0 & 0 & \ell_{33} \end{bmatrix} = LL^T.$$

Write the entries ℓ_{ij} of the lower triangular matrix L explicitly in this Cholesky decomposition.

Following the previous example and the exercise, it is not difficult to write down an algorithm for Cholesky factorisation of a symmetric, positive definite $n \times n$ matrix Σ. In Algorithm 5.8, we present the Cholesky factorisation method and conclude this section.

Algorithm 5.8 Cholesky Factorisation

---

for $k = 1, 2, \ldots, n$ **do**

$$\ell_{kk} = \left(\sigma_{kk} - \sum_{s=1}^{k-1} \ell_{ks}^2 \right)^{1/2} \qquad \text{\% diagonal entries}$$

    for $i = k+1, k+2, \ldots, n$ **do**

$$\ell_{ik} = \frac{1}{\ell_{kk}} \left(\sigma_{ik} - \sum_{s=1}^{k-1} \ell_{is}\ell_{ks} \right) \qquad \text{\% off-diagonal entries}$$

    end for

end for

Outlook

Due to its importance in scientific and, in particular, financial applications, fast generation of random variates from the (standard) normal distribution is highly appreciated. Being one of the oldest transformation methods, the Box-Muller method has now extensively used variants that are combined with many other techniques. We refer to [Thomas *et al.* (2007)] and [Marsaglia and Tsang (2000)] for possible extensions as well as other algorithmic approaches used to generate high quality normal random numbers.

Details of matrix factorisations can be found, for instance, in (Cheney and Kincaid, 1994, Chapter 4), which we find it very helpful, in particular, for the Cholesky factorisation.

5.4 Monte Carlo Integration

Loosely speaking, when numerical integration is considered, generally one thinks about quadrature formulae that are in fact very efficient in integration of functions of one or two variables. However, as the number of variables increases, these methods become inefficient or difficult to implement. An alternative approach is to resort to random sampling based on Monte Carlo integration, or Monte Carlo method.

Consider the problem of computing a multidimensional integral of the form

$$I = \int_A g(x)\, dx,$$

where $A \subset \mathbb{R}^n$ is Lebesgue measurable. We may estimate I by randomly sampling a sequence of points $x_i \in A$, $i = 1, 2, \ldots, N$, and building the estimator

$$\hat{I}_N = \frac{\text{vol}(A)}{N} \sum_{i=1}^{N} g(x_i),$$

where $\text{vol}(A)$ denotes the volume of the region A. Quite often we consider the unit hypercube

$$A = [0,1]^n = [0,1] \times [0,1] \times \cdots \times [0,1],$$

so that $\text{vol}(A) = 1$. The estimator $\hat{I}_N$ is then regarded as the average of the function g on the unit hypercube A. The *strong law of large numbers* implies that

$$\lim_{N \to \infty} \hat{I}_N = I$$

with probability one. See Theorem 5.4 on page 163.

More generally, if X denotes a vector random variable with joint density function $f(x)$, $x \in \mathbb{R}^n$, then the Monte Carlo integration may be used to estimate the *expected value*

$$\mathbb{E}\left[g(X)\right] = \int_{\mathbb{R}^n} g(x) f(x)\, dx$$

of an arbitrary function g of X. The question is how to choose the random sampling to estimate this integral and whether the method converges. Consider a simple case:

$$\int_0^1 g(x)\, dx.$$

This integral may be thought to be the expected value $\mathbb{E}\left[g(U)\right]$ of a uniform random variable $U \sim \mathcal{U}(0,1)$ over the interval $(0,1)$. Then, the idea of Monte Carlo integration is to generate a sequence $\{U_i\}_{i=1}^{N}$ of *independent* samples from the uniform distribution and then to evaluate the sample mean

$$\frac{1}{N} \sum_{i=1}^{N} g(U_i).$$

One of the main advantages of such a method is that it does not require recalculation of the integrand when more samples are needed in order to increase the accuracy of the approximation. Here is an example how the Monte Carlo integration works.

Example 5.4. Consider the integral

$$\int_0^1 4\sqrt{1 - x^2}\, dx = \pi \approx 3.1416.$$

The following MATLAB code,

```
>> clear all, rand('state', 13); g = inline('4.*sqrt(1-x.^2)');
>> app1 = g(rand(1,1000)); pi1 = mean(app1)
pi1 =
    3.0856
```

may be used to obtain an approximation to this integral, which produces 3.0856. Increasing the number of samples used will hopefully yield better results. For instance, another 2000 random numbers can be added to the first one by

```
>> app2 = g(rand(1,2000)); pi2 = mean(app2)
pi2 =
    3.1590
>> mean([app1 app2]) % equals
ans =
    3.1346
>> rand('state', 13); pi3 = mean( g(rand(1,3000)))
pi3 =
    3.1346
```

so that the new approximations to π are 3.1590 and 3.1346 by using, respectively, 2000 and 3000 uniformly distributed random samples. Quite a large number of samples must be taken in this plain Monte Carlo integration for an acceptable estimate.

Although the underlying quantity of interest is an expectation of a random variable, namely an integral, the method of Monte Carlo integration is sometimes called as *Monte Carlo simulation*. In fact, Monte Carlo method may be regarded as a mathematical experiment. These experiments, even the scenarios generated by random sampling, are named as *replications*. You would expect better results if you use larger number of samples, or replications in Monte Carlo method. This is indeed true, as long as the realisations represented by random numbers are really random and independent.

The Monte Carlo method is based on a sound mathematical background: the *strong law of large numbers* and the *central limit theorem*. For a family of independent identically distributed (*i.i.d.*) random variables $\{X_i\}_{i=1}^{\infty}$, the partial sum S_N is defined by

$$S_N = \sum_{i=1}^{N} X_i = X_1 + X_2 + \cdots + X_N. \qquad (5.14)$$

Associated with S_N is the *sample mean* $\bar{X}_N$ which is another random variable given by

$$\bar{X}_N = \frac{1}{N} S_N = \frac{1}{N} \sum_{i=1}^{N} X_i. \tag{5.15}$$

This is an *unbiased* estimator of the parameter

$$\mu = \mathbb{E}\left[X_i\right]$$

of the *i.i.d.* sample X_i. In other words, the expectation of $\bar{X}_N$ is the same as μ, since

$$\mathbb{E}\left[\bar{X}_N\right] = \frac{1}{N}\mathbb{E}\left[S_N\right] = \mathbb{E}\left[X_i\right] = \mu, \tag{5.16}$$

due to the *i.i.d.* sequence $\{X_i\}_{i=1}^{\infty}$. The strong law of large numbers ensures that the sample mean converges to the mean of the *i.i.d.* sequence of random variables almost surely. This theorem reads as follow.

Theorem 5.4 (Strong Law of Large Numbers). *For a family of i.i.d. random variables* $\{X_i\}_{i=1}^{\infty}$, *suppose that the mean* $\mu = \mathbb{E}\left[X_i\right]$ *exists. Then,*

$$\lim_{N \to \infty} \bar{X}_N = \lim_{N \to \infty} \frac{1}{N} \sum_{i=1}^{N} X_i = \mu$$

with probability one.

Remark 5.2. The theorem can also be considered as

$$\mathbb{P}\left\{\lim_{N \to \infty} \frac{S_N}{N} = \mu\right\} = 1.$$

The *weak* version of the law of large numbers gives a similar conclusion, namely,

$$\lim_{N \to \infty} \mathbb{P}\left\{\left|\frac{S_N}{N} - \mu\right| > \epsilon\right\} = 0,$$

for every $\epsilon > 0$.

Moreover, we may quantify the quality of the estimator $\bar{X}_N$ by considering the expectation of the *squared-error* as

$$\begin{aligned}
\mathbb{E}\left[(\bar{X}_N - \mu)^2\right] &= \mathbb{E}\left[\bar{X}_N^2\right] - \left(\mathbb{E}\left[\bar{X}_N\right]\right)^2 \\
&= \mathbb{V}\mathrm{ar}\left[\bar{X}_N\right] = \frac{1}{N^2}\mathbb{V}\mathrm{ar}\left[\sum_{i=1}^{N} X_i\right] \\
&= \frac{1}{N^2}\sum_{i=1}^{N}\mathbb{V}\mathrm{ar}\left[X_i\right] \\
&= \frac{\sigma^2}{N},
\end{aligned} \tag{5.17}$$

where $\sigma^2 = \mathbb{V}\mathrm{ar}\,[X_i]$ may be estimated by a sample variance, say $\bar{\sigma}_N^2$. Here, we emphasise again that the X_i are *i.i.d.* sequence of random variables, and the existence of the finite variance is implicitly assumed. Thus, increasing the number N of the samples, or replications if realisations are considered, improves the estimate in the sense of (5.17).

Therefore, beside an unbiased sample mean $\bar{X}_N$, an unbiased sample variance $\bar{\sigma}_N^2$ may be given as

$$\bar{\sigma}_N^2 = \frac{1}{N-1}\sum_{i=1}^{N}\left(X_i - \bar{X}_N\right)^2 = \frac{N}{N-1}\left(\frac{1}{N}\sum_{i=1}^{N}X_i^2 - \bar{X}_N^2\right). \qquad (5.18)$$

It is not difficult to show that

$$\mathbb{E}\left[\bar{\sigma}_N^2\right] = \mathbb{V}\mathrm{ar}\,[X_i] = \sigma^2$$

holds by using the second equality in (5.18). Hence, $\bar{\sigma}_N^2$ is indeed an unbiased estimator for the sample variance.

On the other hand, based on the central limit theorem, a *confidence interval* is associated with the value $\mu = \mathbb{E}\,[X_i] = \mathbb{E}\left[\bar{X}_N\right]$. In Monte Carlo simulations it is almost always customary to define a confidence interval for the approximations obtained. This is based on the following theorem.

Theorem 5.5 (Central Limit Theorem). *For a family of i.i.d. random variables $\{X_i\}_{i=1}^{\infty}$ with finite mean μ and finite variance $\sigma^2 > 0$, let*

$$Z_N = \frac{S_N - N\mu}{\sigma\sqrt{N}} = \frac{\bar{X}_N - \mu}{\sqrt{\sigma^2/N}}.$$

Then, for $x \in \mathbb{R}$,

$$\lim_{N\to\infty}\mathbb{P}\left\{Z_N \leq x\right\} = \Phi(x) = \frac{1}{\sqrt{2\pi}}\int_{-\infty}^{x}e^{-\xi^2/2}\,d\xi,$$

where Φ is the standard normal distribution function.

Thus, according to the central limit theorem, the probability of the partial sum S_N can be approximated by the normal distribution $\mathcal{N}(N\mu, N\sigma^2)$ with mean $N\mu$ and variance $N\sigma^2$.

Now, a $(1-\alpha)$th level of *confidence interval* for a random variable Z is defined by $[-z_{1-\alpha/2},\, z_{1-\alpha/2}]$ such that the *critical number* $z_{1-\alpha/2}$ is found from the equation

$$\mathbb{P}\left\{-z_{1-\alpha/2} \leq Z \leq z_{1-\alpha/2}\right\} = 1 - \alpha. \tag{5.19}$$

If, further, the random variable Z is standard normally distributed, then it is possible to rewrite (5.19) as

$$1 - \alpha = \Phi(z_{1-\alpha/2}) - \Phi(-z_{1-\alpha/2}) = 2\,\Phi(z_{1-\alpha/2}) - 1.$$

In other words,

$$\Phi(z_{1-\alpha/2}) = 1 - \alpha/2. \tag{5.20}$$

Therefore, the critical number $z_{1-\alpha/2}$ for the $(1-\alpha)$th level of confidence for standard normally distributed random variable Z can be obtained by inverting the distribution function. Using the *inverse* of the *error function*, erf^{-1}, the critical number is given by

$$z_{1-\alpha/2} = \Phi^{-1}\left(1 - \alpha/2\right) = \sqrt{2}\,\mathrm{erf}^{-1}(1-\alpha). \tag{5.21}$$

Among the critical numbers there are two of them that are most commonly used. These correspond to the choices $\alpha = 0.05$ and $\alpha = 0.01$. That is,

$$z_{0.975} = \Phi^{-1}\left(1 - 0.05/2\right) \approx 1.96, \quad \text{for} \quad \alpha = 0.05, \tag{5.22}$$

$$z_{0.995} = \Phi^{-1}\left(1 - 0.01/2\right) \approx 2.58, \quad \text{for} \quad \alpha = 0.01, \tag{5.23}$$

for the $(1-\alpha)$th level of confidence interval for a standard normally distributed random variable.

Thus, if the number of samples N is large enough, then the random variable

$$Z = \frac{\bar{X}_N - \mu}{\sqrt{\bar{\sigma}_N^2/N}}$$

can be considered to be *approximately* standard normally distributed by the central limit theorem. Note that the unbiased estimator $\bar{\sigma}_N^2$ for the variance is used. Therefore,

$$1 - \alpha \approx \mathbb{P}\left\{-z_{1-\alpha/2} \leq \frac{\bar{X}_N - \mu}{\sqrt{\bar{\sigma}_N^2/N}} \leq z_{1-\alpha/2}\right\}$$

$$= \mathbb{P}\left\{\bar{X}_N - z_{1-\alpha/2}\sqrt{\bar{\sigma}_N^2/N} \leq \mu \leq \bar{X}_N + z_{1-\alpha/2}\sqrt{\bar{\sigma}_N^2/N}\right\}$$

implies that an approximate $(1 - \alpha)$th level confidence interval for the parameter $\mu = \mathbb{E}\left[X_i\right]$ may be computed from the sample mean $\bar{X}_N$ and the sample variance $\bar{\sigma}_N^2$ as

$$\left[\bar{X}_N - z_{1-\alpha/2}\sqrt{\bar{\sigma}_N^2/N},\ \bar{X}_N + z_{1-\alpha/2}\sqrt{\bar{\sigma}_N^2/N}\right]. \tag{5.24}$$

The idea is that if we repeat the sampling and the estimation procedure over and over in Monte Carlo simulations, the percentage of cases in which the "true" value falls within the interval in (5.24) should approximately be $100 \times (1 - \alpha)$ in Monte Carlo simulations.

The length of the confidence interval in (5.24) is $2z_{1-\alpha/2}\sqrt{\bar{\sigma}_N^2/N}$, which tends to zero as N increases if the sample variance is bounded. This also implies that the rate of convergence of Monte Carlo method is of order $\mathcal{O}\left(\sqrt{\bar{\sigma}_N^2/N}\right)$. Moreover, the rate may be improved by reducing the sample variance $\bar{\sigma}_N^2$. Variance reduction techniques for option pricing will be introduced later in this chapter.

Outlook

Monte Carlo integration methods [Hammersley and Handscomb (1964)] are regarded as algorithms for the approximate evaluation of definite integrals, usually multidimensional ones. Monte Carlo methods, however, randomly choose the points at which the integrand is evaluated so that the estimation of the integral is based on the central limit theorem. Some of the references we may refer to are [Caflisch (1998); Glasserman (2004); Kwok (1998); Niederreiter (1992)], which also include techniques to reduce the variance of the samples used in integration. Some of these techniques to reduce the variance are discussed also in Section 5.6 and Section 5.7 for pricing options by Monte Carlo methods.

5.5 Option Pricing by Monte Carlo Simulation

An extremely useful property of the Black-Scholes option valuation is that the price may be regarded as the discounted average (expected) payoff, under the risk-neutrality condition, that is, when $\mu = r$. In other words, you may reproduce the option value by setting $\mu = r$ in the asset model and computing the average of the payoff over all possible asset paths. In practice, this may be done by Monte Carlo simulation, averaging the payoff values obtained by using a large number of asset paths. Particularly for European options, the asset prices at maturity are enough to calculate the payoff values; computations of the whole paths are not necessary unless the options are path dependent.

For path dependent options, however, for each replication in Monte Carlo method, necessarily the whole path of the underlying asset prices has to be calculated. The payoff values, which depend on the history, are then obtained at maturity. *Monte Carlo* method for pricing European options is summarised in Algorithm 5.9, which shows some possible actions to be taken when applying the method. In fact, this algorithm is a generic one, and it might need modifications depending not only on the properties of the option contract, but also on the model for the asset prices.

Algorithm 5.9 Monte Carlo Simulation for European Options

Given: S_0, r, σ, T, N

Assumption: $dS = rS\,dt + \sigma S\,dW$

for $k = 1, 2, \ldots, N$ **do**

  if the option is *path dependent* **then**

    simulate a path to get $(S_T)_k$ % by numerical methods for SDEs

    calculate the *payoff*, V_k

  else

    draw $Z_k \sim \mathcal{N}(0,1)$

    $(S_T)_k = S_0 \exp\left\{\left(r - \tfrac{1}{2}\sigma^2\right)T + \sigma Z_k \sqrt{T}\right\}$

    calculate the *payoff*, V_k

  end if

end for

$\widehat{\mathbb{E}}(V) = \frac{1}{N}\sum_{k=1}^{N} V_k$ % estimate of risk-neutral expectation

$\widehat{V} = e^{-rT}\widehat{\mathbb{E}}(V)$ % discounted variable

Return: $\widehat{V}$ % approximate value of option

The resulting $\widehat{V}$ of Algorithm 5.9 is the desired approximate option price. That is,

$$\widehat{V} = e^{-rT}\widehat{\mathbb{E}}(V) \approx V(S_0, 0) = e^{-rT}\mathbb{E}_{\mathbb{Q}}\left[V(S_T, T)\right],$$

where e^{-rT} is the discounting factor. Also, the risk-neutral expectation of the payoff in the continuous model is approximated by the sample mean denoted by $\widehat{\mathbb{E}}(V)$.

Moreover, recall that in the risk-neutral valuation principle for modelling of options the return rate μ of the asset prices S_t has to be replaced by the risk-free interest rate r. Following this principle,[4] Algorithm 5.9 assumes that the paths of the asset prices S_t follow a geometric Brownian motion of the form

$$dS_t = rS_t \, dt + \sigma S_t \, dW_t,$$

with a given initial price S_0 at time $t = 0$.

In this simple form, the Monte Carlo method can only be applied to European options. Note that Algorithm 5.9, although it includes some sort of path dependence, does not check whether the option is preferable to be exercised before maturity. Pricing American options by Monte Carlo simulation needs greater efforts and is an active research area.

Example 5.5. Now, we use the Monte Carlo method to value a European call option with payoff $V(S_T, T) = \max\{S_T - K, 0\}$. We will use the Black-Scholes closed-form solution formula to compute the exact value and see how well the Monte Carlo method performs. The parameters related to asset prices as well as the option are given in the MATLAB script shown in Fig. 5.7.

Actually, the Monte Carlo method is driven by the function in Fig. 5.8, which use only the final values of the asset price. It is also possible to obtain these values by simulating the paths of a geometric Brownian motion. This can be done either by using the closed-form solution or by numerical integration of SDEs. Such a simulation using the solution of the geometric Brownian motion was given in Fig. 3.12 on page 104. However, in most cases paths may be approximated numerically by Euler-Maruyama method for instance. Recall that this method was introduced in Chapter 3 and implemented by a MATLAB script shown in Fig. 3.7 on page 81.

In Fig. 5.9, the values obtained by Monte Carlo method are depicted. The corresponding 95% confidence intervals to the number of replications used by the method are shown by vertical line segments in the figure. Such a graph may be useful to illustrate the convergence of the Monte Carlo method to the closed-form solution shown by the horizontal line.

---

[4]A formal, or a more mathematical approach includes the equivalent measures (or martingale measures) which we try to avoid in this book. So, we refer to advanced texts for equivalent measures and change of measures in integration.

```
____________________ MC_Call_Eg.m ____________________
% test MC_Call
clear all, close all, randn('state',13);
S0 = 10; K = 9; sigma = 0.1; r = 0.06; T = 1; M = 17;

for i = 1:M
    NRepl = 2^(i+4);
    [P, CI] = MonteCarlo_Call(S0,K,r,sigma,T,NRepl);
    Price(i) = P; confInterval(i,:) = CI;
end
format long; Price, confInterval
[C, Cdelta, P, Pdelta] = CallPut_Delta(S0,K,r,sigma,T);
plot([1:M], Price, 'o'), hold on
plot([0:M+1], ones(1,M+2)*C, 'r')
for i=1:M
    plot([i,i], confInterval(i,:), 'g--' )
end
xlabel('M (2^{M+4} Number of Samples)','FontSize',12), ylabel('V','FontSize',12)
print -r900 -deps '../figures/MC_Call_eg'
```

Fig. 5.7   Monte Carlo simulation for different number of sample paths. The code uses the function in Fig. 5.8

```
____________________ MonteCarlo_Call.m ____________________
function [Price, CI] = MonteCarlo_Call(S0,K,r,sigma,T,NRepl)
% NRepl : number of replications (paths)

muT = (r - 0.5*sigma^2)*T; sigmaT = sigma * sqrt(T);
DiscPayoff = exp(-r*T) * max( 0, S0*exp(muT+sigmaT*randn(NRepl,1)) - K );
% Matlab command for the Mean and Standard Deviation and the Confidence Interval
%[Price, SDev, CI] = normfit(DiscPayoff);
Price = mean(DiscPayoff); width = 1.96*std(DiscPayoff)/sqrt(NRepl);
CI = [Price-width, Price+width];
```

Fig. 5.8   Monte Carlo simulation for European call

The following example illustrates the Monte Carlo method in case the option payoff depends on the history of asset prices. Beside this path dependence, the model for the asset prices is not a geometric Brownian motion any more. Moreover, it involves a stochastic volatility governed by a mean reverting process. Thus, it is more convenient to apply numerical integration of SDEs, such as Euler-Maruyama method, rather than looking for a closed-form solution, if there is any.

Example 5.6. Consider an Asian option that is also European: the price of an Asian option depends on the average and, hence, the history of the process S_t. One of the possible ways of taking an average is the *arithmetic mean*: Assume that the price S_t is observed at discrete times $t = t_i$ for $i = 1, 2, \ldots, N$ with equidistant time interval $\Delta t := T/N$, where T is the maturity. Hence, $t_i = i \Delta t$ for $i = 0, 1, \ldots, N$. Then, the arithmetic mean,

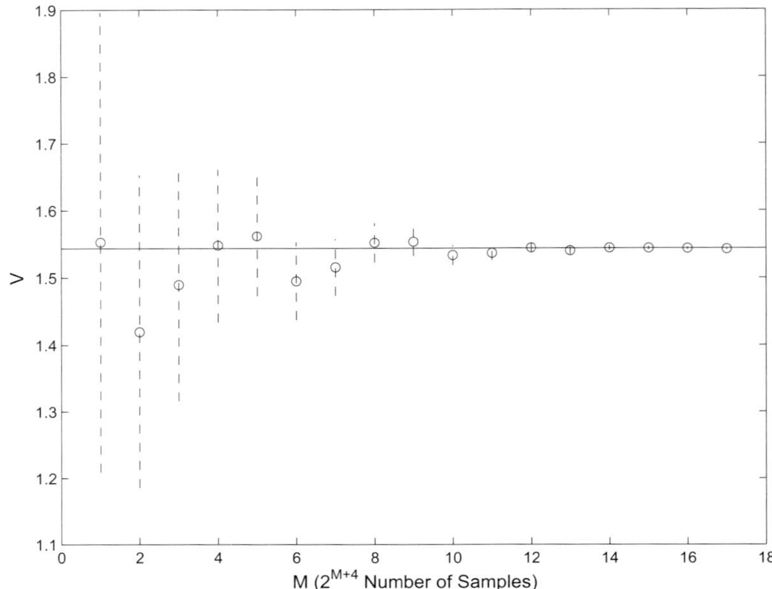

Fig. 5.9   Convergence of Monte Carlo approximations, Algorithm 5.9, to European call

$\bar{S}_t$, becomes

$$\bar{S}_t = \frac{1}{N} \sum_{i=1}^{N} S_{t_i} = \frac{1}{T} \sum_{i=1}^{N} \Delta t \, S_{t_i}.$$

On the other hand, the arithmetic mean $\bar{S}_t$ can also be regarded as an average of the continuously sampled observation until time T. In other words, it may be considered to be an approximation to the integral

$$\hat{S} = \frac{1}{T} \int_0^T S_t \, dt.$$

In this example, a 2-dimensional stochastic process is assumed to be the market model described by the following SDEs

$$\begin{aligned}
dS_t &= \mu S_t \, dt + \sigma_t \sqrt{S_t} \, dW_t^S, \\
d\sigma_t &= (\sigma_0 - \sigma_t) \, dt + \sqrt{\sigma_t} \, dW_t^\sigma,
\end{aligned} \tag{5.25}$$

where W_t^S and W_t^σ are *independent* Wiener processes. The initial condition is given by

$$S_{t=0} = S_0, \qquad \sigma_{t=0} = \sigma_0.$$

For the simulation of the paths, the Euler-Maruyama method is applied to the 2-dimensional stochastic process in (5.25). Monte Carlo simulation seems to be the most reasonable method to approximate the value $e^{-rT}\,\mathbb{E}\,[V(S_T, T)]$ of the *arithmetic mean Asian option* with the payoff

$$V(S_T, T) = \max\left\{\bar{S}_t - K,\, 0\right\}.$$

The MATLAB script given in Fig. 5.10 is an implementation of the Monte Carlo method, in which Euler-Maruyama method is used for numerically solving the underlying SDEs. The code is vectorised over the replications; and the realisations of the paths of (5.25) are not stored, since the sum of the asset prices is necessary and sufficient to calculate the payoff.

```
————————————————— Asian_Arithmetic.m ——————————
% Euler-Maruyama: Asian option with Arithmetic Mean
clear all, close all, randn('state',13)
K = 1; r = 0.05; T = 1; N = 2^8; dt = T/N; M = 10000;
mu = r; S_0 = 1; sigma_0 = 0.8;
S = S_0*ones(M,1); Sigma = sigma_0*ones(M,1); sumOfS = S;
for j = 1:N
    dW_1 = sqrt(dt)*randn(M,1); dW_2 = sqrt(dt)*randn(M,1); % independent of dW_1
    % To be safe!
    S = abs(S + dt*mu*S + sqrt(S).*Sigma.*dW_1);
    Sigma = abs(Sigma + dt*(sigma_0 - Sigma) + sqrt(Sigma).*dW_2);
    sumOfS = sumOfS + S;
end
meanOfX = sumOfS/(N+1); Price = exp(-r*T)*mean(max(0,meanOfX-K))
```

Fig. 5.10 Approximation of an Asian Option: using the Euler-Maruyama method and then applying the Monte Carlo Method

Readers are encouraged to finalise the implementation in Fig. 5.10 by including a confidence interval for the approximated option price.

Exercise 5.4. The payoff of a *lookback* option depends on the maximum or minimum value of the asset price S_t reaches during the life time of the option. For example, if we denote $S^{max} := \max_{0 \le t \le T} S_t$, then

- a *fixed strike lookback call* has the payoff

$$(S^{max} - K)^+ := \max\{S^{max} - K,\, 0\},$$

- a *floating strike lookback put* has the payoff $S^{max} - S_T$.

Write down the similar definitions, using $S^{min} := \min_{0 \le t \le T} S_t$, for *fixed strike put* and *floating strike call*. Write a Monte Carlo method to price any of such lookback options.

Exercise 5.5. Monte Carlo methods can also be used to calculate the delta, Δ, of options. This can be achieved by using a small value of h and applying a *finite difference* approximation,

$$\frac{\partial V(S,t)}{\partial S} \approx \frac{V(S+h,t) - V(S,t)}{h}.$$

Thus, write a Monte Carlo algorithm to approximate the time-zero Δ (i.e., at $S = S_0$) for a vanilla call option, and compare it with the exact value.

5.5.1   *Correlated Assets*

Assume that asset prices $S_t^{(i)}$ follow geometric Brownian motions with returns μ_i and *volatility vector*, denoted by $b_i = (b_{i1}, b_{i2}, \ldots, b_{in})$. Then, the volatility matrix, say B, is defined as

$$B(t) = (b_{ij}(t))_{i,j=1}^n = \begin{bmatrix} b_{11}(t) & b_{12}(t) & \cdots & b_{1n}(t) \\ b_{21}(t) & b_{22}(t) & \cdots & b_{2n}(t) \\ \vdots & \vdots & \ddots & \vdots \\ b_{i1}(t) & b_{i2}(t) & \cdots & b_{in}(t) \end{bmatrix}.$$

With such a volatility matrix at hand, it is possible to consider an n-factor market model by assuming that the number of assets and the number of driving, independent Wiener processes are the same. The Geometric Brownian motion for each of the assets, therefore, can be written as

$$dS_t^{(i)} = S_t^{(i)} \left(\mu_i(t)\, dt + \sum_{j=1}^n b_{ij}(t)\, dW_t^{(j)} \right), \quad i = 1, 2, \ldots, n, \quad (5.26)$$

where μ_i is the instantaneous drift of the ith asset. Hence, it is easy to show that the solutions $S_t^{(i)}$ of (5.26) are given by

$$S_t^{(i)} = S_0^{(i)} \exp \left\{ \int_0^t \left(\mu_i - \frac{1}{2} \sum_{j=1}^n b_{ij}^2 \right) ds + \sum_{j=1}^n \int_0^t b_{ij}\, dW_s^{(j)} \right\}. \quad (5.27)$$

In particular, when $\mu_i(t) \equiv \mu_i$ and $b_{ij}(t) \equiv b_{ij}$ are constant, these can further be simplified to

$$S_t^{(i)} = S_0^{(i)} \exp \left\{ \left(\mu_i - \frac{1}{2} \sum_{j=1}^n b_{ij}^2 \right) t + \sum_{j=1}^n b_{ij} W_t^{(j)} \right\}. \quad (5.28)$$

Often, it is plausible to have a scalar volatility σ_i for the asset $S_t^{(i)}$ process rather than a volatility vector b_i. Thus, a *total volatility* for the ith asset process is defined to be

$$\sigma_i = \sqrt{\sigma_{ii}} = \sqrt{b_{i1}^2 + b_{i2}^2 + \cdots + b_{in}^2}. \tag{5.29}$$

On the other hand, a possible correlation between the assets is generally given by a symmetric positive definite matrix $\Sigma = (\sigma_{ij})_{i,j=1}^n$. The entries of this matrix define the correlation between the ith and the jth assets with respective correlation coefficients ρ_{ij} such that

$$\sigma_{ii} = \sigma_i^2, \quad \sigma_{ij} = \rho_{ij}\sigma_i\sigma_j.$$

Here, σ_i is the (total) volatility corresponding to the ith asset, and hence, it has to be defined similarly as in (5.29).

Fortunately, the Cholesky factorisation of the matrix Σ may be helpful. Let the Cholesky decomposition of Σ be $\Sigma = LL^T$, where $L = (\ell_{ij})_{i,j=1}^n$ is the lower triangular matrix so that $\ell_{ij} = 0$ for all $j > i$. Then, the identity

$$\ell_{kk} = \left(\sigma_{kk} - \sum_{s=1}^{k-1} \ell_{ks}^2\right)^2$$

for the diagonal entries in Algorithm 5.8 implies that

$$\sum_{j=1}^n \ell_{ij}^2 = \sigma_{ii} = \sigma_i^2, \quad i = 1, 2, \ldots, n. \tag{5.30}$$

This is in accordance with the meaning of total volatility in (5.29).

Therefore, defining the volatility matrix B as the lower triangular matrix L such that $\Sigma = LL^T$, the correlation between the assets can be inserted into the n-factor model. In fact, this is not a surprise, since correlation between the asset prices can only be explained by correlated Wiener processes that drive the asset prices.

To sum up, the n-factor model for correlated asset prices by a given symmetric positive definite correlation matrix Σ takes the form

$$dS_t^{(i)} = S_t^{(i)}\left(\mu_i\,dt + \sum_{j=1}^n \ell_{ij}\,dW_t^{(j)}\right), \quad i = 1, 2, \ldots, n. \tag{5.31}$$

Here, the matrix $L = (\ell_{ij})_{i,j=1}^{n}$ is the lower triangular matrix such that $\Sigma = LL^{T}$. By (5.28) and the fact (5.30), it follows that the solution of (5.31) can easily be represented by

$$
S_t^{(i)} = S_0^{(i)} \exp\left\{ \left(\mu_i - \frac{1}{2}\sigma_i^2 \right) t + \sum_{j=1}^{n} \ell_{ij} W_t^{(j)} \right\} \tag{5.32}
$$

for each $i = 1, 2, \ldots, n$.

Furthermore, from the solutions of the asset prices $S_t^{(i)}$ given by (5.32), it is easy to calculate the expectations of the log-prices, $\log S_t^{(i)}$ as well as the covariances between $\log S_t^{(i)}$ and $\log S_t^{(k)}$. The expectations of the log-prices are almost trivially done by taking the logarithms of $S_t^{(k)}$ and then applying the expectation operator. Hence,

$$
\mathbb{E}\left[\log S_t^{(i)} \right] = \left(\mu_i - \frac{1}{2}\sigma_i^2 \right) t + \log S_0^{(i)}, \quad i = 1, 2, \ldots, n.
$$

The calculation of the covariances of the log-prices, on the other hand, is a bit tiresome:

$$
\begin{aligned}
\mathrm{Cov}\left[\log S_t^{(i)}, \log S_t^{(k)} \right] &= \mathrm{Cov}\left[\sum_{j=1}^{n} \ell_{ij} W_t^{(j)}, \sum_{s=1}^{n} \ell_{ks} W_t^{(s)} \right] \\
&= \sum_{j=1}^{n} \ell_{ij} \, \mathrm{Cov}\left[W_t^{(j)}, \sum_{s=1}^{n} \ell_{ks} W_t^{(s)} \right] \\
&= \sum_{j=1}^{n} \ell_{ij} \sum_{s=1}^{n} \ell_{ks} \, \mathrm{Cov}\left[W_t^{(j)}, W_t^{(s)} \right].
\end{aligned}
$$

Since the Wiener processes $W_t^{(i)}$ are uncorrelated, it follows that

$$
\mathrm{Cov}\left[W_t^{(j)}, W_t^{(s)} \right] = \delta_{js}\, t,
$$

where δ_{js} is the Kronecker's delta defined by

$$
\delta_{js} = \begin{cases} 0, \; j \neq s, \\ 1, \; j = s. \end{cases}
$$

Therefore,

$$
\mathrm{Cov}\left[\log S_t^{(i)}, \log S_t^{(k)} \right] = \sum_{j=1}^{n} \ell_{ij} \sum_{s=1}^{n} \ell_{ks}\, \delta_{js}\, t = \sum_{j=1}^{n} \ell_{ij}\ell_{kj}\, t.
$$

Finally, recall the multiplication rule for the two matrices L and L^T which yields the matrix Σ. That is,

$$\sigma_{ik} = \sum_{j=1}^{n} \ell_{ij}\ell_{kj}$$

for all $i, k = 1, 2, \ldots, n$. Consequently, the covariances of the log-prices are given by

$$\mathbb{C}\mathrm{ov}\left[\log S_t^{(i)}, \log S_t^{(k)}\right] = \sigma_{ik}\, t,$$

To put it simply, the covariance matrix for the logarithm of the asset prices is given by $L\left(t I_n\right) L^T = \Sigma\, t$.

The following example illustrates the Monte Carlo method for an option price where the option depends on correlated asset prices.

Example 5.7. With this example we would like to price a call option on the spread between two assets $S^{(1)}$ and $S^{(2)}$, based on the payoff,

$$V(S_T^{(1)}, S_T^{(2)}; T) = \left(S_T^{(1)} - S_T^{(2)} - K\right)^{+}$$

with a strike price K. The assets are modelled by geometric Brownian motions, however, we will assume that these assets are correlated by a correlation coefficient ρ between them. Hence, the covariance matrix of the assets is

$$\Sigma = \begin{pmatrix} \sigma_{11} & \sigma_{12} \\ \sigma_{21} & \sigma_{22} \end{pmatrix} = \begin{pmatrix} \sigma_1^2 & \rho\sigma_1\sigma_2 \\ \rho\sigma_1\sigma_2 & \sigma_2^2 \end{pmatrix}.$$

Although this option can be priced in closed-form solution, we will try to understand how the paths of the two assets that are correlated are described by the geometric Brownian motion, and then apply the Monte Carlo method for pricing.

Without the correlation between the assets the solution paths of the vector geometric Brownian motion,

$$dS_t^{(i)} = S_t^{(i)}\left(\mu_i\, dt + \sigma_i\, dW_t^{(i)}\right), \qquad i = 1, 2,$$

with independent $W_t^{(i)}$, would be

$$S_{t_{i+1}}^{(1)} = S_{t_i}^{(1)} \exp\left\{\left(\mu_1 - \frac{1}{2}\sigma_1^2\right)(t_{i+1} - t_i) + \sigma_1\sqrt{t_{i+1} - t_i}\, Z^{(1)}\right\},$$

$$S_{t_{i+1}}^{(2)} = S_{t_i}^{(2)} \exp\left\{\left(\mu_2 - \frac{1}{2}\sigma_2^2\right)(t_{i+1} - t_i) + \sigma_2\sqrt{t_{i+1} - t_i}\, Z^{(2)}\right\},$$

for $i = 1, 2, \ldots, M - 1$ so that $M\Delta t = T = t_M$. The samples $Z^{(i)}$ are independent and from the standard normal distribution, $Z^{(i)} \sim \mathcal{N}(0, 1)$.

However, in order to have correlation between the assets the driving Brownian motions $W_t^{(i)}$ must be correlated. In other words, the normal variates $Z^{(1)}$ and $Z^{(2)}$ must be correlated. Therefore, we should introduce this correlation into the asset price model.

In particular, the system for $n = 2$ turns out to be

$$
\begin{aligned}
dS_t^{(1)} &= S_t^{(i)} \left(\mu_1 \, dt + \sigma_1 \, dW_t^{(1)} \right), \\
dS_t^{(2)} &= S_t^{(i)} \left(\mu_2 \, dt + \sigma_2 \left(\rho \, dW_t^{(1)} + \sqrt{1 - \rho^2} \, dW_t^{(2)} \right) \right),
\end{aligned}
$$

by using the Cholesky decomposition,

$$
\Sigma = \begin{pmatrix} \sigma_1^2 & \rho\sigma_1\sigma_2 \\ \rho\sigma_1\sigma_2 & \sigma_2^2 \end{pmatrix} = \begin{pmatrix} \sigma_1 & 0 \\ \rho\sigma_2 & \sigma_2\sqrt{1 - \rho^2} \end{pmatrix} \begin{pmatrix} \sigma_1 & \rho\sigma_2 \\ 0 & \sigma_2\sqrt{1 - \rho^2} \end{pmatrix} = L\,L^T.
$$

Therefore, the discrete paths of the system can be written as

$$
S_{t_{i+1}}^{(1)} = S_{t_i}^{(1)} \exp\left\{ \left(\mu_1 - \frac{1}{2}\sigma_1^2 \right)(t_{i+1} - t_i) + \sigma_1 \sqrt{t_{i+1} - t_i}\,\bar{Z}^{(1)} \right\},
$$

$$
S_{t_{i+1}}^{(2)} = S_{t_i}^{(2)} \exp\left\{ \left(\mu_2 - \frac{1}{2}\sigma_2^2 \right)(t_{i+1} - t_i) + \sigma_2 \sqrt{t_{i+1} - t_i}\,\bar{Z}^{(2)} \right\},
$$

where $\bar{Z}^{(1)} = Z^{(1)}$ and $\bar{Z}^{(2)} = \rho Z^{(1)} + \sqrt{1 - \rho^2} Z^{(2)}$ are correlated standard normal variates with correlation ρ and the variates $Z^{(i)} \sim \mathcal{N}(0, 1)$ are uncorrelated.

The MATLAB script in Fig. 5.11 illustrates the use of Monte Carlo method for pricing a spread option where the underlying assets are correlated. The code should be modified to include confidence intervals. Notice also that, only the values of the paths at maturity are computed for both asset prices rather than the whole path in $[0, T]$.

Exercise 5.6. This exercise considers *basket* options that depends on several underlying stocks, like the spreads.

(1) Consider a two-asset European basket call option on the stocks $S^{(1)}$ and $S^{(2)}$ with volatilities $\sigma_1 = 0.25$, $\sigma_2 = 0.35$ and the correlation coefficient $\rho_{12} = -0.65$. The risk-free interest rate is $r = 0.045$. Assume that stocks *do not* pay dividends. The payoff of such an option is given by

$$
P(S^{(1)}, S^{(2)}; T) = \max\left\{ n_1 S^{(1)} + n_2 S^{(2)} - K, \, 0 \right\},
$$

```
───────────────────── SpreadOption_MC.m ─────────────────────
% At maturity the payoff from a call spread option is max(S1-S2-K,0)
% At maturity the payoff from a put spread option is max(K-S1+S2,0)
clear all, close all, randn('state', 13)

flag_CallPut = 'c'; S1 = 110; S2 = 100; K = 1; r = 0.06; sum=0;
mu1 = r; mu2 = r; sigma1 = .2; sigma2 = .3; rho = .5; T = 1; nPaths = 10000;
if flag_CallPut == 'c'
    z = 1; %  Will return call option value
else
    z = -1;   % Will return put option value
end
drift1 = (mu1 - sigma1^2 / 2) * T; drift2 = (mu2 - sigma2^2 / 2) * T;
sigma1Sqrdt = sigma1 * sqrt(T); sigma2Sqrdt = sigma2 * sqrt(T);
for i = 1:nPaths,
    Z1 = randn; Z2 = rho * Z1 + randn * sqrt(1 - rho ^ 2);
    St1 = S1 * exp(drift1 + sigma1Sqrdt * Z1);
    St2 = S2 * exp(drift2 + sigma2Sqrdt * Z2);
    sum = sum + max(z * (St1 - St2 - K), 0);
end
Price = exp(-r * T) * (sum / nPaths)
```

Fig. 5.11   Monte Carlo simulation for a spread of two assets

at time $T = 1$, where $K = 100$ is the strike price and $n_1 = 0.58$ and $n_2 = 0.42$ are the weights of the assets in the basket. Assume that $S_0^{(1)} = S_0^{(2)} = 100$ are given initially, and apply a Monte Carlo method to price the option.

(2) By changing your code (and of course the payoff), include another asset $S^{(3)}$ in the basket with additional parameters, $\sigma_3 = 0.2$, $\rho_{23} = 0.5$, $\rho_{31} = 0.25$, and $S_0^{(3)} = 100$. Now, the weights are $n_1 = 0.38$, $n_2 = 0.22$, and $n_3 = 0.40$. Note that, when the number of assets increases the use of Cholesky decomposition algorithm should be preferred.

(3) Write a Monte Carlo method to include the possibility of *paying (continuously compounding) dividends*. You may take $\delta_1 = 0.05$, $\delta_2 = 0.07$, and $\delta_3 = 0.04$ for the dividend yields.

Outlook

Monte Carlo method, or as it was originally known, the *method of statistical sampling*, is not only used in finance, but it has been applied successfully in applications of linear algebra, differential and integral equations for years.

However, since [Boyle (1977)], Monte Carlo simulation has been used for pricing financial derivatives by many researchers in their articles, monographs and books. For practitioners the method, although its low rate of convergence, is very valuable due to pricing complex and exotic options whose closed-form solutions are not available. Some of the texts that covers Monte Carlo simulation for finance and financial engineers include [Brandimarte (2002); Glasserman (2004); Higham (2004); Jäckel (2002); Kwok (1998); Seydel (2002); Wilmott *et al.* (1993)].

5.6 Variance Reduction Techniques

As it has been seen that the central limit theorem predicts a convergence rate of order $\mathcal{O}\left(\sqrt{\bar{\sigma}_N^2/N}\right)$, where $\bar{\sigma}_N^2$ is the sample variance in Monte Carlo simulations. As long as the variance of the underlying distribution is bounded, in the limit, the order is $\mathcal{O}\left(1/\sqrt{N}\right)$. This rate of convergence cannot be improved by stochastic simulations unless one use deterministic sequence of samples. The method that uses deterministic sequences of numbers for which the rate is improved will be discussed in Section 5.7.

However, for finitely many replications in Monte Carlo simulations it is possible to *reduce the sample variance*. Hence, if not the order of convergence, the accuracy obtained by the Monte Carlo method may be improved. This is sometimes desired for some important applications in financial engineering. Moreover, increasing the number of independent *replications* may not even be possible as the sequences of random numbers generated by computers have finite periods and are surely predictable.

5.6.1 *Antithetic Variates*

A first approach in order to reduce the sample variance is rather easy to apply and does not require a deep knowledge of what is simulated. It is the technique of *antithetic variates*, or *antithetic sampling*. In the plain Monte Carlo approach a sequence of independent samples was used. However, inducing some correlation may be helpful.

Consider the idea of generating two sequences of independent identically distributed samples,

$$\left\{X_i^1\right\}_{i=1}^N = \left\{X_1^1, X_2^1, \ldots, X_N^1\right\}, \quad \left\{X_i^2\right\}_{i=1}^N = \left\{X_1^2, X_2^2, \ldots, X_N^2\right\}. \tag{5.33}$$

These samples may separately be used in Monte Carlo simulations, and so may the pair-averaged samples

$$X_i = \frac{1}{2}\left(X_i^1 + X_i^2\right), \qquad i = 1, 2, \ldots, N. \tag{5.34}$$

Since the average-pair sample $\{X_i\}_{i=1}^{N}$ is also *i.i.d.*, by the central limit theorem we may build a sample mean $\bar{X}_N$ and a *confidence interval* based on it.

Thus, assume a correlation between the samples as

$$\mathbb{Cov}\left[X_i^1, X_i^2\right] < 0,$$

for each $i = 1, 2, \ldots, N$. By using the identity

$$\left|\mathbb{Cov}\left[X_i^1, X_i^2\right]\right| \le \frac{1}{2}\left\{\mathbb{Var}\left[X_i^1\right] + \mathbb{Var}\left[X_i^2\right]\right\},$$

it follows that

$$\mathbb{Var}\left[X_i\right] = \frac{1}{4}\left\{\mathbb{Var}\left[X_i^1\right] + \mathbb{Var}\left[X_i^2\right] + 2\,\mathbb{Cov}\left[X_i^1, X_i^2\right]\right\}$$
$$\le \frac{1}{2}\left\{\mathbb{Var}\left[X_i^1\right] + \mathbb{Var}\left[X_i^2\right]\right\}.$$

Hence, the variance of X_i becomes smaller if X_i^1 and X_i^2 are negatively correlated. Note that in this case, the sample variance satisfies the inequality,

$$\mathbb{Var}\left[\bar{X}_N\right] = \mathbb{Var}\left[\frac{1}{N}\sum_{i=1}^{N}X_i\right]$$
$$= \frac{1}{N}\mathbb{Var}\left[X_i\right] \le \frac{1}{2N}\left\{\mathbb{Var}\left[X_i^1\right] + \mathbb{Var}\left[X_i^2\right]\right\}.$$

This is the idea of *antithetic* variates.

However, in application of the Monte Carlo method, a problem arises in choosing the antithetic variates. That is, how one should choose the so-called antithetic variates X_i^2 that are negatively correlated with the variates X_i^1, without knowing either. For instance, in option pricing they represent the prices that come out from the replications in a Monte Carlo simulation. To resolve this problem is not so easy without knowing extra information on the underlying dynamics. Nevertheless, in applying Monte Carlo simulations we may induce a correlation on the replications and hope that the results will be negatively correlated.

To induce a negative correlation, first, we may use the sequence $\{Z_k\}$ of random samples drawn from the underlying distribution to obtain a sample, replication. Then, the sequence $\{-Z_k\}$ (without any cost in drawing) may be used to obtain another sample, replication. Since the *input* streams (random samples from the underlying distribution) are negatively correlated, we "hope" that the *output* streams (replications) will be negatively correlated, too. Finally, these two results may be averaged to obtain the pair-averaged so that the variance of the new sample will hopefully be reduced.

Indeed, according to the arguments above the method has no guarantee to reduce the variance, however, the method of antithetic variates in option pricing may slightly improve the results when compared to the plain Monte Carlo method. Rarely, the results may slightly be deteriorated by additional calculation of antithetic variates.

Example 5.8. This example uses the *antithetic variates* to price a specific barrier option: *up-and-in* call option, where the underlying asset is governed by the geometric Brownian motion. Since the option payoff depends on the paths of the asset, simulation of the asset paths is necessary. The final values S_T as well as the values S_{t_i} are important for such barrier options, where $t_i = i\,\Delta t$, $i = 1, 2, \ldots, M$ and $M\Delta t = T$ as usual.

A pseudo-code for the up-and-in call option is shown in Algorithm 5.10, however, the idea behind the algorithm for antithetic variate is similar for other types of options.

Algorithm 5.10 Up-and-In Call, with *antithetic variates*

    Given: M, N, S_0, r, σ, B, K

   for $i = 1, 2, \ldots, M$ **do**

      for $j = 0, 1, \ldots, N - 1$ **do**

         $Z_j \sim \mathcal{N}(0, 1)$

         $S_{j+1} = S_j \exp\left\{\left(r - \tfrac{1}{2}\sigma^2\right)\Delta t + \sigma Z_j \sqrt{\Delta t}\right\}$ % introduce

         $\hat{S}_{j+1} = \bar{S}_j \exp\left\{\left(r - \tfrac{1}{2}\sigma^2\right)\Delta t - \sigma Z_j \sqrt{\Delta t}\right\}$ % correlation

      end for

      $S_i^m = \max\limits_{0 \le j \le N} S_j, \quad \hat{S}_i^m = \max\limits_{0 \le j \le N} \hat{S}_j$

      if $S_i^m > B$ **then**

         $V_i^1 = e^{-rT} \max\{S_N - K, 0\},$ **else** $V_i^1 = 0$

      end if

      if $\hat{S}_i^m > B$ **then**

         $V_i^2 = e^{-rT} \max\{\hat{S}_N - K, 0\},$ **else** $V_i^2 = 0$ % antithetic variates

      end if

      $V_i = \tfrac{1}{2}\left(V_i^1 + V_i^2\right)$ % pair-averaged sample

   end for

$$\bar{V}_M = \frac{1}{M}\sum_{i=1}^{M} V_i, \quad \bar{\sigma}_M^2 = \frac{1}{M-1}\sum_{i=1}^{M}(V_i - \bar{V}_M)^2$$

An implementation of Algorithm 5.10 is illustrated in Fig. 5.12. Here, we present a table of confidence intervals for comparison of the use of antithetic variates with plain Monte Carlo method in pricing this up-and-in call option. It can also be deduced from Table 5.1 that *for this example* the use of antithetic variates, *luckily*, improved the plain Monte Carlo method, by a factor of 1.5 for the ratios of the confidence interval.

Table 5.1   A comparison of the confidence intervals for plain Monte Carlo and the use of Antithetic Variates

M	Monte-Carlo (Plain)	Monte-Carlo (Antithetic Variates)	Ratio (Widths)
10^2	[0.0754, 0.3857]	[0.1392, 0.3709]	1.3387
10^3	[0.1740, 0.2656]	[0.2055, 0.2716]	1.3843
10^4	[0.2372, 0.2696]	[0.2356, 0.2570]	1.5150
10^5	[0.2411, 0.2511]	[0.2417, 0.2485]	1.4799

```
                      ________ MC_Antithetic_UpIn_Eg.m ________
% Up-and-in call option: uses Monte Carlo with antithetic variates
clear all, close all, randn('state',13)

S = 5; E = 6; sigma = 0.3; r = 0.05; T = 1; B = 8; dt = 1e-4; N = T/dt; M = 1e3;
V = zeros(M,1); Vanti = zeros(M,1);
for i = 1:M
    samples = randn(N,1);
    % standard Monte Carlo
    Svals = S*cumprod(exp((r-0.5*sigma^2)*dt+sigma*sqrt(dt)*samples));
    Smax = max(Svals);
    if Smax > B
       V(i) = exp(-r*T) * max(Svals(end)-E,0);
    end
    % antithetic path
    Svals2 = S*cumprod(exp((r-0.5*sigma^2)*dt-sigma*sqrt(dt)*samples));
    Smax2 = max(Svals2); V2 = 0;
    if Smax2 > B
       V2 = exp(-r*T) * max(Svals2(end)-E,0);
    end
    Vanti(i) = 0.5*(V(i) + V2);
end
PriceV = mean(V); StdV = std(V);
CI = [PriceV - 1.96*StdV/sqrt(M), PriceV + 1.96*StdV/sqrt(M)]
PriceVanti = mean(Vanti); StdVanti = std(Vanti);
CIanti = [PriceVanti - 1.96*StdVanti/sqrt(M), ...
    PriceVanti + 1.96*StdVanti/sqrt(M)]
ratio = ( CI(2)-CI(1) ) / ( CIanti(2)-CIanti(1) )
```

Fig. 5.12   An implementation of Monte Carlo simulation that uses Antithetic Variates

5.6.2 *Control Variates*

Antithetic variates in Monte Carlo method do not require much knowledge of the system that is simulated. A second approach to reduce the sample variance is the use of *control variates*. Better results might be obtained by *controlling* the variates and using some additional knowledge of the system.

Suppose that we wish to estimate the parameter

$$\theta = \mathbb{E}\left[X\right]$$

of a random variable and that there is another random variable Y with a known expected value

$$\nu = \mathbb{E}\left[Y\right].$$

Assume that Y is somewhat correlated with X. The random variable Y is called the *control variable*, or *control variate*. This additional information on the control variate Y may be exploited by introducing the *controlled estimator*,

$$X_c = X + c\left(Y - \nu\right), \tag{5.35}$$

where c is a parameter that has to be chosen later.

The expectation and the variance of the controlled estimator are

$$\mathbb{E}\left[X_c\right] = \mathbb{E}\left[X\right] = \theta$$

and

$$\mathbb{V}\mathrm{ar}\left[X_c\right] = \mathbb{V}\mathrm{ar}\left[X\right] + c^2\,\mathbb{V}\mathrm{ar}\left[Y\right] + 2c\,\mathbb{C}\mathrm{ov}\left[X, Y\right],$$

respectively. The first formula indicates that for any choice of c, the controlled estimator X_c is an unbiased estimator of the parameter $\theta = \mathbb{E}\left[X\right]$. The use of the control estimator X_c in Monte Carlo simulation is known as the *control variate* approach. On the other hand, the second formula suggests that by a suitable choice of c, the variance of the estimator can further be reduced.

In fact, since $\mathbb{V}\mathrm{ar}\left[X_c\right]$ is a quadratic function of c, the unique value of the minimum variance occurs at c^* such that

$$0 = 2c^*\,\mathbb{V}\mathrm{ar}\left[Y\right] + 2\,\mathbb{C}\mathrm{ov}\left[X, Y\right],$$

for $\mathbb{V}\mathrm{ar}\left[Y\right] > 0$. Hence,

$$c^* = -\frac{\mathbb{C}\mathrm{ov}\left[X, Y\right]}{\mathbb{V}\mathrm{ar}\left[Y\right]}.$$

At this optimal case, when $c = c^*$, the variance of the controlled estimator becomes

$$\mathbb{V}\mathrm{ar}\left[X_c^*\right] = \mathbb{V}\mathrm{ar}\left[X\right] + (c^*)^2 \,\mathbb{V}\mathrm{ar}\left[Y\right] + 2c^* \,\mathbb{C}\mathrm{ov}\left[X,Y\right], \qquad (5.36)$$

where $X_c^* = X + c^*\left(Y - \nu\right)$. Inserting c^* into (5.36) and using the correlation coefficient ρ_{XY},

$$\rho_{XY} = \frac{\mathbb{C}\mathrm{ov}\left[X,Y\right]}{\sqrt{\mathbb{V}\mathrm{ar}\left[X\right]}\sqrt{\mathbb{V}\mathrm{ar}\left[Y\right]}},$$

we deduce that

$$\frac{\mathbb{V}\mathrm{ar}\left[X_c^*\right]}{\mathbb{V}\mathrm{ar}\left[X\right]} = 1 - \rho_{XY}^2. \qquad (5.37)$$

This shows that the value of the variance $\mathbb{V}\mathrm{ar}\left[X_c^*\right]$ is not greater than the value of the variance $\mathbb{V}\mathrm{ar}\left[X\right]$. Moreover, due to the quadratic behaviour of $\mathbb{V}\mathrm{ar}\left[X_c\right]$, $\mathbb{V}\mathrm{ar}\left[X_c\right] < \mathbb{V}\mathrm{ar}\left[X\right]$ if and only if c lies between zero and $2c^*$, where c^* may be either negative or positive.

In practice, the optimal value of c must be estimated since the covariance $\mathbb{C}\mathrm{ov}\left[X,Y\right]$, and possibly $\mathbb{V}\mathrm{ar}\left[Y\right]$, are not known. Of course, a set of *pilot* replications can be used to estimate $\mathbb{C}\mathrm{ov}\left[X,Y\right]$ as well as $\mathbb{V}\mathrm{ar}\left[Y\right]$. However, it would be tempting to use these replications both for selecting c^* and to estimate θ. It is better to avoid pilot replications, as suggested in [Brandimarte (2002)], when using the control variate approach, since you may induce some bias in the estimate of the parameter θ. So, unless suitable statistical techniques are used or theoretical results are available, the pilot replications should only be used to estimate c^*. However, remember that the controlled estimator is an unbiased estimator of θ no matter what the parameter c is.

Example 5.9. In this example, we consider pricing an Asian option with the payoff

$$\max\left\{\frac{1}{N}\sum_{i=1}^{N} S_{t_i} - K,\, 0\right\},$$

where the option maturity is T years, $t_i = i\,\Delta t$, and $\Delta t = T/N$. In a plain Monte Carlo approach, we must simply generate asset price paths and estimate the discounted payoff as usual. Such an implementation is shown in Fig. 5.13.

```
────────────────────── MC_ArithmeticAsian.m ──────────────────────
function [P,CI] = MC_ArithmeticAsian(S0,K,r,sigma,T,NSamples,NRepl)

Payoff = zeros(NRepl,1);
for i=1:NRepl
   Path=AssetPaths_gBM(S0,r,sigma,T,NSamples,1);
   Payoff(i) = max(0, mean(Path(2:(NSamples+1))) - K);
end
% for simplicity use
[P,approxsigma,CI] = normfit( exp(-r*T) * Payoff);
```

Fig. 5.13   An implementation of Monte Carlo simulation applied to Arithmetic Asian Option

The plain Monte Carlo sampling may be improved by using *control variates*, however. As a control variate Y, take the following sum of the asset prices:

$$Y = \sum_{i=0}^{N} S_{t_i}.$$

This is seemingly a suitable control variate since it is clearly correlated with the option payoff. It is possible to compute the expected value of Y:

$$\mathbb{E}\left[Y\right] = \mathbb{E}\left[\sum_{i=0}^{N} S_{t_i}\right] = \sum_{i=0}^{N} \mathbb{E}\left[S_{i\Delta t}\right]$$

$$= \sum_{i=0}^{N} S_0 e^{ri\Delta t} = S_0 \sum_{i=0}^{N} \left(e^{r\Delta t}\right)^{i} = S_0 \frac{e^{r(N+1)\Delta t} - 1}{e^{r\Delta t} - 1},$$

where the formula

$$\sum_{i=0}^{N} \alpha^i = \frac{\alpha^{N+1} - 1}{\alpha - 1}$$

is used. Here, we assume a geometric Brownian motion for the asset prices with return rates r, the risk-free interest rate.

The MATLAB script in Fig. 5.14 checks the improvement obtained by applying the control variates, and the algorithm for pricing the arithmetic average Asian option is shown in Fig. 5.15. Also, Table 5.2 summarises the results obtained by Monte Carlo method with and without the use of control variates.

In pricing arithmetic average price Asian call option of the example above, it is possible to use *geometric* average price Asian call option with payoff

$$\max\left\{\left(\prod_{i=1}^{N} S_{t_i}\right)^{1/N} - K,\, 0\right\}$$

```
————————————————————— test_ControlVariate_Sums —————————————
% test MC and Control Variate with Asset Sums
clear all, close all, rand('state', 13), randn('state', 13)
howMany = 5;
for k=2:howMany
    [Pmc,CI] = MC_ArithmeticAsian(50,50,0.1,0.4,5/12,5,5*10^k);
    [Pcv,CIcv] = MC_ArithmeticAsian_Control_SumOfS( ...
        50,50,0.1,0.4,5/12,5,5*10^k,5*10^(k-1));
    TC = [k, CI(1), CI(2), CIcv(1), CIcv(2), ...
        ( CI(2)-CI(1) ) / ( CIcv(2)-CIcv(1) ) ]
end
```

Fig. 5.14   A MATLAB code for testing the improvement in applying the method of Control Variate

```
————————————————————— MC_ArithmeticAsian_Control_SumOfS.m —————————
function [P,CI] = MC_ArithmeticAsian_Control_SumOfS(...
    SO,K,r,sigma,T,NSamples,NRepl,NPilot)

% pilot replications to set control parameter
TryPath=AssetPaths_gBM(SO,r,sigma,T,NSamples,NPilot);
StockSum = sum(TryPath,2); PP = mean( TryPath(:,2:(NSamples+1)), 2 );
TryPayoff = exp(-r*T) * max(0, PP - K);
MatCov = cov(StockSum, TryPayoff); c = - MatCov(1,2) / var(StockSum);
dt = T / NSamples;
ExpSum = SO * (1 - exp((NSamples + 1)*r*dt)) / (1 - exp(r*dt));
% MC run
ControlVars = zeros(NRepl,1);
for i=1:NRepl
    StockPath = AssetPaths_gBM(SO,r,sigma,T,NSamples,1);
    Payoff = exp(-r*T) * max(0, mean(StockPath(2:(NSamples+1))) - K);
    ControlVars(i) = Payoff + c * (sum(StockPath) - ExpSum);
end
[P,approxSigma,CI] = normfit(ControlVars);
```

Fig. 5.15   An implementation of Monte Carlo simulation applied to Arithmetic Asian Option using Control Variates as the sum of S

as a *control* variate. This is due to the fact that the geometric average price

$$S^{ga} = \left(\prod_{i=1}^{N} S_{t_i} \right)^{1/N}$$

stays *lognormally* distributed as long as the stock price S_t follows the geometric Brownian motion,

$$S_t = S_0\, e^{\left(r - \frac{1}{2}\sigma^2\right)t + \sigma W_t}.$$

Therefore, a closed-form formula for the value of a geometric average price option can be derived. Using

$$S_{t_i} = S_0\, e^{\left(r - \frac{1}{2}\sigma^2\right)t_i + \sigma W_{t_i}},$$

Table 5.2 A comparison of the confidence intervals for plain Monte Carlo and the use of Control Variates in Fig. 5.14

Replications	Pilot Replications	Monte-Carlo (Plain)	Monte-Carlo (Control Variate)	Ratio (Widths)
$5 \cdot 10^2$	$5 \cdot 10^1$	[3.1562, 4.1555]	[3.8204, 4.2510]	2.3207
$5 \cdot 10^3$	$5 \cdot 10^2$	[3.7335, 4.0564]	[3.9444, 4.0817]	2.3501
$5 \cdot 10^4$	$5 \cdot 10^3$	[3.9182, 4.0224]	[3.9536, 3.9971]	2.3991
$5 \cdot 10^5$	$5 \cdot 10^4$	[3.9467, 3.9796]	[3.9574, 3.9710]	2.4117

where $t_{i+1} = t_i + \Delta t$, $t_0 = 0$ and $t_N = T$, one can easily obtain

$$S^{ga} = S_0 \, \exp\left\{ \left(r - \frac{1}{2}\sigma^2 \right) \frac{1}{N} \sum_{i=1}^{N} t_i + \frac{\sigma}{N} \sum_{i=1}^{N} W_{t_i} \right\}.$$

Note that the sum, $\sum_{i=1}^{N} W_{t_i}$, of normally distributed random variables, W_{t_i}, is again normally distributed: it is not difficult to show that

$$\mathbb{E}\left[\sum_{i=1}^{N} W_{t_i} \right] = 0$$

and

$$\mathbb{V}\mathrm{ar}\left[\sum_{i=1}^{N} W_{t_i} \right] = \sum_{i=1}^{n} \left[2n - (2i - 1) \right] t_i$$

so that

$$\sum_{i=1}^{N} W_{t_i} \sim \mathcal{N}\left(0, \ \sum_{i=1}^{n} \left[2n - (2i - 1) \right] t_i \right).$$

Therefore, using the well-known identities

$$\sum_{i=1}^{N} i = \frac{N(N+1)}{2} \quad \text{and} \quad \sum_{i=1}^{N} i^2 = \frac{N(N+1)(2N+1)}{6},$$

together with $t_i = i \Delta t$ for all $i = 0, 1, \ldots, N$, it follows that

$$\mathbb{E}\left[\log S^{ga}/S_0 \right] = \left(r - \frac{1}{2}\sigma^2 \right) \frac{N+1}{2N} T$$

and

$$\mathbb{V}\mathrm{ar}\left[\log S^{ga}/S_0 \right] = \frac{\sigma^2}{N^2} \frac{(N+1)(2N+1)}{6} T,$$

where $T = N\Delta t$ is the time to maturity. Thus,

$$\log S^{ga}/S_0 \sim \mathcal{N}\left(\left(\hat{\mu} - \frac{1}{2}\hat{\sigma}^2\right)T,\ \hat{\sigma}^2 T\right),$$

where

$$\hat{\sigma} = \frac{\sigma^2}{N^2}\frac{(N+1)(2N+1)}{6} \tag{5.38}$$

and

$$\hat{\mu} = \left(r - \frac{1}{2}\sigma^2\right)\frac{N+1}{2N} + \frac{1}{2}\hat{\sigma}^2. \tag{5.39}$$

Now, it remains to adapt the Black-Scholes closed-form formula (4.35) for a vanilla call option written on the underlying lognormally distributed asset S. Here, the underlying is considered to be the geometric average price S^{ga}. It follows therefore from (4.35) that if $V^{ga}(S_0, 0)$ denotes the value of the geometric average price Asian call option, then we have

$$V^{ga}(S_0, 0) = S_0 e^{(\hat{\mu}-r)T}\Phi(\hat{d}_1) - Ke^{-rT}\Phi(\hat{d}_2), \tag{5.40}$$

where Φ is the distribution function of the standard normal distribution, r is the risk-free interest rate and

$$\hat{d}_1 = \frac{\log(S_0/K) + \left(\hat{\mu} + \frac{1}{2}\hat{\sigma}^2\right)T}{\hat{\sigma}\sqrt{T}}, \tag{5.41}$$

$$\hat{d}_2 = = d_1 - \hat{\sigma}\sqrt{T} = \frac{\log(S_0/K) + \left(\hat{\mu} - \frac{1}{2}\hat{\sigma}^2\right)T}{\hat{\sigma}\sqrt{T}}. \tag{5.42}$$

On the other hand, the following exercise may be regarded as a generalisation of the Black-Scholes formulae for options on the underlying that is lognormally distributed.

Exercise 5.7. Let X be a random variable that is lognormally distributed. Show that

$$\mathbb{E}\left[\max\{X - K, 0\}\right] = \mathbb{E}\left[X\right]\Phi(a) - K\Phi(b)$$

where

$$a = \frac{\log(\mathbb{E}\left[X\right]/K) + \mathbb{V}\mathrm{ar}\left[\log X\right]/2}{\sqrt{\mathbb{V}\mathrm{ar}\left[\log X\right]}},$$

$$b = \frac{\log(\mathbb{E}\left[X\right]/K) - \mathbb{V}\mathrm{ar}\left[\log X\right]/2}{\sqrt{\mathbb{V}\mathrm{ar}\left[\log X\right]}}.$$

Using the result, derive the Black-Scholes formulae for vanilla call and put options, as well as the value of the geometric average price Asian option given by (5.40).

Exercise 5.8. Write a program that uses the geometric average price Asian call option as a control variate in Monte Carlo method to approximate the value of the arithmetic average price Asian call option. That is, use

$$Y = e^{-rT} \max\left\{S^{ga} - K,\, 0\right\}$$

as the control variate and the result of Example 5.7 in order to reduce the variance.

Outlook

Many textbooks on Monte Carlo simulation include the variance reduction techniques beside [Brandimarte (2002); Higham (2002)] that influenced the content presented in this section. In order to improve the rate of convergence of the (plain) Monte Carlo method, there have been developed many other methods on variance reduction, such as *stratified* and *importance sampling*, *conditional Monte Carlo*, etc.. They are extensively used in valuation of financial derivatives, particularly, in pricing path-dependent exotic or American options when either the closed-form solutions are not available or the convergence of the plain Monte Carlo is inefficient.

For general information and detailed discussions on the variance reduction techniques we refer to [Glasserman (2004)] and [Hammersley and Handscomb (1964); Hull (2000); Ripley (2006)]. To accompany these references, texts on practical issues of pricing financial derivatives include [Boyle *et al.* (1997); Jäckel (2002); Kwok (1998); Wilmott *et al.* (1993)].

5.7   Quasi-Monte Carlo Simulation

In order to improve the convergence of plain Monte Carlo method, the use of variance reduction techniques have been considered. These techniques depend on the idea that the random sampling was *really* random and independent of one another. However, random number generators produce pseudo-random numbers that are not random at all!

A problem with random number generators is that they may fail to generate numbers that are distributed uniformly. In principle, the generators are expected to produce numbers for which the *deviation* from being uniform is minimal. This deviation from uniformity is then called *discrepancy*. The sequence of numbers with *low discrepancy* is *quasi-random* numbers, although the generation is fully deterministic. To be more specific, the following two definitions (Seydel, 2002, pp. 68–69) are given.

Definition 5.2. *Discrepancy of a set* $\{x_1, x_2, \ldots, x_N\}$ *of points is defined to be*

$$D_N := \sup_Q \left| \frac{\operatorname{card}(Q)}{N} - \operatorname{vol}(Q) \right|,$$

where the supremum is taken over the rectangles $Q \subseteq \mathbb{R}^m$, $\operatorname{card}(Q)$ and $\operatorname{vol}(Q)$ denote the number of points in Q and the volume of Q, respectively.

Definition 5.3. A sequence $\{x_i\}_{i=1}^{\infty}$ of points in $\mathbb{R}^m$ is called a *low-discrepancy sequence* if there is a constant C_m, which does not depend on N, such that

$$D_N \leq C_m \frac{(\log N)^m}{N}$$

holds for all N. Furthermore, a sequence of numbers satisfying this bound is called a sequence of *quasi-random numbers*.

Since $\log N$ grows modestly as N increases, a low-discrepancy sequence essentially has the property that $D_N \approx \mathcal{O}\left(\frac{1}{N}\right)$ as long as the dimension m is not too large. If, further, the quasi-random numbers preserve some "uniform randomness" and "independence", then a Monte Carlo simulation can be carried out by using these numbers. In this case, the method is called a *quasi*-Monte Carlo method.

In the sequel, such a sequence of quasi-random numbers is presented and applied in pricing an option by the quasi-Monte Carlo method.

5.7.1 *Halton Sequences*

Halton low-discrepancy sequences are based on a simple idea for the generation of *van der Corput* sequences:

(1) Represent an integer number n in a given base b, where b is (usually) a *prime number*, as follows:

$$n = (d_m \cdots d_4 d_3 d_2 d_1 d_0)_b = \sum_{k=0}^{m} d_k b^k.$$

(2) Reflect the digits and add a radix point in this base to obtain another number: the nth term in the van der Corput sequence with base b is in the interval $[0, 1]$ and defined by

$$h(n, b) = (0.d_0 d_1 d_2 d_3 d_4 \cdots d_m)_b = \sum_{k=0}^{m} d_k b^{-(k+1)}.$$

The Halton sequence is then a generalisation of the van der Corput sequence to higher dimensions. If the b_i for $i = 1, 2, \ldots, m$ are (relatively) prime bases for van der Corput sequences $\{h(n, b_i)\}_{n=1}^{\infty}$, then the m-dimensional Halton sequence $\{x_n\}_{n=1}^{\infty}$ is defined as the sequence of vectors

$$x_n = [h(n, b_1), h(n, b_2), \ldots, h(n, b_m)]^T$$

in $\mathbb{R}^m$ with bases $b_1, b_2, \ldots, b_m$. In particular, van der Corput sequences are one-dimensional Halton sequences, hence, we will simply do not distinguish the two and simply call both as Halton sequences.

Here is an example to show how the nth term of a van der Corput sequence with a given base b is obtained. The number b, which is usually a prime number, may be regarded as the *seed* of the van der Corput sequence so that the terms can be regenerated whenever necessary.

Example 5.10. Let the prime number $b = 3$ be a chosen base. Then, the integers can be written in this base as

$$1 = (1)_3, \ 2 = (2)_3, \ 3 = (10)_3, \ 4 = (11)_3, \ 5 = (12)_3, \ 6 = (20)_3, \ \ldots.$$

So, the following numbers are the first 6 terms of the Halton sequence with base 3:

$$\begin{aligned}
h(1,3) &= (0.1)_3 = 1/3, & h(2,3) &= (0.2)_3 = 2/3, \\
h(3,3) &= (0.01)_3 = 1/9, & h(4,3) &= (0.11)_3 = 4/9, \\
h(5,3) &= (0.21)_3 = 7/9, & h(6,3) &= (0.02)_3 = 2/9.
\end{aligned}$$

An implementation of Halton sequences, presented in (Brandimarte, 2002, pp. 237), for a given prime base is shown in Fig. 5.16. In order to see how the points in a low-discrepancy sequence are placed, for instance in $\mathbb{R}^2$, the plots in Fig. 5.17 compare the points in Halton sequence with the ones generated by the MATLAB built-in function **rand**.

Example 5.11. Although there is nothing special with this example, it should be emphasised that the use Halton sequences in option pricing needs transforming the points to samples from a normal distribution. For the purpose of uniform samples the Box-Muller or the Marsaglia's polar method can be used. In this example we have chosen the former despite some discussions in literature on quasi-Monte Carlo methods.

The MATLAB function in Fig. 5.18 applies the Monte Carlo method to price a European call and also returns the confidence interval associated with the sample mean. Indeed, in order to use *statistics* in quasi-Monte

```
———————————————————— getHaltonSequence.m ————————————
function Seq = getHaltonSequence(Base, howMany)

Seq = zeros(howMany,1); NumBits = 1+ceil(log(howMany)/log(Base));
b = Base.^(-(1:NumBits)); d = zeros(1,NumBits);
for i = 1:howMany
      j = 1; ok = 0;
      while (ok == 0)
          d(j) = d(j)+1;
          if ( d(j) < Base )
              ok = 1;
          else
              d(j) = 0; j = j+1;
          end
      end
      Seq(i) = dot(d, b);
end
```

Fig. 5.16　An implementation of the *Halton Sequence*

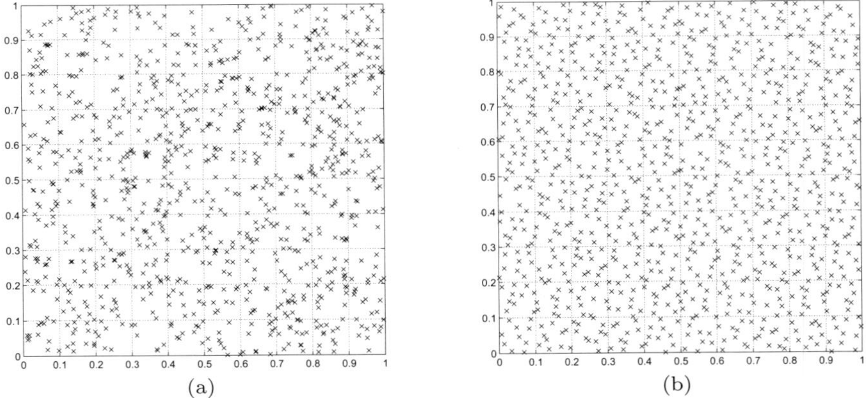

Fig. 5.17　Covering of the unit square with the use of (a) the MATLAB **rand** function, (b) the Halton Sequence with prime bases 2 and 7

Carlo simulations, the quasi-random numbers must be randomised by some means since they seem to be predictable due to their construction.

In order to transform two Halton sequences with their respective bases to samples from a uniform distribution, Box-Muller algorithm is used. Alternatively, one might prefer to use the polar method of Marsaglia. Nevertheless, it is important to note that these two van der Corput sequences that are transformed must be independent of each other. This is achieved by choosing (relatively) prime bases for each sequence.

———— qMC_Halton_Call.m ————

```
function [Price, CI] = qMC_Halton_Call(S0,X,r,sigma,T,NPoints, Base1,Base2)
% Base1, Base2 are two bases (primes) for Halton Sequences

nuT = (r - 0.5*sigma^2)*T; siT = sigma * sqrt(T);
% Halton Sequences
H1 = getHaltonSequence(Base1, ceil(NPoints/2));
H2 = getHaltonSequence(Base2, ceil(NPoints/2));

% Use Box-Muller to generate standard normals
sqLog = sqrt(-2*log(H1));
Norm1 = sqLog .* cos(2*pi*H2); Norm2 = sqLog .* sin(2*pi*H2);
Norm = [Norm1 ; Norm2]; Norm = Norm(1:NPoints);

% Pricing
DiscPayoff = exp(-r*T) * max( 0, S0*exp(nuT+siT*Norm) - X );
Price = mean(DiscPayoff);
% assuming a statistical error
width = 1.96*std(DiscPayoff)/sqrt(NPoints);
CI = [Price-width, Price+width];
```

Fig. 5.18   An implementation of quasi-Monte Carlo method using *Halton Sequences*

Finally, it is advisable to read this example along with Example 5.5. In particular, comparison of Fig. 5.9 and Fig. 5.19 gives an idea for the convergence rates of both quasi- and plain Monte Carlo methods.

Outlook

Due to their dependent generations, quasi-random numbers or low discrepancy sequences are often called *deterministic* sequences. In fact, the *quasi* modifier is used to indicate more clearly that the values of a low-discrepancy sequence are neither random nor pseudo-random. Although such sequences share some properties of random variables, in certain applications, such as the (stochastic) Monte Carlo method, their lower discrepancy is an important advantage to increase the rate of convergence. See, for instance, [Joy *et al.* (1996); Niederreiter (1992)].

However, when using such deterministic sequences there is a need to randomise them in order to apply the Monte Carlo method and then use *statistical* methods for errors such as the confidence interval. In this respect, the confidence intervals depicted in Fig. 5.19 do not represent the correct statistics. The error bounds for quasi-Monte Carlo methods as well as randomising the low-discrepancy sequences that will enable the use of statistical error bounds are given in standard textbooks on Monte Carlo methods, such as [Glasserman (2004); Caflisch (1998); Niederreiter (1992); Tezuka (1995)]. For the use of randomised quasi-Monte Carlo in pricing

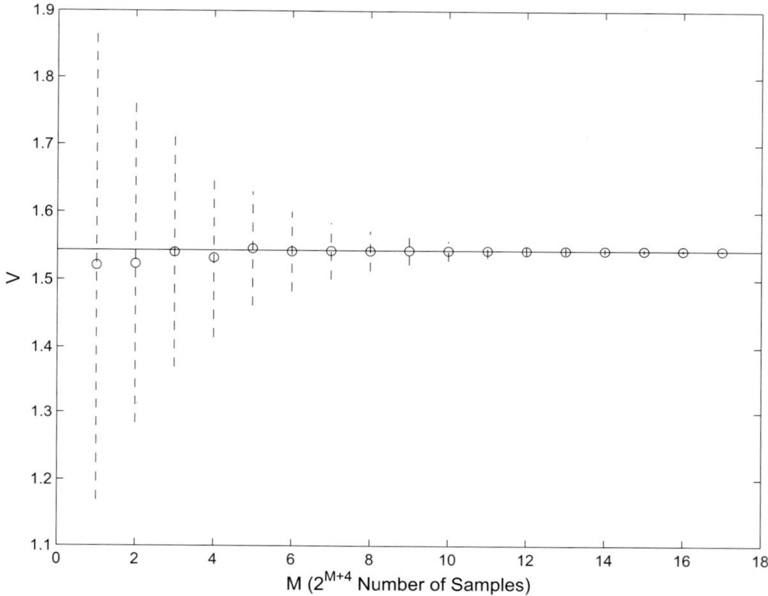

Fig. 5.19   Convergence of Monte Carlo approximations, using Halton Sequences, to a European Call.   Compare the convergence rates depicted in this figure with the one in Fig. 5.9 on page 170

financial derivatives, in particular, we refer to [Ökten and Eastman (2004); Tan and Boyle (2000)] and the references therein.

Constructions of low-discrepancy sequences require some knowledge in *number theory*, however, we refer to (Brandimarte, 2002, Chapter 4) for an introduction and MATLAB implementations to construct *Sobol* (low-discrepancy) sequences. Some other low-discrepancy sequences are called after their founders, for instance, *Faure, Hammersley, Sobol, Niederreiter* as well as *van der Corput* and *Halton* sequences.

Chapter 6

Option Pricing by Partial Differential Equations

Partial differential equations (PDEs) play a major role in financial engineering. Due to close connection between the option price and its equivalent PDE, as is derived for the Black-Scholes framework, PDEs have become an important tool in option valuation. Indeed, PDEs can provide a powerful and consistent framework for pricing rather complex financial derivatives. However, since closed-form solutions like the Black-Scholes formulae are not available in general, one must often resort to numerical methods.

Solving PDEs numerically is a common tool in mathematical physics and engineering, and quite sophisticated methods have been developed. The complexity of these methods also depends on the *specific* types of PDEs, classified as *hyperbolic, parabolic,* and *elliptic,* for which numerical solutions are sought. However, this chapter deals with relatively simple and straightforward *finite difference methods,* which are based on the natural idea of approximating partial derivatives with their discrete versions: *difference quotients.* The resulting discrete equation is therefore a *difference equation.*

In this chapter, these finite difference methods will be applied only to parabolic PDEs. However, the idea of finite differences is applicable to other PDEs in general. The heat equation, which is also known as the *diffusion* equation, is the basic example of a parabolic PDE. The Black-Scholes equation, on the other hand, is also parabolic, and it can be reduced to the heat equation.

Therefore, in the sequel, the finite difference methods are introduced, particularly, for the heat equation. Then, having investigated their stability analysis, the methods will be applied to the problem of pricing options by numerically solving the heat as well as the Black-Scholes equations. The methods included in this chapter are the *explicit, implicit* and the *Crank-*

Nicolson methods for solving parabolic PDEs. The stability analysis of the methods plays an important role in solutions of PDEs numerically, hence, a special care must be taken. Careless use of these finite difference methods may cause unreasonable results.

Due to early exercise possibility of *American* options, the governing PDEs, better to say, *inequalities*, need a special treatment. Early exercise possibility is best explained mathematically in terms of *free boundary* problems. A free boundary separates the regions of *exercise* and *continuation*: in the region of exercise an American option must be exercised. Hence, the associated Black-Scholes PDE must be solved in the region of continuation. Some of the possible approaches to pricing American options by solving numerically the related Black-Scholes equation and the free boundary problem will be presented in this chapter.

Finally, by the end of the chapter, an almost trivial relation between finite difference methods and the *tree methods* will be shown.

6.1 Classification of PDEs

The Black-Scholes PDE was introduced in Chapter 4 to find the theoretical price $V(S, t)$ of a derivative security depending on the price S of an underlying asset at time t. Using a stochastic model for the dynamics of the underlying asset and using the no-arbitrage principle, it was found that the value $V = V(S, t)$ for European options must satisfy the equation

$$\frac{\partial V}{\partial t} + \frac{1}{2}\sigma^2 S^2 \frac{\partial^2 V}{\partial S^2} + (r - \delta)S\frac{\partial V}{\partial S} - rV = 0. \tag{6.1}$$

Here, r is the risk-free interest rate, δ is the dividend yield, and σ is the asset price volatility. In order to price a particular option, the Black-Scholes equation (6.1) must be considered with suitable terminal and boundary conditions.

The Black-Scholes PDE in (6.1) has various mathematical classifications: it is *second-order*, *linear*, and *parabolic*. The *order* of a PDE is the highest order of the derivatives involved in the equation. For instance, an equation of the form,

$$a(x, y)\frac{\partial u}{\partial x} + b(x, y)\frac{\partial u}{\partial y} + c(x, y)u + d(x, y) = 0,$$

is a first-order PDE. Here, the coefficients $a, b, c,$ and d are given functions of the *independent variables* x and y, and the function $u = u(x, y)$ is the *dependent* variable. Furthermore, the PDE above is *linear*. This is because the functions a, b, c, and d depend only on these independent variables, but not on the function u; the derivatives and the function u itself appear as a linear combination. Thus, the Black-Scholes equation is a second-order linear equation. An example of a first-order *nonlinear* equation may be, for instance,

$$u\,u_x + (u_y)^2 = 1,$$

where we have used the notation: $u_\xi = \frac{\partial u}{\partial \xi}$. Another example of a nonlinear, but second-order, equation is

$$a(x, y, u_x)u_{xx} + b(x, y, u_y)u_{yy} + e(x, y, u_y)u_y + f(x, y, u)u = g(x, y, u_x).$$

Although it is nonlinear, the highest-order derivatives, u_{xx} and u_{yy}, occur linearly, but in a different way: the coefficients of these derivatives depend only on the lower-order derivatives as well as the independent variables. In such cases, the PDE is called a *quasilinear* equation.

For the sake of simplicity and, of course, because of the Black-Scholes equation, we will only deal with linear equations. It should be noted that while the Black-Scholes equation is linear, nonlinear versions may be obtained by relaxing some of the assumptions behind the Black-Scholes model. For example, a nonlinear equation arises when the transaction costs are introduced. Fortunately, the technique of finite differences of this chapter can be applied to those equations, but possibly with small modifications.

On the other hand, the Black-Scholes equation is classified as being a parabolic one. It is customary to classify a linear (or a quasilinear) second-order PDE of the form

$$a\frac{\partial^2 u}{\partial x^2} + b\frac{\partial^2 u}{\partial x \partial y} + c\frac{\partial^2 u}{\partial y^2} + d\frac{\partial u}{\partial x} + e\frac{\partial u}{\partial y} + fu + g = 0. \qquad (6.2)$$

This classification is based on the sign of the expression, $b^2 - 4ac$, which is called the *discriminant*:

- if $b^2 - 4ac > 0$, then the equation (6.2) is called *hyperbolic*,
- if $b^2 - 4ac = 0$, then the equation (6.2) is called *parabolic*,
- if $b^2 - 4ac < 0$, then the equation (6.2) is called *elliptic*.

The idea behind the classification is that with the hyperbolic equations there are two distinct curves in the xy-plane, called the *characteristics*, along which the PDE can be transformed into an *ordinary differential equation*. Parabolic equations have one characteristic, elliptic equations have none. We should also note that depending on the coefficients a, b, and c, a PDE may be of one type in a region of the plane and of another type in another region.

A typical example for an elliptic PDE is the *Laplace equation*,

$$\frac{\partial^2 u}{\partial x^2} + \frac{\partial^2 u}{\partial y^2} = 0.$$

Here, $a = c = 1$ and $b = 0$, so that $b^2 - 4ac = -4 < 0$. The *wave equation*,

$$\frac{\partial^2 u}{\partial t^2} - \rho^2 \frac{\partial^2 u}{\partial x^2} = 0,$$

where t represents time, and ρ is a specific constant, is a typical example of a hyperbolic equation, since the discriminant is $4\rho^2 > 0$. Finally, the *heat equation*, or the diffusion equation,

$$\frac{\partial u}{\partial t} = k \frac{\partial^2 u}{\partial x^2},$$

is an example of a parabolic equation, where t is the time and k is a specific constant. Note that $b^2 - 4ac = 0$. By a simple change of variables, $\tau = kt$, the equation may even be transformed into the dimensionless form,

$$\frac{\partial u}{\partial \tau} = \frac{\partial^2 u}{\partial x^2},$$

which is what we have already seen previously. The closed-form solutions to the Black-Scholes equation were given by solving this diffusion equation. Indeed, the Black-Scholes equation, due to $b = c = 0$, is *parabolic*. Such a close relation between the heat and the Black-Scholes equation can be explained by the characteristic curves. In fact, the use of the characteristic curves transforms the equations into their simpler forms: the *canonical forms*. Herewith, it is the diffusion equation for the Black-Scholes equation. As a matter of fact, although there are no real characteristic curves for elliptic equations, it is still possible to find such transformations by considering the characteristic curves in the complex plane.

Roughly speaking, a PDE must be accompanied with either an initial condition or boundary conditions, or both in order to have a solution in some certain class of functions. As an example, assume that $u(x, t)$ is the *temperature* at the point $x \in [0, 1]$ of a rod of length 1 at time t; the end points $x = 0$ and $x = 1$ are kept at a constant temperatures a and b, respectively. Suppose the initial temperature $f(x) = u(x, 0)$ of the rod is given over all of its length, $0 \le x \le 1$. Hence, the heat conduction problem must be equipped with *initial* and *boundary* conditions. Then, a "meaningful" solution may be drawn from the governing equations,

$$\frac{\partial u}{\partial t} = \frac{\partial^2 u}{\partial x^2}, \qquad 0 < x < 1, \quad t > 0,$$
$$u(x, 0) = f(x), \qquad 0 \le x \le 1,$$
$$u(0, t) = a, \quad u(1, t) = b, \qquad t \ge 0,$$

which is called an *initial boundary value problem*. Here, the *domain* of the PDE is bounded with respect to the spatial variable x and unbounded with respect to time variable t.

In financial problems, the initial condition is usually replaced by a *terminal* condition, as the option payoff is known at the expiration time T. Therefore, the domain is bounded with respect to the time variable, whereas the domain with respect to the price of the underlying asset may be unbounded (in principle, but not necessarily in practical applications in financial markets). The readers are advised to write the corresponding terminal and boundary conditions for the Black-Scholes equation (6.1) for European call or put options.

A final remark concerns whether or not a given problem is *well-posed*. A problem is called well-posed if

- there is a solution,
- the solution is unique,
- the solution depends continuously on the initial data.

Since the existence and uniqueness of PDEs are out of the scope of this book, all the problems we consider are implicitly assumed to be well-posed. In fact, our main focus will be on solving PDEs numerically by finite difference methods in the following sections.

Outlook

This introductory section is highly influenced by [Brandimarte (2002)] due to its simplified presentation. However, a more complete classical book on partial differential equations is considered to be [John (1991)]. On the other hand, for numerical solutions of partial differential equations by finite difference methods we refer to [Morton and Mayers (1995); Thomas (1995)].

6.2   Finite Difference Methods for Parabolic Equations

Finite difference methods to solve PDEs are based on the simple idea of approximating each partial derivative by a difference quotient. This transforms the functional equation into a set of algebraic equations. As in many numerical algorithms, the starting point is a finite series approximation: in most cases, the *Taylor polynomials*. Under suitable continuity and differentiability hypotheses, Taylor's theorem states that a function $f(x)$ may be expressed as

$$f(x+h) = f(x) + hf'(x) + \frac{1}{2}h^2 f''(x) + \frac{1}{6}h^3 f'''(x) + \mathcal{O}\left(h^4\right).$$

If the terms of order h^2 and higher are neglected, then the series gives

$$f'(x) = \frac{f(x+h) - f(x)}{h} + \mathcal{O}\left(h\right),$$

so that an approximation to $f'(x)$ can be obtained as

$$f'(x) \approx \frac{1}{h}\left[f(x+h) - f(x)\right].$$

This is the so-called *forward difference* approximation and it is of order $\mathcal{O}\left(h\right)$.

There are alternative ways to approximate first-order derivatives. Consider, for instance, the Taylor's formula for $f(x-h)$ with $h > 0$, that is,

$$f(x-h) = f(x) - hf'(x) + \frac{1}{2}h^2 f''(x) - \frac{1}{6}h^3 f'''(x) + \mathcal{O}\left(h^4\right).$$

Then, one could prefer to use this form of the series to obtain the finite difference formula,

$$f'(x) = \frac{f(x) - f(x-h)}{h} + \mathcal{O}\left(h\right).$$

So, an alternative to the forward difference, the *backward difference* approximation,

$$f'(x) \approx \frac{1}{h}\left[f(x) - f(x-h)\right],$$

can be used, which is again of order $\mathcal{O}\left(h\right)$.

On the other hand, subtracting the Taylor series for $f(x+h)$ and $f(x-h)$, another finite difference formula,

$$f'(x) = \frac{1}{2h}\left[f(x+h) - f(x-h)\right] + \mathcal{O}\left(h^2\right),$$

can be achieved. In fact, this is a *better* approximation than the preceding two, since the *truncation error* is of order $\mathcal{O}\left(h^2\right)$ in approximating $f'(x)$ by

$$f'(x) \approx \frac{1}{2h}\left[f(x+h) - f(x-h)\right].$$

This is the so-called *central difference* formula for $f'(x)$.

It should be emphasised that there are many other finite difference formulae to approximate $f'(x)$ with different truncation orders. Table 6.1 shows some of the other commonly used finite difference formulae, and the readers are encouraged to derive them by using the Taylor's expansion.

Table 6.1   Commonly used finite difference formulae for approximating derivatives

Derivative	Finite Difference	Order
$f'(x)$	$\dfrac{-f(x+2h) + 4f(x+h) - 3f(x)}{2h}$	$\mathcal{O}\left(h^2\right)$
	$\dfrac{3f(x) - 4f(x+h) + 3f(x-2h)}{2h}$	$\mathcal{O}\left(h^2\right)$
$f''(x)$	$\dfrac{f(x+2h) - 2f(x+h) - 3f(x)}{h^2}$	$\mathcal{O}\left(h\right)$
	$\dfrac{f(x) - 2f(x-h) + f(x-2h)}{h}$	$\mathcal{O}\left(h\right)$
	$\dfrac{-f(x+3h) + 4f(x+2h) - 5f(x+h) + 2f(x)}{h^2}$	$\mathcal{O}\left(h^2\right)$
$\dfrac{\partial^2 u(x,y)}{\partial x \partial y}$	$\dfrac{u(x+h,y) - u(x+h,y-k) - u(x,y) + u(x,y-k)}{hk}$	$\mathcal{O}\left(h\right) + \mathcal{O}\left(k\right)$
	$\dfrac{u(x+h,y+k) - u(x+h,y-k)}{4hk}$	
	$+\dfrac{-u(x-h,y+k) + u(x-h,y-k)}{4hk}$	$\mathcal{O}\left(h^2\right) + \mathcal{O}\left(k^2\right)$

Remark 6.1. Although central difference is better when compared to forward or backward differences, this may not imply a better method you get

when applied to a particular problem. Careless use of these finite differences may cause *unstable* algorithms.

The derivation of the finite difference formulae for higher-order derivatives is quite similar. Indeed, to apply the finite difference formulae to the Black-Scholes equation, an approximation to the second-order derivative is needed. This can easily be achieved by adding the Taylor's expansions of $f(x+h)$ and $f(x-h)$ as

$$f(x+h) + f(x-h) = 2f(x) + h^2 f''(x) + \mathcal{O}\left(h^4\right).$$

Rearranging the terms yields

$$f''(x) = \frac{1}{h^2}\left[f(x+h) - 2f(x) + f(x-h)\right] + \mathcal{O}\left(h^2\right)$$

and, hence, the *central difference* approximation for the second-derivative f'' at x is

$$f''(x) \approx \frac{1}{h^2}\left[f(x+h) - 2f(x) + f(x-h)\right].$$

Some other finite difference formulae that are commonly used are shown in Table 6.1.

In order to use these finite difference formulae for functions of several variables, when approximating the partial derivative with respect to a variable, the other variables are kept constant. Therefore, if $u = u(x,y)$ is a function of two variables, for instance, then the variable y is kept constant when we consider approximating the partial derivative $u_x(x,y)$ with respect to x. Therefore,

$$u_x(x,y) = \frac{1}{h}\left[u(x+h,y) - u(x,y)\right] + \mathcal{O}\left(h\right)$$

is a *forward* finite difference formula for $u = u(x,y)$. Of course, this can be obtained by using the Taylor series for functions of several variables, such as,

$$u(x+h,y) = u(x,y) + hu_x(x,y) + \frac{1}{2}h^2 u_{xx}(x,y) + \mathcal{O}\left(h^3\right).$$

Similarly, a *central* difference formula for the second derivative of u with respect to x can be given by

$$u_{xx}(x,y) = \frac{1}{h^2}\left[u(x+h,y) - 2u(x,y) + u(x-h,y)\right] + \mathcal{O}\left(h^2\right).$$

An approximation to a *mixed* partial derivative u_{xy}, where $u = u(x, y)$ for instance, can be derived from the Taylor series,

$$u(x + h, y + k) = u(x, y) + hu_x(x, y) + ku_y(x, y)$$
$$+ \tfrac{1}{2} \left(h^2 u_{xx}(x, y) + 2hk u_{xy}(x, y) + k^2 u_{yy}(x, y) \right) + \cdots .$$

However, it is also possible to derive a finite difference formula for a mixed derivative by using the forward difference formulae for both u_x and u_y. This can be calculated as follows:

$$u_{xy}(x, y) = \frac{\partial}{\partial x}\left(\frac{\partial u}{\partial y} \right) \approx \frac{\partial}{\partial x}\left(\frac{u(x, y + k) - u(x, y)}{k} \right)$$
$$\approx \frac{1}{k}\left(\frac{u(x + h, y + k) - u(x, y + k)}{h} - \frac{u(x + h, y) - u(x, y)}{h} \right)$$
$$= \frac{u(x + h, y + k) - u(x, y + k) - u(x + h, y) + u(x, y)}{hk}.$$

The order of this finite difference formula can be shown to be $\mathcal{O}(h) + \mathcal{O}(k)$. Some other finite difference formulae are shown in Table 6.1.

In order to apply the idea of finite differences to a PDE, we need first a *griding* strategy. Second, an interpolation of the discrete solutions obtained at those grid points in the domain of the PDE is required. Since it is possible to apply a linear interpolation as long as the *grid* used is sufficiently *fine*, we mainly focus on the finite difference solutions to PDEs.

In the sequel, the basic finite difference methods as well as their *stability* analysis will be discussed. The canonical form of parabolic equations, namely the diffusion, or the heat equation will be at the centre of the derived methods. However, the idea of finite differences can easily be extended to be used for other types of PDEs: hyperbolic, elliptic and even for quasilinear or nonlinear equations. The corresponding methods and the algebraic equations and, moreover, the stability analysis of those methods differ for sure.

6.2.1　*An Explicit Method*

With some effort, the Black-Scholes equation was transformed into the heat equation and then the closed-form solutions for the European call and put options were given in Chapter 4. So, it is worthwhile to investigate this equation first, and study how finite difference methods can be obtained for numerical solutions of PDEs. Then, it is possible to apply the finite difference techniques to the original Black-Scholes equation for options. Of course, one can choose to apply the methods directly to the heat equation and interpret the results for the Black-Scholes equation by using the necessary transformations that convert the former to the latter.

Let us now consider the diffusion equation, that is, the heat equation in its dimensionless form

$$\frac{\partial u}{\partial t} = \frac{\partial^2 u}{\partial x^2}, \qquad a < x < b, \quad t > 0. \tag{6.3}$$

The domain of interest is $x \in [a, b]$ and $t \geq 0$, that is, the strip $(x, t) \in [a, b] \times [0, \infty)$. Practically, the domain with respect to the time variable t will also be restricted to a finite horizon, $0 \leq t \leq T$, and we will be interested in the solution at time $t = T$. For a well-posed heat problem the governing partial differential equation (6.3) must be associated with initial and boundary conditions. So, let the *initial condition* be

$$u(x, 0) = f(x), \qquad a \leq x \leq b, \tag{6.4}$$

defined for $t = 0$, and let the *boundary conditions* be

$$u(a, t) = \alpha(t), \quad u(b, t) = \beta(t), \qquad t \geq 0, \tag{6.5}$$

for $x = a$ and $x = b$. Here, the functions f, α, and β may or may not be related to finance.

In order to apply the finite difference formulae the interval $[a, b]$ is discretized by a step length,

$$\Delta x = \frac{b - a}{N}, \qquad N \in \mathbb{N},$$

so that

$$x_i = a + i\,\Delta x, \qquad i = 0, 1, \ldots, N$$

are the points of the interval $[a, b] = [x_0, x_N]$. Similar discretization for the time interval $[0, T]$ is considered and the corresponding points in $[0, T]$ are defined by

$$t_j = t_0 + j\,\Delta t, \qquad j = 0, 1, \ldots, M,$$

where $t_0 = 0$. Here, the time step length may be given by

$$\Delta t = \frac{T}{M}, \qquad M \in \mathbb{N},$$

so that $t_M = t_0 + M\,\Delta t = T$. Thus, the grid points,

$$(x_i, t_j), \qquad i = 0, 1, \ldots, N \ \text{ and } \ j = 0, 1, \ldots, M,$$

are defined, which is also called the *mesh*. The discretization is shown in Fig. 6.1.

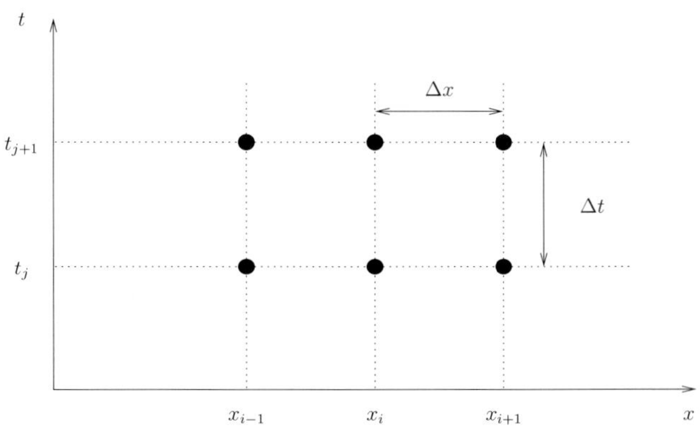

Fig. 6.1   The mesh and the grid points

On the mesh, the aim is to approximate the values of the unknown function u. In other words, the values

$$u_{ij} := u(x_i, t_j)$$

are of interest for every $0 \leq i \leq N$ and $0 \leq j \leq M$, both being integers.

A first possibility for coping with this heat equation is to approximate the derivative with respect to time t by a forward difference, and the second-derivative with respect to the spacial variable x by a central difference. Inserting these finite difference formulae into the heat equation (6.3) gives

$$\frac{u_{i,j+1} - u_{ij}}{\Delta t} + \mathcal{O}\left(\Delta t\right) = \frac{u_{i+1,j} - 2u_{ij} + u_{i-1,j}}{(\Delta x)^2} + \mathcal{O}\left((\Delta x)^2\right), \qquad (6.6)$$

for each $i = 1, 2, \ldots, N - 1$ and $j = 0, 1, \ldots, M - 1$. Discarding the error terms, $\mathcal{O}\left(\Delta t\right)$ and $\mathcal{O}\left((\Delta x)^2\right)$, and denoting the approximations to u_{ij} by

$$w_{ij} \approx u_{ij} := u(x_i, t_j),$$

the truncated version of the heat equation (6.3) turns into

$$\frac{w_{i,j+1} - w_{ij}}{\Delta t} = \frac{w_{i+1,j} - 2w_{ij} + w_{i-1,j}}{(\Delta x)^2}.$$

Now, denoting the term $\frac{\Delta t}{(\Delta x)^2}$ by λ as

$$\lambda := \frac{\Delta t}{(\Delta x)^2}, \tag{6.7}$$

the method can be written compactly in the form

$$w_{i,j+1} = \lambda w_{i-1,j} + (1 - 2\lambda)w_{ij} + \lambda w_{i+1,j}, \tag{6.8}$$

for each $i = 1, 2, \ldots, N - 1$ and $j = 0, 1, \ldots, M - 1$.

Fig. 6.2 accentuates the grid points that are connected by the formula (6.8). Such a graphical pattern that illustrates the structure of the method, is called *stencil*, or a *molecule*.

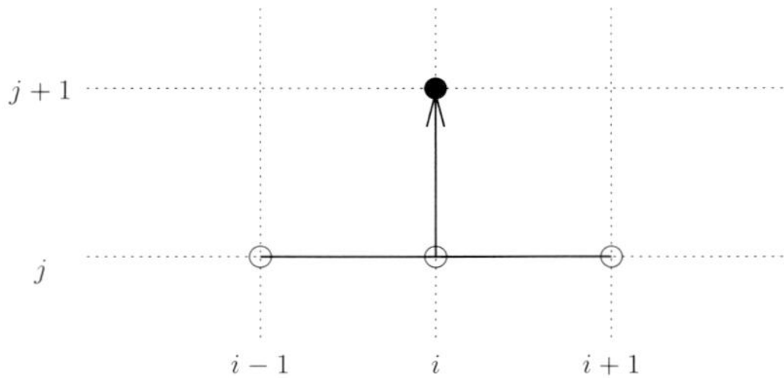

Fig. 6.2   Stencil (molecule) of the Explicit Finite Difference Method

Equation (6.8) and Fig. 6.2 corresponding to it suggest an evaluation according to the *time levels*. All grid points with the same index j form the jth time level. For a fixed j the values $w_{i,j+1}$ for all i of the time level $j+1$ are calculated from the values of the time level j, and we advance to the next time level. This formula is an explicit expression for each of the $w_{i,j+1}$: the values of w at level $j+1$ are not coupled and provides an explicit formula for all $w_{i,j+1}$, where $i = 0, 1, \ldots, N$. This method is, therefore, called an *explicit method*, or a *forward-difference method* to emphasise the forward time step. The method is also known as the *Euler method* for the diffusion equation.

The explicit Euler method starts with the values $w_{i,0}$ for $j = 0$ that are given by the initial condition,

$$w_{i,0} = u(x_i, 0) = f(x_i), \qquad i = 0, 1, \ldots, N. \qquad (6.9)$$

Moreover, the $w_{0,j}$ and $w_{N,j}$ for all $j = 1, 2, \ldots, M$ are known by the conditions at the boundaries $x = x_0$ and $x = x_N$,

$$\begin{aligned} w_{0,j} &= u(x_0, t_j) = u(a, t_j) = \alpha_j, \\ w_{N,j} &= u(x_N, t_j) = u(b, t_j) = \beta_j, \end{aligned} \qquad j = 1, 2, \ldots, M. \qquad (6.10)$$

An implementation of the explicit method is shown in Fig. 6.3 as a MATLAB function, which takes the initial and boundary conditions as input functions. See Fig. 6.4 for the implementation of these functions in MATLAB.

```
                        ─── heatExplicit.m ───
function sol = heatExplicit(f, alpha, beta, a, b, dx, dt, tmax)
% f, alpha, beta : functions of initial, (left and right, resp.) boundaries
% a, b : x \in [a,b]

N = round((b-a)/dx); M = round(tmax/dt);
sol = zeros(N+1,M+1); lambda = dt / (dx)^2; dLambda = 1-2*lambda;
x = a + dx*[0:N]; t = dt*[0:M];

% initial and boundary from f, alpha, beta
sol(:,1) = feval(f, x); % t=0
sol(1,:)   = feval(alpha, t); % x = a
sol(end,:) = feval(beta, t); % x = b

% solution in the domain
for j=1:M    % for t
   for i=2:N % for x
      sol(i,j+1) = lambda*sol(i-1,j) + dLambda*sol(i,j) + lambda*sol(i+1,j);
   end
end
```

Fig. 6.3   An implementation of the *explicit method* for the heat conduction problem

To illustrate the explicit method, we perform an artificial example below, where the initial and the boundary conditions are not related to finance, but to the heat diffusion problem on a rod of unit length.

Example 6.1. Consider the following initial boundary value problem for the heat equation,

$$\begin{aligned} u_t &= u_{xx}, & 0 < x < 1, \quad t > 0, \\ u(x, 0) &= \sin(\pi x), & 0 \leq x \leq 1, \\ u(0, t) &= u(1, t) = 0, & t > 0. \end{aligned}$$

```
————————————————— heatInitialFunction.m —————————————————
function f = heatInitialFunction(x)
% x : possible a vector

f = sin(pi*x);
```

```
————————————————— heatLeftBoundary.m —————————————————
function alpha = heatLeftBoundary(t)
% t : is possible a vector

alpha = zeros(size(t));
```

```
————————————————— heatRightBoundary.m —————————————————
function beta = heatRightBoundary(t)
% t : is possible a vector

beta = zeros(size(t));
```

Fig. 6.4　Initial and boundary functions for the heat problem

Our aim is to calculate an approximation w for u at the points (x, t), for example $(x, t) = (0.2, 0.5)$. The exact solution to the heat equation above is, in fact, known in closed-form:

$$u(x, t) = e^{-\pi^2 t} \sin(\pi x),$$

which can be obtained by simple techniques, such as *separation of variables*, for solving PDEs. Thus, the exact value we like to estimate is

$$u(0.2, 0.5) = 0.004227\dots.$$

The explicit finite difference method implemented in Fig. 6.3 is called by the MATLAB script shown in Fig. 6.5. The script is run for different values of Δt in order to check the behaviour of the numerical solution for a variety of $\lambda = \frac{\Delta t}{(\Delta x)^2}$. The output of the script is collected in Table 6.2.

Table 6.2　Several solutions of the heat equation at $x = 0.2$, with $\Delta x = 0.1$ obtained by the explicit method

$\lambda = \frac{\Delta t}{(\Delta x)^2}$	Δt	$w(0.2, 0.5)$
0.05	0.0005	0.0043
0.10	0.0010	0.0043
0.30	0.0030	0.0041
0.50	0.0050	0.0039
0.70	0.0070	3.5596
1.00	0.0100	-6.5593×10^5

The graph shown in Fig. 6.6(a) depicts how the exact and the approximate solutions $u(x, t)$ behave at time $t = 0.5$ for $\lambda = 0.05$. In Fig. 6.6(b),

```
________________________ testHeatSolutions.m ________________________
% testHeatSolutions
clear all, close all,
% exact Solution
u = inline('exp(-pi^2*t)*sin(pi*x)', 'x', 't');
a = 0; b = 1; tmax = 0.5; dx = 0.1; dt = 0.0005; % dt = 0.01;

f = @heatInitialFunction;
alpha = @heatLeftBoundary; beta = @heatRightBoundary;
 w = heatExplicit(f, alpha, beta, a, b, dx, dt, tmax);
% w = heatImplicit(f, alpha, beta, a, b, dx, dt, tmax);
% w = heatCrankNicolson(f, alpha, beta, a, b, dx, dt, tmax);

[m,n] = size(w); x = linspace(a,b,m); t = linspace(0,tmax,n);
w(3,end), u(0.2,0.5), lambda = dt/dx^2 % at x = 0.2, t = 0.5

figure(1), plot(x, u(x,tmax)), hold on % exact solution
plot(x, w(:,end), 'rx'),    % approx
xlabel('x','FontSize',12), ylabel('w(:,end)','FontSize',12), hold off
print -r900 -depsc -cmyk '../figures/testHeatExplicit_a'
figure(2), mesh(x,t,w'), xlabel('x','FontSize',12), ylabel('t','FontSize',12),
zlabel('w(x,t)','FontSize',12), hold off
print -r300 -depsc -cmyk '../figures/testHeatExplicit_b'
```

Fig. 6.5   A script file that test the *explicit method* for the heat conduction problem

the surface $u = u(x,t)$ approximated by the explicit method is shown using the same λ.

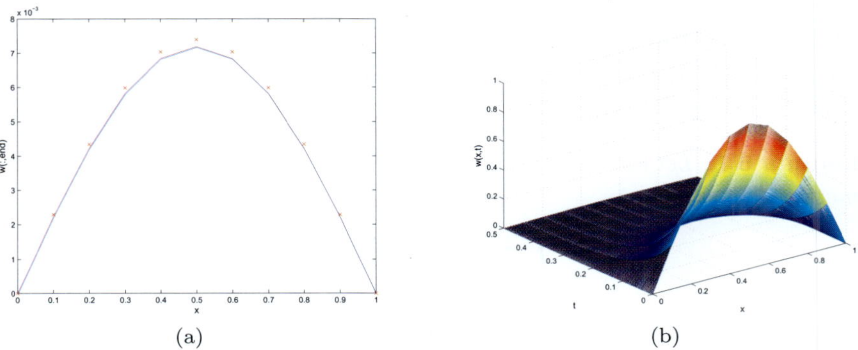

(a)   (b)

Fig. 6.6   Comparison of the exact solution with the approximate solutions at the final time (a), and the whole surface (b) obtained by the *explicit method*

It turns out that for sufficiently small choices of Δt the method leads to a reasonable approximation to the exact solutions. This is true as long as λ is about $1/2$. On the other hand, when λ gets bigger in magnitude the explicit method is no longer trusted. Moreover, it causes a disaster when $\lambda = 1$, for example! This happens, because the explicit method is used blindly, without investigating its stability. It seems, there is a relation between the discretization and the method's stability, a *stability condition.*

Stability Analysis of the Explicit Method

We start with a theorem that is useful for investigating the existence of a fixed point of a function (or an operator); in this case, it is considered to be linear and of the form, $h(x) = Qx + c$, where Q is a matrix and x, c are vectors of suitable dimensions. The theorem and its proof can be found in (Cheney and Kincaid, 1994, p. 188).

Theorem 6.1. *For the iteration formula*

$$x^{(k)} = Qx^{(k-1)} + c$$

to produce a sequence converging to $(I - Q)^{-1} c$, where I is the identity matrix, for any starting vector $x^{(0)}$, it is necessary and sufficient that the spectral radius of Q be less than one.

The spectral radius $\rho(Q)$ of a matrix Q is defined by the maximum length of the eigenvalues of Q. That is,

$$\rho(Q) := \max \left\{ |\lambda| \; : \; \det(Q - \lambda I) = 0 \right\}.$$

The following lemma will prove useful in the sequel when computing the eigenvalues of the matrices arising from the finite difference methods of finite differences.

Lemma 6.1. *Let $\theta_k = \frac{k\pi}{n+1}$ for each $k = 1, 2, \ldots, n$, and let G be an $n \times n$ matrix defined by*

$$G = \begin{pmatrix} 2 & -1 & 0 & \cdots & 0 & 0 \\ -1 & 2 & -1 & \cdots & 0 & 0 \\ 0 & -1 & 2 & \cdots & 0 & 0 \\ \vdots & \vdots & \vdots & \ddots & \vdots & \vdots \\ 0 & 0 & 0 & \cdots & 2 & -1 \\ 0 & 0 & 0 & \cdots & -1 & 2 \end{pmatrix}.$$

Then, the eigenvalues of the matrix G are

$$\mu_k = 2 - 2\cos\theta_k,$$

associated with the corresponding eigenvectors,

$$v_k = [\sin\theta_k,\, \sin(2\theta_k),\, \ldots,\, \sin(n\theta_k)]^T.$$

Proof. The proof follows simply from $Gv_k = \mu_k v_k$ by direct substitution. Let G_i be the ith row of G, and denote the jth component of v_k by $v_{k,j}$. That is, $v_{k,j} = \sin(j\theta_k)$. For simplicity, assume that $1 < i < n$. Then,

$$\begin{aligned}
G_i v_k &= -v_{k,i-1} + 2v_{k,i} - v_{k,i+1} \\
&= -\sin((i-1)\theta_k) + 2\sin(i\theta_k) - \sin((i+1)\theta_k) \\
&= (2 - 2\cos\theta_k)\sin(i\theta_k) \\
&= \mu_k v_{k,i}.
\end{aligned}$$

Similar relations also hold for the special cases when $i = 1$ and $i = n$. Therefore, combining $G_i v_k = \mu_k v_{k,i}$ for all $i = 1, 2, \ldots, n$ shows that $Gv_k = \mu_k v_k$ for each $k = 1, 2, \ldots, n$, and completes the proof. $\square$

Exercise 6.1. Let $\xi, \eta, \gamma \in \mathbb{R}$ be such that $\gamma/\eta \geq 0$, and let

$$G = \begin{pmatrix}
\xi & \eta & 0 & \cdots & 0 & 0 \\
\gamma & \xi & \eta & \cdots & 0 & 0 \\
0 & \gamma & \xi & \cdots & 0 & 0 \\
\vdots & \vdots & \vdots & \ddots & \vdots & \vdots \\
0 & 0 & 0 & \cdots & \xi & \eta \\
0 & 0 & 0 & \cdots & \gamma & \xi
\end{pmatrix}$$

be a tridiagonal $n \times n$ matrix. Verify that the eigenvalues μ_k and the eigenvectors v_k of G are

$$\mu_k = \xi + 2\eta\sqrt{\frac{\gamma}{\eta}}\cos\theta_k,$$

$$v_k = \left[\sqrt{\frac{\gamma}{\eta}}\sin\theta_k,\, \left(\sqrt{\frac{\gamma}{\eta}}\right)^2\sin(2\theta_k),\, \ldots,\, \left(\sqrt{\frac{\gamma}{\eta}}\right)^n\sin(n\theta_k)\right]^T,$$

where $\theta_k = \frac{k\pi}{n+1}$ for each $k = 1, 2, \ldots, n$.

Therefore, for the stability analysis it is useful to write the explicit method (6.8), together with the initial values in (6.9) and the boundary conditions in (6.10), in the matrix-vector form. To do so, notice that the explicit method defined by (6.8) can be written as a system of equations,

$$w_{1,j+1} = \lambda w_{0,j} + (1 - 2\lambda)w_{1,j} + \lambda w_{2,j},$$

$$w_{2,j+1} = \lambda w_{1,j} + (1 - 2\lambda)w_{2,j} + \lambda w_{3,j},$$

$$\vdots$$

$$w_{N-1,j+1} = \lambda w_{N-2,j} + (1 - 2\lambda)w_{N-1,} + \lambda w_{N,j}.$$

This system holds for every $j = 0, 1, \ldots, M - 1$. Note also that the values $w_{0,j}$ and $w_{N,j}$ are known from (6.10). Thus, if at the time level j the unknown values $w_{1,j}, w_{2,j}, \ldots, w_{N-1,j}$ are collected in the vectors

$$w^{(j)} := \begin{bmatrix} w_{1,j} \\ w_{2,j} \\ \vdots \\ w_{N-1,j} \end{bmatrix},$$

then the coefficient matrix of the system becomes

$$A = \begin{bmatrix} 1 - 2\lambda & \lambda & 0 & \cdots & 0 & 0 \\ \lambda & 1 - 2\lambda & \lambda & \cdots & 0 & 0 \\ 0 & \lambda & 1 - 2\lambda & \cdots & 0 & 0 \\ \vdots & \vdots & \vdots & \ddots & \vdots & \vdots \\ 0 & 0 & 0 & \cdots & 1 - 2\lambda & \lambda \\ 0 & 0 & 0 & \cdots & \lambda & 1 - 2\lambda \end{bmatrix}.$$

Hence, the explicit method can be written neatly in the matrix-vector form,

$$w^{(j+1)} = A\,w^{(j)} + b^{(j)}, \qquad j = 0, 1, \ldots, M - 1, \tag{6.11}$$

where the $b^{(j)}$ are the column vectors defined by

$$b^{(j)} = \begin{bmatrix} \lambda w_{0,j} \\ 0 \\ \vdots \\ 0 \\ \lambda w_{N,j} \end{bmatrix} = \lambda \begin{bmatrix} \alpha_j \\ 0 \\ \vdots \\ 0 \\ \beta_j \end{bmatrix}, \tag{6.12}$$

which consists of the known boundary values. This formulation in (6.11) with the matrix A is needed only for theoretical purposes. An actual computer implementation of the explicit method should generally use the iterative scalar equation (6.8) together with the initial and boundary data from equations (6.9) and (6.10), respectively. Even if the matrices above are used in implementation, there is no need to store the zeros appearing in the *tridiagonal* matrix A.

In order to understand what *stability* of a method means let us denote by $e^{(0)}$ the error introduced to the system initially at $j = 0$. This error can be defined by the difference

$$e^{(0)} = w^{(0)} - \tilde{w}^{(0)},$$

where $w^{(0)}$ is the value that is free of the introduced error, and $\tilde{w}^{(0)}$ is the value that includes the error. The latter is used in the actual calculations by the computers or algorithms that use the prescribed method. The stability analysis is therefore interested in the propagation of this error to the future stages of the method. Therefore,

$$e^{(j)} = w^{(j)} - \tilde{w}^{(j)}, \tag{6.13}$$

is the accumulated error defined for each integer $j > 0$, where $w^{(j)}$ represents the value that is free of the error, and $\tilde{w}^{(j)}$ is the value that includes the introduced error. In other words, if the explicit method is considered, then

$$w^{(j+1)} = A\, w^{(j)} + b^{(j)},$$
$$\tilde{w}^{(j+1)} = A\, \tilde{w}^{(j)} + b^{(j)},$$

holds for every $j = 0, 1, \ldots, M - 1$. Therefore, the accumulated errors satisfy the *recurrence* relation

$$e^{(j)} = A\, w^{(j-1)} - A\, \tilde{w}^{(j)} = A\, e^{(j-1)}.$$

Hence, recursive application of this relation for each $j > 0$ yields

$$e^{(j)} = A^j\, e^{(0)}, \tag{6.14}$$

which relates the accumulated error $e^{(j)}$ to the introduced error $e^{(0)}$. As long as the error $e^{(j)}$ is *bounded* we call the method *stable*. If the accumulated error is *unbounded* then the method is said to be *unstable*. Such a stability analysis is called a *matrix stability analysis*.

According to Theorem 6.1, therefore, the explicit method is stable if and only if the spectral radius of the coefficient matrix A of the method is less than one, unity. Moreover, if this is the case, the error $e^{(j)}$ vanishes as j tends to infinity, that is,

$$\lim_{j \to \infty} e^{(j)} = 0.$$

Therefore, the eigenvalues of the matrix A must be investigated whether they are less than unity in absolute value. To do so, either Lemma 6.1 or Exercise 6.1 can be used, however, the former is preferred in the following analysis.

Note that the matrix A of the explicit method is of size $(N-1)\times(N-1)$, and it can be written as follows:

$$A = I - \lambda G,$$

where G is an $(N-1) \times (N-1)$ matrix that has the form in Lemma 6.1. Therefore, if μ^G represents an eigenvalue of G then it is easy to see that an eigenvalue of A is of the form

$$\mu^A = 1 - \lambda \mu^G.$$

Hence, due to Lemma 6.1 all the eigenvalues μ_k^A of A are found to be

$$\mu_k^A = 1 - \lambda \mu_k^G = 1 - 4\lambda \sin^2 \frac{k\pi}{2N}, \quad k = 1, 2, \ldots, N-1.$$

Here, we use a trigonometric identity to calculate

$$\mu_k^G = 2 - 2\cos \frac{k\pi}{N} = 4\lambda \sin^2 \frac{k\pi}{2N}.$$

Therefore, the stability requirement $\left| \mu_k^A \right| < 1$ can be written as

$$\left| 1 - 4\lambda \sin^2 \frac{k\pi}{2N} \right| < 1, \quad k = 1, 2, \ldots, N-1.$$

Fortunately, this implies the two inequalities,

$$\lambda > 0 \quad \text{and} \quad -1 < 1 - 4\lambda \sin^2 \frac{k\pi}{2N},$$

the former of which is trivially satisfied since Δx and Δt are assumed to be positive. The latter, on the other hand, can be rearranged to give

$$\frac{1}{2} > \lambda \sin^2 \frac{k\pi}{2N}, \quad k = 1, 2, \ldots, N-1.$$

The greatest restriction on λ occurs when $\frac{k\pi}{2N} = \frac{\pi}{2}$. However, this never happens, but $\sin^2 \frac{k\pi}{2N}$ becomes very close to one when $k = N-1$ for N being too large. Therefore, we must require $\lambda \leq 1/2$.

Thus, following the argument above, we conclude that the *explicit method*,

$$w^{(j+1)} = A w^{(j)} + b^{(j)}, \quad j = 0, 1, \ldots, M-1,$$

is *stable* for the values of $\lambda = \frac{\Delta t}{(\Delta x)^2}$ that satisfy

$$0 < \lambda \le \frac{1}{2}. \tag{6.15}$$

In view of $\lambda = \frac{\Delta t}{(\Delta x)^2}$, this stability condition in (6.15) bounds the time step lengths Δt to the spacial step lengths Δx by the inequality

$$0 < \Delta t \le \frac{(\Delta x)^2}{2}.$$

This means, one has to choose Δt so small that the method stays in the stability region. Conversely, this could also be interpreted as follows: for a given *small* time step length Δt one has to take a *relatively big* step Δx in the spacial variable. However, this may cause *inefficient* discretization, no matter the stability condition holds.

6.2.2 *An Implicit Method*

When the explicit method was introduced in the previous section, the time derivative of the unknown function was approximated by a forward difference. Now, instead, the *backward* finite difference formula,

$$\frac{\partial u_{ij}}{\partial t} = \frac{u_{ij} - u_{i,j-1}}{\Delta t} + \mathcal{O}\left(\Delta t\right),$$

of order $\mathcal{O}\left(\Delta t\right)$ is going to be used. The second order derivative with respect to the spacial variable x is again the central difference approximation. As before, denote the approximations to u_{ij} by

$$w_{ij} \approx u_{ij} = u(x_i, t_j),$$

within the same framework of mesh defined by

$$x_i = a + i\,\Delta x, \qquad i = 0, 1, \ldots, N,$$
$$t_j = t_0 + j\,\Delta t, \qquad j = 0, 1, \ldots, M, \quad t_0 = 0.$$

Discarding the error terms of order $\mathcal{O}\left(\Delta t\right)$ and $\mathcal{O}\left((\Delta x)^2\right)$, the alternative finite difference method for the heat problem,

$$\frac{\partial u}{\partial t} = \frac{\partial^2 u}{\partial x^2}, \qquad a < x < b, \quad t > 0, \tag{6.16}$$

can be written as

$$-\lambda w_{i-1,j} + (2\lambda + 1)w_{ij} - \lambda w_{i+1,j} = w_{i,j-1}, \tag{6.17}$$

for each $i = 1, 2, \ldots, N - 1$ and $j = 1, 2, \ldots, M$. Here, the meaning of λ is again the same, and $\lambda := \frac{\Delta t}{(\Delta x)^2}$.

The method (6.17) relates the time level j to the time level $j - 1$. For the transition from the $(j - 1)$st level to the next, only the value $w_{i,j-1}$ on the right hand side of (6.17) is known; however, on the other hand side, the values $w_{i-1,j}$, w_{ij}, and $w_{i+1,j}$ are all unknown. The corresponding stencil is depicted in Fig. 6.7.

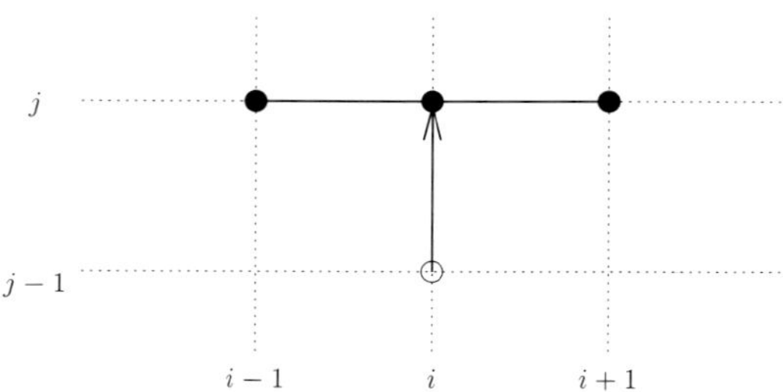

Fig. 6.7   Stencil (molecule) of the Implicit Finite Difference Scheme

There is no simple explicit formula with which the unknown can be computed one after the other. Rather, if possible, they all have to be determined at once. Fortunately, the representation of the method (6.17) consists of $N - 1$ linear equations in the unknown variables, $w_{1,j}, w_{2,j}, \ldots, w_{N-1,j}$ at the jth time level. Thus, all these equations related to the model (6.17) can be solved for the unknown values to pass to the next time level.

A matrix-vector notation reveals the structure of the method: the linear equations associated to the method are given by

$$-\lambda w_{0,j} + (2\lambda + 1)w_{1,j} - \lambda w_{2,j} = w_{1,j-1},$$
$$-\lambda w_{1,j} + (2\lambda + 1)w_{2,j} - \lambda w_{3,j} = w_{2,j-1},$$
$$\vdots$$
$$-\lambda w_{N-2,j} + (2\lambda + 1)w_{N-1,j} - \lambda w_{N,j} = w_{N-1,j-1}.$$

Equivalently, if the coefficient matrix is

$$A = \begin{bmatrix} 2\lambda+1 & -\lambda & 0 & \cdots & 0 & 0 \\ -\lambda & 2\lambda+1 & -\lambda & \cdots & 0 & 0 \\ 0 & -\lambda & 2\lambda+1 & \cdots & 0 & 0 \\ \vdots & \vdots & \vdots & \ddots & \vdots & \vdots \\ 0 & 0 & 0 & \cdots & 2\lambda+1 & -\lambda \\ 0 & 0 & 0 & \cdots & -\lambda & 2\lambda+1 \end{bmatrix}$$

and the vectors of unknowns and the boundary data are

$$w^{(j)} = \begin{bmatrix} w_{1,j} \\ w_{2,j} \\ \vdots \\ w_{N-1,j} \end{bmatrix} \quad \text{and} \quad b^{(j-1)} = \begin{bmatrix} \lambda w_{0,j} \\ 0 \\ \vdots \\ 0 \\ \lambda w_{N,j} \end{bmatrix} = \lambda \begin{bmatrix} \alpha_j \\ 0 \\ \vdots \\ 0 \\ \beta_j \end{bmatrix},$$

then the method can be written simply in matrix-vector notation as

$$A\,w^{(j+1)} = w^{(j)} + b^{(j)}, \qquad j = 0, 1, \ldots, M - 1. \qquad (6.18)$$

Notice the shifting of the index so as to make it similar in appearance to the explicit method! Hence, for each time level j a system of equations must be solved to advance to the $(j+1)$st level. This method is called *fully implicit method*, or simply *implicit method*. It is also called *backward-difference*, or the *backward Euler* method. An implementation of the algorithm is shown in Fig. 6.8.

```
                          heatImplicit.m
function sol = heatImplicit(f, alpha, beta, a, b, dx, dt, tmax)
% f, alpha, beta : functions of initial, (left and right, resp.) boundaries
% a, b : x \in [a,b]

N = round((b-a)/dx); M = round(tmax/dt); sol = zeros(N+1,M+1);
lambda = dt / (dx)^2; dLambda = 1+2*lambda;
x = a + dx*[0:N]; t = dt*[0:M];

% initial and boundary from f, alpha, beta
sol(:,1) = feval(f, x); % t=0
sol(1,:)   = feval(alpha, t); % x = a
sol(end,:) = feval(beta, t); % x = b

A = diag((dLambda) * ones(N-1,1)) - ...
    diag(lambda*ones(N-2,1),1) - diag(lambda*ones(N-2,1),-1);
[L, U] = lu(A);

bj = zeros(N-1,1);
for j=1:M
    bj(1) = lambda*sol(1,j+1); bj(end) = lambda*sol(end,j+1);
    sol(2:N,j+1) = U \ ( L \ (sol(2:N,j)+bj) );
end
```

Fig. 6.8   An implementation of the fully *implicit method* for the heat conduction problem

In this implicit method, at each time step, although a system of linear equations has to be solved, the cost of applying the method is low, since the matrix A is constant: it does not depend on the time level j. Since the matrix A is independent of the time levels j, an *LU-decomposition* of A is calculated only once at the initialisation stage of the implementation in Fig. 6.8. An *LU*-decomposition of the matrix A has the form

$$A = L\,U,$$

where L is a lower and U is an upper triangular matrix of the same size as of A.[1] Existence of such a factorisation, of course, depends on the properties of the matrix. The algorithm behind the *LU*-decomposition is based on the *Gaussian elimination*. In the case of the implicit method, it is easy to show the existence of such a factorisation for the tridiagonal symmetric matrix A. Even, one can try using the Cholesky decomposition.

Using the *LU*-decomposition, it is easy to solve the system (6.18) by using the matrices L and U. First, introducing the temporary variable $y^{(j+1)} := Uw^{(j+1)}$, the system

$$L\,y^{(j+1)} = w^{(j)} + b^{(j)}$$

must be solved by a method called *forward substitution*. Denote this substitution method, formally, by

$$y^{(j+1)} = L^{-1}\left(w^{(j)} + b^{(j)}\right),$$

although the inverse L^{-1} is never computed numerically. Then, the solution $w^{(j+1)}$ is obtained by using a similar method called *backward substitution*, which may be denoted by

$$w^{(j+1)} = U^{-1}y^{(j+1)}.$$

Therefore, combining the forward and backward substitutions, the solution to the system of linear equations can be written, formally,

$$w^{(j+1)} = U^{-1}\left\{L^{-1}\left(w^{(j)} + b^{(j)}\right)\right\}$$

in terms of U and L.

Before the stability analysis of the fully implicit method (6.18) let us apply the method to the heat equation of Example 6.1 in Section 6.2.1. In the example below, you may wish to check what happens when $\lambda = 1$, the disastrous case!

Example 6.2. Consider again the problem in Example 6.1, where the heat conducting problem

$$u_t = u_{xx}, \qquad 0 < x < 1, \quad t > 0,$$

$$u(x,0) = \sin(\pi x), \qquad 0 \le x \le 1,$$

$$u(0,t) = u(1,t) = 0, \qquad t > 0,$$

---

[1]An *LU*-decomposition (or factorisation) of A is generally written as $PA = LDU$, where P is a permutation matrix, and D is a diagonal matrix.

was considered. The discretization by the choices, $\Delta x = 0.1$ and $\Delta t = 0.01$ were used so that $\lambda = 1$, but the explicit method of Section 6.2.1 produced an unsatisfactory result. See Table 6.2. In this example, however, a similar table of values is to be presented by the fully implicit method of this section. These results are shown in Table 6.3 for different choices of λ.

Table 6.3 Several solutions of the heat equation at $x = 0.2$, with $\Delta x = 0.1$ obtained by the fully implicit method

$\lambda = \frac{\Delta t}{(\Delta x)^2}$	Δt	$w(0.2, 0.5)$
0.05	0.0005	0.0045
0.10	0.0010	0.0045
0.30	0.0030	0.0047
0.50	0.0050	0.0049
0.70	0.0070	0.0053
1.00	0.0100	0.0055

The explicit method was unstable for some choices of the step lengths, however, the implicit method is now stable, even for the case $\lambda = 1$. Calculation of the desired value for $\lambda = 1$ shows that $w_{2,50} \approx 0.0055$, which is relatively good for the approximation to the exact value. In fact, the values in Table 6.3 can be improved by choosing smaller steps Δx. Moreover, it seems that there is no restriction on the step sizes that can be chosen, unlike the *conditional stability* of the explicit method, given by the relation in (6.15).

Stability Analysis of the Implicit Method

The fully implicit method has the form $A\, w^{(j+1)} = w^{(j)} + b^{(j)}$, which can also be written as

$$w^{(j+1)} = A^{-1}\left(w^{(j)} + b^{(j)}\right) \tag{6.19}$$

as long as the matrix A is nonsingular. Hence, in order to determine the conditions for stability, the eigenvalues of the matrix A^{-1} have to be investigated. Fortunately, since $A = I + \lambda G$, where G is the matrix defined in Lemma 6.1, the eigenvalues $\mu^{A^{-1}}$ can be calculated from those of A: the eigenvalues μ^A of the $(N-1) \times (N-1)$ matrix A are then given by

$$\mu_k^A = 1 + \lambda \mu_k^G,$$

where μ_k^G are the eigenvalues of G, that is,

$$\mu_k^G = 2 - 2\cos\theta_k.$$

Here, again $\theta_k = \frac{k\pi}{N}$ for each $k = 1, 2, \ldots, N-1$.

Thus, one can easily calculate to verify that

$$\mu_k^A = 1 + 4\lambda \sin^2 \frac{k\pi}{2N} > 1, \quad k = 1, 2, \ldots, N-1$$

for every $\lambda > 0$. In fact, this ensures the existence of A^{-1}. Moreover, the desired eigenvalues $\mu_k^{A^{-1}}$ of A^{-1} satisfy the relation,

$$\left| \mu_k^{A^{-1}} \right| = \left| \frac{1}{1 + 4\lambda \sin^2 \frac{k\pi}{2N}} \right| < 1,$$

for all $k = 1, 2, \ldots, N-1$, and for any λ. Hence, the implicit method is *unconditionally stable*, meaning that there is no condition on the choice of the step sizes Δx and Δt.

6.2.3 *Crank-Nicolson Method*

For the methods previously obtained, the discretization of $\frac{\partial u}{\partial t}$ are of order $\mathcal{O}(\Delta t)$. One would prefer a method where this time discretization has a better order, for instance $\mathcal{O}\left((\Delta t)^2\right)$, and the stability is still unconditional. Crank and Nicolson suggested to average the forward and the backward difference methods, namely the explicit and the implicit schemes derived for the heat equation,

$$\frac{\partial u}{\partial t} = \frac{\partial^2 u}{\partial x^2}.$$

Consider the forward time finite difference,

$$\frac{w_{i,j+1} - w_{ij}}{\Delta t} = \frac{w_{i+1,j} - 2w_{ij} + w_{i-1,j}}{(\Delta x)^2} \tag{6.20}$$

at the time level j, that discretize the heat equation at the node (x_i, t_j). Here, the central difference is used in the space variable x. Further, consider the discretization at the node (x_i, t_{j+1}) by using, now, the backward finite difference in time:

$$\frac{w_{i,j+1} - w_{ij}}{\Delta t} = \frac{w_{i+1,j+1} - 2w_{i,j+1} + w_{i-1,j+1}}{(\Delta x)^2}, \tag{6.21}$$

where, again, the central difference is used in x.

In fact, the methods described by (6.20) and (6.21) are the methods of previous sections. That is, they are, respectively, the explicit and the implicit methods to approximate the heat equation. However, by adding these two equations, namely, (6.20) and (6.21), another method can be described as

$$\frac{w_{i,j+1} - w_{ij}}{\Delta t} = \frac{1}{2(\Delta x)^2}\Big[w_{i+1,j} - 2w_{ij} + w_{i-1,j} \\ + w_{i+1,j+1} - 2w_{i,j+1} + w_{i-1,j+1} \Big]. \tag{6.22}$$

Combining the similar terms on each side yields the so-called *Crank-Nicolson* method for the heat equation. The method is defined by

$$-\lambda w_{i-1,j+1} + 2(1+\lambda)w_{i,j+1} - \lambda w_{i+1,j+1} \\ = \lambda w_{i-1,j} + 2(1-\lambda)w_{ij} + \lambda w_{i+1,j} \tag{6.23}$$

for all $i = 1, 2, \ldots, N - 1$ and $j = 0, 1, \ldots, M - 1$. Here, λ has again the usual definition: $\lambda = \frac{\Delta t}{(\Delta x)^2}$. In Fig. 6.9, the corresponding stencil of the method is depicted. The Crank-Nicolson method relates the unknown values $w_{i-1,j+1}, w_{i,j+1}$, and $w_{i+1,j+1}$ at the time level $j + 1$ to the corresponding known ones at the level j. Thus, all the unknown values must be determined at once, and hence, it is another *implicit* method.

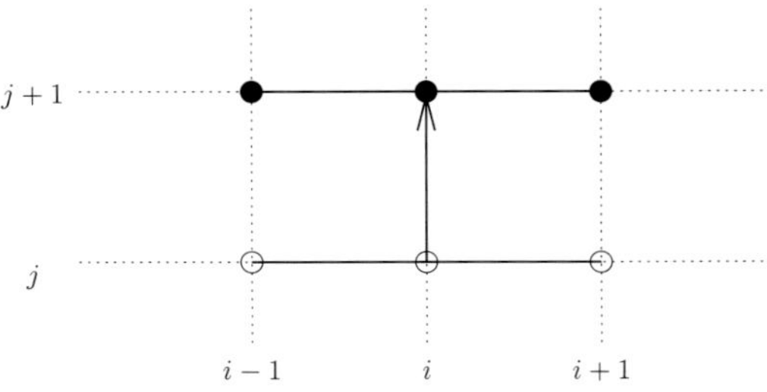

Fig. 6.9   Stencil (molecule) of the Crank-Nicolson Scheme

Remark 6.2. The Crank-Nicolson method can also be obtained by using a *convex* combination of the explicit and the implicit methods. That is, for $0 \le \theta \le 1$, the method

$$\frac{w_{i,j+1} - w_{ij}}{\Delta t} = \frac{1}{(\Delta x)^2} \left\{ \theta \left(w_{i-1,j+1} - 2w_{i,j+1} + w_{i+1,j+1} \right) \right.$$
$$\left. + (1 - \theta) \left(w_{i-1,j} - 2w_{ij} + w_{i+1,j} \right) \right\} \tag{6.24}$$

is sometimes called the *θ-averaged method*, or simply the θ-method for the heat equation. Taking this method for granted, one can obtain

- the explicit method by choosing $\theta = 0$,
- the (fully) implicit method by choosing $\theta = 1$, and
- the Crank-Nicolson method by choosing $\theta = \frac{1}{2}$.

In order to determine the order of the Crank-Nicolson method, a practical notation for the central difference formula for u_{xx} is used:

$$\delta_x^2 w_{ij} := \frac{w_{i+1,j} - 2w_{ij} + w_{i-1,j}}{(\Delta x)^2},$$

which is of order $\mathcal{O}\left((\Delta x)^2\right)$. Hence, one can show that

$$\delta_x^2 u_{ij} = \frac{\partial^2}{\partial x^2} u_{ij} + \frac{h^2}{12} \frac{\partial^4}{\partial x^4} u_{ij} + \mathcal{O}\left(h^4\right)$$

holds by using the Taylor series,

$$u_{i\mp 1,j} = u_{ij} \mp h \frac{\partial}{\partial x} u_{ij} + \frac{h^2}{2!} \frac{\partial^2}{\partial x^2} u_{ij} \mp \frac{h^3}{3!} \frac{\partial^3}{\partial x^3} u_{ij} + \frac{h^4}{4!} \frac{\partial^4}{\partial x^4} u_{ij}$$
$$\mp \frac{h^5}{5!} \frac{\partial^5}{\partial x^5} u_{ij} + \mathcal{O}\left(h^6\right),$$

for sufficiently smooth u, where $h = \Delta x$. Therefore, in the case of the Crank-Nicolson method defined by (6.22), the local discretization error, say ε, can be written as

$$\varepsilon := \frac{u_{i,j+1} - u_{ij}}{\Delta t} - \frac{1}{2} \left\{ \delta_x^2 u_{ij} + \delta_x^2 u_{i,j+1} \right\}.$$

The truncation error describes how well the exact solution u of a differential equation satisfies the corresponding difference method. Applying the meaning of δ_x^2 one can easily obtain that

$$\varepsilon = \mathcal{O}\left((\Delta t)^2\right) + \mathcal{O}\left((\Delta x)^2\right),$$

by using the fact that $u_t = u_{xx}$. We suggest readers that they should try the calculations to derive the conclusion: the Crank-Nicolson method is of order $\mathcal{O}\left((\Delta t)^2\right) + \mathcal{O}\left((\Delta x)^2\right)$.

The equations involved in the Crank-Nicolson method (6.23) can be written explicitly for each i so as to form the matrix-vector equation for the method. Hence, defining the unknown vector, as usual, by

$$w^{(j)} = \begin{bmatrix} w_{1,j} \\ w_{2,j} \\ \vdots \\ w_{N-1,j} \end{bmatrix}$$

at the jth time level, the Crank-Nicolson method becomes

$$Aw^{(j+1)} = Bw^{(j)} + b^{(j)}, \tag{6.25}$$

for $j = 0, 1, \ldots, M - 1$. The tridiagonal matrices involved in the method are then defined as

$$A = \begin{bmatrix} 2(1+\lambda) & -\lambda & 0 & \cdots & 0 & 0 \\ -\lambda & 2(1+\lambda) & -\lambda & \cdots & 0 & 0 \\ 0 & -\lambda & 2(1+\lambda) & \cdots & 0 & 0 \\ \vdots & \vdots & \vdots & \ddots & \vdots & \vdots \\ 0 & 0 & 0 & \cdots & 2(1+\lambda) & -\lambda \\ 0 & 0 & 0 & \cdots & -\lambda & 2(1+\lambda) \end{bmatrix},$$

and

$$B = \begin{bmatrix} 2(1-\lambda) & \lambda & 0 & \cdots & 0 & 0 \\ \lambda & 2(1-\lambda) & \lambda & \cdots & 0 & 0 \\ 0 & \lambda & 2(1-\lambda) & \cdots & 0 & 0 \\ \vdots & \vdots & \vdots & \ddots & \vdots & \vdots \\ 0 & 0 & 0 & \cdots & 2(1-\lambda) & \lambda \\ 0 & 0 & 0 & \cdots & \lambda & 2(1-\lambda) \end{bmatrix}.$$

The vectors $b^{(j)}$, on the other hand, are

$$b^{(j)} = \begin{bmatrix} \lambda w_{0,j} + \lambda w_{0,j+1} \\ 0 \\ \vdots \\ 0 \\ \lambda w_{N,j} + \lambda w_{N,j+1} \end{bmatrix} = \lambda \begin{bmatrix} \alpha_j + \alpha_{j+1} \\ 0 \\ \vdots \\ 0 \\ \beta_j + \beta_{j+1} \end{bmatrix}.$$

The $b^{(j)}$ are computed from the boundary conditions of the heat problem. An implementation of the Crank-Nicolson method described by (6.25) is shown in Fig. 6.8.

```
────────────────────────── heatCrankNicolson.m ──────────────────────────
function sol = heatCrankNicolson(f, alpha, beta, a, b, dx, dt, tmax)
% f, alpha, beta : functions of initial, (left and right, resp.) boundaries
% a, b : x \in [a,b]

N = round((b-a)/dx); M = round(tmax/dt); sol = zeros(N+1,M+1);
lambda = dt / (dx)^2; dA = 2*(1+lambda); dB = 2*(1-lambda);
x = a + dx*[0:N]; t = dt*[0:M];

% initial and boundary from f, alpha, beta
sol(:,1) = feval(f, x); % t=0
sol(1,:)   = feval(alpha, t); % x = a
sol(end,:) = feval(beta, t); % x = b

A = diag((dA) * ones(N-1,1)) - ...
    diag(lambda*ones(N-2,1),1) - diag(lambda*ones(N-2,1),-1);
B = diag((dB) * ones(N-1,1)) + ...
    diag(lambda*ones(N-2,1),1) + diag(lambda*ones(N-2,1),-1);
[L, U] = lu(A);

bj = zeros(N-1,1);
for j=1:M
    bj(1) = lambda*(sol(1,j)+sol(1,j+1));
    bj(end) = lambda*(sol(end,j)+sol(end,j+1));
    sol(2:N,j+1) = U \ ( L \ ( B*sol(2:N,j) + bj ) );
end
```

Fig. 6.10   An implementation of the *Crank-Nicolson method* for the heat conduction problem

Stability Analysis of the Crank-Nicolson Method

An important observation here is that, since $\lambda = \frac{\Delta t}{(\Delta x)^2} > 0$, the eigenvalues of the matrix A are located in the left-half of the complex plane. Indeed, since the matrix A is *symmetric*, the eigenvalues lie in the real interval $[2, 2+4\lambda]$. This is due to the well-known theorem of *Gerschgorin*, for which one may refer to (Cheney and Kincaid, 1994, p. 240). The eigenvalues of A must be in the (Gerschgorin) disks,

$$|z - 2(1 + \lambda)| \leq \lambda \quad \text{and} \quad |z - 2(1 + \lambda)| \leq 2\lambda,$$

where z is a complex number. The *Gerschgorin disks* are shown in Fig. 6.11. Thus, this rules out a *zero* eigenvalue of A, and so A must be *nonsingular* and the solution of the linear system is uniquely defined.

For the stability analysis of the method, therefore, the eigenvalues of the matrix $A^{-1}B$ must be investigated. However, it is easy to see that the eigenvalues, say μ_k, of $A^{-1}B$ satisfy the relation,

$$\mu_k = \frac{2 - 4\lambda \sin^2 \frac{k\pi}{2N}}{2 + 4\lambda \sin^2 \frac{k\pi}{2N}},$$

for all $k = 1, 2, \ldots, N - 1$. Hence, $|\mu_k| < 1$ for any $\lambda > 0$. This shows that the Crank-Nicolson method is *unconditionally stable*.

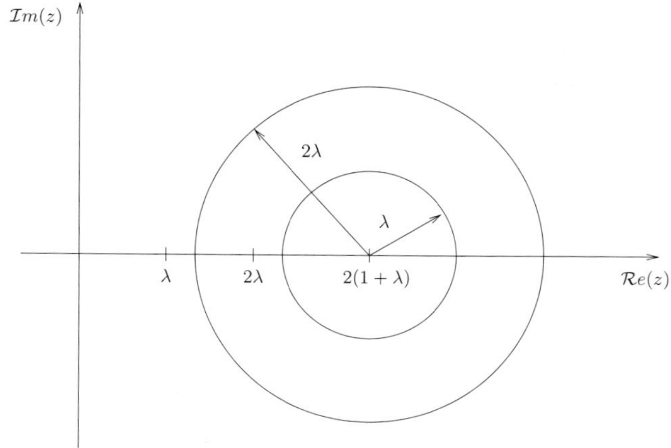

Fig. 6.11   Gerschgorin disks: $|z - 2(1 + \lambda)| \leq \lambda$ and $|z - 2(1 + \lambda)| \leq 2\lambda$

The unconditional stability of the Crank-Nicolson method is illustrated by the following example.

Example 6.3. Consider again the problem in Example 6.1, where the heat conducting problem

$$u_t = u_{xx}, \qquad 0 < x < 1, \quad t > 0,$$
$$u(x, 0) = \sin(\pi x), \qquad 0 \leq x \leq 1,$$
$$u(0, t) = u(1, t) = 0, \qquad t > 0,$$

was considered. Table 6.4 compares some of the values obtained by the Crank-Nicolson and the fully implicit methods for different time steps Δt. Besides the stability, the table shows that the time discretization error for the Crank-Nicolson method is less than that of the implicit method.

Outlook

Despite its simplicity, finite difference method is fundamental in numerical solutions of partial differential equation. This section, however, just introduces the method and confines itself to the solution of the classical heat equation for the sake of simplicity. Introductory texts such as [Brandimarte (2002); Higham (2004); Seydel (2002); Wilmott *et al.* (1995)] that include numerical solutions of PDEs for financial engineers are among the ones we have appreciated throughout this section.

Table 6.4 Several solutions of the heat equation at $(x, t) = (0.2, 0.5)$, with $\Delta x = 0.1$.

$\lambda = \frac{\Delta t}{(\Delta x)^2}$	Δt	Fully Implicit	Crank-Nicolson
1.00	0.0100	0.0055	0.0044
0.70	0.0070	0.0053	0.0045
0.50	0.0050	0.0049	0.0044
0.30	0.0030	0.0047	0.0044
0.10	0.0010	0.0045	0.0044
0.05	0.0005	0.0045	0.0044

Classical textbooks on finite difference methods [Morton and Mayers (1995); Thomas (1995)] we refer to also include the well-known *Lax Equivalence Theorem*: it simply states that *provided that the PDE is well-posed, the discretized numerical scheme is convergent if and only if it is stable. Consistency*, however, is a concept related to the numerical scheme with vanishing *truncation error*. Hence, the Lax Equivalence theorem ensures that for the complete analysis of the numerical (finite difference) method that is consistent, it suffices to study its stability.

Finite difference method is not the only method for approximating solutions of partial differential equations: *finite elements* and *finite volume* are among the most commonly used techniques to solve PDEs numerically in physical and engineering applications. An introduction to finite elements for financial engineers we recommend [Seydel (2002)].

6.3 Option Pricing by the Heat Equation

The Black-Scholes PDE,

$$\frac{\partial V}{\partial t} + \frac{1}{2}\sigma^2 S^2 \frac{\partial^2 V}{\partial S^2} + (r - \delta)S\frac{\partial V}{\partial S} - rV = 0,$$

for pricing European options, as it has been shown, boils down to the classical heat conduction problem,

$$\frac{\partial u}{\partial \tau} = \frac{\partial^2 u}{\partial x^2},$$

by the change of variables defined by (4.16) in Section 4.2.1. For ease of reference, these transformations were given by

$$S = K\, e^x, \qquad\qquad t = T - \frac{\tau}{\sigma^2/2},$$
$$V(S,t) = K\, v(x,\tau), \qquad v(x,\tau) = e^{-\gamma x - (\beta^2 + \ell)\tau}\, u(x,\tau). \tag{6.26}$$

Here, the constants γ, β and ℓ were defined as in (4.15). Namely,

$$\kappa = \frac{r-\delta}{\sigma^2/2}, \qquad\qquad \ell = \frac{\delta}{\sigma^2/2},$$
$$\gamma = \frac{1}{2}(\kappa - 1), \qquad \beta = \frac{1}{2}(\kappa + 1) = \gamma + 1. \tag{6.27}$$

By these transformations, the original domain

$$\mathcal{D}_V = \{(S,t) \,:\, S > 0, \quad 0 \le t \le T\}$$

of the Black-Scholes PDE is mapped to

$$\mathcal{D}_u = \left\{ (x,\tau) \,:\, -\infty < x < \infty, \quad 0 \le \tau \le \frac{\sigma^2}{2}T \right\}.$$

Hence, while the solution $V(S,t)$ of the Black-Scholes PDE is sought in $\mathcal{D}_V$, the solution $u(x,\tau)$ of the classical heat equation is to be defined for all (x,τ) in $\mathcal{D}_u$. Moreover, the terminal condition at time $t = T$ for the Black-Scholes PDE turns out to be an initial condition at $\tau = 0$ for the heat equation. These terminal conditions for European call and put options were given, respectively, by the equations in (4.21) and (4.22) as

$$V_C(S,T) = \max\{S - K,\, 0\}, \tag{6.28}$$
$$V_P(S,T) = \max\{K - S,\, 0\}. \tag{6.29}$$

The initial conditions for the heat equations, however, were transformed to the ones in (4.23) and (4.24):

$$u_C(x,0) = \max\{e^{\beta x} - e^{\gamma x},\, 0\}, \tag{6.30}$$
$$u_P(x,0) = \max\{e^{\gamma x} - e^{\beta x},\, 0\}, \tag{6.31}$$

respectively, for European call and put options.

On the other hand, to apply finite difference methods for numerical solutions to the heat equation it is necessary to define *boundary conditions* on a *truncated* domain. Indeed, this is practically the case for options at the market: generally, an upper and a lower bound for the underlying asset prices are considered. These boundary conditions must be mapped by the transformations defined in (6.26), if we consider numerical solutions to the heat equation. This gives us an *initial and boundary value* problem. Therefore, we truncate the infinite interval, $-\infty < x < \infty$, and consider the rectangular domain

$$\bar{\mathcal{D}}_u = \left\{ (x, \tau) \; : \; x_{min} \leq x \leq x_{max}, \quad 0 \leq \tau \leq \frac{\sigma^2}{2} T \right\}, \qquad (6.32)$$

where x_{min} and x_{max} stand for the too small and too high asset prices, respectively, due to the fact that $S = Ke^x$.

In order to solve the heat equation in the truncated domain $\bar{\mathcal{D}}_u$, boundary conditions must be defined on the lines $x = x_{min}$ and $x = x_{\max}$ in the $x\tau$-plane. Hence, we should consider the option values for small and large values of the underlying asset prices. To this end, the following notation is useful:

- $S_{max} = K\,e^{x_{max}}$ represents the *large* values of asset prices,
- $S_{min} = K\,e^{x_{max}}$ represents the *small* values of asset prices.

Of course, the domain of the Black-Scholes PDE for a particular option should always be kept in mind. For instance, in case of vanilla options, S_{max} accounts for the large values of S, while S_{min} represents the line $S = 0$. However, for a *down-and-out* option, with the barrier at $S = B$, the meaning of S_{max} stays the same though, the meaning of S_{min} is changed to $S_{min} = B$. In the latter, the domain of the Black-Scholes PDE is $[B, S_{max}] \times [0, T]$. Hence, we will consider the truncated domain for the Black-Scholes equation as

$$\bar{\mathcal{D}}_V = \{ (S, t) \; : \; S_{min} \leq S \leq S_{max}, \quad 0 \leq t \leq T \}. \qquad (6.33)$$

Now, consider a European call option for which the underlying asset price S tends to $S_{min} \approx 0$. Hence, the call option is out of the money and assumes the value zero for all $t \in [0, T]$. That is, the condition

$$V_C(S_{min}, t) = 0 \qquad (6.34)$$

holds as long as $S_{min} \approx 0$. Hence, by the transformations in (6.26) it is easy to see that

$$u_C(x_{min}, \tau) = 0, \qquad (6.35)$$

which is the left boundary condition, at $x = x_{min}$, for the corresponding heat equation. Note that x_{min} tends to negative infinity as S_{min} approaches zero.

Similarly, if a European put option is considered, the option will be out of the money, hence worthless, as the asset price S increases to S_{max} that stands for the positive infinity. That is,

$$V_P(S_{max}, t) = 0 \qquad (6.36)$$

holds for the right boundary of the truncated domain $\bar{\mathcal{D}}_V$ for the Black-Scholes equation. Again, by the transformations in (6.26), it follows that the right boundary condition, at $x = x_{max}$, for the heat equation is

$$u_P(x_{max}, \tau) = 0. \qquad (6.37)$$

The conditions at the other ends of the truncated region can now be obtained by considering the *put-call* parity,

$$V_P(S, t) - V_C(S, t) + Se^{-\delta(T-t)} = Ke^{-r(T-t)}, \qquad (6.38)$$

for the European call and put options, where r is the risk-free interest rate, and δ is the dividend rate paid by the underlying asset. For instance, when $S = S_{max}$, the put-call parity yields

$$V_C(S_{max}, t) = S_{max}e^{-\delta(T-t)} - Ke^{-r(T-t)}, \qquad (6.39)$$

by using the condition (6.36). On the other hand, for a European put option, the put-call parity gives the boundary condition

$$V_P(S_{min}, t) = Ke^{-r(T-t)} - S_{min}e^{-\delta(T-t)} \qquad (6.40)$$

as $S = S_{min}$, where S_{min} assumes the value zero.

The corresponding boundary conditions for the solution of the heat equation can be obtained by using the transformations in (6.26). For instance, by using the relations $T - t = \frac{\tau}{\sigma^2/2}$ and $S_{max} = Ke^{x_{max}}$, it follows from (6.39) that

$$u_C(x_{max}, \tau) = e^{\gamma x_{max}+(\beta^2+\ell)\tau}\frac{1}{K}V_C(S_{max}, t)$$

$$= e^{\gamma x_{max}+(\beta^2+\ell)\tau}\left\{e^{x_{max}-\delta\frac{\tau}{\sigma^2/2}} - e^{-r\frac{\tau}{\sigma^2/2}}\right\}.$$

Carrying out the calculations by using the constants in (6.27), particularly, the relations $\beta = \gamma + 1$ and $\gamma = \frac{1}{2}(\kappa - 1)$, we obtain the right boundary condition for the heat equation as

$$u_C(x_{max}, \tau) = e^{\beta x_{max}+\beta^2\tau} - e^{\gamma x_{max}+\gamma^2\tau} \qquad (6.41)$$

for all $\tau \in [0, \frac{\sigma^2}{2}T]$.

Similarly, the left boundary condition for u that solves the heat equation is found to be

$$u_P(x_{min}, \tau) = e^{\gamma x_{max}+\gamma^2\tau} - e^{\beta x_{max}+\beta^2\tau}. \qquad (6.42)$$

To sum up, the boundary conditions that the option price $V(S,t)$ for a vanilla call and a put option must satisfy at $S = S_{min}$ and $S = S_{max}$ are collected in Fig. 6.12 together with the terminal conditions, the payoffs. On the other hand, Fig. 6.13 shows the corresponding transformed initial and boundary conditions that the solution $u = u(x, \tau)$ of the heat equation must satisfy.

```
─────────────────── BlackScholes_Payoff_CP.m ───────────────────
function f = BlackScholes_Payoff(S,K)

% f = max(S-K,0); % call
f = max(K-S,0); % put
```

```
─────────────── BlackScholes_LeftBoundary_CP.m ───────────────
function leftB = BlackScholes_LeftBoundary(t, T,r,K, Smin, div)

% leftB = zeros(size(t)); % at S = 0 (Call)
leftB = K*exp(-r*(T-t)) - Smin*exp(-div*(T-t)); % at S = 0 (Put)
```

```
─────────────── BlackScholes_RightBoundary_CP.m ───────────────
function rightB = BlackScholes_RightBoundary(t,T,r,K, Smax, div)

% rightB = Smax*exp(-div*(T-t))  - K*exp(-r*(T-t)); % at S = Smax (Call)
rightB = zeros(size(t)); % at S = Smax (Put)
```

Fig. 6.12   Payoffs and boundary functions for call and put options for numerical solution of Black-Scholes PDE in its original form

```
―――――――――――――――― heat_BlackScholes_InitialFunction.m ――――――――
function f = heat_BlackScholes_InitialFunction(x, gamma, beta)

% f = max( exp( beta*x) - exp(gamma*x), 0 ); % call
f = max( exp( gamma*x) - exp(beta*x), 0 );   % put
```

```
――――――――――――――――― heat_BlackScholes_LeftBoundary.m ――――――――――
function leftB = heat_BlackScholes_LeftBoundary(t, gamma, beta, xmin)

% leftB = zeros(size(t)); % call
leftB = exp( gamma^2 .* t ) .* exp (gamma * xmin) - ...
    exp( beta^2 .* t ) .* exp (beta * xmin); % put
```

```
―――――――――――――――― heat_BlackScholes_RightBoundary.m ――――――――――
function rightB = heat_BlackScholes_RightBoundary(t, gamma, beta, xmax)

% rightB = exp( beta^2 .* t ) .* exp (beta .* xmax) - ...
%     exp( gamma^2 .* t ) .* exp (gamma .* xmax); % call
rightB = zeros(size(t)); % put
```

Fig. 6.13   Initial and boundary functions for for call and put options of the transformed
Black-Scholes PDE

The MATLAB script given in Fig. 6.14 applies the transformation and
solves the resulting heat equation by the Crank-Nicolson method shown
in Fig. 6.15. Here, the Crank-Nicolson method is a modification of the one
for heat equation and includes just the necessary parameters. Fig. 6.13
also shows how these parameters are used for the transformed terminal
conditions as well as the boundary conditions for both put and call options.

The graph shown in Fig. 6.16(a) depicts how the exact solution as well
as the approximations behave. In Fig. 6.16(b) the surface $V = V(S,t)$ for
the put option is shown. Although the discretization used for the spatial
variable x is uniform, the discretization for the asset prices S becomes
nonuniform due to the transformation $S = e^x$. Unfortunately, this gives
rise to clustered nodes near $S_{min} \approx 0$, but the nodes are separated from
each other near S_{max}. Hence, a drawback of these transformations may be
that the resulting grid is not uniform for the asset prices.

In the sequel, the idea of finite difference methods will be applied to the
Black-Scholes PDE in its original form. This, at least, allows us to obtain
a uniform grid for the asset prices, and the resulting numerical schemes are
hoped to give "satisfactory" results over such a grid. Of course, one can
always choose a nonuniform grid when solving the heat equation so as to
get a uniform one in the asset prices. Suppose that for $N \in \mathbb{N}$,

$$\Delta S = S_{i+1} - S_i, \quad i = 0, 1, \ldots, N$$

is the given constant step size in the asset prices, where $S_0 =: S_{min} > 0$
is some given lower bound for the prices. The corresponding bound in the

```matlab
% testHeat_BlackScholes
clear all, close all
S0 = 10; K = 10; r = 0.25; sigma = 0.6; div = 0; div = 0.2; T = 1;
% Transformations
kappa = (r-div)/(sigma^2/2); ell = div/(sigma^2/2);
gamma = 0.5*(kappa - 1); beta = gamma+1; x0 = log(S0/K); tmax = 0.5*sigma^2*T;

xmin = -5; xmax = 5; dx = 0.05; dt = 0.00005; % dt = 0.01;
f = @heat_BlackScholes_InitialFunction; % but transformed from option data
leftB = @heat_BlackScholes_LeftBoundary; rightB = @heat_BlackScholes_RightBoundary;
w = heat_BlackScholes_CrankNicolson(f, leftB, rightB, ...
    xmin, xmax, dx, dt, tmax, gamma, beta);

[m,n] = size(w); x = linspace(xmin,xmax,m); tau = linspace(0,tmax,n);
S = K*exp(x); t = T - 2*tau/sigma^2; j = 1;
for time = tau % another defn of a "for" loop
    inExp = exp( -gamma*x' );
    inExp = inExp .* exp( -(beta^2 + ell)*time );
    V(:,j) = K * inExp .* w(:,j); j = j + 1;
end
[C, Cdelta, P, Pdelta] = CallPut_Delta(S,K,r,sigma,T,div); u = P;
[C, Cdelta, P, Pdelta] = CallPut_Delta(S,K,r,sigma,0,div); payoff = P;
figure(1), plot(S, u), hold on % exact solution
plot(S, V(:,end), 'rx-'), plot(S, payoff, 'k-.'); hold on
axis([0 30 0 10]); legend('Closed-Form', 'PDE Solution', 'Payoff');
xlabel('S','FontSize',12), ylabel('V(:,end)','FontSize',12), hold off
print -r900 -depsc -cmyk '../figures/testHeat_BlackScholes_CrankNicolson_2D'
figure(2), mesh(S(1:135),t,V(1:135,:)')
xlabel('S','FontSize',12), ylabel('t','FontSize',12),
zlabel('V(x,t)','FontSize',12), hold off
print -r300 -depsc -cmyk '../figures/testHeat_BlackScholes_CrankNicolson'
```

Fig. 6.14   An implementation that tests the *Crank-Nicolson method* for the transformed Black-Scholes PDE

variable x is then $x_{min} := x_0 = \log S_{min} > -\infty$. Thus, the discretization of the heat equation in the spatial variable $x = \log S$ can be written as

$$\Delta x_i := x_{i+1} - x_i = \log(S_{i+1}) - \log(S_i) = \log\left(\frac{S_{i+1}}{S_i}\right),$$

for each $i = 0, 1, \ldots, N$. Therefore, for a given ΔS, the varying step sizes in x may be chosen by

$$\Delta x_i = \log\left(\frac{S_i + \Delta S}{S_i}\right) = \log\left(1 + \frac{\Delta S}{S_{min} + i\Delta S}\right).$$

However, over such a nonuniform grid, the construction of the finite difference methods for the heat equation may not be as easy as the one over a uniform grid. Nevertheless, in many cases, the transformations of the initial and boundary conditions are required if one insists on the solution to the heat equation. After having solved the equation numerically, a back

```
_______________________ heat_BlackScholes_CrankNicolson.m _______________
function sol = heat_BlackScholes_CrankNicolson(f, leftB, rightB, ...
     a, b, dx, dt, tmax, gamma, beta)
% f, alpha, beta : functions of initial, (leftB and rightB, resp.) boundaries
% a, b : x \in [a,b]

N = round((b-a)/dx); M = round(tmax/dt); sol = zeros(N+1,M+1);
lambda = dt / (dx)^2; dA = 2*(1+lambda); dB = 2*(1-lambda);
x = a + dx*[0:N]; t = dt*[0:M];
sol(:,1) = feval(f, x, gamma, beta); % t=0
sol(1,:)   = feval(leftB, t, gamma, beta, a); % x = a
sol(end,:) = feval(rightB, t, gamma, beta, b); % x = b

A = diag((dA) * ones(N-1,1)) - ...
    diag(lambda*ones(N-2,1),1) - diag(lambda*ones(N-2,1),-1);
B = diag((dB) * ones(N-1,1)) + ...
    diag(lambda*ones(N-2,1),1) + diag(lambda*ones(N-2,1),-1);
bj = zeros(N-1,1); [L, U] = lu(A);
for j=1:M
    bj(1) = lambda*(sol(1,j)+sol(1,j+1));
    bj(end) = lambda*(sol(end,j)+sol(end,j+1));
    sol(2:N,j+1) = U \ ( L \ ( B*sol(2:N,j) + bj ) );
end
```

Fig. 6.15   An implementation of the *Crank-Nicolson method* for the transformed Black-Scholes PDE

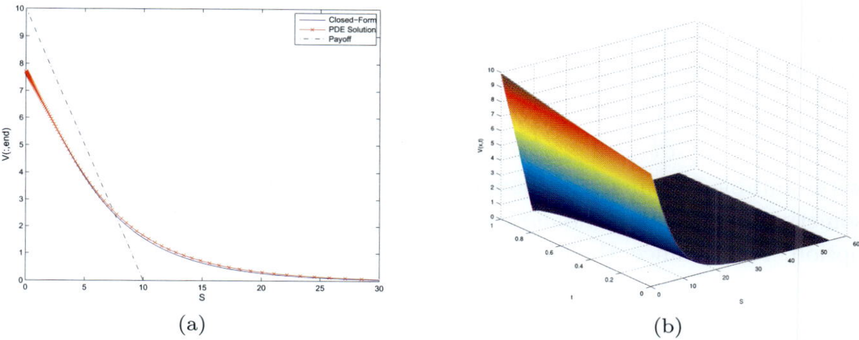

(a)   (b)

Fig. 6.16   Vanilla put option: (a) comparison of the exact solution with the approximate solutions at the final time, (b) the whole surface obtained by the *Crank-Nicolson method* for the transformed heat equation

transformation must be applied to interpret the solution in terms of option values. See the implementation in Fig. 6.15.

On the other hand, the terminal and boundary conditions, which are parts of the option contracts, are more commonly used than the corresponding initial and boundary conditions for the heat equation. Thus, applying the finite differences directly to the Black-Scholes equation gives the possibility to use the terminal and boundary conditions of the option directly, without any transformation. Moreover, in this case, it is possible to take a uniform discretization in the asset prices and apply the finite differences to the derivatives involved in the Black-Scholes PDE.

Outlook

This section may be regarded as an application of numerical solutions of the heat equation by finite difference method. However, the initial and boundary conditions are emphasised and transformed to mimic the boundaries of the option that is to be valued. In order to carry out numerical methods the truncation of the domain has been necessary together with the boundary conditions so that the problem is then well-posed. We refer to [Seydel (2002); Nielsen (1999); Wilmott *et al.* (1995)] for more information on option pricing by the transformed heat equation, where the transformations used may slightly vary.

6.4   Option Pricing by the Black-Scholes Equation

Recall that the value V of a European option at time t, written on an underlying asset with price S, satisfies the Black-Scholes equation,

$$\frac{\partial V}{\partial t} + \frac{1}{2}\sigma^2 S^2 \frac{\partial^2 V}{\partial S^2} + (r - \delta)S\frac{\partial V}{\partial S} - rV = 0, \tag{6.43}$$

with suitable terminal and boundary conditions. All such conditions are sometimes called the *boundaries of the option*, since they characterise the option. For instance, the terminal condition at expiry is given by the payoff

$$V_C(S, T) = \max\{S - K,\ 0\}$$

for a European call option with a strike price K. Similarly, for a European put option, the payoff at maturity is

$$V_P(S, T) = \max\{K - S,\ 0\}.$$

On the other hand, the boundary conditions with respect to asset prices over a truncated domain were given by

$$V_C(S_{min}, t) = 0, \quad V_C(S_{max}, t) = S_{max}e^{-\delta(T-t)} - Ke^{-r(T-t)},$$

and

$$V_P(S_{max}, t) = 0, \quad V_P(S_{min}, t) = Ke^{-r(T-t)} - S_{min}e^{-\delta(T-t)},$$

respectively for vanilla call and put options.

Having obtained these terminal and boundary conditions for a particular option, it becomes easy to associate them into the discrete version of the Black-Scholes PDE obtained by applying the finite differences. The following sections will apply the well-known finite differences to the Black-Scholes PDE in its original form (6.43). The corresponding finite difference methods will be called as usual, that is, the *explicit, implicit,* and the *Crank-Nicolson* methods for solving the Black-Scholes PDE.

6.4.1 *Pricing by an Explicit Method*

In order to derive an explicit method for the Black-Scholes PDE, it is crucial to note that the time t should run backward. Namely, knowing the solution at $t = T$ from the terminal conditions should allow us to compute the solution at time $t = t_0$ for any $0 \le t_0 < T$, in particular, at $t_0 = 0$. This suggests using a *backward* finite difference in time, such as

$$\frac{\partial V(S,t)}{\partial t} = \frac{V(S,t) - V(S, t - \Delta t)}{\Delta t} + \mathcal{O}\left(\Delta t\right),$$

where $\Delta t > 0$ is either the given time step or computed from the relation,

$$\Delta t = \frac{T - t_0}{M} \quad \text{so that} \quad t_j = t_0 + j\Delta t, \quad j = 0, 1, \ldots, M,$$

for given t_0 and $M \in \mathbb{N}$.

On the other hand, a *second-order* finite difference formula can be used for approximating the second derivative of V with respect to S, for instance, the central difference formula. However, in the original Black-Scholes PDE (6.43) there is also the first-order derivative of V with respect to the asset price S. The use of a *second-order* finite difference formula for approximating this term is advisable and, moreover, it is consistent with the use of a second-order central difference approximation used for the second-order derivative. These central difference formulae for the derivatives with respect to S are then taken as

$$\frac{\partial^2 V(S,t)}{\partial S^2} = \frac{V(S + \Delta S, t) - 2V(S,t) + V(S - \Delta S, t)}{(\Delta S)^2} + \mathcal{O}\left((\Delta S)^2\right)$$

and

$$\frac{\partial V(S,t)}{\partial S} = \frac{V(S + \Delta S, t) - V(S - \Delta S, t)}{2\,\Delta S} + \mathcal{O}\left((\Delta S)^2\right).$$

Here the step length ΔS is either given or determined from

$$\Delta S = \frac{S_{max} - S_{min}}{N} \quad \text{so that} \quad S_i = S_{min} + i\Delta S, \quad i = 0, 1, \ldots, N.$$

Notice that $S_{min} = S_0$ is implicitly assumed, and it does *not* stand for the asset price *today*!

Now, denoting the approximations to V_{ij} by w_{ij},

$$w_{ij} \approx V_{ij} = V(S_i, t_j),$$

at the grid points (S_i, t_j) and dropping the order terms in the discrete version of the Black-Scholes PDE, we obtain an *explicit* method:

$$\frac{w_{ij} - w_{i,j-1}}{\Delta t} + (r - \delta)S_i \frac{w_{i+1,j} - w_{i-1,j}}{2\,\Delta S}$$
$$+ \tfrac{1}{2}\sigma^2 S_i^2 \frac{w_{i+1,j} - 2w_{ij} + w_{i-1,j}}{(\Delta S)^2} - rw_{ij} = 0,$$

which is of order $\mathcal{O}\left(\Delta t\right) + \mathcal{O}\left((\Delta S)^2\right)$. This is indeed an *explicit method*, since the time runs backward. For $j = M$, the w_{iM} are known from the payoff, and recursively, one can determine $w_{i,j-1}$ for all $j = M, M-1, \ldots, 1$ so that the resulting $w_{i,0}$ is an approximation for the option price at the nodes of the grid. It easy to see this if the resulting method is written as

$$w_{i,j-1} = a_i w_{i-1,j} + b_i w_{ij} + c_i w_{i+1,j}, \qquad (6.44)$$

for every $i = 1, 2, \ldots, N-1$ while $j = M, M-1, \ldots, 1$ after having collected the similar terms. Here, the coefficients are defined as

$$a_i = \frac{1}{2}\Delta t \left\{ \sigma^2 \left(\frac{S_i}{\Delta S}\right)^2 - (r - \delta)\frac{S_i}{\Delta S} \right\},$$
$$b_i = 1 - \Delta t \left\{ \sigma^2 \left(\frac{S_i}{\Delta S}\right)^2 + r \right\}, \qquad (6.45)$$
$$c_i = \frac{1}{2}\Delta t \left\{ \sigma^2 \left(\frac{S_i}{\Delta S}\right)^2 + (r - \delta)\frac{S_i}{\Delta S} \right\}.$$

An implementation of the explicit method in (6.44) is shown in Fig. 6.17. It is important to note that in Fig. 6.17, a *linear interpolation* is used

```
________________________ BlackScholes_Explicit.m ________________________
function [sol, price] = BlackScholes_Explicit(S0, K, r, D, sigma, T, ...
     f, alpha, beta, Smin, Smax, dS, dt)
% f, alpha, beta : functions of initial, (left and right, resp.) boundaries
% price : linearly interpolated

N = round((Smax-Smin)/dS); M = round(T/dt);
sol = zeros(N+1,M+1); S = Smin + dS*[0:N]; t = dt*[0:M];
% payoff and boundary from f, alpha, beta
sol(:,end) = feval(f, S,K); % t = T
sol(1,:)   = feval(alpha, t,T,r,K,Smin, D); % S = Smin
sol(end,:) = feval(beta, t,T,r,K,Smax, D); % S = Smax

mS = S/dS;
a = 0.5*dt*(mS.*(sigma^2*mS - (r-D)));
b = 1 - dt*( sigma^2*mS.^2 + r);
c = 0.5*dt*(mS.*(sigma^2*mS + (r-D)));
for j=M:-1:1    % for t
    for i=2:N % for S
        sol(i,j) = a(i)*sol(i-1,j+1) + ...
        b(i)*sol(i,j+1) + c(i)*sol(i+1,j+1);
    end
end
% linear interpolation
down = floor((S0-Smin)/dS); up = ceil((S0-Smin)/dS);
if (down == up)
    price = sol(down+1,1);
else
    price = sol(down+1,1) + ...
        (sol(up+1,1) - sol(down+1,1))*(S0-Smin - down*dS)/dS;
end
```

Fig. 6.17   An implementation of the *explicit method* in (6.44)

to approximate the value of the option with the underlying asset in case today's value, say s_0 at time t_0, of the asset is not on the grid points S_i.

Example 6.4. In this example we consider a European call option. The boundaries of the option are given as in Fig. 6.12, but for the call option, the parameters involved in the option, such as the strike price, volatility, interest rate and time to maturity is given in Fig. 6.18. At time $t_0 = 0$ the underlying asset assumes the value that is $s_0 = 50$.

The graphs shown in Fig. 6.19 depict how the exact solution as well as the approximations behave. As it can be seen clearly, the numerical results are relatively satisfactory when they are compared to the approximate solutions obtained by heat equation. Moreover, the grid used here is uniform for the asset prices. Unfortunately however, the grid size ΔS in S cannot be reduced for a given Δt as we like due to the conditional stability of the explicit method.

We should always keep in mind that we have to interpolate the data if we are interested in pricing an option for a given today's price s_0 of

```
_________________________ testBlackScholes_Explicit.m _________________________
% test Black-Scholes Solutions
clear all, close all,
S0 = 50; K = 50; D = 0; sigma = 0.4; r = 0.1; T = 5/12;
Smin = 0; Smax = 150; % Smin = 40; for barrier option

dS = 2; dt = 1/1200;
f = @BlackScholes_Payoff_Exp;
alpha = @BlackScholes_LeftBoundary_Exp; beta = @BlackScholes_RightBoundary_Exp;
[w,p] = BlackScholes_Explicit(S0, K, r, D, sigma, T, ...
    f, alpha, beta, Smin, Smax, dS, dt);
% [w,p] = BlackScholes_Implicit(S0, K, r, D, sigma, T, ...
%    f, alpha, beta, Smin, Smax, dS, dt);
% [w,p] = BlackScholes_CrankNicolson(S0, K, r, D, sigma, T, ...
%     f, alpha, beta, Smin, Smax, dS, dt);

[m,n] = size(w); S = linspace(Smin,Smax,m); t = linspace(0,T,n);
% Closed-Form Solution
[call,cdelta,put,pdelta] = CallPut_Delta(S, K, r, sigma, T);

figure(1), plot(S, w(:,1), 'rx'), hold on, plot(S, call),
xlabel('S','FontSize', 12), ylabel('V(S,0)','FontSize', 12),
legend('Explicit Method','Closed-Form'), hold off
print -r900 -depsc -cmyk '../figures/testBS_Explicit_2D'
figure(2), mesh(S,t,w'), xlabel('S','FontSize',12), ylabel('t','FontSize',12),
zlabel('V(S,t)','FontSize',12)
print -r300 -depsc -cmyk '../figures/testBS_Explicit'

fprintf('PDE Solution...........: %f\n', p);
% Exact solution from a closed-form formula for S0
[cclosed,cdclosed,pclosed,pdclosed] = CallPut_Delta(S0, K, r, sigma, T);
fprintf('Closed-Form Solution...: %f\n', cclosed);
```

Fig. 6.18   Part of the script for running the finite difference methods for the Black-Scholes PDE

the underlying. Interpolation of the results is necessary in cases when s_0 is not a point on the grid. Here a linear interpolation is used. However, interpolation of the solution by higher order polynomials or splines is also possible, however, a careless use of interpolation may cause undesirable effects like oscillations! As long as the grid used is fine it is preferable to be on the "safe" side and use a linear interpolation.

It would be a good exercise to investigate the *stability analysis* of the explicit method in (6.44), but we will trust our numerical experiments for that. However, it will be helpful, later in the sequel, to derive the corresponding matrix-vector form of the iterations (6.44) for the explicit method. Let us denote the jth time level vector of approximations $w_{1,j}, w_{2,j}, \ldots, w_{N-1,j}$

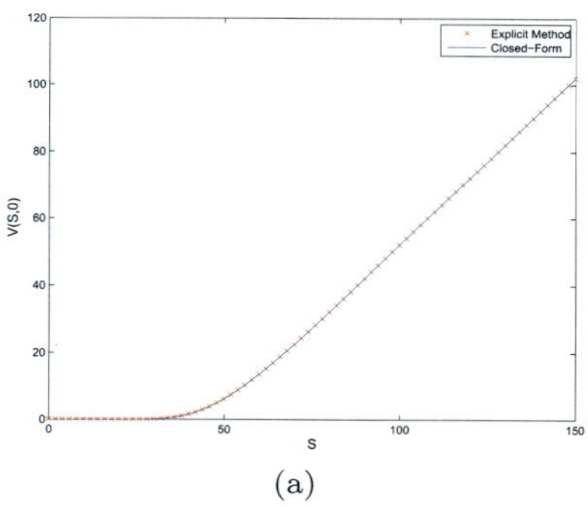

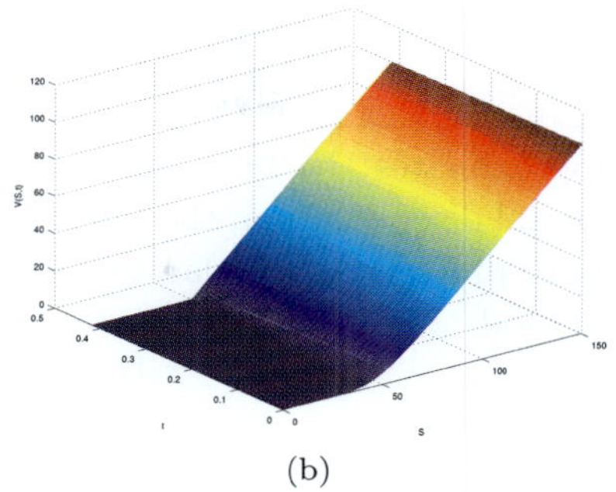

(a)   (b)

Fig. 6.19   *Explicit method*: (a) comparison of the exact solution with the approximate solutions at the final time, (b) the surface $V = V(S, t)$ for a vanilla call option

by the column vector

$$w^{(j)} = \begin{bmatrix} w_{1,j} \\ w_{2,j} \\ \vdots \\ w_{N-1,j} \end{bmatrix}.$$

Writing the equations, explicitly for each i, in (6.44), it is easy to obtain the following matrix-vector equation:

$$w^{(j-1)} = Aw^{(j)} + b^{(j)}, \quad j = M, M-1, \dots, 1, \qquad (6.46)$$

where

$$A = \begin{bmatrix} b_1 & c_1 & 0 & \cdots & 0 & 0 \\ a_2 & b_2 & c_2 & \cdots & 0 & 0 \\ 0 & a_3 & b_3 & \cdots & 0 & 0 \\ \vdots & \vdots & \vdots & \ddots & \vdots & \vdots \\ 0 & 0 & 0 & \cdots & b_{N-2} & c_{N-2} \\ 0 & 0 & 0 & \cdots & a_{N-1} & b_{N-1} \end{bmatrix}, \quad b^{(j)} = \begin{bmatrix} a_1 w_{0,j} \\ 0 \\ \vdots \\ 0 \\ c_{N-1} w_{N,j} \end{bmatrix}.$$

Here, the vectors $b^{(j)}$ consist of the data from the boundary conditions. Furthermore, the vector $w^{(M)}$ is known from the terminal condition, the payoff of the option at maturity.

6.4.2   *Pricing by an Implicit Method*

In order to obtain an *implicit* method, a *forward* finite difference in time is used. That is,

$$\frac{\partial V(S,t)}{\partial t} = \frac{V(S, t + \Delta t) - V(S,t)}{\Delta t} + \mathcal{O}\left(\Delta t\right)$$

approximates the first-order derivative with respect to time t. For the spacial discretization, the central finite differences are used. Inserting these finite difference formulae to the Black-Scholes equation yields an *implicit* method:

$$\frac{w_{i,j+1} - w_{i,j}}{\Delta t} + (r - \delta) S_i \frac{w_{i+1,j} - w_{i-1,j}}{2\,\Delta S}$$
$$+ \tfrac{1}{2}\sigma^2 S_i^2 \frac{w_{i+1,j} - 2w_{ij} + w_{i-1,j}}{(\Delta S)^2} - r w_{ij} = 0,$$

where $w_{ij} \approx V_{ij} = V(S_i, t_j)$. A simpler form of this implicit method can be obtained by collecting the similar terms as follows:

$$a_i w_{i-1,j} + b_i w_{ij} + c_i w_{i+1,j} = w_{i,j+1}, \tag{6.47}$$

for every $i = 1, 2, \ldots, N - 1$ while $j = M - 1, M - 2, \ldots, 0$. Here, however, the coefficients are defined as

$$a_i = \frac{1}{2}\Delta t \left\{ (r - \delta)\frac{S_i}{\Delta S} - \sigma^2 \left(\frac{S_i}{\Delta S}\right)^2 \right\},$$
$$b_i = 1 + \Delta t \left\{ \sigma^2 \left(\frac{S_i}{\Delta S}\right)^2 + r \right\}, \tag{6.48}$$
$$c_i = -\frac{1}{2}\Delta t \left\{ (r - \delta)\frac{S_i}{\Delta S} + \sigma^2 \left(\frac{S_i}{\Delta S}\right)^2 \right\}.$$

Compare these coefficients with the ones defined for the explicit method in (6.45).

The matrix-vector form of the implicit method, on the other hand, can be written as a system of linear equations:

$$A w^{(j)} = w^{(j+1)} + b^{(j+1)}, \quad j = M - 1, M - 2, \ldots, 0, \tag{6.49}$$

where

$$A = \begin{bmatrix} b_1 & c_1 & 0 & \cdots & 0 & 0 \\ a_2 & b_2 & c_2 & \cdots & 0 & 0 \\ 0 & a_3 & b_3 & \cdots & 0 & 0 \\ \vdots & \vdots & \vdots & \ddots & \vdots & \vdots \\ 0 & 0 & 0 & \cdots & b_{N-2} & c_{N-2} \\ 0 & 0 & 0 & \cdots & a_{N-1} & b_{N-1} \end{bmatrix}, \quad b^{(j+1)} = \begin{bmatrix} -a_1 w_{0,j} \\ 0 \\ \vdots \\ 0 \\ -c_{N-1} w_{N,j} \end{bmatrix}.$$

By computing the eigenvalues of A^{-1}, one can show that this implicit method is *unconditionally stable*. An implementation of this *implicit method* is illustrated in Fig. 6.20.

```
―――――――――――――――――― BlackScholes_Implicit.m ――――――
function [sol, price] = BlackScholes_Implicit(S0, K, r, D, sigma, T, ...
    f, alpha, beta, Smin, Smax, dS, dt)
% f, alpha, beta : functions of initial, (left and right, resp.) boundaries
% price : linearly interpolated

N = round((Smax-Smin)/dS); M = round(T/dt);
sol = zeros(N+1,M+1); S = Smin + dS*[0:N]; t = dt*[0:M];
sol(:,end) = feval(f, S,K); % t = T
sol(1,:)   = feval(alpha, t,T,r,K,Smin, D); % S = Smin
sol(end,:) = feval(beta, t,T,r,K,Smax, D); % S = Smax

mS = S/dS;
a = 0.5*dt*(mS.*((r-D) - sigma^2*mS));
b = 1 + dt*(sigma^2*mS.^2 + r);
c = -0.5*dt*(mS.*((r-D) + sigma^2*mS));
A = diag(a(3:N),-1) + diag(b(2:N)) + diag(c(2:N-1),1);
[L U] = lu(A);

bj = zeros(N-1,1);
for j = M:-1:1 % for t
    bj(1) = -a(2)*sol(1,j); bj(end) = -c(end-1)*sol(end,j);
    sol(2:N,j) = U \ ( L \ (sol(2:N,j+1) + bj) );
end
down = floor((S0-Smin)/dS); up = ceil((S0-Smin)/dS);
if (down == up)
    price = sol(down+1,1);
else
    price = sol(down+1,1) + ...
        (sol(up+1,1) - sol(down+1,1))*(S0-Smin - down*dS)/dS;
end
```

Fig. 6.20   An implementation of the *implicit method* in (6.47)

Example 6.5. This example considers now a vanilla put option pricing by applying the implicit method. The parameters of the option and the method are as the same as the ones in Example 6.4. However, since the implicit method is unconditionally stable this example uses a step size $\Delta S = 0.2$, without changing the time step $\Delta t = 1/1200$.

We use a very similar MATLAB script as in Fig. 6.18. The graphs of the option price V are depicted in Fig. 6.21 for an illustration.

6.4.3 *Pricing by the Crank-Nicolson Method*

In order to obtain the *Crank-Nicolson* method, the explicit and the implicit methods are combined as it has been done for the heat equation. By

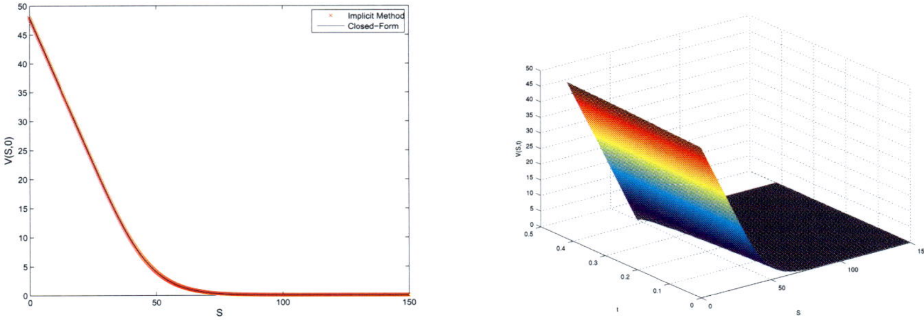

Fig. 6.21 *Implicit method*: (a) comparison of the exact solution with the approximate solutions at the final time, (b) the surface $V = V(S, t)$ for a vanilla put option

taking the arithmetic average of these methods defined by equations (6.44) and (6.47), it is easy to derive the Crank-Nicolson method

$$-a_i w_{i-1,j-1} + (1 - b_i) w_{i,j-1} - c_i w_{i+1,j-1}$$
$$= a_i w_{i-1,j} + (1 + b_i) w_{i,j} + c_i w_{i+1,j}, \qquad (6.50)$$

for every $i = 1, 2, \ldots, N - 1$ while $j = M - 1, M - 2, \ldots, 1$. The coefficients of this method, however, are defined as

$$a_i = \frac{1}{4} \Delta t \left\{ \sigma^2 \left(\frac{S_i}{\Delta S} \right)^2 - (r - \delta) \frac{S_i}{\Delta S} \right\},$$

$$b_i = -\frac{1}{2} \Delta t \left\{ \sigma^2 \left(\frac{S_i}{\Delta S} \right)^2 + r \right\}, \qquad (6.51)$$

$$c_i = \frac{1}{4} \Delta t \left\{ \sigma^2 \left(\frac{S_i}{\Delta S} \right)^2 + (r - \delta) \frac{S_i}{\Delta S} \right\}.$$

In terms of matrix-vector notation the method can be written as

$$A w^{(j-1)} = B w^{(j)} + b^{(j)}, \qquad j = M - 1, M - 2, \ldots, 1, \qquad (6.52)$$

where

$$
A = \begin{bmatrix}
1-b_1 & -c_1 & 0 & \cdots & 0 & 0 \\
-a_2 & 1-b_2 & -c_2 & \cdots & 0 & 0 \\
0 & -a_3 & 1-b_3 & \cdots & 0 & 0 \\
\vdots & \vdots & \vdots & \ddots & \vdots & \vdots \\
0 & 0 & 0 & \cdots & 1-b_{N-2} & -c_{N-2} \\
0 & 0 & 0 & \cdots & -a_{N-1} & 1-b_{N-1}
\end{bmatrix},
$$

$$
B = \begin{bmatrix}
1+b_1 & c_1 & 0 & \cdots & 0 & 0 \\
a_2 & 1+b_2 & c_2 & \cdots & 0 & 0 \\
0 & a_3 & 1+b_3 & \cdots & 0 & 0 \\
\vdots & \vdots & \vdots & \ddots & \vdots & \vdots \\
0 & 0 & 0 & \cdots & 1+b_{N-2} & c_{N-2} \\
0 & 0 & 0 & \cdots & a_{N-1} & 1+b_{N-1}
\end{bmatrix},
$$

and the vectors that contain the boundary data

$$
b^{(j)} = \begin{bmatrix}
a_1(w_{0,j-1} + w_{0,j}) \\
0 \\
\vdots \\
0 \\
c_{N-1}(w_{N,j-1} + w_{N,j})
\end{bmatrix}.
$$

By computing the eigenvalues of $A^{-1}B$, one can show that the Crank-Nicolson method here is *unconditionally stable*. An implementation of the *Crank-Nicolson method* is illustrated in Fig. 6.22.

Example 6.6. Now, the Crank-Nicolson method is applied to a down-and-out put option derived from Example 6.5. In this example, only the barrier $B = 40$ is introduced for S_{min}. Namely, $S_{min} = B = 40$.

Since the option is worthless in case the asset prices touch or fall below the barrier, the domain of the Black-Scholes PDE is restricted to where $S > B$ and, for S below the barrier the option has the zero value. Due to the barrier the down-and-out put option is cheaper than its corresponding vanilla put option. This can easily be seen in Fig. 6.23.

Exercise 6.2. Consider an artificial option whose payoff function $P_{sc}(S, T)$ at maturity T is given by

$$
P_{sc}(S, T) = \begin{cases}
\sqrt{R^2 - (S - K)^2}, & |S - K| \le R, \\
0, & \text{otherwise,}
\end{cases}
$$

```
———————————————— BlackScholes_CrankNicolson.m ————————————————
function [sol, price] = BlackScholes_CrankNicolson(S0, K, r, D, sigma, T, ...
    f, alpha, beta, Smin, Smax, dS, dt)
% f, alpha, beta : functions of initial, (left and right, resp.) boundaries
% price : linearly interpolated

N = round((Smax-Smin)/dS); M = round(T/dt);
sol = zeros(N+1,M+1); S = Smin + dS*[0:N]; t = dt*[0:M];

sol(:,end) = feval(f, S,K); % t = T
sol(1,:)   = feval(alpha, t,T,r,K,Smin, D); % S = Smin
sol(end,:) = feval(beta, t,T,r,K,Smax, D); % S = Smax

mS = S/dS;
a = 0.25*dt*(mS.*(sigma^2*mS - (r-D)));
b = -0.5*dt*(sigma^2*(mS.^2) + r);
c = 0.25*dt*(mS.*(sigma^2*mS + (r-D)));
A = -diag(a(3:N),-1) + diag(1-b(2:N)) - diag(c(2:N-1),1);
B =  diag(a(3:N),-1) + diag(1+b(2:N)) + diag(c(2:N-1),1);
[L U] = lu(A);

bj = zeros(N-1,1);
for j = M:-1:1 % for t
    bj(1) = a(2) * (sol(1,j) + sol(1,j+1));
    bj(end) = c(end-1) * (sol(end,j) + sol(end,j+1));
    sol(2:N,j) = U \ ( L \ ( B*sol(2:N,j+1) + bj ) );
end
down = floor((S0-Smin)/dS); up = ceil((S0-Smin)/dS);
if (down == up)
    price = sol(down+1,1);
else
    price = sol(down+1,1) + ...
        (sol(up+1,1) - sol(down+1,1))*(S0-Smin - down*dS)/dS;
end
```

Fig. 6.22   An implementation of the *Crank-Nicolson method* in (6.47)

such that $K - R \geq 0$. As the payoff represents a semi-circle, let us call the option *semi-circle option* with strike price $K > 0$ and radius $R > 0$.

Applying a finite difference method, preferably the Crank-Nicolson, obtain an approximate solution to the option price by imposing suitable boundary conditions.

Outlook

One of the most cited references for pricing financial derivatives by finite difference methods applied to the Black-Scholes equation may be regarded as [Tavella and Randall (2000)]. Indeed, aiming at practitioners, the book contains many examples of pricing options (on a single or many assets) by finite differences to demonstrate the capabilities of the methodology. However, for an introduction we refer to [Brandimarte (2002); Higham (2004)]

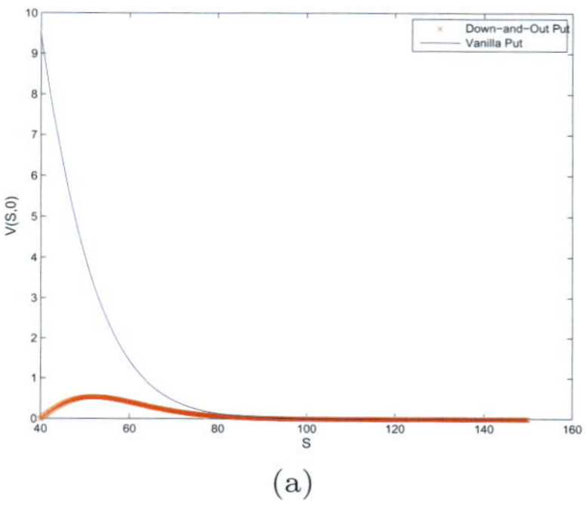

(a)

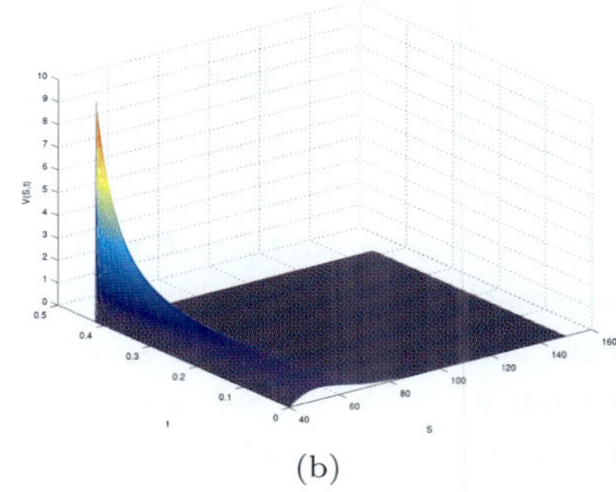

(b)

Fig. 6.23   Down-and-out put option: (a) Comparison of vanilla put with the approximate solution, (b) The surface, obtained by the *Crank-Nicolson method*

which also present MATLAB codes for finite difference methods of this section.

We emphasise that the transformation we have presented to convert the Black-Scholes equations into the heat equation may not be easy to apply for some complex options (with complex boundaries). Thus, it might be better to discretize the Black-Scholes PDE, as in this section, despite the variable coefficients which may be liable to numerical errors. There are some alternative finite difference methods, such as *upwind* scheme, that can be used instead; see, for instance, [Morton and Mayers (1995); Thomas (1995)].

6.5   Pricing American Options

Finite difference methods have proved useful and satisfactory in pricing European options. In fact, many of the options considered until now do have closed-form solutions, however, solutions for American options cannot be written in such forms, in general. Moreover, applying Monte-Carlo methods is quite difficult and is currently an active research area. The use of binomial methods or other tree methods, is too costly and, for some type of options, they are not preferred.

As long as the finite difference methods can be applied to pricing of American options, we will benefit from the advantages of numerical solutions of PDEs. The main difficulty in valuing American options is due to the possibility of an early exercise. To avoid arbitrage opportunities at each grid point in the (S, t)-plane, the value of an American option can never be less than the *intrinsic* value, the immediate payoff in case the option is exercised.

The situation can be best explained by a *free boundary* problem. Consider Fig. 6.24(a), which depicts the graphs of $V = V^{Am}(S, t)$ of an American and a European vanilla *put* option at some specific time t before maturity T. The *contact point* $S_f(t)$ in Fig. 6.24(a) moves as time increases and approaches to T, and hence $S = S_f(t)$ defines a curve in the (S, t)-plane that is similar to the one shown in Fig. 6.24(b). In other words, there is a region where $V^{Am}(S, t)$ coincides with the option payoff, and if $S \leq S_f(t)$, the put option should be exercised. In fact, it would then be possible to sell the underlying asset and let the money earn the risk-free interest rate r.

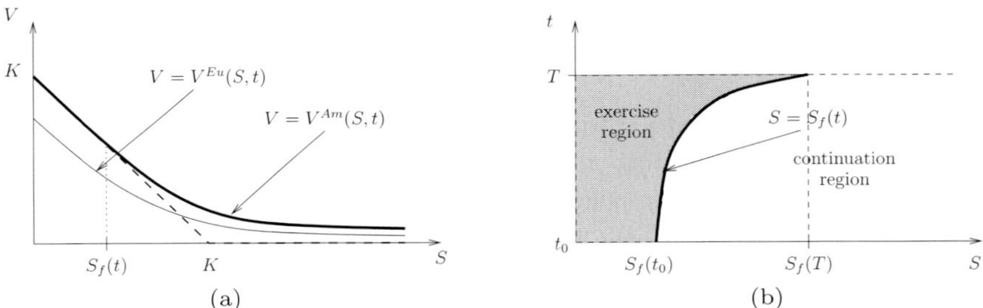

Fig. 6.24   For a typical vanilla put option: (a) option values $V^{Am}(S, t)$ and $V^{Eu}(S, t)$, (b) exercise and continuation regions for American option and the curve $S = S_f(t)$

The region

$$\Omega_E := \{(S, t) \ : \ S \leq S_f(t), \ t_0 \leq t \leq T\}$$

in Fig. 6.24(b), where the value $V^{Am}(S, t)$ coincides with the payoff, is called the region of *exercise*. Indeed, the holder of the option should exercise as soon as the asset price equals $S_f(\tau)$ at time τ, which is called a *stopping time*. On the other hand, if $V^{Am}(S, t)$ is more than the intrinsic value, early exercise means a loss; therefore the option should never be exercised in the region

$$\Omega_C := \{(S, t) \ : \ S > S_f(t), \ t_0 \leq t \leq T\},$$

which is called the *continuation region*. See Fig. 6.24(b).

Only if the curve $S = S_f(t)$ is known would we solve the corresponding Black-Scholes PDE in the region of continuation Ω_C. Unfortunately, *a priori* the location of $S_f(t)$ at time t is unknown and it must be determined along with the solution $V^{Am}(S, t)$ in Ω_C. Such a problem is called a *free boundary problem*, because the boundary of the domain Ω_C, in which the PDE is to be solved, is changing as time passes.

In order to solve the free boundary problem, we will use the idea in binomial lattices, where the option value is compared with the intrinsic value for the possibility of an early exercise. If $P(S_i, t_j)$ is the intrinsic value of an American option whose value is $V^{Am}(S_i, t_j)$ at time level j, then the inequality

$$V_{ij}^{Am} := V^{Am}(S_i, t_j) \geq P(S_i, t_j) =: P_{ij} \qquad (6.53)$$

must hold for all S_i at that time level j. So, starting from the utmost time level $j = M$, in other words, maturity T, possible candidates $\hat{V}_{ij}^{Am}$ for the price of an American option are computed as if there is no free boundary. Then, the possibility of exercise is checked by the maximum of the candidate and the intrinsic value of the payoff,

$$V_{ij}^{Am} = \max\left\{ \hat{V}_{ij}^{Am}, \ P_{ij} \right\}. \qquad (6.54)$$

Note that if the maximum is P_{ij} in (6.54), then the point (S_i, t_j) is likely to be in the region of exercise Ω_E, otherwise it is in the continuation region Ω_C. This has been the approach used in the binomial model and proved useful in pricing American options, at least in the discrete model.

We will first take this simple, naïve approach in (6.54) granted for pricing American options. To begin with, by a simple modification in the finite difference methods for European options the condition (6.54) can be taken into account. A candidate $\hat{V}_{ij}^{Am}$ for the price of an American option is calculated as if there were no free boundary. This stage can be done by any of the methods that have been obtained for the Black-Scholes equation in the previous sections. Then, the condition (6.54) is used to update this candidate at each time level before passing to the next.

In the following example, in order to take the advantages of stability and truncation order, the *Crank-Nicolson method* is applied to find the candidate for the price of an American option. Note that, because the method is an implicit one, all the values of the candidates $\hat{V}_{ij}^{Am}$ at time level

j are updated by the condition (6.54), just before passing to the $(j+1)$st time level.

Example 6.7. Consider an American put option on the underlying asset with price $S_0 = 50$. Assume the option has the strike price $K = 50$ and maturity at $T = 3$. The volatility of the asset is assumed to be $\sigma = 0.4$ and the risk-free interest rate is $r = 0.1$. Here, we also introduce a dividend rate $\delta = 0.1$ to compare the values with the corresponding option where the underlying pays no dividend.

The modified Crank-Nicolson method for American options that deals with the condition (6.54) is implemented by the MATLAB function shown in Fig. 6.25. This function is indeed almost a copy of the one for European options implemented in Fig. 6.22 that we suggest readers to compare both. In the implementation, lower and upper bounds of asset prices are taken to be, respectively, $S_{min} = 0$ and $S_{max} = 200$, while the step size is $\Delta S = 0.25$. The time step size, on the other hand, is assumed to be $\Delta t = 0.001$.

In Fig. 6.26(a), the solution curves represent the prices of the considered options. When compared with European options, American option is more expensive and the values are never less than its final payoff. The surface $V = V(S,t)$ is depicted in Fig. 6.26(b).

For small values of asset prices, the American put option has the value as its payoff, hence, the option must be exercised. However, as the asset prices increases the solution curve of the American put option leaves the payoff curve at a certain *contact point*. For values of S more than this point the option should not be exercised. This contact point separates the S-axis into two intervals: on the left is the interval of *exercise* and on the right is the interval of *continuation* for the American put option. As time to maturity changes these intervals change, too. In Fig. 6.27(a) shows some solution curves of American put option for different remaining times to maturity. As the time to maturity approaches the contact points move on the payoff towards the strike price K. Hence, this behaviour of the contact points as time t and asset prices S change defines the curve, so-called *free boundary*, $S = S_f(t)$ on the (S,t)-plane. Fig. 6.27(b) depicts the free boundary that separates the regions of *exercise* and the *continuation* of the American put option.

Exercise 6.3. Consider an American *call* option on an underlying asset that pays dividend with yield $\delta \geq 0$. Draw the free boundary curve that separates the (S,t)-plane into exercise and continuation regions. Note also that, if the underlying asset pays no dividend, namely $\delta = 0$, then the

```
________________________ BlackScholes_CrankNicolson_Am.m ________________________
function [sol, price] = BlackScholes_CrankNicolson_Am(S0, K, r, D, sigma, T, ...
    f, alpha, beta, Smin, Smax, dS, dt, Am)
% f, alpha, beta : functions of initial, (left and right, resp.) boundaries
% price : linearly interpolated

N = round((Smax-Smin)/dS); M = round(T/dt);
sol = zeros(N+1,M+1); S = Smin + dS*[0:N]; t = dt*[0:M];
sol(:,end) = feval(f, S,K); % t = T
sol(1,:)   = feval(alpha, t,T,r,K,Smin, D); % S = Smin
sol(end,:) = feval(beta, t,T,r,K,Smax, D); % S = Smax

mS = S/dS;
a = 0.25*dt*(mS.*(sigma^2*mS - (r-D)));
b = -0.5*dt*(sigma^2*(mS.^2) + r);
c = 0.25*dt*(mS.*(sigma^2*mS + (r-D)));
A = -diag(a(3:N),-1) + diag(1-b(2:N)) - diag(c(2:N-1),1);
B =  diag(a(3:N),-1) + diag(1+b(2:N)) + diag(c(2:N-1),1);
[L U] = lu(A);

bj = zeros(N-1,1);
for j = M:-1:1 % for t
    bj(1) = a(2) * (sol(1,j) + sol(1,j+1));
    bj(end) = c(end-1) * (sol(end,j) + sol(end,j+1));
    sol(2:N,j) = U \ ( L \ ( B*sol(2:N,j+1) + bj ) );
    sol(:,j) = max( sol(:,j), feval(f, S, K)' );
end
down = floor((S0-Smin)/dS); up = ceil((S0-Smin)/dS);
if (down == up)
    price = sol(down+1,1);
else
    price = sol(down+1,1) + ...
        (sol(up+1,1) - sol(down+1,1))*(S0-Smin - down*dS)/dS;
end
```

Fig. 6.25   An implementation of the *Crank-Nicolson method* for American options

values of American and European *call* options coincide. This means, it is
not optimal to exercise an American call before maturity. Illustrate this fact
by letting δ approach zero and drawing the corresponding free boundary
curves.

6.5.1   *Projected SOR Method for American Options*

There is an alternative method that considers the condition (6.54) during
the calculation of $\hat{V}_{ij}^{Am}$, the candidate for the price. Such an alternative
approach, which we will consider next, includes *iterative solutions* of linear
system of equations. Indeed, since the idea of using the condition (6.54)
seems to work in the above example, one starts to think of replacing the
direct method with an *iterative one* for solving linear system of equations.
This is desirable and, moreover, it would then be possible to include the

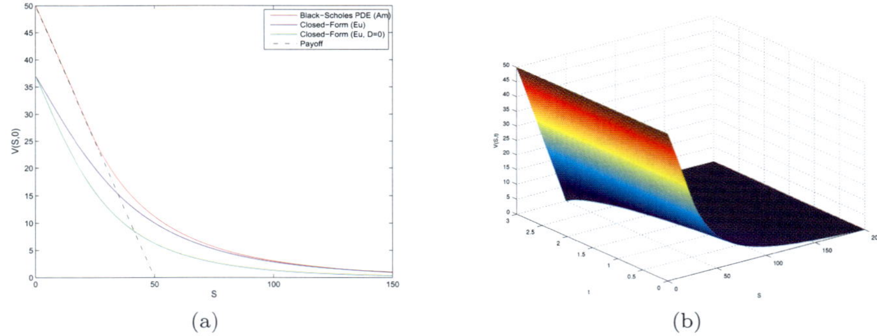

Fig. 6.26   Solution of the American put option at time $T = 3$: (a) solutions curves are compared with variant options, (b) solution surface

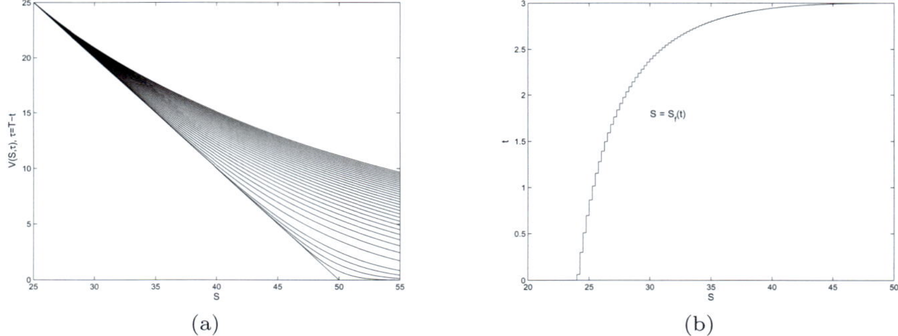

Fig. 6.27   *free boundary*: (a) solution curves as the time to maturity decreases, (b) free boundary curve $S = S_f(t)$ for an American put option

condition (6.54) at the stage when iteratively computing a candidate for the value of an American option.

Of course, it is possible to use iterative solvers for linear systems only if certain conditions for convergence hold. Fortunately, the method presented in the sequel is based on the *Gauss-Seidel* algorithm for solving linear systems iteratively, and it will be proved to converge to the true solution of the system. Even more, in order to accelerate convergence of the method a technique, called the *successive overrelaxation* (SOR), will be used. However, in order to price an American option, one has to modify such an iterative method to take care of the condition (6.54). The modified SOR method in this case is called *projected SOR*.

Let us, first, investigate how a system of linear equations can be solved via iterative methods, in particular, the so-called *Gauss-Seidel* method. Let the system of linear equations be

$$A x = b, \tag{6.55}$$

where

$$A = \begin{bmatrix} a_{11} & a_{12} & \cdots & a_{1n} \\ a_{21} & a_{22} & \cdots & a_{2n} \\ \vdots & \vdots & \ddots & \vdots \\ a_{n1} & a_{n2} & \cdots & a_{nn} \end{bmatrix}, \quad x = \begin{bmatrix} x_1 \\ x_2 \\ \vdots \\ x_n \end{bmatrix}, \quad b = \begin{bmatrix} b_1 \\ b_2 \\ \vdots \\ b_n \end{bmatrix}.$$

The Gauss-Seidel iterative method is then defined as follows: for a given initial guess $x^{(0)} = [x_1^{(0)}, x_2^{(0)}, \ldots, x_n^{(0)}]^T$, the components of the next iterate are computed recursively by

$$x_i^{(k+1)} = \frac{1}{a_{ii}} \left\{ b_i - \sum_{j=1}^{i-1} a_{ij} x_j^{(k+1)} - \sum_{j=i+1}^{n} a_{ij} x_j^{(k)} \right\} \tag{6.56}$$

for every $i = 1, 2, \ldots, n$ and $k = 1, 2, \ldots$. The iterates $x^{(k)}$ are then called Gauss-Seidel iterates. Of course, depending on some criteria the iterative algorithm should stop for some finite positive integer k. The Gauss-Seidel iterates are known to converge to the solution of the linear system in (6.55) under certain conditions on the coefficient matrix A. In fact, a sufficient condition on A so that the Gauss-Seidel iterates converge is that the matrix A should be *diagonally dominant*. That is,

$$|a_{ii}| > \sum_{\substack{j=1 \\ j \neq i}}^{n} |a_{ij}| \tag{6.57}$$

should hold for every $i = 1, 2, \ldots, n$. Fortunately, this condition is fulfilled by the matrices obtained for the finite difference methods[2] of the previous sections. So, the iterates will converge and

$$\lim_{k \to \infty} x^{(k)} = x.$$

Successive overrelaxation, however, modifies (6.56) and introduces a *relaxation* parameter $\omega \in (0, 2)$. Starting with $x^{(k)}$ the algorithm reads:

---

[2]Readers should recall that those matrices were even *tridiagonal* and the summations in (6.56) can further be simplified.

$$x^{(k+1)} = x^{(k)} + \omega \left(x_{GS}^{(k+1)} - x^{(k)} \right) = (1 - \omega)x^{(k)} + \omega x_{GS}^{(k+1)}, \qquad (6.58)$$

where $x_{GS}^{(k+1)}$ is the $(k+1)$st Gauss-Seidel iterate. Evidently, one can think of this scheme as taking a weighted average of the current and the next Gauss-Seidel iterate. If $\omega < 1$ the scheme is called *underrelaxation*, and if $\omega > 1$ it is *overrelaxation*. Note also that the case $\omega = 1$ is exactly the Gauss-Seidel method. The iterations defined in (6.58) can also be written by using the components of each iterate $x^{(k+1)}$ as

$$x_i^{(k+1)} = x_i^{(k)} + \frac{\omega}{a_{ii}} \left\{ b_i - \sum_{j=1}^{i-1} a_{ij} x_j^{(k+1)} - \sum_{j=i}^{n} a_{ij} x_j^{(k)} \right\} \qquad (6.59)$$

for every $i = 1, 2, \ldots, n$. The successive overrelaxation method is shown in Algorithm 6.1.

Algorithm 6.1 The SOR Method

    Given: $x^{(0)}$, $A = (a_{ij})$, b, ω, n

    Optional: $\omega = 1$ % for Gauss-Seidel

    for $k = 0, 1, 2, \ldots$ **do**

      for $i = 1, 2, \ldots, n$ **do**

$$x_i^{(k+1)} = x_i^{(k)} + \frac{\omega}{a_{ii}} \left\{ b_i - \sum_{j=1}^{i-1} a_{ij} x_j^{(k+1)} - \sum_{j=i}^{n} a_{ij} x_j^{(k)} \right\}$$

    end for

  end for

  Return: $x^{(k+1)}$ as an approximate solution of $Ax = b$.

Nevertheless, our aim is to modify the SOR algorithm to include the condition (6.54) for an American option rather than finding the solution of the corresponding linear system. The idea of the *projected SOR* algorithm for valuing American options is to enforce the condition (6.54) whenever a SOR iterate is available: update the current iterate and use it to calculate the next one.

Suppose that the Crank-Nicolson method is used in order to discretize the Black-Scholes equation so that the resulting linear equations are

$$Aw^{(j-1)} = Bw^{(j)} + b^{(j)} =: y^{(j)}, \qquad (6.60)$$

where the matrices A and B are tridiagonal and the vectors $b^{(j)}$ involves the boundary data. A similar system of equations arises if the fully implicit method is used, in which B stands for the identity matrix I. From the time level j, advancing to the next, $(j-1)$st, requires to solve a linear system. The solution of this linear system is now to be approximated by an iterative method, such as SOR, but it has to be modified to include the condition (6.54) for pricing American options.

Let us denote the components of the vectors $w^{(j)}$ by $w_{i,j}$ at the time level j, for simplicity. The imposed condition (6.54) for American options now reads as

$$w_{i,j}^{Am} = \max\left\{\hat{w}_{i,j}^{Am}, \ P_{ij}\right\}, \qquad (6.61)$$

where the $\hat{w}_{i,j}^{Am}$ denote the possible candidates for the prices that are calculated as if there is no free boundary, and the P_{ij} are the intrinsic values at the (S_i, t_j) nodes. Thus, the modified SOR method that cares the imposed condition (6.61) while solving (6.60) iteratively is shown in Algorithm 6.2. The algorithm is the so-called *projected* SOR method for pricing American options.

An implementation of Algorithm 6.2 is shown in Fig. 6.28, which is almost another copy of the Crank-Nicolson method for European options. However, instead of solving the set of equations, the successive overrelaxation is modified to include the side condition (6.61) at each iteration. Moreover, the SOR iterations in the implementation is continued only if two consecutive iterates are not close to each other. For a given tolerance ϵ, the SOR iteration $x^{(k+1)}$ is assumed to be good enough if

$$\left\| x^{(k+1)} - x^{(k)} \right\| \leq \epsilon,$$

since further iterations will slightly improve the iterates.

Example 6.8. This example illustrates the computation of the Delta Greek, $\Delta(S,t)$, where the option considered is the one in Example 6.7 on page 247. Knowing the values $V(S_i, t_j)$ of the option at each node (S_i, t_j) gives us the possibility of calculating several Greeks easily by applying the finite difference formulae.

Algorithm 6.2 The projected SOR Method for American Options

> **Given:** $A = (a_{ij})$ % coefficient matrix as in (6.60), for instance
> **for** $j = M, M - 1, \ldots, 1$ **do**
> $(y_{i,j}) = B\,(w_{i,j}) + (b_{i,j})$ % right-hand side vector as in (6.60)
>   **for** $k = 0, 1, 2, \ldots, K - 1$ **do**
>   **for** $i = 1, 2, \ldots, N - 1$ **do**
> $$\hat{w}_{i,j}^{(k+1)} = w_{i,j}^{(k)} + \frac{\omega}{a_{ii}} \left\{ y_{i,j} - \sum_{s=1}^{i-1} a_{is} w_{s,j}^{(k+1)} - \sum_{s=i}^{n} a_{is} w_{s,j}^{(k)} \right\}$$
> $$w_{i,j}^{(k+1)} = \max\left\{ \hat{w}_{i,j}^{(k+1)},\, P_{ij} \right\} \qquad \text{\% American Option!}$$
>   **end for**
>   **end for**
>   **for** $i = 1, 2, \ldots, n$ **do**
> $$w_{i,j-1} = w_{i,j-1}^{(0)} = \max\left\{ w_{i,j}^{(K)},\, P_{i,j-1} \right\} \qquad \text{\% American Option!}$$
>   **end for**
> **end for**
> **Return:** $(w_{i,j})$.   % Values at nodes (S_i, t_j)

The MATLAB script shown in Fig. 6.29 calculates the surface $\Delta = \Delta(S, t)$ and the free boundary $S = S_f(t)$ of the American option. The surface as well as the free boundary are depicted in Fig. 6.30.

Exercise 6.4. Consider the *semi-circle option* of Exercise 6.2, however, assume now that it is of American type and you have the option to exercise it at any time until maturity.

Compare the values of an American semi-circle option with the corresponding European version by applying a finite difference scheme.

Outlook

Pricing American options are very much linked to solving *variational inequalities* and *linear complementarity problems*: in this section, we have considered

(1) the Black-Scholes inequality
$$\frac{\partial V^{Am}}{\partial t} + \frac{1}{2}\sigma^2 S^2 \frac{\partial^2 V^{Am}}{\partial S^2} + (r - \delta)S\frac{\partial V^{Am}}{\partial S} - rV \leq 0, \quad (S, t) \in \Omega_E \cup \Omega_C\,;$$

(2) due to the no-arbitrage argument, the inequality
$$V^{Am}(S, t) \geq P(S, t), \text{ for all } (S, t) \in \Omega_E \cup \Omega_C\,;$$

```
———————————— BlackScholes_CrankNicolson_pSOR.m ————————————
function [sol, price] = BlackScholes_CrankNicolson_pSOR(SO, K, r, D, sigma, T, ...
    f, alpha, beta, Smin, Smax, dS, dt, omega, tol)
% f, alpha, beta : functions of initial, (left and right, resp.) boundaries
% price : linearly interpolated

N = round((Smax-Smin)/dS); M = round(T/dt);
sol = zeros(N+1,M+1); S = Smin + dS*[0:N]; t = dt*[0:M];
sol(:,end) = feval(f, S, K); % t = T
sol(1,:)   = feval(alpha, t,T,r,K,Smin, D); % S = Smin
sol(end,:) = feval(beta, t,T,r,K,Smax, D); % S = Smax

mS = S/dS;
a = 0.25*dt*(mS.*(sigma^2*mS - (r-D)));
b = -0.5*dt*(sigma^2*(mS.^2) + r);
c = 0.25*dt*(mS.*(sigma^2*mS + (r-D)));
B =  diag(a(3:N),-1) + diag(1+b(2:N)) + diag(c(2:N-1),1); %[L U] = lu(A);

bj = zeros(N-1,1); P = feval(f, S(2:end-1), K)';
for j = M:-1:1 % for t
    bj(1) = a(2) * (sol(1,j) + sol(1,j+1));
    bj(end) = c(end-1) * (sol(end,j) + sol(end,j+1));
    yj = B*sol(2:N,j+1) + bj;
    SOR = sol(2:end-1, j+1)'; error = realmax;   % start with a huge number
    while ( tol < error )
        AmSOR(1) = SOR(1) + omega/(1-b(2)) * ( yj(1) - ...
            (1-b(2))*SOR(1) + c(2)*SOR(2) );
        AmSOR(1) = max( AmSOR(1), P(1) );
        for i = 2:N-2
            AmSOR(i) = SOR(i) + omega/(1-b(i+1)) * ( yj(i) + ...
                a(i+1)*AmSOR(i-1) - (1-b(i+1))*SOR(i) + c(i+1)*SOR(i+1) );
            AmSOR(i) = max( AmSOR(i), P(i) );
        end
        AmSOR(N-1) = SOR(N-1) + omega/(1-b(N)) * ( yj(N-1) + ...
            a(N)*AmSOR(N-2) - (1-b(N))*SOR(N-1) );
        AmSOR(N-1) = max( AmSOR(N-1), P(N-1) );
        error = norm(AmSOR - SOR); SOR = AmSOR;
    end
    sol(:,j) = max([sol(1,j) AmSOR sol(end,j)], feval(f, S, K) );
end
down = floor((SO-Smin)/dS); up = ceil((SO-Smin)/dS);
if (down == up)
    price = sol(down+1,1);
else
    price = sol(down+1,1) + ...
        (sol(up+1,1) - sol(down+1,1))*(SO-Smin - down*dS)/dS;
end
```

Fig. 6.28 An implementation that uses *projected SOR* method for pricing American options by the *Crank-Nicolson method*

(3) the fact that one of the inequalities above are at *equality*; that is, either we *hold* the option, or *exercise* it.

Due to the unknown free boundary that arises as a result of the linear complementarity problem, iterative solutions of linear systems are imposed. See [Brandimarte (2002); Seydel (2002)], for example. For general itera-

```
———————————————————————— testAm_pSOR.m ————————————————
% test Black-Scholes Solutions
clear all, close all
S0 = 50; K = 50; D = 0.1; sigma = 0.4; r = 0.1; Smin = 0; Smax = 200;
T = 3; dS = 0.25; dt = 0.001; omega = 1.0; tol = 1e-8;

f = @BlackScholes_Payoff_Am;
alpha = @BlackScholes_LeftBoundary_Am; beta = @BlackScholes_RightBoundary_Am;
[w,p] = BlackScholes_CrankNicolson_pSOR(S0, K, r, D, sigma, T, ...
    f, alpha, beta, Smin, Smax, dS, dt, omega, tol);

[n,m] = size(w); S = linspace(Smin,Smax,n); t = linspace(0,T,m);
Sf = zeros(1,m); DeltaW = zeros(size(w));
for j = 1:m-1
    difference = w(:,j) - feval(f, S, K)';
    tFirst = find(difference, 1,'first'); Sf(j) = S(tFirst);
end
DeltaW(1:end-1,:) = ( w(2:end,:) - w(1:(end-1),:) ) ./ dS;
mesh(S, t, DeltaW'), xlabel('S','FontSize',12),
ylabel('t','FontSize',12), zlabel('\Delta(S,t)','FontSize',12), hold on,
plot3([Sf((1:end-1)) K],t(1:end), zeros(size(w)), 'k-', 'LineWidth', 2),
print -r300 -depsc -cmyk '../figures/testAm_pSOR_Delta'
fprintf('PDE Solution.................: %f\n', p);
```

Fig. 6.29 A MATLAB script calculates the Delta Greek of an American option

tive algorithms to solve matrix equations we refer to [Cheney and Kincaid (1994)].

For more details of the variational inequalities and the linear complementarity problems, the texts [Achdou and Pironneau (2005); Forsyth and Vetzal (2002); Rogers and Talay (1997); Seydel (2002); Wilmott *et al.* (1995)] are good resources for both advanced readers and beginners. A classical reference on free and moving boundary problems is [Elliott and Ockendon (1982)].

6.6 Tree Methods and Finite Differences

This section presents some relations between finite differences and tree methods. The explicit finite difference method, in particular, can be considered as a trinomial tree or as the previously investigated binomial method. In fact, these emerge from a common sense: the stencil for the explicit finite difference resembles a one-period trinomial tree. A binomial tree is then obtained by imposing only two outcomes, up and down. In the sequel, the idea will become more clear when the related finite difference method is introduced.

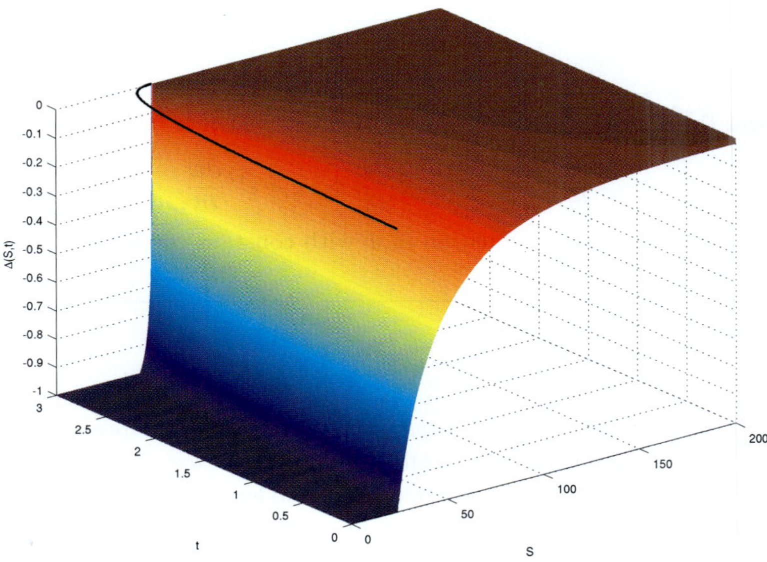

Fig. 6.30 The Delta Greek, $\Delta = \frac{\partial V}{\partial S}$, of an American put option, and the black curve is the free boundary, $S = S_f(t)$, associated with the option

Consider the Black-Scholes equation,

$$\frac{\partial V}{\partial t} + \frac{1}{2}\sigma^2 S^2 \frac{\partial^2 V}{\partial S^2} + rS\frac{\partial V}{\partial S} - rV = 0,$$

where $V = V(S,t)$ is the value of a European option. As we have seen, a transformation of the form

$$x = \ln S, \qquad (6.62)$$

can easily convert the Black-Scholes equation into a *constant coefficient* one. Using the relations

$$\frac{\partial V}{\partial S} = \frac{1}{S}\frac{\partial V}{\partial x} \quad \text{and} \quad \frac{\partial^2 V}{\partial S^2} = \frac{1}{S^2}\left(\frac{\partial^2 V}{\partial x^2} - \frac{\partial V}{\partial x}\right), \qquad (6.63)$$

it is not difficult to obtain this constant coefficient equation as

$$\frac{\partial v}{\partial t} + \frac{1}{2}\sigma^2 \frac{\partial^2 v}{\partial x^2} + \left(r - \frac{1}{2}\sigma^2\right)\frac{\partial v}{\partial x} - rv = 0, \qquad (6.64)$$

where

$$v = v(x,t) = V(e^x, t).$$

Furthermore, the application of the transformation

$$v(x,t) = e^{rt}w(x,t) \tag{6.65}$$

removes the term rv in (6.64), due to the fact that

$$\frac{\partial v}{\partial t} = re^{rt}w + e^{rt}\frac{\partial w}{\partial t} = rv + e^{rt}\frac{\partial w}{\partial t}.$$

The resulting differential equation in w with constant coefficients can then be written as

$$\frac{\partial w}{\partial t} + \frac{1}{2}\sigma^2\frac{\partial^2 w}{\partial x^2} + \left(r - \frac{1}{2}\sigma^2\right)\frac{\partial w}{\partial x} = 0. \tag{6.66}$$

Now, for a wish to apply an *explicit method* in order to approximate the partial differential equation in (6.66), we use a *backward* difference in time t and central differences in space x at the time level $j + 1$, but not j. The explicit method for the PDE in (6.66) becomes

$$\begin{aligned}
\frac{w_{i,j+1} - w_{ij}}{\Delta t} &+ \frac{1}{2}\sigma^2\frac{w_{i+1,j+1} - 2w_{i,j+1} + w_{i-1,j+1}}{(\Delta x)^2} \\
&+ \left(r - \frac{1}{2}\sigma^2\right)\frac{w_{i+1,j+1} - w_{i-1,j+1}}{2\Delta x} = 0,
\end{aligned} \tag{6.67}$$

where Δt and Δx are the step lengths taken, respectively, in time and in space. Note that w_{ij} stands for the approximation to $w(x_i, t_j)$, that is $w_{ij} \approx w(x_i, t_j)$. Collecting the similar terms in (6.67) it is possible to rewrite the method in the following simple form:

$$w_{ij} = aw_{i-1,j+1} + bw_{i,j+1} + cw_{i+1,j+1}, \tag{6.68}$$

where

$$\begin{aligned}
a &= \frac{1}{2}\Delta t\left\{\left(\frac{\sigma}{\Delta x}\right)^2 - \left(r - \frac{1}{2}\sigma^2\right)\frac{1}{\Delta x}\right\}, \\
b &= \Delta t\left\{\frac{1}{\Delta t} - \left(\frac{\sigma}{\Delta x}\right)^2\right\} = 1 - \Delta t\left(\frac{\sigma}{\Delta x}\right)^2, \\
c &= \frac{1}{2}\Delta t\left\{\left(\frac{\sigma}{\Delta x}\right)^2 + \left(r - \frac{1}{2}\sigma^2\right)\frac{1}{\Delta x}\right\}.
\end{aligned} \tag{6.69}$$

Using the transformation (6.65) we may return back to the approximations for v_{ij} as

$$v_{ij} = e^{-r\Delta t}\left\{av_{i-1,j+1} + bv_{i,j+1} + cv_{i+1,j+1}\right\}, \qquad (6.70)$$

for $j = M-1, M-2, \ldots, 0$ and $i = 1, 2, \ldots, N-1$, where $\Delta t = t_j - t_{j-1}$. In other words, the approximations

$$v_{ij} \approx v(x_i, t_j) = e^{rt_j} w(x_i, t_j) \approx e^{rt_j} w_{ij}$$

satisfy the equations in (6.70). However, (6.70) stands for an *explicit finite difference method*, and this method will be the basis for the tree methods presented in the sequel. Moreover, one may go further back to the approximate solutions V_{ij} of $V = V(S_i, t_j)$, that is, $V_{ij} \approx V = V(S_i, t_j)$. Only if it is necessary, transforming x back to S by

$$S_i = e^{x_i}$$

will approximate the solutions of the original Black-Scholes equation.

Remark 6.3. In this setting, it should be noted that time runs backward and the explicit method starts from maturity, $t_M = T$. That is, initial values for the recurrence relation (6.70) are computed from the payoff of the option: for instance for a call option with a strike K, the payoff is converted to

$$v_{iM} = \max\left\{e^{x_i} - K,\ 0\right\} = \max\left\{S_i - K,\ 0\right\}$$

for every $i = 0, 1, \ldots, N$. The boundary conditions can be treated similarly to obtain $v_{0,j}$ and $v_{N,j}$ for every $j = 0, 1, \ldots, M$.

In the following, we shall investigate two cases that we may relate this explicit finite difference method to the tree methods in literature: a trinomial tree and a binomial one. The latter is what we have investigated in this book. Therefore, we may start with the trinomial tree which may be regarded as an additional new method presented here for pricing options.

6.6.1 *A Trinomial Tree*

In order to relate the explicit method in (6.70) to a trinomial tree it is enough to give a meaning to the coefficients a, b and c: let

$$p_u = c, \quad p_0 = b, \quad \text{and} \quad p_d = a.$$

With these notations at hand, the explicit method, or the tree method in fact, is

$$v_{ij} = e^{-r\Delta t} \left\{ p_u v_{i+1,j+1} + p_0 v_{i,j+1} + p_d v_{i-1,j+1} \right\}. \qquad (6.71)$$

In this representation, p_u and p_d denote the probabilities of up-movement and down-movement of the option value v, respectively. On the other hand, p_0 is the probability that v stays the same within the time interval Δt. A stencil is shown in Fig. 6.31.

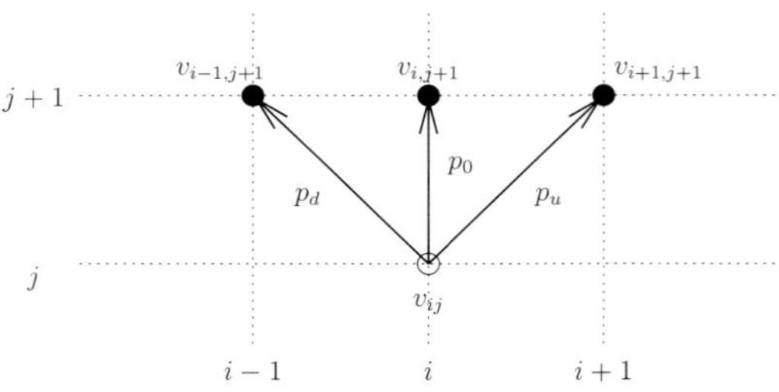

Fig. 6.31   Stencil for the Trinomial tree

It is interesting to see that

$$p_u + p_d = \Delta t \left(\frac{\sigma}{\Delta x} \right)^2 = 1 - p_0,$$

which implies that those probabilities, in fact, sum up to one:

$$p_u + p_0 + p_d = 1. \qquad (6.72)$$

Therefore, the recursion (6.71) represents a *discounted, expected value of v after Δt time step*. The discount factor is the continuously compounding risk-free interest rate, that is, $e^{-r\Delta t}$.

6.6.2   *A Binomial Tree*

The basic difference between a binomial tree and a trinomial one is that we have only two possibilities in the former. This suggests us that we should break down one of the connections shown in Fig. 6.31. In other words, the probability that v stays the same must be zero. To do so, we assume that we can choose

$$\Delta t = \left(\frac{\Delta x}{\sigma}\right)^2 \tag{6.73}$$

so that p_0 vanishes, $p_0 = b = 0$, in the trinomial tree (6.71), or in the explicit finite difference method in (6.70). That is, only up- and down-movements of v are allowed.

The assumption in (6.73) is indeed a heuristic one: recall the conditional stability of the explicit method, for instance. Such an assumption might destroy the stability of the algorithm. For the sake of constructing a binomial lattice, however, such a heuristic assumption is assumed for now. In fact, it turns out that this assumption is valid and it does *not* destroy the stability of the method.

Under the assumption (6.73), the explicit finite difference method in (6.70) can be rewritten as

$$v_{ij} = e^{-r\Delta t}\left\{qv_{i+1,j+1} + (1-q)v_{i-1,j+1}\right\}, \tag{6.74}$$

where q is obtained from p_u by using the assumption (6.73), and it reads

$$\begin{aligned} q &= \frac{1}{2} + \frac{1}{2}\left(r - \frac{1}{2}\sigma^2\right)\frac{\Delta x}{\sigma^2} \\ &= \frac{1}{2}\left\{1 + \sqrt{\Delta t}\left(\frac{r}{\sigma} - \frac{\sigma}{2}\right)\right\}. \end{aligned} \tag{6.75}$$

Note also that p_d becomes $1-q$ so that $p_u + p_d = 1$ in this particular case. Hence, q represents the probability of an *up*-movement, while $1 - q$ stands for that of a *down*-movement. A stencil for the corresponding explicit finite difference, which can be thought as a binomial method, is shown in Fig. 6.32.

Of course, the crucial point whether or not it is possible to choose

$$\Delta t = \left(\frac{\Delta x}{\sigma}\right)^2$$

still remains to be resolved. Indeed, one can show that such an assumption is possible and it does not violate the stability of the explicit method. An analysis through the stability of the explicit method in (6.71) shows that the method is stable only if the condition

$$\Delta t \leq \left(\frac{\Delta x}{\sigma}\right)^2 \tag{6.76}$$

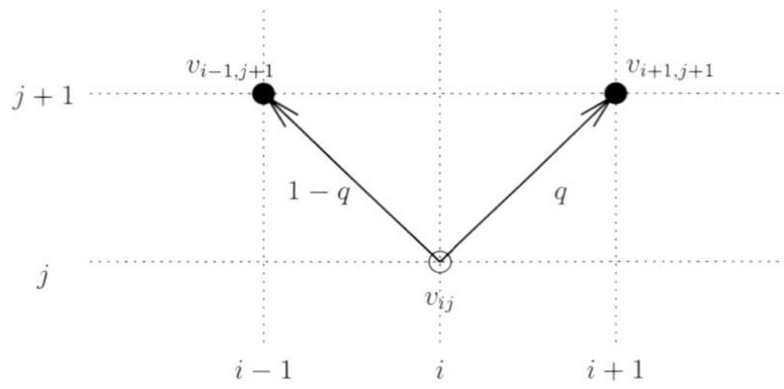

Fig. 6.32   Stencil for the Binomial tree

holds. This condition bounds the step lengths Δx and Δt, and it is similar to the one previously obtained for the stability of the explicit method for the dimensionless heat equation. This means, on the other hand, the method constructed here by choosing the condition (6.73) is *stable*. However, it is near the border that separates the stability and instability regions.

Exercise 6.5. Show that the explicit method defined by (6.71) is stable only if, the condition (6.76) holds.

Outlook

A more complete treatment of the connection between tree methods and finite difference approximations can be found in [Forsyth and Vetzal (2002); Kwok (1998)]. In addition, for tree methods, in particular, we refer to the classical texts in finance, such as [Cox *et al.* (1979); Higham (2002); Hull (2000); Wilmott *et al.* (1995)].

Appendix A

A Short Introduction to Matlab

Matlab,[1] which stands for "MATrix LABoratory", was originally developed to provide as easy access to matrices and vectors. It became popular for both teaching and research projects and involved into commercial software package.

It contains many built-in functions that are designed for matrix-vector computations. There are many other extremely efficient routines that can work and perform operations on matrices. There are, on the other hand, extensive library that can handle with two- or three-dimensional graphics. All these "state-of-the-art" built-in functions make Matlab an integrated environment for *computation, simulation* and *visualisation*.

Moreover, having provided almost all of the "data types" and the "control structures", Matlab is, nowadays, considered to be a *programming language* to develop serious applications in science and technology. Hence, all the built-in functions and predefined variables can be modified or overwritten. In fact, to extend the capabilities of Matlab, many toolboxes are created. A *toolbox* is a collection of functions, variables and scripts that extends the integrated development environment for a particular area of applications.

This appendix gives a quick way to become familiar with the most important parts of Matlab. The ease of implementing and visualising when necessary make Matlab an appropriate framework for exploring the contents and algorithms written in this book.[2]

---

[1] Matlab® is a registered trademark of *The MathWorks, Inc.*

[2] For sure, there are possible alternatives to Matlab: among them are *Scilab* and *Octave*, which are freely distributed and very similar to Matlab.

A.1 Getting Started

The simplest way to start with MATLAB is to use it for simple calculations. Having a wide range of built-in functions and constants, MATLAB can handle with real and complex numbers and operations on them. Here are some obvious examples, where the comma (,) separates the calculations.

```
>> (-1+2+3)*4 - 5/6, exp(log(2)), sqrt((-2)^3)
ans =
   15.1667
ans =
     2
ans =
        0 + 2.8284i
```

Unlike other programming languages, such as *C/C++*, *Java*, *Fortran*, etc., MATLAB calculates 5/6 as real (in *double* precision). The built-in functions `exp` and `log` are the natural exponential and logarithm functions. As you may have noticed above that `i` is used for complex number, $i = \sqrt{-1}$. Similarly, `j` is also used for the complex number i. There are other predefined constants such as `pi` and `eps`. The former stands for the mathematical constant π and the latter is the *machine epsilon*, ε_m, that is about 10^{-16}, but depends on the machine MATLAB is installed.

MATLAB has a comprehensive online documentation, which can be accessed by typing the command `help`. In fact, for a specific function or constant you may simply type `help` followed by the name of the function or constant, such as

```
>> help elfun, help matfun, ...
help sin, help pi, ...
help format, help datatypes
```

The first two, `elfun` and `matfun`, correspond to, respectively, elementary and matrix functions. The other two are specific built-in function and constant. The command `format`, followed by `long`, or `short`, or `bank` and so on, sets the format of the output. For instance, many of the outputs given in this book is obtained by using `format compact`, which suppresses extra line-feeds. Note that the three dots (...) allows the user to continue on a new line. All *data types* that MATLAB can handle is listed by the command `help datatypes`.

A.1.1 *Variables*

Although these built-in functions and constants are predefined in MATLAB, it is possible to overwrite their definitions. This may be done in two ways: defining a *variable* or a MATLAB *function* with the same name. For example, defining variable names i, eps, and sin will change the predefined definitions. They regain their predefined roles when the variables are *cleared* from the *Workspace* of MATLAB by the command clear followed by the variable name.

```
>> i = cos(pi), eps = 10^(-8), sin = 5
i =
    0.2837
eps =
    1.0000e-08
sin =
     5
>> sin(pi)
??? Index exceeds matrix dimensions.
>> clear sin
```

We will deal with functions later in this appendix. They are structured *files*, called *m-files*, which work for some specific purpose.

Variable names in MATLAB must start with a letter and may follow by a combination of letters and numbers. Since it is not possible to use *spaces* in variable names, you may simply separate long variable names by using *underscore*. For instance, Variable_123_Name is a valid variable name in MATLAB. The built-in variable ans holds the last computed values, but not assigned to a variable. For example,

```
>> clear all
>> myVar = 1 + 2*4, -cos(pi); myVar2 = myVar + ans
myVar =
     9
myVar2 =
    10
```

After having cleared all the variables from the Workspace, myVar holds the value 9, ans holds the value of $-\cos(\pi)$, and the sum of myVar and ans is assigned to myVar2. As you may have noticed that the semicolon (;) suppresses the output. Further, you may use the command who, or whos for the long form of who, to see the list of all the variables in the current workspace. For instance,

```
>> who
```

```
Your variables are:

ans       myVar    myVar2

>> whos
  Name           Size                   Bytes  Class

   ans            1x1                       8  double array
   myVar          1x1                       8  double array
   myVar2         1x1                       8  double array

Grand total is 3 elements using 24 bytes
```

Until now, we have been typing MATLAB commands and functions in the *command window*. It is possible to save all (or some of) *workspace* variables to a *binary* file by typing

```
>> save myFileName myVars
```

This will save the variable(s) `myVars` in a file named `myFileName.mat`, which can then be loaded to the workspace by the `load` command of MATLAB. The option `-ascii` can be used if binary is not desired. The `-append` option may be used to add variables to an existing file.

MATLAB also provides a command `diary` in order to save the current *command window* (and the output therein) to a file. Its usage is rather simple. See the following example as well as the file `myDiaryFile.txt` to which the output is appended.

```
>> diary myDiaryFile.txt
>> inDiary = 5
inDiary =
     5
>> diary off
>> notInDiary = 0;
>> diary on
>> inDiary = 6;
>> diary off
```

A.2 Matrices and Vectors

Matrices, in particular vectors, are crucial and fundamental in MATLAB. In fact, these are two- and one-dimensional arrays, respectively. Although it is possible to define multi-dimensional arrays, the matrices and vectors, and standard operations on them will be emphasised in this section.

An $m \times n$ *matrix* in MATLAB is a two-dimensional array of size (m, n).

An *n-vector* is either an $n \times 1$ or $1 \times n$ matrix, depending whether a column or a row vector is considered. A *scalar* in MATLAB is, therefore, a 1×1 matrix. There are many ways to construct and initialise matrices. Here are some of them.

```
>> M = [1,2,3; 6,5,4; 7,8,9], col_v = [1;2;3],...
row_v = [4,5,6]
M =
       1     2     3
       6     5     4
       7     8     9
col_v =
       1
       2
       3
row_v =
       4     5     6
>> col_v2 = row_v'
col_v2 =
       4
       5
       6
```

First, a 3×3 matrix M is constructed and then, a column and a row vector, respectively, `col_v` and `row_v` are constructed. The transpose operator (`'`) is used to convert `row_v` vector and the result is assigned to the variable `col_v2`.

The standard operations, such as *addition* and *multiplication*, of matrices are defined as usual: following the previously defined matrices and vectors, here are some examples.

```
>> rand('state', 13); MT = M'; A = MT + M;
>> b = MT * ( 2*col_v - rand(3,1) ) + 5
b =
    66.9998
    70.5823
    74.1648
```

The command `rand('state', 13)` initialises the *random number genera-tor*, `rand`, with the *seed* that is 13. The random number generator produces *uniform* random numbers between 0 and 1, if it is called simply as `rand` with no input arguments. However, if it is called with parameters, such as, `rand(m,n)`, where m and n are integers, then the output is an $m \times n$ matrix whose entries are random numbers that are uniformly distributed. For instance, `rand(3,1)` in the second line generates a column vector of size 3×1. There is also another random number generator, `randn`, which works very similar to **rand**. However, **randn** generates random numbers that are standard normally distributed.

The second line in the MATLAB environment above creates a column vector b: apart from a usual matrix multiplication or the multiplication of a matrix by a scalar, an addition of a matrix (in fact, a vector) and a scalar is presented. This is not an error in MATLAB. The second line above may be rewritten as follows:

```
>> b = MT * ( 2*eye(3)*col_v - rand(3,1) ) + 5*ones(3,1);
```

Here, **ones(3,1)** is a 3×1 matrix with entries that are equal to *one*. Likewise, the MATLAB function **eye(m,n)** generates a matrix whose main diagonal consists of *ones*. In particular, **eye(m)** generates the $m \times m$ *identity* matrix. One can also initialise an $m \times n$ matrix with zeros by simply typing **zeros(m,n)**. Further assistance on elementary matrices and matrix manipulation can be obtained by **help elmat**.

It is also easy to solve linear systems of equations of the form

$$A x = b,$$

where A is an $m \times n$ matrix and b is m-vector. Here, the solution vector x is to be sought. Computationally, finding a solution is not so easy that one has to resort to *numerical methods* for solutions of linear systems. However, MATLAB introduces a very useful operator $(\backslash)$, the *backslash* operator. In MATLAB, **A\b** is the matrix division of **A** into **B**, which is roughly the same as **inv(A)*b**, except it is computed in a different way. The vector **x = A\b** is the solution in the *least squares* sense to the system above. Below is an example, where x solves the system of equations in the least squares sense and the *residual* $r = b - A x$ is almost a zero vector.

```
>> L = [1 0 0; 2 3 0; 4 5 6]; A = L*L'; b = [3 2 1]';
>> x = A \ b, r = b - A*x
x =
    3.9691
   -0.2438
   -0.1204
r =
   1.0e-15 *
        0
   -0.4441
        0
```

Note also that the matrix A formed above is invertible and the command **inv(A)*b** computes $x = A^{-1} b$ as the solution of the system. However, when the coefficient matrix A of the system is *singular*, consequently, **inv(A)** will not work as expected. In fact, in numerical computations, the inverse of a matrix is hardly needed!

Accessing the entries of a matrix in MATLAB is easily accomplished by specifying its location in the array. For instance, if `A` is a matrix of some certain size, then the entry on the `m`th row and the `n`th column is `A(m,n)`. Not only a single entry of a matrix can one access, but also selection of a block (a submatrix) out of a matrix is possible. Associated with the usage `A(m,n)`, it is important to emphasise that the variables `m` and `n` may be vectors that contain the row and the column indices, respectively. This will be clear in the sequel.

MATLAB has a built-in *colon* operator, `(:)`, for constructing vectors as well as accessing entries of a matrices. The operator, in general, has the form

$$\boxed{\texttt{inital:stepsize:final}}$$

This is indeed a row vector whose components starts with the `initial` value. The second component of the vector is then computed by adding the *nonzero* value of the `stepsize` to the `initial` value. The next component is obtained again by adding the *stepsize* to the current only if the result obtained does not exceed the `final` value. Consequently, the `final` value may or may not be included in the vector. Note that there is no restriction on the sign of the `stepsize`; however, if the `stepsize` is positive (respectively, negative), then the value of `final` should not be less (respectively, greater) than that of the `initial`.

Another common usage of the colon operator is that one may use the *default* `stepsize`, which is 1. In this case,

$$\boxed{\texttt{inital:final}}$$

generates a row vector with components starting with the `initial` value and ending with the `final` value.

Here is an example that illustrates some of the basic use of the colon operator.

```
>> randn('state', 13); A = randn(10,15);
>> m = 3:8, n = 2:4:15, r = 0:0.25:1
m =
     3     4     5     6     7     8
n =
     2     6    10    14
r =
        0    0.2500    0.5000    0.7500    1.0000
```

```
>> B = A(m,n)
B =
    1.5319   -0.3251   -0.4470    0.1747
   -0.1009   -1.9545    0.8423    1.7590
   -0.7548    0.0018    1.8984    0.2954
   -0.6805    0.1140    1.6201    1.8069
    1.1651   -0.9739    2.0801   -0.9937
    1.1551    0.7506   -0.0007    0.6790
>> A(4,10), m(2), n(3), B(2,3)
ans =
    0.8423
ans =
     4
ans =
    10
ans =
    0.8423
>> B(2,:)
ans =
   -0.1009   -1.9545    0.8423    1.7590
```

Here, B(2,:) is a row vector whose components are the *second* row of the
matrix B. Similarly, B(:,j) will be a column vector, the jth column of B,
only if j is assigned to a *scalar*. Otherwise, if j is a vector of indices of
certain columns of B, then B(:,j) is a matrix consisting of those columns
only.

Initialising or changing the entries of a matrix follow similar rules. For
instance, the following MATLAB codes simply changes the jth column of
the matrix B.

```
>> rand('state',13); A = rand(3,5);
>> B = zeros(size(A)); j = 3;
>> B(:,j) = A(:,5), i = [1 3];
B =
         0         0    0.8187         0         0
         0         0    0.4153         0         0
         0         0    0.4270         0         0
>> B(i,:) = [ 1 2 3 4 5; 6:10 ]
B =
    1.0000    2.0000    3.0000    4.0000    5.0000
         0         0    0.4153         0         0
    6.0000    7.0000    8.0000    9.0000   10.0000
```

Note that it is also possible to change several columns or rows at the same
time. Above, the first and the third rows of B are assigned to another
matrix.

A.2.1 *Operations on Matrices*

Apart from the usual addition and multiplication of matrices, MATLAB defines similar operations and functions on the *entries* of matrices. For instance, you may wish to take the square of each entry of a matrix, but not the square of the matrix itself. The latter, for square matrices, is easy: A^2 calculates the matrix multiplication, A*A. The former, on the other hand, requires accessing each entry of the matrix which need not be a square one.

There are *element-by-element* versions of taking a power of a matrix and multiplying two matrices: `power` and `times`, respectively. Rather these functions, we prefer to use the built-in binary operators, simply denoted by .^ and .*. The element-by-element division is made by the operator ./ or the function `rdivide`. In general, these operators (or corresponding functions) works on two matrices having the same size *unless one of them is a scalar*. Note that a period (.) is not used in the usual addition + and subtraction – due to the fact that they are already element-by-element operations.

Below is an example to illustrate some element-by-element operations on matrices.

```
>> x = linspace(-pi,pi,5), y = x.^2, z = x.*y, y2 = z ./ x
x =
    -3.1416    -1.5708         0    1.5708    3.1416
y =
     9.8696     2.4674         0    2.4674    9.8696
z =
   -31.0063    -3.8758         0    3.8758   31.0063
Warning: Divide by zero.
y2 =
     9.8696     2.4674       NaN    2.4674    9.8696
>> [1 2; 3 4] .^ [4 3; 2 1]
ans =
     1     8
     9     4
```

The MATLAB built-in function `linspace` above takes three arguments as input: `linspace(a, b, n)`. The last one, n, is *optional* and its default value is 100. The function generates n linearly equally spaced points between a and b.

Readers may note the warning: dividing zero by zero by zero produces *Not-a-Number* (NaN). See MATLAB documentation for NaN (as well as Inf which stands for the *infinity*) for further details.

In MATLAB many built-in functions, such as `sin`, `cos`, `exp`, `log`, acts on the entries of the matrices given as input. For instance, `exp(A)` generates a matrix that consists of the exponential of each entries in `A`, but *not* the mathematical definition of e^A for A being a square matrix. Here are some cases when the argument is either a vector or a matrix.

```
>> x = linspace(-pi,pi,5); y = sin(x), z = exp(x)
y =
   -0.0000   -1.0000        0    1.0000    0.0000
z =
    0.0432    0.2079    1.0000    4.8105   23.1407
>> t = atan( [x; y; z] ), e = exp( t )
t =
   -1.2626   -1.0039        0    1.0039    1.2626
   -0.0000   -0.7854        0    0.7854    0.0000
    0.0432    0.2050    0.7854    1.3658    1.5276
e =
    0.2829    0.3665    1.0000    2.7289    3.5347
    1.0000    0.4559    1.0000    2.1933    1.0000
    1.0441    1.2275    2.1933    3.9190    4.6071
```

A.3 Graphics

MATLAB provides a wide range of graphics facilities which are collected in a set of functions with many options. You may start with typing `help graph2d` for two-dimensional graphics and then may wish to see help on `graph3d` or `specgraph` for more. Unfortunately, however, this section covers only a very few of those functions and options for plotting two- or three-dimensional plots.

The most common plotting function in MATLAB may be the `plot`, which takes several forms. For example,

$$\boxed{\texttt{plot(x, y)}} \qquad \text{or} \qquad \boxed{\texttt{plot(x, y, style)}}$$

plots the vector `y` versus the vector `x`. In case when `x` and `y` are matrices, then the kth column of `y` is plotted versus the kth column of `x`. Plotting is then repeated for all pairs of columns. Here, `style` is a character string that specifies options for colours, symbols or line types for plotting. Here is an example.

```
>> x1 = linspace(0,2*pi,20); x2 = 0:pi/20:2*pi;
>> y1 = sin(x1); y2 = cos(x2); y3 = exp(-abs(x1-pi));
>> plot(x1, y1), hold on
>> plot(x2, y2, 'r+:'), plot(x1, y3, '-.o')
```

```
>> plot([x1; x1], [y1; y3], '-.x'), hold off
>> print -depsc -r900 -cmyk '../figures/appendixPlot_1'
```

There are a few points that have to be clarified in the example above, whose graph is given in Fig. A.1

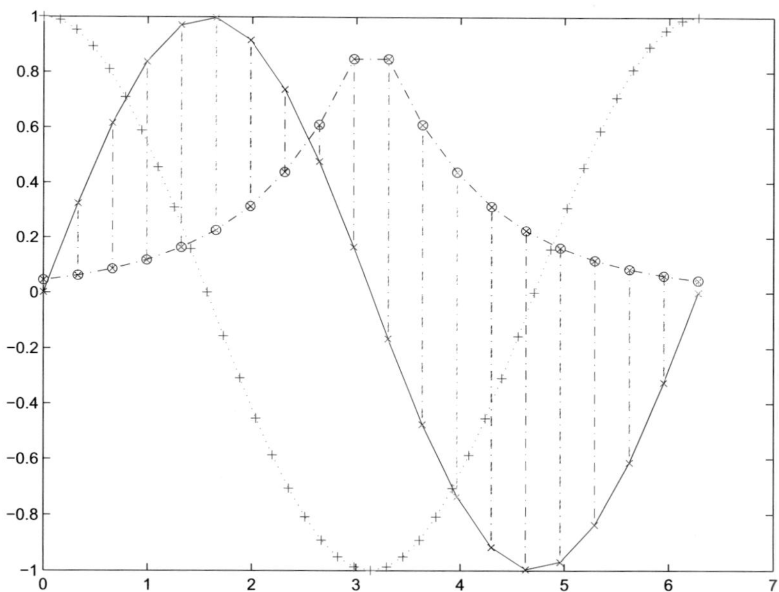

Fig. A.1   Superimposed two-dimensional plots: Using `plot`

First, the function `plot` pops up a *figure window* and draws the given data with specified option. The figure window can be used to edit the properties. The command `hold on` (or the function `hold`) is used to ensure that subsequent graphing commands add to the existing graph. On the other hand, one can combine several drawings in a single `plot` function as

$$\boxed{\texttt{plot(x1, y1, style1, x2, y2, style2, ...)}}$$

The command `hold off` returns to the default mode whereby subsequent plotting erases what has been created before and draws the new graphics.

Another issue is the string parameter for style of current drawings. Generally, for styling there are three separate groups: *colours, points,* and *lines.* One can choose one symbol from one or all of these groups. Some of the commonly used symbols and their meanings are given in Table A.1.

Table A.1 Some of the style parameters in plotting graphs

	Colours		Points		Lines
b	blue	.	point	–	solid
g	green	o	circle	:	dotted
r	red	x	x-mark	–.	dashdot
c	cyan	+	plus	––	dashed
m	magenta	*	star		no line
y	yellow	s	square		
k	black	d	diamond		
		v	triangle (down)		

The last point that needs an emphasis is that although the *figure window* can be used to edit and save the drawings, there are MATLAB commands and functions which are used for the same purpose. The command `print`, for instance, is used for saving (or printing) the figure. In the example above, the format of the figure that has to be saved under a folder with a given name is specified by the *device* option: `-depsc` stands for the *encapsulated colour PostScript* format (EPS). The option `-r900` is used for *dots-per-inch resolution*, which is 900 in this case; and `-cmyk` ensures the use of *CMYK* colours instead of *RGB*. One may also add *TIFF* preview by adding the option `-tiff` so that the saved figure (with extension .eps) may be viewed in a *Word document*. For more information on `print`, see MATLAB documentation, or simply type `help print`.

Among many other functions for plotting there are some special ones that are used in many graphics, such as `title`, `xlabel`, `ylabel`, and so on. One can easily display text inside a plot by using the function `text` or `gtext`. Below, we present another example that uses some of these functions as well as `subplot`, the latter of which splits the figure window into grids.

```
>> x = linspace(0,2*pi);
>> subplot(2,2,1); plot(x, sin(x), x, cos(x), '--')
>> xlabel('x'), ylabel('y'), title('Place (1,1)'), grid on
>> subplot(2,2,2); plot(exp(i*x)), title('Place (1,2): z = e^{ix}')
>> axis square, text(0,0, 'i is complex')
>> subplot(2,2,3); polar(x, ones(size(x))), title('Place (2,1)')
>> subplot(2,2,4); semilogx(x,sin(x), x,cos(x), '--')
>> title('Place: (2,2)'), grid on
>> legend('sin', 'cos', 'Location', 'SouthWest')
```

The figure as an output of the example is given in Fig. A.2

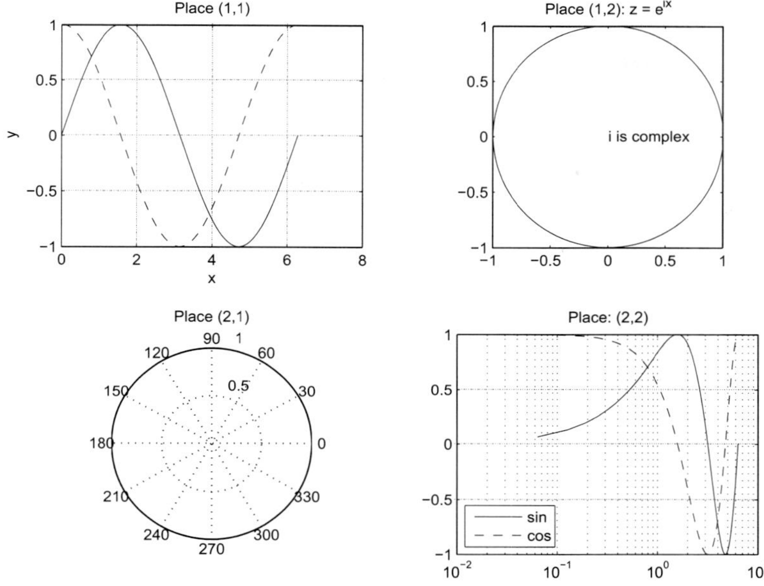

Fig. A.2   Figure window split into 2×2 sub-windows by using `subplot`

A.3.1   *Three-Dimensional Plots*

In order to create three-dimensional surfaces or contour plot of surfaces, it is necessary to evaluate the function f that represents the surface $z = f(x, y)$ on a rectangular grid (mesh) on the xy-plane. In other words, the values of z must be obtained for all values of (x, y) on the grid. This can be done in MATLAB by using the function `meshgrid`. Here we give a small example to see what it really does.

```
>> x = linspace(-2,2); y = linspace(-2,2,50);
>> [X, Y] = meshgrid(x,y); whos
   Name        Size                    Bytes  Class

   X           50x100                  40000  double array
   Y           50x100                  40000  double array
   x           1x100                     800  double array
   y           1x50                      400  double array

Grand total is 10150 elements using 81200 bytes

>> X(1:5, 1:5), Y(1:5, 1:5)
ans =
```

```
        -2.0000    -1.9596    -1.9192    -1.8788    -1.8384
        -2.0000    -1.9596    -1.9192    -1.8788    -1.8384
        -2.0000    -1.9596    -1.9192    -1.8788    -1.8384
        -2.0000    -1.9596    -1.9192    -1.8788    -1.8384
        -2.0000    -1.9596    -1.9192    -1.8788    -1.8384
ans =
        -2.0000    -2.0000    -2.0000    -2.0000    -2.0000
        -1.9184    -1.9184    -1.9184    -1.9184    -1.9184
        -1.8367    -1.8367    -1.8367    -1.8367    -1.8367
        -1.7551    -1.7551    -1.7551    -1.7551    -1.7551
        -1.6735    -1.6735    -1.6735    -1.6735    -1.6735
```

Now that the function f, say $f(x,y) = x^2 + y^2$, has to be calculated at every mesh point (x,y), it is necessary to use the matrices $\mathtt{X}$ and $\mathtt{Y}$ in the following calculation.

```
>> z = X.^2 + Y.^2; whos z
  Name        Size                      Bytes  Class

  z           50x100                    40000  double array

Grand total is 5000 elements using 40000 bytes
```

Now, $\mathtt{z}$ is also a matrix of size 50×100 which holds the values of f on the mesh (points). We emphasise that $\mathtt{x}$ and $\mathtt{y}$ are vectors while $\mathtt{X}$ and $\mathtt{Y}$ generated by $\mathtt{[X,Y] = meshgrid(x,y)}$ are matrices.

There are many functions that can be used in three-dimensional graphs: **mesh** and **surf** are the two commonly used functions to plot surfaces, after having done the preparations above. Readers are encouraged to type **help graph3d** for more on these functions as well as many others. Here are some examples on how these functions are used in three-dimensional drawings.

```
>> subplot(2,2,1), mesh(x,y,z), xlabel('x'), ylabel('y')
>> zlabel('z'), hold on, contour(x,y,z), title('mesh + contour')
>> subplot(2,2,2), surf(x,y,z), xlabel('x'), ylabel('y')
>> zlabel('z'), shading interp, title('surf + shading')
>> myZ = z .* exp(-z);
>> subplot(2,2,3), contour3(x,y,myZ,20), xlabel('x'), ylabel('y')
>> zlabel('myZ'), title('contour3')
>> subplot(2,2,4), H = contour(x,y,myZ); xlabel('x'), ylabel('y')
>> zlabel('myZ'), title('contour + clabel'), clabel(H)
>> print -depsc -r300 -cmyk '../figures/appendixPlot_3D'
```

The output of this example is given in Fig. A.3. We should remark that although the vectors $\mathtt{x}$ and $\mathtt{y}$ are used in $\mathtt{mesh(x,y,z)}$ (or $\mathtt{surf(x,y,z)}$), the same output would be obtained if the corresponding matrices $\mathtt{X}$ and $\mathtt{Y}$, where $[X,Y]$ = `meshgrid(x,y)`, were used.

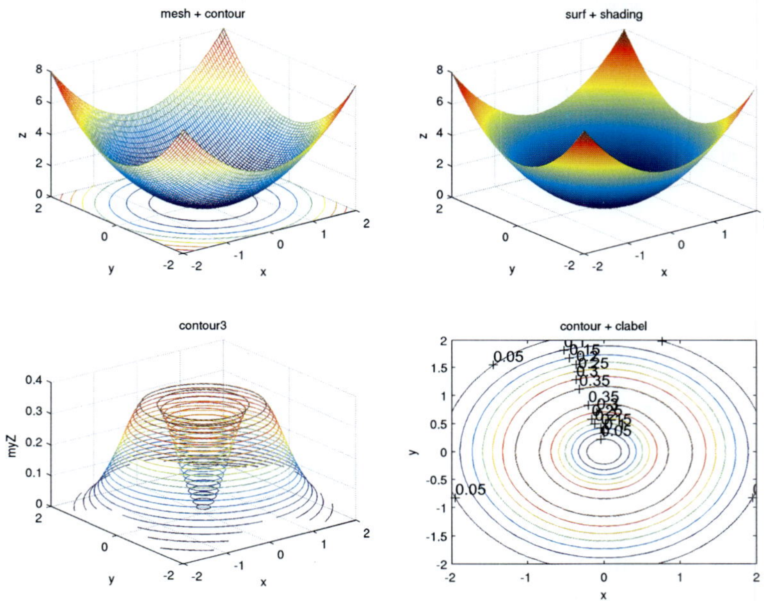

Fig. A.3   Three-dimensional graphics in MATLAB

There is also one other function in MATLAB which is a three-dimensional analogue of `plot`. This is, no surprise, `plot3`: plots curves (or lines) in three-dimensional space. For example, for $\theta \in [0, 2\pi]$,

$$r = 2(1 + \cos\theta)$$

defines a *cardioid* in polar coordinates, where

$$x = r\cos\theta, \quad y = r\sin\theta.$$

Now, if we let $z = \theta$, then we have a parametric curve in 3-dimensional space. See Fig. A.4. Here is an example that plots these curves.

```
>> t = linspace(0,2*pi); r = 2 * ( 1 + cos(t) );
>> x = r .* cos(t); y = r .* sin(t); z = t;
>> subplot(1,2,1), plot(x, y, 'r'), xlabel('x'), ylabel('y')
>> axis square, grid on, title('cardioid')
>> subplot(1,2,2), plot3(x, y, z), xlabel('x'), ylabel('y'), hold on
>> axis square, grid on, title('in 3-D'), zlabel('z = t')
>> plot3(x, y, zeros(size(x)), 'r'), view(-40, 60)
```

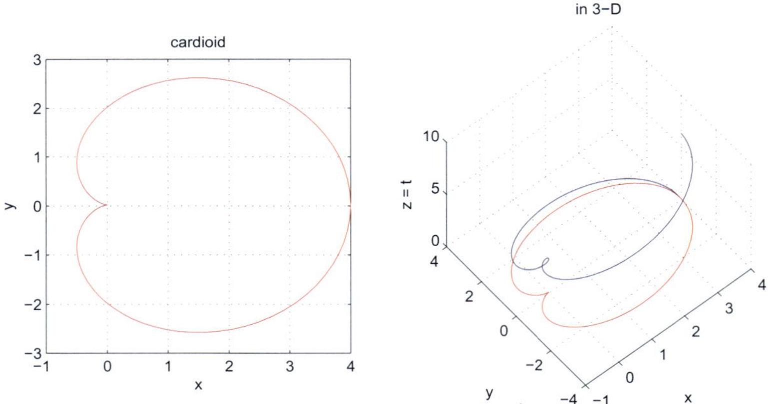

Fig. A.4   Parametric curves in two- and three-dimensions

A.4   Programming in Matlab: *Scripts* and *functions*

To use the *command window* all the time is not efficient if you want to write your own programs of more than a few lines and programs or functions you might want to call repeatedly. Thus, in Matlab you can easily write all necessary commands and functions you need in a file, so called an *m-file*, which is a text file whose name ends with the extension .m. Upon typing the name of the file in the command window of Matlab, those commands in the m-file are executed as if they had been entered at the keyboard. The m-files you write must be located in the current working directory or in any of the directories in which Matlab automatically looks for m-files. Type `help path` to learn how to add a directory to the working path.

Now, suppose that the m-file in Fig. A.5 is accessible by Matlab: the file has the name `myScript.m` and contains just a sequence of Matlab commands and functions. To run this sequence of commands it is enough to type the name of the file without the extension .m in the command window. Here is how we start typing the file and running it.

```
>> edit myScript.m
>> myScript
ans =
     0.0058

Your variables are:

ans     myMat   n
```

Note that the value of the output variable **ans** differs from run to run and the variables defined in the script file is now available to MATLAB.

```
─────────────────────── myScript.m ───────────────────────
% This script computes the determinant of
% a randomly chosen square matrix

n = 10; % chosen dimension of the square matrix
myMat = rand(n); % random matrix
det(myMat) % no semi-colon (;) at the end, so displays the output
```

Fig. A.5   Simple structure of a MATLAB script file

In most cases, the command **edit** followed by the file name will open the MATLAB *editor* (or the one introduced in the preferences). Since it is just a text file, using any text editor of yours is fine. However, the MATLAB editor can also be used for *debugging* purposes.

The first two lines in the file **myScript.m** is ignored by MATLAB. Any line starting with the reserved symbol **%** is a *comment*. If **help myScript** is typed in command window those lines that starts with **%** at the *very* beginning of the file will be displayed. Thus, it is important to describe what the script file is about and how it works at the beginning. On the other hand, on any line, the symbol **%** indicates that the rest of the line is a comment, probably, on that line it appears.

Much more powerful than script files are *functions*, which allow us to create new MATLAB programs, simply commands. A *function* in MATLAB is defined generally by an m-file that begins with a line of the following form:

```
function outArguments = NameOfFunAsYouLike(inArguments)
```

The rest of the file is similar to script files. Thus, the keyword **function** indicates that the m-file is a function. The **inArguments** and the **outArguments** are comma separated lists of input and output variables. However, the latter must be inside the brackets [and] in case the number of output arguments are more than one.

The name of the function above, on the other hand, is given by **NameOfFunAsYouLike**, which is generally the name of the *m-file*, but not necessary. *The functions in* MATLAB *are called by the m-file names rather than the names you write when defining the functions in an m-file.* In Fig. A.6 a simple MATLAB function, which is saved in the m-file **myFunction.m**, is shown. Therefore, the function is accessible only by its file name.

```
————————————————————— myFunction.m —————————————————————
function [argOut1, argOut2] = NameOfFunAsYouLike(argIn1, argIn2)
% This function computes the determinant of
% a randomly chosen square matrix
%
% argIn1  : dimension of the matrix
% argIn2  : seed to the random number generator
% argOut1 : the determinant of the matrix
% argOut2 : the random matrix
%
% Usage : [myVar1, myVar2] = myFunction(myInput1, myInput2)

rand('state', argIn2); % initialise the rand
argOut2 = rand(argIn1); % random matrix
argOut1 = det(argOut2); % output depends how you call the function
```

Fig. A.6   Simple structure of a MATLAB function

The commented lines following the function description in the file
`myFunction.m` are displayed if `help myFunction` is typed in the command
window. The function takes in two arguments, `argIn1` and `argIn2`, and depending on how it is called outputs two arguments, `argOut1` and `argOut2`.
None of these arguments (variables) are accessible by MATLAB workspace.
They can only be used inside the function. In other words, MATLAB creates
a *local* workspace when the function is invoked and destroys it afterwards.
Here is an example.

```
>> clear all
>> myFunction(2,13)
ans =
     0.1341
>> [detA, A] = myFunction(2,13), whos
detA =
     0.1341
A =
     0.8214     0.2119
     0.6159     0.3221
   Name        Size                     Bytes  Class

     A         2x2                         32  double array
     ans       1x1                          8  double array
     detA      1x1                          8  double array

 Grand total is 6 elements using 48 bytes

>> detA = myFunction(2,13)
detA =
     0.1341
```

It must be emphasised that functions in MATLAB can also be defined by using the `inline` command. However, this approach should be used only if the expression defining the function is relatively simple. For example,

```
>> myFun = inline('sin(2*pi*x + theta)', 'x', 'theta')
myFun =
     Inline function:
     myFun(x,theta) = sin(2*pi*x + theta)
>> myFun(1.5, pi)
ans =
   -4.8986e-16
```

Type `help inline` or see its documentation for further information on constructing inline functions.

A.4.1 *Programming*

The capabilities of MATLAB can be extended to include your own scripts and functions written in MATLAB *programming language*. Indeed, MATLAB provides its programming language that includes *looping* statements, *conditional* statements and *relational* and *logical* operators for constructing conditions. Moreover, it is also possible to use subroutines or programs, or even, objects written in other programming languages, such as Java, C/C++ or Fortran within MATLAB. However, we will restrict ourselves to programming in MATLAB and illustrate basic control structures.

The most commonly used looping structure is the *for loops*. The basic syntax is

$$
\begin{array}{l}
\texttt{for}\ variable = matrix \\
\quad statements \\
\texttt{end}
\end{array}
$$

The *statements*, which are valid MATLAB statements, are executed with *variable* taking as its value the successive columns of *matrix*. The function in Fig. A.7 calculates the mean of a sequence of numbers.

Here is an example that illustrates the `for` statement in the function described in `myMean.m`.

```
>> clear all
>> a = rand(1e7,1);
>> tic, myMean(a), toc
ans =
     0.5000
Elapsed time is 0.074817 seconds.
>> tic, mean(a), toc
```

```
————————————————————————————— myMean.m —————
function myMean = myMean( vector )
%
myMean = 0; n = length(vector);
for i = 1:n
    myMean = myMean + vector(i);
end
myMean = myMean ./ n;
```

Fig. A.7   A simple **for** loop in MATLAB

```
ans =
    0.5000
Elapsed time is 0.052202 seconds.
```

Note that the function **myMean** works only on vectors, however, the MATLAB built-in function **mean** works on matrices. It should not be difficult to modify **myMean** to take this fact into account by looping over the columns of the given matrix, which is left as an exercise to encourage readers.

Another looping structure in MATLAB is constructed by using **while** statements. Its basic syntax is

> **while** *expression*
> *statements*
> **end**

statements inside the loop are executed as long as the *expression* is (evaluated to be) *true* or any value that is nonzero. If the expression is *false* or *zero*, then the *statements* in the loop are not executed any more or not at all. Some of the logical operators used in MATLAB are shown in Table A.2.

Table A.2   Some of the logical operators in MATLAB

Operator	Meaning
<, <=, >, >=	less than, less than or equal to, etc.
==, ~=	equal to, not equal to
&	logical AND
|	logical OR
~	logical NOT

An example of **while** loop is illustrated in a MATLAB script shown in Fig. A.8. The script file **myNewton.m** describes two inline functions: **myFun** and **myFunDer**. They stand for the functions

$$f(x) = x - \sin(x), \quad \text{and} \quad f'(x) = 1 + \cos(x),$$

respectively. The *Newton's root finding* algorithm approximately computes the solution of the equation

$$f(x) = 0$$

around a given point x_0. In other words, a zero near x_0 of f is calculated. The method is a simple *iterative* method defined by the *Newton iterates*

$$x_{n+1} = x_n - \frac{f(x_n)}{f'(x_n)}, \quad n = 0, 1, 2, \ldots.$$

The iterations starts with the given x_0 until some certain *convergence* criteria hold. Here, we have chosen the criterion

$$|x_{n+1} - x_n| > \epsilon.$$

This means in `myNewton.m` that while two consecutive iterates, x_{n+1} and x_n, are not close to each other within the given tolerance ϵ the statements inside the `while` loop are executed to find the next Newton iterate.

```
——————————— myNewton.m ———————————
% calculates a zero of the function around x0 upto a tolerance eps
myFun = inline('x - cos(x)', 'x');
myFunDer = inline('1 + sin(x)', 'x');
x0 = 0; dx = 1; % eps = 1e-8; % if you like.
disp('   x0              dx');
while ( abs(dx) > eps )
    dx = -myFun(x0) / myFunDer(x0);
    x0 = x0 + dx;
    fprintf('%6.4f \t %12.8e\n', x0, dx);
end
```

Fig. A.8   Newton's root finding by using `while` loop in MATLAB

There is also a built-in function **fzero** in MATLAB that tries to find a zero of the given function. See the following example and type **help fzero** for details.

```
>> myNewton
   x0              dx
1.0000           1.00000000e+00
0.7504          -2.49636132e-01
0.7391          -1.12509769e-02
0.7391          -2.77575261e-05
0.7391          -1.70123407e-10
0.7391          -0.00000000e+00
>> fzero(myFun, 0)
ans =
    0.7391
```

Again, we encourage readers to modify the file `myNewton.m` so that it defines a function, say `myNewton`, which takes in two functions `myFun` and `myFunDer` and one initial guess `x0` for an approximate zero of `myFun`. You may even consider `eps` as an input for the tolerance. Then, the function should calculate an approximate zero within the given tolerance.

In order to control the flow of a program *conditional statements* are very important in any programming language. In MATLAB, the `if` statements has the following syntax:

  `if` *expression1*
    statements1
  `elseif` *expression2*
    statements2

     $\vdots$

  `else`
    statements
  `end`

The meaning is trivial: the *statements* are executed as long as the *expressions* are *true*. In case when none of the `if` or `elseif` *expressions* are true, then the *statements* after the *else* are executed. It is important to note that `elseif` is one-word: changing `elseif` to `else if` dramatically changes the meaning for sure.

Here is an example that uses the function `myPi` shown in Fig. A.9.

```
>> myPi(); myPi('Monte Carlo'); myPi('MC',1e4);
Value of "pi" in Matlab: 3.1416
You want to calculate "pi" by the method: Monte Carlo
Value of pi = acos(-1): 3.1416
>> myPi('');
Enter the value of "pi" yourself: 3
>> myPi([]);
Enter the value of "pi" yourself: 3.14
>> myPi([], 10);
Value of pi = acos(-1): 3.1416
```

There are several issues to be discussed in the example above. First, the MATLAB built-in variable `nargin` holds the number of function input arguments. Similarly, `nargout` holds the number of function output arguments. Second, the function `input` is sometimes useful if a value is needed to be entered during the execution of a program. So, in the example above, the values 3 and 3.14 are entered at the keyboard. Finally, the syntax `''`

```
────────────────────────── myPi.m ──────────────────────────
function myPi = calculatePi(method, nPoints)
% calculates approximate value of pi

if nargin < 1
    myPi = pi;
    disp(['Value of "pi" in Matlab: ', num2str(myPi)]);
elseif ( nargin < 2 & ~isempty(method) )
    disp(['You want to calculate "pi" by the method: ', num2str(method)])
elseif nargin == 2
    myPi = acos(-1);
    disp(['Value of pi = acos(-1): ', num2str(myPi)]);
else
    myPi = input('Enter the value of "pi" yourself: ');
end
```

Fig. A.9   Simple structure of `if` conditional statements in MATLAB

represents an empty *string* and [] stands for an empty *array* in MATLAB programming language.

Another rarely used conditional statement is `switch`. The systax for `switch` is

$$
\begin{array}{l}
\texttt{switch } \textit{switch_expression} \\
\qquad \texttt{case } \textit{case_expression1} \\
\qquad\qquad \textit{statements1} \\
\qquad \texttt{case } \textit{case_expression2} \\
\qquad\qquad \textit{statements2} \\
\qquad\qquad \vdots \\
\qquad \texttt{otherwise} \\
\qquad\qquad \textit{statements} \\
\texttt{end}
\end{array}
$$

Note that a complete `switch` statement is constructed with the keywords `case` and `otherwise`. The example below uses the function `optionPrice` shown in Fig. A.10.

```
>> optionPrice('Monte Carlo')
Method to be used is Monte Carlo
>> optionPrice('PDE')
Method to be used is "partial differential equation" (PDE)
>> optionPrice('let it be exact')
Exact Solution
```

```
────────────────────────────── optionPrice.m ──────────────────────────────
function price = optionPrice(method)
% method is a string.

switch lower(method)
    case {'monte carlo', 'quasi-monte carlo', 'mc', 'qmc'}
        disp('Method to be used is Monte Carlo')
    case {'binomial', 'trinomial'}
        disp('Method to be used is a Lattice Method')
    case 'pde'
        disp('Method to be used is "partial differential equation" (PDE)')
    otherwise
        disp('Exact Soultion')
end
```

Fig. A.10   Simple structure of `switch` conditional statements in MATLAB

A.4.2   *Vectorisation*

MATLAB is internally optimised for working with matrices and, in particular, vectors. Consequently, calculations in MATLAB can be greatly speeded up by using vector operations rather than using a loop to repeat a calculation or accessing each element of vector. As a general rule, if a sample of code needs to be executed quickly, `for` loops in MATLAB should be avoided where possible. For example,

```
>> clear all, N = 100000;
>> tic, vec = (1:N) .^ 2; toc
Elapsed time is 0.002010 seconds.
>> tic, for i = 1:N, vec(i) = i^2; end, toc
Elapsed time is 0.138471 seconds.
```

In most cases, a double `for` loop can be replaced by a single one in order to *vectorise* the code and speed up the calculations. However, this must be done with care. Consider the script in Fig. A.11 which multiplies a vector by a matrix. Here, we test the script as

```
>> testMultiplication
Elapsed time is 0.072986 seconds.
Elapsed time is 0.057435 seconds.
Elapsed time is 0.019355 seconds.
```

This shows that vectorisation, herewith over the columns, does not help too much. However, in general, doing so will help reduce the execution time of a program. Consider, for instance, writing a similar script that multiplies two matrices.

Another way of speeding up a MATLAB script is to preallocate the arrays that hold the matrices and vectors. That is, if A is a matrix having m rows

```
——————————————— testMultiplication.m ———————————————
m = 1000; n = 5000; rand('state', 13);
A = rand(m,n); x = rand(n,1); y = zeros(m,1);
tic;
% usual way
for j = 1:n % loop over columns
    for i = 1:m % loop over rows
        y(i) = y(i) + A(i,j)*x(j); % multiplication rule for matrices
    end
end
toc; % disp(num2str(y)), tic;
tic;
% in general, may be slightly better: vectorised over columns
for i = 1:m
    y(i) = A(i,:) * x; % dot product
    % y(i) = dot( A(i,:), x ); % seems to be the worst (why?)
end
toc; % disp(num2str(y)), tic;
tic;
% best one
y = A*x; % Matlab's way of multiplication
toc; % disp(num2str(y))
```

Fig. A.11   Vectorisation in MATLAB: speeding up calculations

and **n** columns, then initialise it by, for example, **A = zeros(m,n)** rather than **A = []**. The latter indicates that **A** is just an array, but it does not allocate a memory to it. However, the former, **A = zeros(m,n)**, *does* initialise the matrix together with appropriate memory allocation. For an extensive discussion on vectorisation, see the related documentations in MATLAB.

Bibliography

Abramowitz, M. and Stegun, I. A. (eds.) (1972). *Handbook of Mathematical Functions with Formulas, Graphs, and Mathematical Tables*, 9th edn. (Dover, New York).

Achdou, Y. and Pironneau, O. (2005). *Computational Methods for Option Pricing* (SIAM).

Acklam, P. J. (2004). An algorithm for computing the inverse normal cumulative distribution function, http://home.online.no/~pjacklam/notes/invnorm.

Arnold, L. (1974). *Stochastic Differential Equations: Theory and Applications* (Wiley, New York).

Barraquand, J. and Pudet, T. (1996). Pricing of American path-dependent contingent claims, *Mathematical Finance* **6**, pp. 17–51.

Baxter, M. and Rennie, A. (1996). *Financial Calculus: An Introduction to derivative Pricing* (Cambridge University Press).

Björk, T. (1998). *Arbitrage Theory in Continuous Time* (Oxford University Press, Oxford).

Black, F. and Scholes, M. (1973). The pricing of options and corporate liabilities, *Journal of Political Economy* **81**, 3, pp. 637–654.

Boyle, P., Broadie, M. and Glasserman, P. (1997). Monte Carlo methods for security pricing, *Journal of Economic Dynamics and Control* **21**, pp. 1267–1321.

Boyle, P. P. (1977). Options: A Monte Carlo approach, *Journal of Financial Economics* **4**, pp. 323–338.

Brandimarte, P. (2002). *Numerical Methods in Finance: a MATLAB-based introduction* (John Wiley & Sons, Inc.).

Breen, R. (1991). The accelerated binomial option pricing model, *J. Financial and Quantitative Analysis* **26**, pp. 153–164.

Brent, R. P. (1994). On the periods of generalized fibonacci recurrences, *Mathematics of Computation* **63**, 207, pp. 389–401.

Brigo, D. and Mercurio, F. (2001). *Interest Rate Models: Theory and Practice* (Springer, Berlin).

Caflisch, R. E. (1998). Monte Carlo and quasi-Monte Carlo methods, *Acta Numerica* **7**, pp. 1–49.

Chakravarti, I., Laha, R. and Roy, J. (1967). *Handbook of Methods of Applied Statistics*, Vol. I (John Wiley and Sons, New York).

Cheney, W. and Kincaid, D. (1994). *Numerical Mathematics and Computing*, 3rd edn. (Brooks/Cole Publishing Co.).

Cox, J. C., Ross, S. A. and Rubinstein, M. (1979). Option pricing: A simplified approach, *Journal of Financial Economics* **7**, pp. 229–263.

Cox, J. C. and Rubinstein, M. (1985). *Options Markets* (Prentice Hall, Englewood Cliffs).

Cyganowski, S., Kloeden, P. and Ombach, J. (2002). *From Elementary Probability to Stochastic Differential Equations with MAPLE* (Springer-Verlag, Berlin).

D'Agostino, R. B. and Stephens, M. A. (eds.) (1986). *Goodness-of-fit techniques* (Marcel Dekker, Inc., New York, NY, USA).

Devroye, L. (1986). *Non-Uniform Random Variate Generation* (Springer-Verlag, New York).

Elliott, C. M. and Ockendon, J. R. (1982). *Weak and Variational Methods for Moving Boundary Problems* (Pitman Advanced Publishing Program, Boston).

Elton, E. J. and Gruber, M. J. (1995). *Modern Portfolio Theory and Investment Analysis*, 5th edn. (Wiley, New York).

Evans, L. C. (2008). An introduction to stochastic differential equations, http://math.berkeley.edu/~evans/SDE.course.pdf, version 1.2.

Fabozzi, F. J. (1997). *Fixed Income Mathematics: Analytical and Statistical Techniques*, 5th edn. (McGraw-Hill, New York).

Fletcher, R. (1987). *Practical Methods of Optimization*, 2nd edn. (Wiley, Chichester, West Sussex, England).

Forsyth, P. A. and Vetzal, K. R. (2002). Quadratic convergence for valuing american options using a penalty method, *SIAM Journal on Scientific Computing* **23**, pp. 2095–2122.

Glasserman, P. (2004). *Monte Carlo Methods in Financial Engineering* (Springer-Verlag, New York).

Gup, B. E. and Brooks, R. (1993). *Interest Rate Risk Management: The Banker's Guide to Using Futures, Options, Swaps, and Other Derivative Instruments* (Irwin Professional Publishing, New York).

Hammersley, J. M. and Handscomb, D. C. (1964). *Monte Carlo Methods* (Chapman and Hall, London & Newyork).

Heath, M. T. (2002). *Scientific Computing*, 2nd edn. (Mc Graw Hill).

Higham, D. J. (2001). An algorithmic introduction to numerical solution of stochastic differential equations, *SIAM Review* **43**, pp. 525–546.

Higham, D. J. (2002). Nine ways to implement the binomial method for option valuation in MATLAB, *SIAM Review* **44**, pp. 661–667.

Higham, D. J. (2004). *An Introduction to Financial Option Valuation: mathematics, stochastics, and computation* (Cambridge University Press).

Higham, D. J. and Mao, X. (2005). Convergence of Monte Carlo simulations involving the mean-reverting square root process, *Journal of Computational Finance* **8**, 3, pp. 35–61.

Hull, J. C. (2000). *Options, Futures, and Other Derivatives*, 4th edn. (Prentice

Hall International Editions, Upper Saddle River).

Hull, J. C. and White, A. (1987). The pricing of options on assets with stochastic volatilities, *Journal of Finance* **42**, pp. 281–300.

Hull, J. C. and White, A. (1994a). Numerical procedures for implementing term structure models i: Single-factor models, *Journal of Derivatives* **2**, 1, pp. 7–16.

Hull, J. C. and White, A. (1994b). Numerical procedures for implementing term structure models ii: Two-factor models, *Journal of Derivatives* **2**, 2, pp. 37–48.

Jäckel, P. (2002). *Monte Carlo Methods in Finance* (Wiley, Chichester).

Jiang, L. and Dai, M. (2004). Convergence of binomial tree methods for european/american path-dependent options, *SIAM Journal on Numerical Analysis* **42**, 3, pp. 1094–1109.

John, F. (1991). *Partial Differential Equations*, 4th edn. (Springer).

Joshi, M. S. (2004). *The Concepts and Practice of Mathematical Finance* (Cambridge University Press).

Joy, C., Boyle, P. P. and Tang, K. S. (1996). Quasi-Monte Carlo methods in numerical finance, *Management Science* **42**, 6, pp. 926–938.

Kahaner, D., Moler, C. and Nash, S. (1989). *Numerical Methods and Software* (Prentice Hall, Englewood Cliffs, New Jersey).

Kijima, M. (2003). *Stochastic Processes with Financial Applications to Finance* (Chapman & Hall/CRC).

Klassen, T. R. (2001). Simple, fast and flexible pricing of asian options, *J. Comp. Finance* **4**, pp. 89–124.

Kloeden, P. E. and Platen, E. (1992). *Numerical Solution of Stochastic Differential Equations* (Springer, Berlin).

Kloeden, P. E., Platen, E. and Schurz, H. (1997). *Numerical Solution of SDE through Computer Experiments* (Springer-Verlag, New York).

Knuth, D. E. (1997). *Seminumerical Algorithms, The Art of Computer Programming*, Vol. 2, 3rd edn. (Addison-Wesley, Reading, Massachusetts).

Korn, R. (1997). *Optimal Portfolios: Stochastic Models for Optimal Investment and Risk Management in Continuous Time* (World Scientific, Singapore).

Korn, R. and Korn, E. (2001). *Option Pricing and Portfolio Optimization: modern methods of financial mathematics* (American Mathematical Society).

Kwok, Y. K. (1998). *Mathematical Models of Financial Derivatives* (Springer, Berlin).

Leisen, D. and Reimer, M. (1996). Binomial models for option valuation — examining and improving convergence, *Applied Mathematical Finance* **3**, pp. 319–346.

Luenberger, D. G. (1998). *Investment Science* (Oxford University Press).

Mao, X. (2007). *Stochastic Differential Equations and Applications*, 2nd edn. (Horwood Publishing Ltd.).

Marsaglia, G. and Tsang, W. W. (2000). The ziggurat method for generating random variables, *Journal of Statistical Software* **5**, 8, pp. 1–7.

Mathews, J. and Walker, R. L. (1970). *Mathematical Methods of Physics*, 2nd edn. (Addison-Wesley).

Mathews, J. H. and Fink, K. D. (2004). *Numerical Methods using* MATLAB, 4th edn. (Pearson Education, Inc.).

Merton, R. C. (1973). Theory of rational option pricing, *Bell Journal of Economics and Management Science* **4**, 1, pp. 141–183.

Merton, R. C. (1990). *Continuous-Time Finance* (Blackwell, Cambridge).

Mikosch, T. (1998). *Elementary Stochastic Calculus: with Finance in View* (World Scientific, Singapore).

Moro, B. (1995). The full Monte, *RISK* , pp. 57–58.

Morton, K. W. and Mayers, D. F. (1995). *Numerical Solution of Partial Differential Equations*, 2nd edn. (Cambridge University Press).

Musiela, M. and Rutkowski, M. (1997). *Martingale Methods in Financial Modelling* (Springer, Berlin).

Nash, S. G. and Sofer, A. (1996). *Linear and Nonlinear Programming* (McGraw-Hill).

Neftci, S. N. (2000). *An Introduction to the Mathematics of Financial Derivatives*, 2nd edn. (Academic Press).

Niederreiter, H. (1992). *Random Number Generation and Quasi-Monte Carlo Methods* (Society for Industrial and Applied Mathematics).

Nielsen, L. T. (1999). *Pricing and Hedging of Derivative Securities* (Oxford University Press, Oxford).

Øksendal, B. (2002). *Stochastic Differential Equations: An Introduction with Applications*, 5th edn. (Springer).

Ökten, G. and Eastman, W. (2004). Randomized quasi-Monte Carlo methods in pricing securities, *Journal of Economic and Control* **28**, pp. 2399–2426.

Park, S. K. and Miller, K. W. (1988). Random number generators: Good ones are hard to find, *Communications of the ACM* **31**, pp. 1192–1201.

Platen, E. (1999). An introduction to numerical methods for stochastic differential equations, *Acta Numerica* , pp. 197–246.

Pliska, S. R. (1997). *Introduction to Mathematical Finance: Discrete Time Models* (Blackwell Publishers, Cambridge).

Ripley, B. D. (2006). *Stochastic Simulation* (Wiley-Interscience).

Rogers, L. C. G. and Talay, D. (eds.) (1997). *Numerical Methods in Finance* (Cambridge University Press, Cambridge).

Seydel, R. (2002). *Tools for Computational Finance* (Springer-Verlag).

Shiryaev, A. N. (1999). *Essentials of Stochastic Finance: Facts, Models, Theory* (World Scientific, Singapore).

Shreve, S. E. (2004a). *Stochastic Calculus for Finance I: The Binomial Asset Pricing Model* (Springer-Verlag, New York).

Shreve, S. E. (2004b). *Stochastic Calculus for Finance II: Continuous-Time Models* (Springer-Verlag, New York).

Steele, J. M. (2001). *Stochastic Calculus and Financial Applications* (Springer, New York).

Sundaram, R. K. (1996). *A First Course in Optimization Theory* (Cambridge University Press, Cambridge).

Sundaresan, S. M. (1997). *Fixed Income Markets and Their Derivatives* (South Western College Publishing, Cincinnati, OH).

Tan, K. S. and Boyle, P. P. (2000). Applications of randomized low discrepancy sequences to the valuation of complex securities, *Journal of Economic Dynamics and Control* **24**, pp. 1747–1782.

Tavella, D. and Randall, C. (2000). *Pricing Financial Instruments: the finite difference method* (John Wiley & Sons, Inc.).

Tezuka, S. (1995). *Uniform Random Numbers: Theory and Practice* (Kluwer Academic Publishers).

Thomas, D. B., Luk, W., Leong, P. H. and Villasenor, J. D. (2007). Gaussian random number generators, *ACM Comput. Surv.* **39**, 4, p. 11, doi:http://doi.acm.org/10.1145/1287620.1287622.

Thomas, J. W. (1995). *Numerical Partial Differential Equations: Finite Difference Methods* (Springer).

Walsh, J. B. (2003). The rate of convergence of the binomial tree scheme, *Finance and Stochastics* **7**, 3, pp. 337–361.

Wilmott, P. (2007). *Paul Wilmott Introduces Quantitative Finance* (Wiley-Interscience, New York, NY, USA).

Wilmott, P., Dewynne, J. and Howison, S. (1993). *Option Pricing: Mathematical Models and Computation* (Oxford Financial Press, Oxford, UK).

Wilmott, P., Howison, S. and Dewynne, J. (1995). *The Mathematics of Financial Derivatives: a student introduction* (Cambridge University Press).

Zhang, P. (1998). *Exotic Options* (World Scientific, Singapore).

Index

duration, 9
  Macaulay, 9
  modified, 9
dynamic programming, 34

efficient frontier, 27, 32
efficient portfolio, 26
error function, 124
Euler-Maruyama, 79
Euler-method, 206
exercise price, 36
expected value, 156, 161
expiration date, 36
explicit method, 206, 222, 236
exponential distribution, 146

face value, 2
fair value, 3
Fibonacci generator, 142, 143
finite difference, 200
forward, 38
forward difference, 200
free boundary, 245
free boundary problem, 246
frictionless market, 113
fundamental solution, 119

Gamma (Greeks), 127
Gauss-Seidel method, 250
gearing effect, 38
generalised inverse, 151
geometric Brownian motion, 45, 99
Girsanov theorem, 116
goodness-of-fit, 144
  χ^2 test, 144
  Kolmogorov Smirnov test, 144
Greeks, 127
  Delta, 127, 130
  Gamma, 127, 130
  Rho, 127, 131
  Theta, 127, 131
  Vega, 127, 131
Green's function, 119
grid, 205

Halton sequence, 190

heat equation, 116, 198
hedging, 38

implicit method, 217, 222, 240
implied volatility, 113
importance sampling, 188
independent increments, 72
integer programming, 34
interest rate, 4
internal rate of return, 6
intrinsic value, 245
inverse transform method, 146
in the money, 67
Itô, 77
  calculus, 99
  integral, 78, 89
  lemma, 112
  process, 78
  product rule, 99
  stochastic differential equation, 77

Jacobian, 152

lagged Fibonacci generator, 142
lattice, 43
Lax Equivalence Theorem, 226
leverage effect, 37
limit in the mean, 86
linear complementarity problems, 255
linear congruential generator, 141
linear programming, 18, 27
lognormal distribution, 45, 82, 99
low-discrepancy sequence, 189
lower triangular matrix, 157
LU-decomposition, 157, 218

market price of risk, 116
Marsaglia's method, 155
martingale property, 90
maturity, 2, 36
mean-variance portfolio, 24, 26
mean reversion, 105
mean vector, 156
mesh, 205
Milstein method, 84
molecule, 206